By SAMUEL J. ANDREWS

CHRISTIANITY AND ANTI-CHRISTIAN-
  ITY 8° $2.00
GOD'S REVELATIONS OF HIMSELF TO
  MAN. 8° $2.00
LIFE OF WILLIAM WATSON ANDREWS
  8° $1.50

G. P. PUTNAM'S SONS
NEW YORK & LONDON

GOD'S REVELATIONS OF HIMSELF TO MEN

AS SUCCESSIVELY MADE IN THE

PATRIARCHAL, JEWISH, AND CHRISTIAN DISPENSATIONS

AND IN

THE MESSIANIC KINGDOM

BY

SAMUEL J. ANDREWS

Republished June, 2019 by:
The Old Paths Publications, Inc.
www.theoldpathspublications.com
TOP@theoldpathspublications.com
ISBN: 978-1-7339247-6-4

SECOND EDITION, REVISED AND ENLARGED

G. P. PUTNAM'S SONS
NEW YORK AND LONDON
The Knickerbocker Press
1901

COPYRIGHT, 1885,
BY S. J. ANDREWS.

COPYRIGHT, 1901,
BY SAMUEL J. ANDREWS.

The Knickerbocker Press, New York

PREFACE TO REVISED EDITION.

IN the present revision few changes have been made. At first thought it may seem that the recent excavations in Babylonia and Egypt, which have carried our knowledge of the history of those regions much farther back—some say to 7000 years B.C.—must be of great importance in our inquiries. But this chronological enlargement gives no new light as to the origin of the earth and man, and his earliest history. If it confirms the belief that the statements in Genesis were based on the Babylonian traditions, it is still to be explained how these traditions originated, and when and how they assumed the shape in which we now find them, and what authority belongs to them. It is no part of the purpose of this book to discuss questions which we have not the knowledge to settle, and which for their adequate treatment demand special treatises. We do not inquire how the Bible became what it is, but assume that it is a true outline of God's actings in human history, without going into examination of details.

But some remarks may be made here in regard to the discussion of the Higher Criticism, printed in the Appendix. All that is there attempted is to state its leading principles and the conclusions to which they lead, as presented by its chief representatives. Many points of detail, which have been so learnedly and laboriously examined, are comparatively of small importance; and with regard to many of those more important, the last word has not yet been said. The historical question which meets us first of all, and is of supreme importance, is to know whether the history of the Hebrews is that of a people standing in a special and unique relation to God, or not. If this relation existed, it must have given to this history a special and unique character; and criticism must recognize this, and give it due weight.

But the more advanced critics wholly deny the existence of any such special relation, on the *a priori* ground that Jehovah, being the one universal Lord, cannot select any one people to be more than the rest the object of His favor. This would be particularism, and inconsistent with His impartial treatment of all. It is said by Kuenen, that "a belief in Israel's selection is not tenable in our day;" and that "Israel is no more the pivot on which the development of the world turns, than the planet which we inhabit the centre of the universe." It is said by Wellhausen, "The relation of Jehovah to Israel was a natural one, not a pact." We must thus give up the belief that the Hebrews were the covenant people, and must treat their history in the same way as that of the peoples around them.[1]

It need not be said that this is a point of vital importance. If the belief that God by His own act stood in special relation to this one people be a delusion, it must greatly change our estimate of the truthfulness and spiritual value of their historical records as we have them. A very large portion must be set aside as unhistoric, especially the supernatural features, and the whole be read as we read other national histories.

It is from this point of view that the more advanced higher critics would rewrite the history of Israel. Their religious education, we are told, was under the same law of historic development as that of the peoples around them. That they were the earliest monotheists proves

[1] A very recent American critic speaks of "the absence of any evidence to warrant the belief that in the case of the Hebrew people the principle of historical development of their religious institutions, illustrated in the history of all other peoples, was departed from."

nothing. Varieties of development, some higher, some lower, no more show that God gives special light and guidance to any, than the varieties of human bodies show His special care for the strongest and most beautiful. The knowledge of Jehovah as the one supreme and holy God did not come through any special revelation made by Him to Israel, but through a gradual moral development which other nations were equally capable of. As one of the leading critics has said : " The religion of Israel is one of the principal religions, nothing less, but also nothing more." The historians, prophets, poets, and wise men of Israel should be read as we read the literature of any other nation.

But it may be said that it is not just to take the critics who deny the covenant relation of Israel, and in general the supernatural, as the truest exponents of the higher criticism. It is said by Professor Briggs ("Higher Criticism of the Hexateuch") that this denial of the supernatural is "a personal feature, and has no necessary connection with the critical analysis of the Pentateuch; and that men of every shade of opinion with regard to the supernatural, and evangelical religion, may be found among the advocates of the theory."

If by this is meant merely that all men, without regard to their religious belief, can judge whether two Biblical statements are directly contradictory, or plainly discrepant, it will be admitted. But such contradictions and discrepancies, however multiplied, form but a very small part of the questions presented by the higher criticism. A great part of its conclusions are inferential, resting upon very uncertain data; and many involve judgments into which the religious element largely enters. If there are critical formulas, like the formulas of the mathematician, which stand in no relation to religion, and which give the same results by whomsoever applied, then indeed it matters not of what shade of opinion the Biblical critic may be. All he has to do is to apply the measuring line,—

and Turk, Jew, Buddhist, agnostic, atheist, can all do this, and one as well as another.

But such a theory of Biblical criticism, none who believe that holy men of old spake as they were moved by the Holy Ghost, and that spiritual things must be spiritually discerned, will admit for an instant. Reverencing the Bible as a sacred book unfolding the great purpose of God in His Son, Christians will not willingly see it made an open tournament field, where a miscellaneous company of "free lances" may fight their intellectual battles.

Whatever may be said of the capability of all men to be Biblical critics, the higher criticism will take in the public mind its distinctive character from those most advanced; and this because they most truly represent its fundamental principles. In regard to the less advanced, almost all show a vagueness and uncertainty which is both confusing and wearisome,—the result of a partial acceptance of principles which they are unwilling to carry out.

But it is agreed by all the school that the Bible stands in great need of a critical revision; for as it now stands it is honeycombed with mistakes and errors. It is said by Professor Briggs: "Ancient Jerusalem lies buried under the rubbish of more than eighteen centuries. . . . Just so the Holy Scriptures, as given by Divine inspiration to holy prophets, lie buried beneath the rubbish of centuries. . . . The valleys of Biblical truth have been filled up with the débris of human dogmas, ecclesiastical institutions, liturgical formulas, priestly ceremonies. . . . Historical criticism is sifting all this rubbish. It will gather out every precious stone. . . . The traditionalists prefer the modern ruins to the ancient city of God, and they battle for every speck of rubbish as if it were the choicest gold. But the old Bible will arise in the reconstruction of Biblical criticism into a splendor and glory greater than ever before." We are reminded of Tolstoi's estimate of the Scriptures, who compares himself to "a man examining a bag of pebbles among which are a few rare pearls."

It is painfully evident that the recent attempts to meet the long-felt difficulties in the Old Testament, historic and other, by minimizing the knowledge of God possessed by Israel, have tended rather to undermine the faith of Christians than to confirm it. And the reason of this is obvious. As the distinction between the Jews and other peoples is effaced, and both are put under the law of historic development, the distinction between the Bible and other sacred books is effaced. What would be rejected as unhistorical, legendary, fictitious, in the latter, must be in the former. And when the disquieted believer asks for a criterion by which he can know how much of the Old Testament he is to receive as true, no answer is given; it is a matter of individual judgment. A considerable part of it is to be regarded as a "no-man's-land," without any defined boundaries, where the critics may roam up and down at their pleasure.

It is also more and more evident that the same uncertainty is beginning to be felt in regard to the truthfulness of the New Testament, and especially of the historic Gospels. Here we are told, that as we find by critical inquiry, much was attributed to Moses that was not his, so much was attributed to Christ which He never did or taught. It is the pious imagination of the second century that presents Him to us as He now appears. When all errors are eliminated, and we get down to exact history, both Old and New Testaments will be reduced to much smaller dimensions, and make less demands upon our faith; and we may safely say, also, that increasing numbers will care less and less for them.

S. J. A.

HARTFORD, CONN., August, 1901.

PREFACE.

This volume is prepared for those who believe that Jesus Christ is the Incarnate Son of God; and that the Bible is a true record of God's purpose in Him, and of the Divine actings to fulfill that purpose. Its aim is simply to set forth that record in its order, and to restore to it that unity in Christ which it claims upon its face, and which was ascribed to it by our Lord, but which with many of its readers it has now lost. (Luke xxiv. 27.) For those who deny the fact of the Incarnation, — that Jesus Christ is, and abides, the God-man forever, — I do not write; much less for those who are seeking proof of the existence of a God. I address myself to believers; for to all others, the Bible, which declares the purpose of God in Christ, must be an insoluble riddle. The Incarnate Son is the centre from which all the actings of the Father, both creative and redemptive, must be seen to be known aright.

This book, therefore, is not critical after the modern fashion; it discusses no textual questions, and enters into no special historical or archæological investigations; and it assumes the substantial truth of the Scriptures as we possess them. It deals only with the outlines of the Divine purpose, not with the details. Its scope is simple, — to set forth the manner in which God is pleased to reveal Himself to men, past, present, and future, as He has made it known. I believe there is in it nothing contrary to catholic truth, nor to the faith of the Church as expressed in her creeds. Nor is there in it any thing distinctively new; or, if there seem to be, it is in the restatement of old truths, and in the consistency with which certain fundamental principles are carried out. In those parts which speak of the still unfulfilled purpose of God in redemption, I believe nothing is affirmed which has not scriptural sanction, and which is not in harmony with that purpose as already fulfilled. Eschatology in its larger meaning, embracing the stages of redemption yet future, has confessedly occupied very little the attention of the Church; and only the most general statements are found in the creeds and confessions of faith.

The number of references to particular passages of Scripture could in most cases have been greatly multiplied, but a single one is generally sufficient to enable a diligent reader to find more; and all who wish to add to these, and to compare passage with passage, have abundant help in any good reference Bible. The revised version of the Old Testament was published too late to be of much use, but the changes in the translation are not for us very important.

I have made no reference to others who have written on these topics, nor citations from them, not as intending to deny my great obligations to them, but because the unity of treatment is thus disturbed, and the attention of the reader diverted. It has demanded some firmness not to enter upon side issues, and to discuss points very nearly related to those treated of, and yet not essential to them, as, e.g., the person and place of "the angel of the covenant." In endeavoring to be brief, I may have sometimes become obscure, and so liable to misapprehension; and I must therefore ask that expressions which are ambiguous, may be interpreted in conformity with the general scope of the book.

I may be permitted to address here a few words to my young friends, students of the Scriptures, and especially to those in theological schools. It was once said by Dean Stanley, that "there are times when we are prone to confound instrumentals with fundamentals, to confound things which are of no importance with things which are of the utmost importance." The present is pre-eminently such a time of confusion as regards religious things. That which is of first importance in Christianity, is the fact of the present existence of Jesus Christ, exalted to the right hand of God, and made Head of the Church, and Ruler over all. You will at once say to me that no Christian denies this. It is declared in all the creeds, and held by all. But we know that not a few who nominally hold the creeds, do disbelieve it; some openly speak of a de-incarnation; and others, as if many incarnations were possible. The tendencies of modern thought are to make the fact of the union of the Divine and human in the person of Jesus Christ, more and more incredible; and if the Incarnation be held, as it doubtless is, by far the larger number, it may be so held as by no means to give it its due place and importance. If Jesus Christ is the Incarnate Son of God, the Word made flesh, now risen from the dead and made immortal, and having all power in heaven and in earth, this is the one supreme fact; it must be recognized, and its transcendent significance be acknowledged. Christianity with the living Christ, and Christianity with a dead Christ, are two things world-wide apart: in the one case, there is a Person and a work; in the other, a book and an ethical system. A mistake here is vital. If He is dead, it is the saddest of delusions to think of Him as sitting in the Father's throne; if He is living, — the man Christ Jesus, the Ruler under God over all His creatures, — it will not do to treat Him as one of the dead, sleeping in His unknown sepulchre. One of these alternatives is true; and with the universal Church we affirm that He who was dead is alive again forever, that He is the Prince of the kings of the earth, the Great High Priest, the Head of the Church. Let, then, His due place and honor be given Him.

Thus taking Christ's present exaltation and dominion as the great central fact of Christianity, what are its bearings on the place of the Bible in the Church, and on biblical criticism? The Bible is an account of what God has done in the past, that we may learn to know both the Father and the Son; and especially to know Christ as the great Actor in man's redemption — who He is, and why He was made man, and what He has done, and is doing, and is yet to do; and thus its records are the chief means of our knowledge. But the Bible cannot be read simply as a history of past events; for its purpose is not merely to enlighten us as to the past, but also to show us the way to Him as now living, that we may go to Him, and that He may work in us His work of salvation. We are not saved through our belief in the past actings of God, but by being in Christ. The book cannot give us life: we must go to Him who, as the Risen One, is the fountain of life. And His existence is not dependent on the existence of the book, any more than the mountain peak upon the existence of the guide-book that describes it, and points out the way to its summit. We may suppose all copies of the Bible to be destroyed: this would not affect Him as now exalted, or His work, past or future; only our knowledge of Him.

What is now demanded of us is, that we put the two, the Bible and Christ, in their right relations to each other. The book is not useless because He lives, as some have said. No words can express its intrinsic value. But it is above all His book; for not only is He its great theme, He is also, through the Spirit whom He has sent, its interpreter. As He explained to His disciples when on earth the things written in it concerning Himself, so must He continue to do down to the end. The Scriptures can be understood only by those whose understandings He opens. (Luke xxiv. 44, 45.) And He will make known their mysteries, the secret counsels of His Father, just so far as His children are spiritually prepared to receive them, and can rightly apply their knowledge. But no wit of man can know what it is God's will to do, before the time when He would make it known. The true and full and harmonious explanation of the Bible can be made only in the Church, wherein is the Spirit of Christ.

Keeping in mind this relation of the Bible to the living Christ, how are we to regard much recent biblical criticism? There are critics of all schools, and of all degrees of faith;

and some who utterly deny the Incarnation, and of course Christ's present existence and exaltation. As an astronomer, who should deny to the sun its central place in the solar system, would wholly fail to explain the order and courses of the planets; so these interpreters of the Scriptures, denying to Christ His central place, cannot see the biblical records in their true order and consistence. But even in this class there are critics and critics. In some is seen a positive hostility to Christ, a determination to pull Him down from the throne in which He sits, and to destroy the faith of men in Him. Their chief motive in studying the sacred records seems to be to prove them full of errors; and to this end they exaggerate differences, and exalt discrepancies into contradictions. The Scriptures are to them only an antiquarian book, whose chief value is that it supplies to them a field on which to display their critical acumen and their powers of invention in new readings of history. If any thing useful in biblical study can be learned from them, it is only in regard to very minor points and small details.

But there are critics of a very different spirit, who holding the Scriptures to be God's word, and Christ to be the Son of God, seek to cast light upon their meaning by a more accurate knowledge and rendering of the texts, by the study of newly discovered or deciphered records, by identification of biblical sites, by archæological investigations, and by diligent use of all external means of knowledge. To these our thanks are due; they approach the Bible, not as a surgeon to dissect a dead body, but carefully to remove some excrescence, or to replace some dislocated limb, that there may be new life and strength.

But the question arises whether the critics of this class do not often fall into the error of which Dean Stanley speaks, of confounding instrumentals with fundamentals, and spend much of their strength in discussions of matters of little moment. There is a sense in which all truth, even in its minutest details, may be said to be of value; but perfect truth is unattainable. Our best knowledge is partial. All events in a single human life can never be written, much less all in the life of a people. There is necessarily a choice between the important and the unimportant. The sacred records are comparatively very brief, yet criticism must here distinguish between the essential and non-essential; a hundred minor questions may remain unanswered. Investigations which concern events intrinsically unimportant — the length of a king's reign, the number of the slain in a battle, the site of a city, the exact date of a prophecy, the authorship of a psalm, and like points, the minima of biblical history — cannot but hold a very subordinate place; they are but instrumentals; we may be ignorant of them, and suffer little loss. The general outlines of the Divine purpose as given in the Bible are clear and unmistakable. As we may know the course of a mountain range, its direction, the order of its summits, and yet cannot see the many little valleys at their feet, so we know the chief facts of the past, their order and significance; and our ignorance of details does not affect what is of chiefest importance to us, our existing relations to God and to His Christ. No knowledge of details, indeed, is to be despised; and he who removes a stone of stumbling out of the King's pathway, or straightens an angle, or cuts down a bush that obstructs the wayfarer's vision, does a service; but he may remember that a hundred generations have trod the pathway before him, and found Him whom they sought. I believe it will be truly said, in a time not very far distant, that many points which now occupy the attention of biblical scholars, and call forth learned dissertations and elaborate treatises, were not worthy of the attention given them; and that their labors will be regarded as the critical tithing of the mint, anise, and cummin.

What is now most necessary, is to hold the Bible in its right relation to the Living Christ. We may dismiss at once all fear that criticism, even the most hostile and deadly, can affect His existence or His work; at most it can only hide Him for a moment from view by the smoke of its learning. The Incarnate Son lives, and Christianity in Him. Do not allow yourselves, my young friends, to be put merely on the defensive; you have something far higher to do than even to maintain the truth and integrity of the Bible against sceptical attacks. What the world would know, and what the Church is set to prove, is that the Son of the Virgin, the Crucified One, is to-day at God's right hand, made Lord over all. How shall the Church prove this? Not simply by appealing to apostolic testimony that He rose from the dead, and ascended to heaven, but by showing forth the power of His resurrection in her children; — in their lives of holiness, in their words of truth, and in their mighty works. It was the prayer of the apostles in the beginning, "Grant unto thy servants, that with all boldness they may speak thy word, by stretching forth thine hand to heal; and that signs and wonders may be done by the name of thy Holy Child Jesus." And this prayer is the prayer of His people unto the end. Christ working from heaven through His Church, is the proof that He is risen, and invested with all power and dominion. Accurate Hebrew and Greek scholarship is desirable in those who can attain to it, but it is only instrumental. Of far more importance is it to be so cleansed and illumined that we have spiritual discernment of the purpose of God; and such faith in His words, and such spirit of self-sacrifice, that we give ourselves to be co-workers with Him and with His Son. The one thing, and the only thing, that will enable the Church to overcome the growing infidelity of the time, is to trust in her Living Head and obey Him, as He trusted in and obeyed the Father. Then will Christ be His own witness from heaven: He will testify to Himself. The temptation of Protestants is to hide Christ behind the Book, that of Roman Catholics to hide Him behind the Church. Let us do neither, but holding both the Bible and the Church in their right relations to Him, keep our eyes ever fastened on Him till He comes forth to fill the earth with the glory of God.

S. J. A.

HARTFORD, CONN., NOV. 6, 1885.

CONTENTS.

	PAGE
INTRODUCTION	1

CHAPTER I.
GOD'S REVELATION OF HIMSELF TO MEN 1

CHAPTER II.
REVELATION AND REDEMPTION 5

PART FIRST.

CHAPTER I.
THE REVELATION OF GOD TO ADAM IN EDEN 9

CHAPTER II.
GOD'S REVELATION OF HIMSELF TO THE PATRIARCHS . . 13

CHAPTER III.
THE THEOCRACY 19

CHAPTER IV.
PURPOSE AND SIGNIFICANCE OF THE THEOCRACY 30

CHAPTER V.
HISTORY OF THE THEOCRATIC PEOPLE TO THE ESTABLISHMENT OF THE MONARCHY 40

CHAPTER VI.
THE ESTABLISHMENT OF THE MONARCHY, AND THE DAVIDIC COVENANT 46

CONTENTS.

CHAPTER VII.
ORIGIN AND ELEMENTS OF THE MESSIANIC BELIEF

CHAPTER VIII.
THE PREPARATION OF THE THEOCRATIC PEOPLE FOR THE MESSIANIC KINGDOM. 62

CHAPTER IX.
HISTORY OF THE KINGDOM FROM DAVID TO ITS DIVISION . 66

CHAPTER X.
HISTORY OF THE TWO KINGDOMS AFTER THE DIVISION   70

CHAPTER XI.
THE MESSIANIC HOPE FROM THE DIVISION OF THE KINGDOM TO THE TIME OF WRITTEN PROPHECY 76

CHAPTER XII.
WRITTEN PROPHECY: ITS PLACE AND SIGNIFICANCE .   79

CHAPTER XIII.
HISTORY OF THE TWO KINGDOMS TO THEIR OVERTHROW . .   91

CHAPTER XIV.
MESSIANIC BELIEF IN THE PROPHETS DOWN TO THE EXILE,   95

CHAPTER XV.
THE NATIONAL OVERTHROW AND THE REMNANT 109

CHAPTER XVI.
MESSIANIC PROPHECIES DURING THE EXILE 124

CHAPTER XVII
THE RETURN FROM THE BABYLONIAN EXILE, AND THE PROPHETS AFTER THE RETURN. 138

CHAPTER XVIII.
MESSIANIC BELIEFS IN THE PSALMS. — MESSIAH AS KING . 152

CHAPTER XIX.

The Presentation in the Law and Prophets and Psalms of a Suffering Messiah 163

CHAPTER XX.

The Dead under the Theocracy 189

CHAPTER XXI.

The Scribes as Successors of the Prophets, and the Messianic Hope 210

CHAPTER XXII.

The Messiah in the Apocryphal and Apocalyptic Books 216

CHAPTER XXIII.

The Resurrection and the Judgment. — The Messianic Kingdom and the World to come. 228

CHAPTER XXIV.

Messianic Beliefs in our Lord's Day as set forth in the Gospels 241

CHAPTER XXV.

The Lord's own Teachings respecting His Messianic Work 250

PART SECOND.

CHAPTER I.

The Messiah in Heaven 259

CHAPTER II.

The New Election, and its Calling as the Body of Christ . . . . .

CHAPTER III.

The Two Elections, Jewish and Christian, compared, 273

CHAPTER IV.
The Church not the Messianic Kingdom 282

CHAPTER V.
The Eternal Life, and the Dead in Christ 299

CHAPTER VI.
The Apostasy and the Anti-Christ 310

PART THIRD.

CHAPTER I.
The Messianic Kingdom: its Nature and Purpose . . 318

CHAPTER II.
The Judicial Actings of Christ as Preparatory to the Kingdom, and the Day of the Lord 325

CHAPTER III.
The Messianic Kingdom in the Book of the Revelation 338

CHAPTER IV.
The Jews in the Kingdom, and the New Covenant . 344

CHAPTER V.
The Last Apostasy and Final Judgment 355

CHAPTER VI.
The New Heavens and New Earth 359

CONCLUSION.
Christianity and Other Religions 369

APPENDIX
The Higher Criticism 379

NOTES FOR REVISED EDITION.

(See Appendix.)

For page 34.—THE MOSAIC RITUAL.

For page 36.—THE THEOCRATIC IDEAL.

For page 86.—THE PROPHET JOEL, DATE OF.

For page 111.—THE CAPTIVITY—ITS MEANING.

GOD'S REVELATIONS OF HIMSELF TO MEN.

INTRODUCTION.—A GENERAL STATEMENT OF PRINCIPLES.

CHAPTER I.

GOD'S REVELATION OF HIMSELF TO MEN.

WE begin our inquiry, which embraces past, present, and future, with the fact — the central one in all God's actings — of the Incarnation. This fact we do not attempt to prove: we assume it. The Church believes and proclaims in all her creeds, that her Head, Jesus Christ, is the God-Man, and that He abides the God-Man forever. From this present fact, as from a high mountain peak, we look backward and forward: from its elevation we trace the winding pathway of Divine history as it leads onward from Eden to Bethlehem, and the pathway of prophecy, till it is lost to view in the splendors of the new heaven and the new earth. In the Incarnate Son is the key to all that God has said or done as recorded in the Scriptures, and we must read them in His light. "Search the Scriptures . . . and they are they which testify of Me."

To those who see in the Incarnate Son the centre of all God's works, "for whom all things were made," and "by whom all things consist," the biblical records will present such unity of purpose, and harmony of utterance, that they will recognize everywhere the one inspiring Spirit of Him who is "the First and the Last, the Beginning and the End."

We thus assume as the teaching of the Scriptures, and the faith of the Church, that the Divine purpose in the creation of man looked forward to the perfect manifestation of God in the person of the Incarnate Son, and that this manifestation is the goal of human history. As preparatory to this manifestation, we find three great stages of Divine actings; and we have to consider first these actings prior to the Incarnation.

God creates the heavens and the earth: He makes man in His own image, and places him in Eden. But how shall man, the finite creature, know God, his infinite and invisible Creator?

The basis of such knowledge must be laid in the nature of man as preconfigured to the Divine image. As made in God's likeness he is able to know Him, and to have communion with Him, and this in ever enlarging degree. But, however great the spiritual capacity of man, we are to remember that the relation between God and men is a personal one, and that, to be known, He must make Himself known. What communion with Him any creature may have, must depend both on its constitution and on His will. It is not enough that man has a religious nature — a faculty to apprehend the Infinite — or even an intuitive belief in His existence as Creator and supreme moral Governor; God must by His own acts enter into personal intercourse with men, must reveal Himself to them, ere they can truly know Him. The possibility of intercourse is not actual intercourse. Likeness to his Creator is the basis and condition of God's personal revelation of Himself to man, but not the revelation itself.

Here is the problem: How can man be so brought into intercourse with God as to know his relations to Him, and the duties which such relations involve? As God has a purpose in man, and as human history moves along the line of that purpose, man needs continually new instruction that he may be a worker together with God. This knowledge cannot come from any study of God's material works around him, nor from any study of his own nature. A God known only by inference is a God afar off. Knowledge of Him and of His will amidst all historic progress must be the result of God's continued personal self-revelation to man, such revelation as shall not only prove His existence and Divine nature, but be, also, an expression of His will as the law of human action. This is God's voluntary act. He comes to man, He speaks and acts; and man both knows that he meets God, and learns what are his relations to Him, and his duties.

In what manner God will reveal Himself to men, and make known His will — whether by spiritual actings in the individual spirit, or through the bodily senses, or both, and to what degree — lies wholly within His own pleasure. But we may believe, that from his creation onward man will not be left in doubt that he is dealing with a Person, One distinct from nature and above it; and that he is subject to a personal will. Recognizing it as the will of God, he is assured that it is the expression of infinite wisdom and goodness, and, therefore, to be obeyed. By obedience to this will as it is made known, he may attain to further knowledge of God, and be prepared to be admitted into closer intercourse with Him.

God having thus placed Himself in personal relation with men, the way to the fuller knowledge of Him is through obedience. The spirit of obedience can be exercised only where there is a law to obey: therefore it is that at the first God met man as the Ruler. He gave him positive commands, and thus taught him the nature and duty of obedience. If obedient as the will of God is made known to him, he is thereby prepared to receive new and fuller revelations, both as to the Divine character, and His purpose in man. The lower service prepares for a higher. Walking in the pathway of obedience man comes ever nearer and nearer to God.

Thus the Scriptures are the record of man's religious education by means of successive Divine revelations beginning in Eden. We learn from them that God not only made man in His own likeness, but condescended to personal intercourse that he might know Him. And from the Fall on men were not left to grope blindly after Him; but He came to them, and dwelt with them, and manifested Himself to them; He put them under His own immediate instruction, and led them up from lower to higher measures of knowledge, each stage being a new revelation of Himself, and demanding as its condition a higher obedience. Thus man's spiritual education is through a series of dispensations, or ages, — æons, — each being preparatory to that which follows it; the end of all being to reveal God more and more, and to bring men into closer and closer union with Him. This is the true progress of the race, — ever enlarging knowledge of God, and higher communion with Him.

CHAPTER II.

REVELATION AND REDEMPTION.

To man unfallen and obedient God could have revealed Himself in ever enlarging measure. The history of a holy people would be one of progressive revelation, for each new expression of His will meets with ready and willing obedience. The more they know of God, and the closer their communion with Him, the more do they grow into His likeness, and His will become the law of their life. But to men fallen and sinful God must come as their Redeemer, delivering them from the law of sin and death, working righteousness within them, and restoring in them His lost likeness, ere He can manifest Himself to them in His glory.

But redemption is not possible without revelation. Without the manifestation of Himself to the fallen, He cannot deliver them. The sinful must know that God is; that He is holy, just, and good; and that He demands of them true repentance, submission, and holiness of life. He must reveal Himself as the Redeemer, and make known to men how He will save them; He must mark out the paths in which they shall walk, and give them commandments which they must keep. By His dealings with them He makes known His purpose, and also brings to light what is in their hearts.

Thus revelation may be without redemption, as with the unfallen and holy angels who always behold the face of God; but redemption cannot be without revelation, and these go hand in hand. In His dealings with sinful men God reveals that He may redeem, and He redeems that He may reveal. Each successive stage of the redemptive work — Patriarchal, Jewish, and Christian — is, also, a higher stage of Divine revelation. The Incarnate Son is both the Redeemer of men and the Revealer of God. But at no stage of the redemptive work does God so reveal Himself to His people as to affect their free and voluntary moral action. He declares His will, but does not compel obedience. It is possible, however bright the light, to close the eyes to it; however manifest His truth, it may be rejected. There is possibility of apostasy from God's covenants in each successive stage till redemption has been completed. Man, therefore, in each period of his redemptive history down to the end, is upon trial whether he will accept his place of subordination and dependence upon God, will acknowledge his sinfulness, will renounce his own will, and co-operate with Him in His purposes of salvation according to his measure of knowledge; or will refuse His grace, and defiantly and persistently reject His authority.

Redemption, from its very nature, is a work limited in time, and will come to an end; but God can never cease to reveal Himself to His redeemed and holy creatures. "Blessed are the pure in heart, for they shall see God," and this forever and forever. We may, therefore, distinguish between the revelations of Himself made by God to men during the time in which He is preparing them to stand before Him in immortality and glory, and those that will then follow. We have thus two great periods, — the first, the redemptive, limited in time; the second, the post-redemptive, and unlimited. In the first, the revelations made by God of Himself are for the salvation of men, and have a character corresponding to this end. Of this redemptive period, and of God's actings in it, we learn through the Scriptures historic and prophetic, — of the past through history, of the future through prophecy. But the prophets of the Old Testament open the future only so far as to show us the acts of God in redemption down to its close: of His glorious manifestations of Himself during the endless ages that will follow, they say little. We, however, know that all done by Him in redemption is only preparatory to the higher revelation afterward to be made, when old things pass away, and all are made new. The foundation of the new creation having been laid in the Incarnation of His Son — very God and very man, in whom is seen through resurrection the new and perfect and immortal form of humanity — He proceeds step by step till the new creation is completed, wherein the fullness of His glory is revealed, and all His redeemed enter into the fullness of heavenly and eternal blessedness. It is only by regarding the redemptive period as a whole; by keeping its preparatory character in mind, and its relation to the ages that follow; and by carefully discriminating its several stages; that we can judge aright of the actings of God as presented in the Scriptures.

I.

THE REVELATIONS OF GOD TO MEN BEFORE AND UNDER THE THEOCRACY.

CHAPTER I.

THE REVELATION OF GOD TO ADAM IN EDEN.

HUMAN history opens with God and man in blessed intercourse. The work of creation is finished. Adam, made in the image of God, dwells in Eden, and here his spiritual education begins. For him God planted a garden in Eden, the land of delight, in which "He made to grow every tree that is pleasant to the sight, and good for food," thus showing His love and care for His creature. Adam from the very first was admitted into personal intercourse with his Creator. He knew that he was not alone in the garden, — there was Another, a higher Being, of whose presence he was sensible. He felt himself under the control of a personal will. The command was given him: "Of every tree of the garden thou mayest freely eat; but of the tree of the knowledge of good and evil, thou shalt not eat of it." The grounds of this command he probably did not understand; but he had the inward assurance that it was not arbitrary; it was given in love. How adequate was his conception of this Being, we need not here ask: it was enough that he knew Him as his Creator and Lord; One who had rightful authority over him, and to whom unreserved obedience was due.

Under what sensible forms God may have manifested Himself to Adam during this period, or in what manner made known His will, we are not told. (Gen. iii. 8.) It has been a current belief in the Church, that there was in the garden some permanent visible symbol of His Presence, perhaps identical with the cloud of Glory, or Shechinah, of later times; and the mention of "the Cherubim" seems to confirm this, since they re-appear in the Jewish Tabernacle and Temple as well-known symbols of the Divine Presence. (Gen. iii. 24.) "I will meet with thee," said God to Moses, "and I will commune with thee . . . from between the Cherubim." It is not unreasonable to believe, that from between the Cherubim in the garden He communed with Adam, declaring His will; and that "the flaming sword," or rather "the infolding fire," was the visible sign of His inhabitation.

It is thought by some to be inconsistent with the spirituality of God, that He should manifest Himself to men under any sensible forms. But when we remember that the great end of all His actings is the revelation of His Son, God manifest in the flesh, "in whom dwelleth all the fullness of the Godhead bodily," we see that His early manifestation of Himself to men through visible symbols, — the pillar of fire, the Glory, — as recorded in the Old Testament, is in perfect harmony with His purpose to reveal Himself in His Son. The local and sensible manifestations of Himself in Eden, at Sinai, and in Jerusalem, were not unworthy of Him whom "the heaven and heaven of heavens cannot contain," for they had their ground in the constitution of man as both material and spiritual; and all pointed forward to Him who is "the visible Image of the invisible God," and to the time when "the earth shall shine with His glory."

Very brief was the period of man's innocence. Adam was tempted and fell. The root of his sin was doubt as to the love of God, — doubt inspired by the serpent; and the result was the lifting up of his own will against the will of God in an act of positive disobedience. Through this his relation to God was radically changed: the state of unconscious innocence gave place to a state of conscious rebellion. In Adam the race came under "the law of sin and death." To convince man of his sinfulness, to awaken in him the desire for redemption, and to make known to him the nature and mode of this redemption, must be henceforth the primary object of the Divine teaching. God will not only be known as the Supreme Ruler, but also as the Holy One who abhors sin, as the Righteous Judge who punishes unrighteousness, and as the Merciful Father who forgives the repentant.

These aspects of God's character we may, therefore, expect to see made prominent in His subsequent dealings with sinful and disobedient men. Man is to be taught the evil that is in him, and which finds its chief expression in the will; and, therefore, he must be put under the law of righteousness. It is now a question of authority, of supremacy of will. Man must be taught the limitations of his nature, and his dependence. But the obedience God seeks is not the outward submission of fear, it is the joyful obedience of love; and, therefore, with the assertion of His authority, He shows Himself, also, merciful and forgiving. Sin He will not spare, but He will give His Son to die for the sinful. But mercy and forgiveness are idle words to him who knows not that he has sinned, who has no consciousness of guilt. To awaken and deepen in men the sense of sin that they may seek deliverance, is now God's primary purpose; and, to this end, men must be made to feel that they are dealing with a righteous personal Ruler. The goal to which human history from this time is moving forward, is the redemption of manhood from sin and the curse, and the establishment of a Kingdom of universal obedience, — the period when "His will shall be done in earth, as it is in heaven."

CHAPTER II.

GOD'S REVELATION OF HIMSELF TO THE PATRIARCHS.

AFTER Adam was expelled from the garden, God placed — "made to dwell," implying permanence — at the east of the garden, Cherubim " to keep the way of the tree of life." (Gen. iii. 24.) How long the Cherubim remained there is not said; many have thought until the Deluge. But, whether the period was longer or shorter, so long as they remained their presence indicated that the garden was still a sacred place. And it is not improbable that in their immediate vicinity the altars of Abel and Cain were built, and that thither, as to a consecrated spot, during the antediluvian period, God's worshippers came to offer their sacrifices and homage.

But, however this may have been, it is plain that there must have been many revelations of Himself, and declarations of His will, to the early Patriarchs. The institutions of the Sabbath and of marriage had been given in Eden. The work of redemption began from the day of the fall of man; and all the subsequent Divine appointments were to the end that men might be convinced of sin, and, being taught their relations to a holy God, might through repentance and faith have assurance of forgiveness. He gave them the rite of animal sacrifice as an element in all pre-Christian worship, thus setting forth the truth that death is the penalty of sin, and prophetically pointing forward to "the Lamb of God which taketh away the sin of the world." Not a few of these early commandments, handed down by tradition, we may believe, were afterwards incorporated into the Mosaic code.

The patriarchal history it is not necessary to trace in detail. The line of distinction between the families obedient to God, and those disobedient, must have been very early drawn. In the first family the separation began, and it widened more and more. The heads of these two lines of development were Cain and Seth. We can see in the children of Seth a sense of sin and a hope of redemption, but these are not seen in the children of Cain. The record that in the days of Enos, the son of Seth, " men began to call upon the name of the Lord," seems to indicate some new and solemn development at that time of the rites of worship among the worshippers of Jehovah. (Gen. iv. 26.) There is no mention of idolatry among the Cainites; and if there was during this period a visible Symbol of Jehovah's presence east of Eden, thus keeping Him in the remembrance of men as the one God, this may be in part an explanation. The especial characteristic of this time was its fleshliness, the indulgence of fleshly lusts. God seems to have left them free to do their own will, and to walk in their own ways. It was a condition of society in which there was little of external authority to restrain human passions. Corruption of manners, and violence, filled the earth. Even to slay a man was counted a light thing. The spirit of the time is well set forth in the song of Lamech, the song of the sword. A man's best defence is not in the protection of God, but in the sharpness of his weapon and the strength of his arm. Against this spirit of violence the peaceful Sethites had little defence. The wickedness of the

Cainites increased continually: as some think, even the boundaries between the realms of men and of evil spirits were passed over. (Gen. vi. 1, etc.) And at last so general was the corruption of the race, that God sent the Flood upon the earth. Only Noah, the tenth in the line of Seth, and his family were delivered.

To what degree during this period the promise of God respecting "the Seed of the woman that should bruise the serpent's head," was known and understood, it is impossible to say. But we can scarcely doubt, that under its figurative terms the early patriarchs saw the promise of a future redemption, — a victory of good over evil to be ultimately obtained by mankind; and this through the mediation of a personal Redeemer. That there was during this period a growing apprehension of the Divine purpose in redemption among the obedient, appears plain from what is told us of Enoch and of Noah, — that they "walked with God," or in His ways; and of the preaching and translation of Enoch, and the preaching of Noah. (Jude 14; Heb. xi. 7; 2 Pet. ii. 5.) The statement in the Epistle to the Hebrews, in which the antediluvian patriarchs are included, — that " these all died in faith, not having received the promises, but having seen them afar off, and were persuaded of them, and embraced them," — can only mean that they had such knowledge of God's purpose in redemption, so far as then revealed, as to be workers together with Him through faith. (xi. 13.)

We may rightly conclude, that, down to the time of the Deluge, God continued to stand in immediate personal relations with the families faithful to Him, making known to them His will, giving them new commandments according to changing circumstances, and using them as His messengers to warn the rebellious of His judgments. The sin of the antediluvians was not, so far as we know, the worship of false gods, but the indulgence of fleshly lusts, the ignoring of His authority, and rejection of His witnesses, ending in the general dissolution of all moral and social bonds. (Gen. vi. 11-13.)

To trace the origin of idolatry after the Flood, to distinguish its forms, and to follow its progress, is no part of our present purpose. We are concerned only with the fact that idolatry, taking different forms in different lands, but essentially nature worship, early became very prevalent. A considerable time anterior to Abraham, we find proofs that polytheism prevailed in Egypt. A multitude of deities of different orders were objects of worship, and polytheism became general in all the region of Chaldæa and Mesopotamia. God was, indeed, not left without witnesses to His unity and supremacy. Such a witness was Melchizedek, who is called a "priest of the Most High God," and who in His name as the "possessor of heaven and earth" blesses Abraham. (Gen. xiv. 18, 19.) And such a witness was Abraham. But scattered individuals or families could not effectually resist the strong tendencies to idolatry everywhere prevailing. The time had come for a new step in the work of redemption, a new manifestation of God to men, an assertion of Himself before all the world as the One Supreme God in opposition to all idols. There is "a fullness of time" in all His actings; and we can see here two elements of this fullness, — the spread of idolatry, and the existence of distinct nations.

So long as the constitution of society had not advanced beyond the patriarchal stage, and the family continued to be the chief element, God's rule over men could be but very imperfectly set forth. His authority could find fit expression only in a nation, whose citizens He could bind together under visible institutions of His own immediate appointment, and to whose laws all must render obedience. He could be best made known to the nations as the Supreme Ruler, at the head of a people; and as the One God, in the unity of their worship. It is probable that there was in the single families at this time a considerable uniformity in religious rites — a residuum of antediluvian tradition; but many scattered family altars could not bear an adequate witness to His unity against the increasing multitude of polytheistic worshippers.

The first step taken by God in this new form of His actings, was the call of Abraham to be the founder of a nation. Already were there nations of high civilization existing; but none of these did He choose, for all were deeply infected with idolatry. It is to be noted, that, with the growth of peoples and the development of national life, the spirit of pride seems to have increased, chiefly, perhaps, because through the unity of many, and consequent consciousness of strength, larger scope was given to human activity, and the will of the ruler became controlling and absolute with the enlargement of the sphere of his rule. In patriarchal times the bonds of union were so few among the several families, there was so little of social order and public law, that individual lawlessness found little to restrain it. But when later, through increase of population, families grew into tribes, and tribes into peoples, and all had one law and one speech, although individual lawlessness on the one hand was restrained, yet, on the other, the scope for personal and despotic rule was enlarged. A great, or perhaps universal, monarchy was now a possibility to the bold and ambitious. The building of the city and tower of Babel was apparently an attempt to unite all the dwellers in that region under one government, perhaps to establish an universal monarchy; and a protest against the Divine purpose of dispersing men in order to "replenish the earth." That the spirit of the movement was evil, is shown by the result: the presumptuous attempt was checked by Divine interposition through the confusion of tongues. (Gen. xi.)

Though Abraham had several children, yet one only was in the elect line of descent; and in the family of Isaac the same was true. But Jacob had twelve sons, and in them was laid the foundation of the nation to which God's purpose from the beginning had looked forward.

CHAPTER III.

THE THEOCRACY.

It has been already remarked that the purpose of God in redemption from the beginning looked beyond individuals, beyond families, to a nation. In the larger communities of nations only could the individual man find his complete development, and also the authority of God be manifested to its full extent. The nation, not the family, is the sphere in which, through its manifold relations and activities, our humanity is brought under influences which touch all its springs, and quicken all its powers into action, and where it finds full scope for all its energies. Nations, therefore, as necessary to individual development, both intellectual and moral, are an integral element of God's purpose towards mankind. New and higher revelations of God's Presence among men and of His righteous rule were, also, dependent upon the existence of nations. The Theocracy could not be established, or its ends be attained, till family life expanded into the larger realm of national life. Through His immediate rule over a people chosen by Him, organized by Him, and obedient to Him, could be made manifest to all the world His personal authority as the one Supreme Ruler over all the earth. Through this theocratic relation could be shown forth in action His divine attributes, and the nations see His righteousness and holiness reflected in the institutions He appointed, and in the character and administration of His government. The preparation for this theocratic kingdom was begun in the election of Abraham, and completed when at Sinai He entered into covenant with the people that had sprung from him, and which had been prepared for its high place by a long process of discipline and trial.

The most important points in God's relations to the Jews may be thus summed up.

First, He separated them from all other peoples by entering into special covenant with them, "putting His name upon them" that they might be unto Him "a people of inheritance." He chose for them a land in which they should dwell, and of which He claimed the exclusive ownership. (Exod. xix. 5, xxiv. 7; Lev. xx. 24, 26, xxv. 23; Deut. vii. 6, xiv. 2.)

Second, Having redeemed them from their bondage in Egypt by mighty judgments upon their oppressors, He led them through the Wilderness, going before them in the cloud and pillar of fire; and, after their land was reached, set up His sanctuary in the place which He had selected, and where He manifested His presence by visible supernatural signs, and which thus became the national civil and ecclesiastical centre. (Exod. vi. 7, xiii. 21, 22.; Lev. xxv. 38; Exod. xxv. 8, xxxiii. 14; Deut. xii. 5.)

Third, He became their Lawgiver and King, all their laws and institutions proceeding directly from Him; and by His direction they acted in all national matters. His will was made known, sometimes by an audible voice, as on Mount Sinai, or by the High Priest through the Urim and Thummim, or through His word spoken by Moses, and later by the prophets. (Exod. iii. 4, 41, xv. 18, xix. 19; Num. x. 35, xxiii. 21; Deut. xxxiii. 5, iv. 12, v. 4; Exod. xxviii. 30; Num. xxvii. 21; Deut. xviii. 18.)

Fourth, If obedient to these laws and institutions,

God would bless them with all temporal blessings, and deliver them from all national evils, from pestilence, and drought and famine, from foreign invasion and conquest, and make them an example to all nations. (Deut. vii. 12, xxviii. 1; Lev. xxvi. 3; Deut. xi. 8, etc.)

Fifth, As God's chosen people, and under His special rule, the Jews were lifted up above all other peoples in honor and blessing; and, as a kingdom of priests, they were set in a mediatorial relation to other nations, and through them in the fullness of time should all the peoples of the earth be blessed. (Deut. iv. 7, 8; Exod. xxxiii. 16, xxxiv. 10; Deut. xxvi. 18, xxviii. 1, etc.)

Sixth, If unholy and disobedient, God would visit them with heavy judgments, even giving them up to national destruction, but would not cast them utterly off; and, when repentant, would bring them again to their own land, would renew His covenant with them, and fulfill to them all His promises of blessing, both temporal and spiritual, and be sanctified in them before the eyes of all nations. (Num. xiv. 11; Lev. xxvi.; Deut. xxviii.)

In this choice of the Jews two relations were established, which it is important to keep clearly in mind, — that of Jehovah to the people, and that of Jehovah to the land.

First, The relation of Jehovah to the people. An attentive consideration of the particulars just enumerated will show that the government of Jehovah over the Jews was, in the fullest sense of the word, a monarchy. The nation was one of His own creation, in the election of its founder, Abraham, in its tribal divisions, and in its unity as established by Moses. Its national birth was through those mighty acts whereby He delivered the people from the Egyptian yoke, and brought them to Sinai. But it was here in the manifestation of Himself, when "His glory was like devouring fire upon the top of the Mount," and He was heard speaking to them and giving them commandments, that the assembled people had incontestable proof that He was present with them as their Lawgiver and King. And the part which Moses then and subsequently took as the mediator to make known His will, bore so plainly the stamp of Divine authentication, that none could doubt that the laws which he gave in the name of Jehovah, were truly His.

We may notice here the fact, that at the first there was under the Theocracy no human executive; no one person, or body of persons, to act as Jehovah's representative. The positions of Moses and of Joshua were clearly exceptional, and their work preparatory; nor could they appoint their successors: and the hereditary princes, the heads of the several tribes, had no such official place or duty. By this, however, is not meant that there were not officers fulfilling civil functions, judicial and executive; for this was as necessary under a Theocracy as under a human government. (Exod. xviii. 13, etc.; Deut. xvi. 18.) And the request of Moses, that God would set a man over the congregation, that it be not as sheep that have no shepherd, showed how strongly he felt the need of a head for the people. (Num. xxvii. 15, etc.) But the fact is plain, that no one did stand after Joshua's death before the united tribes as Jehovah's representative. It is not obvious how we are to explain the absence of such a national head: perhaps it was intended to bring into clearer relief the truth of His immediate rule.

It does not appear that it was God's purpose to set aside tribal distinctions, so emphasized in prophecy, and to fuse all into one. (Gen. xlix.) Their unity should be religious more than political. If pervaded by the true theocratic spirit, this spirit would prove the most powerful bond of national unity, and yet leave full scope for tribal diversities. If unfaithful to Jehovah, no mere political bands could hold them together.

As regards the administration of the theocratic state, it is important to distinguish clearly between the relation of Jehovah to the Jews as their God, and His relation to them as their King. He was, as God, the God of all nations alike, whether they knew and recognized Him as such or not. It was a relation that did not depend on human volition. But the kingly relation was one established by Him with this people only, and with their voluntary assent. (Exod. xix. 5-8.) From this twofold relation of Jehovah to the chosen people, it follows that there must be found in their laws and institutions both permanent and transient elements. Their duties toward Him as their God, and which found their chief expression in their rites of worship, were permanent. The whole ritual, the kinds and order of sacrifice, the priesthood in its several ranks and duties and offices, the sevenfold division of times, the feasts, — all this was unchangeable. No degree of national or individual development could affect them. As typical of higher things to come, they must remain till the antitypes came. And thus it was that Moses was directed to make all these things after the pattern showed him in the Mount, a Divine order which man might not change. (Exod. xxv. 9, 40; Heb. viii. 5, etc.)

As the King of a nation, the laws of Jehovah must be such as were suited to its measure of moral and social development. In one aspect they reflected His own perfections; in another, the imperfections of the people. He dealt with them as a father with his child, condescending for the time to their ignorance and weakness, but ever striving to prepare them, through His teaching and discipline, for the high place to which He had called them. As civil laws, the laws of Jehovah had such penalties attached to their violation as the civil laws of other peoples. Jehovah did not judge and punish acts of disobedience as God, who in His omniscience takes knowledge of the secret motive of the transgressor, and judges according to this, and not to the outward act. This would have made any co-operation of His people in the administration of justice impossible. As under other governments, so here in general, the violation of the laws must be proved by witnesses, and the penalties be inflicted by men. There were, indeed, offences which from their nature could not be so proved; as, for example, eating the blood of a sacrifice: and of such an offender it is said, "I will cut him off from among my people," — a penalty which was understood by the Jews to mean an untimely death supernaturally inflicted. (Lev. xvii. 10.) But this punishment, like the other punishments, was of an act, a transgression of the known law, not punishment of the thought of the heart. Death under the law was a civil penalty, and no more proved the eternal damnation of the offender than it does under human governments. The two spheres of Jehovah's rule — as God, who knows the heart, and whose judgments affect eternity; and as King, who judges according to the outward act, and whose judgments are temporal — must always be kept in mind. We may also notice the distinction between the institutions of the theocratic state and those of other states, springing from the divine Person of the King. A man is sometimes the founder of a state, and stamps his own character upon its political institutions;

but he is still one with the people, — the product of his own time, and its exponent. He can, according to the measure of his sagacity, see the needs of the day, and make some provision for them; but he cannot make provision for the remote future, which he cannot foresee. And, as individual rulers and dynasties are constantly changing, the progress of one generation is often lost in the next. Thus the education of a people under one definite, consistent, and permanent polity becomes impossible. But this was the Divine purpose in the election of the Jews. The theocratic King was the same Person in all the successive generations. And He knew the end from the beginning: He established institutions that looked forward to the attainment of a specific end, and were not to be changed till that end was reached. The laws, in their chief features, were not the gradual outgrowth of the national spirit, but were given to mould and to control that spirit. In Divinely ordered channels should run from the first the currents of national life.

We may thus readily understand why it was that God through Moses did not give His people a few fundamental principles or rudimentary institutions, and leave their further unfolding to circumstances. The Mosaic legislation was a unity. Its several laws were integral parts of a whole: they all combined to the attainment of one end. There was indeed to be growth, but it was organic growth: there was adaptation to changing relations, but ever with the preservation of the organic framework, the new being always in the same line of movement as the old. This was possible, because Moses was taught of God, whose purpose embraced the future no less than the present.

As the great end of the Theocracy was religious, — to bring the people to know and to trust in their God, —

many of its laws appealed to faith; and, if faith was wanting, they would not be observed. Such were those respecting the Sabbatic periods and rest of the land, the keeping of the feasts, the law of tithes and offerings. It was impossible that obedience in many cases could be enforced if the spirit of obedience was wanting.

In its elements the Mosaic legislation must have much in common with contemporaneous legislation of other peoples, because of ideas and customs then universally prevalent. Not a few ancestral usages were tolerated by Moses because of " the hardness of their hearts," as divorce and blood revenge; but these were not to be permanent. (Matt. xix. 8.) The law had in it new elements, which would in time develop themselves, and eliminate all that was unworthy, and prepare the people to receive statutes and ordinances reflecting in a higher degree the perfect justice, wisdom, and holiness of their Divine King.

It was impossible that these two relations of Jehovah to His people, as their God and their King, could be dissevered, and they be faithful in the one and unfaithful in the other. The national life could not be divided into two discordant spheres. Their civil prosperity was dependent on their religious faithfulness. Hence arose the peculiar strength, and also the peculiar weakness, of the Jewish state. Abiding faithful to their covenant, and obeying and worshipping Jehovah, there was nothing conducive to national well-being that was not promised them. Their King was all-powerful, and neither men nor the forces of nature could resist His will. Thus the possibility of unexampled material prosperity and greatness was set before them. But Jehovah did not rule them by force, — their obedience must be voluntary; and therefore He might be among them as a strong man that is bound, unable to bless them, unable even to defend them, because of their moral condition. On the contrary, His presence with them, if they were unfaithful, must bring upon them special judgments. He could not see His laws disobeyed, His sanctuary defiled, without inflicting deserved punishment.

Second, The relation of Jehovah to the Land. His choice of the land of Canaan was announced by Jehovah many years before He gave His people possession, its relative position and physical peculiarities fitting it for His purpose. It wonderfully fulfilled two conditions: First, as a place of training and discipline, — a land where for a time they might be hidden away till prepared to take their proper place among the nations. Defended on all sides by natural barriers, they could "dwell apart." Second, as a land where they could bear their witness to Jehovah, when His time had come. As midway between Egypt and Chaldæa, and adjacent to Asia Minor, the name of Jehovah might be made known through them to the peoples both of the East and the West.

Of this land, Jehovah gave to His people possession, but not ownership. "The land is mine, for ye are pilgrims and sojourners with me." (Lev. xxv. 23.) The whole tenure of landed property was determined by the fact that He was the sole owner, and they only tenants at will, and their possession of it was conditioned upon the fulfillment of their covenant obligations. If faithful to Him, He would defend them from the invasion of enemies; their land should not be visited with drought, nor by devastating insects; there should not be pestilence or famine, but the rain should fall in its season, and the land be filled with plenty. But, if unfaithful, He would visit them with judgments until He had brought the land unto desolation, and scattered the people among the heathen.

As it is necessary in every state that there should be a central seat, a capital where the sovereign dwells, and from whence goes forth the law, so was it here. When the people had taken full possession of the land, Jehovah Himself selected the place where He would dwell, and where should be seen the symbol of His Presence. "I will dwell among the children of Israel, and will be their God." Thus by His Presence the land was hallowed. It had been defiled by its heathen inhabitants, but henceforth it should be holy. "Defile not the land . . . wherein I dwell." As His land, it could not become the permanent possession of any other people; it could not be alienated from the end to which He had designed it. He might, indeed, as a punishment for their sins, scatter His people abroad among the nations, and even give up His own city and temple to overthrow: but His special relation to the land did not cease; it remained His; and no nation could set up in it a stable and prosperous government, or make it the permanent abode of its people. It must remain a land set apart till His purpose is fulfilled in it.

This relation of the Jews to their land, through Jehovah, was a most important element in their history. To be thrust out of it, and to be scattered among the nations, was the heaviest punishment that could be inflicted upon them, since it was inflicted by their King, and was the proof to all the world of their rebellion. Separated from the land, they were separated from Him who had chosen it for them, and who dwelt in it. His temple was there, and only in the temple could the appointed rites of worship be carried on. Nor could the law in many of its chief provisions be executed in any other land. Had it been possible to find another country, and to make it their own, this would not have restored their relation to Jehovah as their King: this relation was inseparably connected with the land He had given them. They could not dwell elsewhere and be His people, and fulfill their calling.

CHAPTER IV.

PURPOSE AND SIGNIFICANCE OF THE THEOCRACY.

The fact of a Theocracy on the earth, the Supreme God ruling a people as its King, is one of deepest interest and importance. We must carefully examine it, that we may understand its high place and scope in the Divine purpose of revelation and redemption.

That God should enter into special covenant relations with one among the peoples of the earth, and that without any merit on its part entitling it to such position, has often been objected to as unworthy of Him who is Ruler over all, and even as self-contradictory, and historically incredible. These objections it is not necessary for us here to consider. The simple statements of the Scriptures are, that God chose the Jews to be His people, not as intrinsically better than others, but because He had a purpose to effect by them. (Deut. ix. 4.) The election of some to be His in a special sense, that He may first reveal Himself to them, and through them reveal Himself to others, is an established mode of His actings in His dealings with men. From the first He has chosen, and prepared, and sent forth, individuals to be His messengers and servants. The peculiarity here is, that He chooses a nation, and sets it among the other nations as the mediator of His truth and grace.

Amongst the ends to be attained by God in this

choice of the Hebrew people, two are especially prominent: first, their education and preparation to be His instruments in a future stage of His work of redemption; second, the present revelation of Himself through them to all nations as the one God, and the Lord of all.

Regarding the Theocracy as primarily an institute for the religious education of the Hebrews, what were the great truths to be taught them, and how were they to be taught? These truths were the nature and character of Jehovah as separate from and above all heathen gods, His unity, His supreme authority, His holiness, His righteousness, His goodness, and His purpose in redemption through His Son; and, learning these truths, they learned to know, also, their own moral character, their sinfulness, ignorance, and weakness, the nature of faith, the duty of obedience, and their place as His helpers in the redemptive work. These truths were to be taught them as a people through His immediate rule over them, and by a common law and ritual; the individual life deriving its form and spirit from the national life. The Hebrew people, in their low moral condition, surrounded by heathen tribes, and continually tempted into idolatry and immorality, must first of all be brought within the sphere of law. A strong barrier must be placed around them to protect them from hostile influences, and they be put under a system of positive prescriptions, embracing the minutest details of civil and religious life; and therefore God was pleased to place Himself to them in the special relation of their King, and to bring them as a people under His immediate authority.

We have here one chief ground of the election of a nation, as distinguished from individuals or families. The nation is pre-eminently the sphere of law. Here can Jehovah reveal Himself as the Lawgiver, the Ruler. His will meets the citizen at every point, and demands submission. Under the Theocracy, therefore, could the Jews be taught the highest lessons of obedience. They were dealing with a living Person, not with abstract principles, nor with a statute-book; and thus a most vivid sense of Jehovah's personality was ineffaceably stamped upon them. And through His rule over them, His attributes — His righteousness, His goodness, His mercy — were revealed in their daily practical application to human needs.

As a member of the Theocratic State, every Jew had in some degree the consciousness of the high national calling, and knowledge of the moral duties it involved. He knew that Jehovah had chosen and set apart His people to be "a kingdom of priests and a holy nation." He knew, also, that a glorious future was before them if they responded to the Divine purpose: thus a strong feeling of national unity was awakened and fostered in his heart. Not to a few individuals, nor to one tribe, but to the whole people, were the promises made; and here was the true counterpoise to tribal rivalries and discords. But, although the election was national, the individual was not swallowed up in the nation. He was reminded in many ways that he stood in a personal relation to Jehovah, and that the eye of his Holy King was ever upon him. The appointed sacrifices were individual as well as national. (Lev. i.–iv.) An ample provision was made that every man might "have a conscience void of offence both toward God and man."

As the purpose of God from the first looked onward to the incarnation of His Son and His atoning sacrifice, and as the Jews were chosen to be the people from whom He should spring, it needs no proof that the appointments of God by Moses had in many respects a typical reference to Him as "the Lamb of God to take away the sin of the world." This prophetic bearing of the Law, its testimonies to Him who should die for men, was not indeed plain to every eye. It could only be spiritually discerned. In proportion as the Jews kept God's commands, and rendered faithful obedience, should they be cleansed in spirit, and be able to discern the deeper imports of the Divine appointments, and their prophetic significance. To do His present will was then, as now and ever, the condition of further knowledge. If obedient, every successive generation would enter into a larger apprehension of the Divine purpose, and be lifted up into higher measures of spiritual knowledge and strength.

It is not necessary to suppose that the elect people had at first any clear knowledge of a suffering Messiah to come, or any distinct consciousness that their sacrifices drew all their virtue from the great Sacrifice He was to offer. But the more spiritually-minded among them could not take part in the appointed rites of worship, without being made to feel that they were sinful, that sin was abhorred of God, and that only through shedding of blood was there atonement and forgiveness. The entrance of the priests only into the Holy Place, and of the high priest alone into the Most Holy, taught them the holiness of God, and that only those whom He chose could minister before Him, and find acceptance. The several laws respecting ceremonial pollution, and the necessary external purifications, no less than the demands for moral purity, kept them ever in mind that Jehovah dwelling among them is holy, and seeks holiness in them.

It was thus through His Presence with them, and His statutes and ordinances embracing every region of life, and not through didactic teaching, that God would prepare His people for their future work. Although a shadow of the better things to come, the legal rites were not merely prophetic: the cleansing and grace to which they pointed through the great Sacrifice to be offered, were in a measure conveyed to all who were obedient and true-hearted. The elect people were not dealing with empty forms and idle symbols, for God was dwelling among them, "the Fountain of living waters;" and every ordinance of His appointment was a channel of spiritual blessing. The Holy Spirit was there to convict of sin, to cleanse, to give knowledge of God's will, and strength to fulfill it. What depths of spiritual self-knowledge, what purity and holiness and devotion, were in fact attained to by the Jewish saints, and what earnest desires for higher communion with God were awakened, is sufficiently attested by their utterances in the Prophets and the Psalms.

But the moral and spiritual development of those under the Theocracy, which was essential to the fulfillment of its purpose, could not be without obedience. Righteousness could be wrought in His people only through the means He had appointed, not in ways of their own choosing. It was in keeping His statutes and ordinances that He could bless them. Nothing was commanded by Him that was idle, and therefore nothing could be neglected. If faith failed among the people, His laws might fall into desuetude; but as fixed elements in the Divine legislation, they abide, and will in due time, when faith revives, answer their appointed end.

As their King, and through His rule over them, Jehovah made known to His people the principles of His moral government. It was well said by Mr. Gladstone that "the State is a moral agency which aims at character through conduct;" and this was in the highest sense true of the Theocratic State. Through the laws regulating personal and social relations, its citizens were to be educated in the practice of morality and justice. Not as speculative principles, nor as theological dogmas, did the great truths of religion meet them, but as embodied in laws and ritual, and enforced by Personal authority. God was not a God afar off, but a God dwelling among them. Through obedience to His statutes and ordinances, through acts of worship, and the practice of righteousness, should they attain true ethical and spiritual knowledge.

Thus under His own immediate instruction and discipline Jehovah began to prepare a people for the coming Messiah, and for their place in His kingdom. He did not reveal to them the future in its fullness; this was impossible: and what knowledge of the Messiah they might at this time have had, is a matter of question; but He gave them in the present every thing necessary to prepare them for the near future. More distinct revelations respecting the Person and work of the Deliverer would be made as they were able to receive them. If they failed to be a people spiritually prepared for the promised One, when the time for His appearing should come, it would be because of their willful rejection of God's grace.

The second great end to be accomplished in the choice of the Jews as the theocratic people, was the present revelation of Jehovah through them to all nations. (1 Kings viii. 60.) As the Head of the nation He could bring Himself in the most conspicuous manner upon the theatre of the world, and under His rule His people might be the noblest actors in its drama. If the elect people should walk in obedience, and be blessed with the rich blessings spiritual and temporal He had promised them, He would as their King be honored in them before all the world.

Let us note more particularly the nature of the witness to Jehovah, which, as the theocratic people, they should bear. It was impossible in the nature of the case that the Jews could be long in the community of nations, and their peculiar form of polity, and their distinctive religious position, not be known. All the neighboring lands had, it is true, their local and special deities, and their State religions. But not as a mere national Deity — one God among many — did Jehovah rule over them. It was a part of their witness to the world that He was the one Supreme God; all other gods were idols; He alone had power to bless and to punish. If His rule was now limited in its visible exercise to the one people only among whom He dwelt, it was not because He did not claim universal dominion, and possess absolute power, but that through this one people He might make Himself known to all, and in due time extend His rule over all. Thus separated, and dwelling apart in the land which He had given them, under laws and institutions proceeding immediately from Himself, having His sanctuary and dwelling-place among them, supernaturally protected and blessed by Him, obeying Him as their King, and worshipping Him as their God, the theocratic people could bear such public and world-wide witness to Him, as was not otherwise possible. In all periods of their history, if they fulfilled in any high measure their calling, it must have been known that their place was unique among the nations.

Let us suppose that the Jews had so lived under the Theocracy that God's promises to them, embracing both spiritual and temporal blessings, could have been fulfilled, what a spectacle would they have presented to all the neighboring peoples! Here was a people professing its faith in one Supreme God, and affirming that He alone should be worshipped, and that all other gods

were vanity; and more than this, that He had chosen
them as His holy people, that He was dwelling among
them as their King, that all their laws and rites of worship came immediately from Him, and that in supernatural ways He directed them in all their national acts.
They affirmed, that under His protection neither pestilence nor famine, nor any destructive forces of nature,
had power to hurt them, and that in war He would
defend them from all enemies. And these blessings
were not to be confined to themselves only. Jehovah's
purpose looked onward to the blessing of all nations.
His temple at Jerusalem was to be "an house of prayer
for all peoples;" and the time would come when one
of their lineage sent of Him, a just and mighty Prince,
would reign in righteousness over all the earth, and all
nations would worship Jehovah, and holiness and peace
everywhere prevail. Such a testimony, one not of word
only, but illustrated and confirmed by God's dealings
with them, could not have been unheard or ignored.
Whatever its moral effect upon the idolatrous nations
in proving the supremacy of Jehovah, and in bringing
them to acknowledge and to worship Him, the very
existence of such a monotheistic people must have
awakened general attention, and been to all receptive
hearts a fact of profoundest interest.

Bishop Butler, in the chapter in his "Analogy" on
the Moral Government of God, refers to the Jewish
people as an illustration of the influence which a kingdom, administered with highest wisdom and perfect
righteousness, would have on the face of the earth. "It
would be plainly superior to any other, and the world
must gradually come under its empire. . . . The head
of it would be an universal monarch; . . . and the East-
ern style would be literally applicable to him, that all
peoples, nations, and languages should serve him." In

the fullest sense would this have been realized in the Jews abiding as a faithful people under the Theocracy. An example of the highest form of national life, just, virtuous, peaceful, and prosperous, undisturbed by internal strifes, invincible, yet not ambitious or aggressive, their influence must have been felt throughout all nations; and the truth of their religion, their conceptions of God, of His unity, wisdom, holiness, goodness, and power, must have found wide recognition in all lands. In due time all peoples would have recognized them as the just and holy nation; their land as " a delightsome land," and their God as worthy the reverence and adoration of all. Thus through the theocratic relation, and as the Head of a nation, could Jehovah present Himself as the King to whom all rulers on the earth owed obedience, and as the God whom all should worship. As the beams from the lighthouse tower penetrate the thick darkness, and are seen afar, so from His throne in Jerusalem should the light of His truth penetrate the darkened spirits of men, even in the most distant lands. However bitterly opposed was the defiled spirit of heathenism to the pure religion of Jehovah, many would have been found among all peoples who would have hearkened willingly to spiritual truth coming to them from a people which illustrated it in all its national acts, and in the holy and blameless lives of its citizens. The words of the prophet would early have found the beginning of their fulfillment: " Many people shall go and say, Come ye, and let us go up to the mountain of the Lord, to the house of the God of Jacob; and He will teach us of His ways, and we will walk in His paths." (Isa. ii. 3.)

Well might Moses ask, " What nation is there so great, who hath God so nigh unto them, as the Lord our God is in all things that we call upon Him for? And what nation is there so great, that hath statutes and judgments so righteous as all this law, which I set before you this day?"

But if on the contrary the people were unfaithful and disobedient, then would Jehovah be manifested to the nations as the Holy and Just One through the judgments He would inflict upon them. In their subjection to their enemies, the burning of their cities, the desolation of their land, His name would be magnified, and His righteousness be declared. All the nations beholding His judgments would say, "Wherefore hath the Lord done thus unto this land? what meaneth the heat of this great anger?" (Deut. xxix. 24.) His dealings with them, whether in acts of blessing or of punishment, would be so wonderful that they would draw to them the attention of the world, and so serve to make known to all His purpose in them, and in the end to exalt and glorify His name. (Jer. xxii. 8, 9; Ezek. v. 8; Mal. iii. 12.)

CHAPTER V.

HISTORY OF THE THEOCRATIC PEOPLE TO THE ESTABLISHMENT OF THE MONARCHY.

THE national witness which the Jews were called to bear to Jehovah as the One, Supreme, Holy and Righteous God, they could not bear till the spirit of His government had fully penetrated and pervaded their own national life. As those to whom were committed the oracles of God, they must receive the truth into their own hearts ere they could become teachers of others: they must themselves offer pure and acceptable worship ere their temple could become "an house of prayer for all peoples."

It was made evident at Mount Sinai that there was needed a preliminary period of discipline and proof ere the elect people could be brought into the land chosen for them. The tribes showed the impress, intellectually and morally, of their hard bondage in Egypt, and their unpreparedness for their high calling. The subsequent long wandering in the Wilderness — the punishment of their unbelief — resulted in the education of a generation in good degree obedient, and which Moses and Joshua could lead forward to take possession of their land. To take this possession was the first duty of the covenant people; but since Jehovah had chosen it, in virtue of His absolute lordship over all lands, and had given it to them, it was His own special work to settle them in it.

But it was a work in which they must co-operate. It was necessary that those dwelling in it should be driven out, for their sins had been such as to draw upon them the just anger of God. How should this be done? His purpose did not demand their destruction, for they might voluntarily have left the land; but it did demand that they be driven beyond its boundaries. The land must be purged of its inhabitants who had defiled it. (Lev. xviii. 24-27; Deut. xviii. 12.) The promise of Jehovah to His people was, "the Lord your God shall lay the fear of you and the dread of you upon all the land," — a fear and dread springing from the knowledge of His presence with them, as shown in His mighty acts in their deliverance from Egypt, and during their wanderings in the Wilderness. Such was the effect of the destruction of the Egyptian hosts at the Red Sea, and of the signs — the pillar of cloud and of fire — that went before them in their march. (Exod. xiv., xv.) Their solemn entrance into the land by the passage of the Jordan dry-shod, showed to all its inhabitants that no obstacles of nature could hinder their progress. (Josh. iii. 13.) To these proofs of the presence and power of their God, was added that of the capture of Jericho, — a capture that showed strikingly the futility of all armed resistance. Nothing was needed but obedience and faith to enable Joshua and the people rapidly to complete their conquest, for these Divine interpositions foreshadowed what Jehovah would do for them if they trusted in Him. The victory over Amalek, their first enemy, was a type showing how they might prevail over all their enemies. (Exod. xvii. 8.) Had they been true to their calling, we may believe that there would have been such signal displays of His power, that none of the heathen tribes would have dared to contend with them, but, yielding to them the quiet possession of the land, would have sought new homes elsewhere. (Deut. ix. 3; Josh. ii. 9.)

But disobedience and want of faith speedily brought with them merited defeat. The courage of the Canaanites revived, and their fear of Jehovah gradually diminished. He did not, indeed, forsake His people, and they were in general victorious under Joshua; but the conquest of the land was very imperfectly effected, and this after a protracted and bloody struggle. They learned by a bitter experience, that without Jehovah's help their strength availed little, and that faith and obedience on their part were the necessary conditions of His interpositions.

This inability to drive out the idolatrous inhabitants, and their consequent cohabitation with them, was a sin the evil effects of which were seen in all their subsequent history. Because of this intercourse with the heathen, "the anger of the Lord was hot against Israel, and He gave them into the hand of their enemies." It is not necessary to recite the facts so distinctly stated in the books of Joshua and the Judges. Long periods of servitude and oppression, with occasional wonderful deliverances, and attempts at reformation under the leadership of the Judges, marked this stage of their history.

It can scarcely be questioned that the Hebrews were in some considerable degree infected with idolatry when they came out of Egypt, and thus were especially exposed to temptation from the idolaters around them. It is not, indeed, probable that the golden calf made by Aaron at Sinai was a copy of any Egyptian deity. (Exod. xxxii. 4.) It was rather a reminiscence of the Cherubim as placed east of Eden, a symbol of the Divine Presence. But, if not directly idolatrous, it was contrary to God's commandment, and showed that intercourse with the heathen around them could not fail to stimulate the tendencies to idolatry. Their safeguard was in driving the idolatrous tribes wholly from the land, and in the complete and permanent separation, through ceremonial laws, from the adjacent nations. Thus made "to dwell alone" till the spirit of their calling had taken possession of all departments of national life, they had been prepared to take their place among the nations, under Jehovah, and to bear their witness to Him as the One Righteous and Holy God.

The whole period from Joshua's death to Samuel, the tribes were without a head, and all their actions were marked by a want of unity. In their contest for the land each tribe acted for itself, and so with very partial success; and probably there was little of united worship. There was strong temptation to each tribe to have its own sanctuaries and high places; although there seems to have been a general recognition that the appointed worship was to be carried on at Shiloh. It is possible, also, that the old patriarchal priesthood long maintained a not altogether illicit existence by the side of the Aaronic priesthood, until experience of its tendencies to disintegration and idolatry led to the final execution of the Mosaic laws in their completeness.

During the long period of the struggle with the Canaanites for mastery, Jehovah could not dwell as King in His own land. Not till it had been taken into full possession, and been cleansed and sanctified as His dwelling-place, could the movable tent — the symbol of wandering — give place to the temple, — the symbol of permanent habitation. Till then Jehovah, dwelling in a tabernacle like Abraham, Isaac, and Jacob, "sojourned in the land of promise, as in a strange country." For a considerable time this tent was in Shiloh, where Jehovah manifested His presence. But both Psalmist and Prophet speak of the increasing apostasy of the people at this period, of their high places and their graven images, so that "He was wroth, and greatly abhorred Israel; so that He forsook the tabernacle of Shiloh, ... and delivered His strength into captivity, and His glory into the enemy's hand." There could be no one central seat of worship, where all might go up, so long as idolaters ruled over the Hebrews in some parts of the land, or remained in other parts of it unsubdued. Thus it was that worship in the high places, not improbably of pre-Mosaic origin, was carried on and tolerated, — an abuse sure to lead, as it did, to great evil, and which it was most difficult in after-times to root out. It was not till later, when the whole land was conquered under David, and all heathen rule put down, that the temple could be erected at Jerusalem, and the promise of God be fulfilled, "Here will I dwell, for I have desired it." Not till this time was it possible for all to keep the feasts without molestation, and to fulfill at the one altar the prescribed rites of worship: hitherto the elect people had rather encamped in the land than possessed it.

But a change was at hand. The long discipline of suffering was producing a wholesome effect, which was especially manifested in a growing desire for greater unity, and in a deeper sense of their covenant relations to Jehovah. And we must not suppose that, in all the public disorders and religious confusion of these years, there was not much genuine piety, and true reverence and zeal for the law. There was, in general, purity in family life, and obedience to God's commands, and faith in the fulfillment of His promises. There were many, doubtless, who deeply felt the evils of their times, and who earnestly prayed for deliverance. And, before the time of Samuel, there were signs of a re-action, and of a turning again to Jehovah. The gift of prophetic utterance, which had been very rare, became more frequent. In the Spirit Hannah, the mother of Samuel, prayed; and her utterances show how strongly, in this hour of national distress and humiliation, the sense of the holiness and majesty of Jehovah had impressed itself on the pious mind. (1 Sam. ii. 1–10.)

CHAPTER VI.

THE ESTABLISHMENT OF THE MONARCHY AND THE DAVIDIC COVENANT.

WE now reach a most important change in the theocratic constitution. The advanced years of Samuel, and the bad character of his sons, added to the vivid remembrance of all the evils they had suffered under the Judges, led the Jewish people to ask for a king. (1 Sam. viii.) They said to Samuel, "Make us a king to judge us like all the nations." This was a wrong step, in that it was in substance a rejection of the immediate rule of Jehovah. "They have rejected me, that I should not be King over them," said God to Samuel. A king as His ruler over men was undoubtedly intended by Him from the first; for the Divine purpose had its culminating point in the Incarnate Son and in His kingdom, and from a line of kings should He spring. Early had it been said to Abraham, "Kings shall come out of thee;" and in the organic law provision was made for such a change in the original constitution. (Deut. xvii. 14; Num. xxvii. 16.) But all this did not justify the present action of the people, since they should have waited for God to bring forth His king in His own time and way. Gideon long before had rightly and wisely refused the proffered throne, saying, "The Lord shall rule over you." (Judg. viii. 23.) Such action by the people was an assertion that their evil condition was not the fruit of their own sins, but of a defect in the theocratic constitution, which they would in this way remedy. To desire a king, that they might be "like the nations around them," showed at least their belief that they would then be in a better position to meet their enemies than as now under Jehovah.

The remonstrances of Samuel were in vain. He foresaw that a king set over them in their then condition of unbelief would become their oppressor, not their deliverer and protector, since they would rely on him rather than on God, and thus, on the one side, provoke Jehovah to anger, and, on the other, beget in the king a spirit of pride inconsistent with his position. The personal character of the ruler, always of highest importance in Oriental states, would very deeply affect the religious life of the people, and might become a great power for evil. The prophet warns them how much they might suffer from his arbitrary acts, and how he might make their interests subordinate to his own ambition. "And ye shall cry out in that day because of your king which ye shall have chosen you; and the Lord will not answer you in that day." A king could be a blessing only when he himself was obedient to Jehovah, and ruled over a people in whom the same spirit of obedience was found. But at last by Divine direction Samuel yielded to their desire, and Saul was set over them. He was, however, chosen by Jehovah, and not by popular election; for this change in the form of polity did not abrogate the covenant made at Sinai, or set aside Jehovah as the Supreme Ruler. (1 Sam. ix. 17.) He continued to be their King, and all steps taken to establish the new monarchy were under His direction.

In this newly established unity of the tribes under one civil head, there was nothing intrinsically incompatible with the kingly place of Jehovah: not as an independent ruler, but as His servant, His king, to execute His will, should the new magistrate administer the government: "To the Holy One of Israel belongs our king." (Rev. Ver., Ps. lxxxix. 18.) He could not make his personal authority the rule of civil action, or of himself originate laws. His place was to execute the law of Moses, and to carry out such special directions as he might receive from God, and in general to maintain political and social order. He could not perform the sacrificial acts appointed to the priests, and certain sacrifices said to be offered by him seem to have been offered by the priests in his presence. (2 Sam. vi. 17; 1 Kings viii. 62. See iii. 4.) It may be admitted that a kind of priestly character belonged to the king in virtue of his place as chief ruler of a priestly people. He had a general supervision of ecclesiastical matters, to see that worship was properly performed, the temple and its furniture kept in order, and legal provision made for the priests. To him especially belonged the office of judge in the last resort; and he was the leader of the armies, and, with the advice and aid of the princes and priests and prophets, made war and peace. His temptation was twofold,- to forget the peculiar calling of the people whom God was training for a special spiritual purpose, and to treat them as like the nations around them; and also to forget his subordination to Jehovah, and to attempt to rule over Israel in the tyrannical spirit of the heathen kings, trusting in his armies and fortresses and political alliances. And this was the rock on which Saul, the first king, made shipwreck. He did not fully recognize and accept his position of subordination, and "hearken unto the voice of the words of the Lord," and forfeited his throne through his disobedience.

It is apparent that an obedient and faithful king, who fully realized the theocratic calling of the people; one who maintained in all points the authority of Jehovah, and gave in himself an example of submission, would have proved a most effectual instrument in preparing the people for higher measures of Divine blessing. But if, on the other hand, he were not himself in unity with Jehovah, if His honor was not his chief aim, if he were selfish and self-willed, unjust and tyrannical, or inclined to idolatry, his position would make him a powerful instrument of evil. Thus the personal character of the king came in, from this time onward, as a most influential factor in determining the future destinies of the nation.

In the second king, David, God found "a man after His own heart," — not a man without sin, but one who was willing to take his due place, and to execute the will of Jehovah. For a long period after his anointing by the prophet, he waited till the providence of God should open to him the way to the throne, treating Saul with all honor and reverence as the Lord's anointed, and following in all points the Divine directions. (2 Sam. xxii. 22, etc.) His life was by no means without offence; and his crimes are not concealed in the historic records, and his last days were embittered by the domestic dissensions which they had caused. But, in the general administration of his government, he had done that which he charged his son Solomon to do, — he had kept "the charge of the Lord, to walk in His ways, to keep His statutes, and His commandments, and His judgments, and His testimonies, as it is written in the law of Moses." It was from this cause that God was pleased to enter into a covenant with him, that He would establish his house and his kingdom forever. (2 Sam. vii.) The throne of Israel was thus given in perpetuity to the family of David. In its substance the promise was unconditional. The purpose of God embraced the Jewish nation as a permanent element in His work of redemption, and He now declares that at the head of this nation should stand a king of Davidic lineage. "Thy throne shall be established for ever." "His seed also will I make to endure for ever, and his throne as the days of heaven." (Ps. lxxxix. 29.) But this promise did not exclude sore judgments upon any of his children who should prove unfaithful. "If his children forsake my law, and walk not in my judgments, . . . then will I visit their transgression with the rod, and their iniquity with stripes." The throne might be overturned, and the nation cease to exist as a nation for a time; but it should be restored, and the Davidic throne re-established. Its fortunes were from this time inseparably bound up with the fortunes of this elect family. "My covenant will I not break, nor alter the thing that is gone out of my lips." Thus through the Davidic covenant, the monarchy became the permanent form of the Jewish government. The earlier promises of Jehovah had assured His people, if faithful to Him, of the continual possession of His land, and of all temporal blessings. To these was now added the blessing that would follow from the righteous administration of the government through His chosen and anointed king. In him the nation was headed up, and he stood before the world as the visible representative of its unity.

It may be admitted that the form of the promise to David does not necessarily limit it to an individual: it may be applied to a succession of rulers, or a dynasty. (2 Sam. vii. 12–16.) But, even if so, it finds its complete fulfillment in one who is especially The Anointed. If we here assume that a dynasty is spoken of, there is to be a succession of kings, — all of them, indeed, Jehovah's kings, His sons, His anointed, but whose official relations to Him do not necessarily preserve them from disobedience. They may commit sin, and deserve chastisement. (Ps. lxxxix. 30–32.) All are mortal and fallible men. It need scarcely be said that the kingdom thus administered could not but be very imperfect. It could not, at best, rise much above the measure of the kingdom under David and Solomon. Did not the Divine purpose look beyond this? How could the idea of duration without end be predicated of such a succession?

Although not very fully expressed, we cannot well doubt that the Messianic Kingdom, administered in perfect righteousness, holy and universal, as afterwards set forth by the prophets, was involved in the covenant with David, and designed by God to be the object of national hope. But here, as always in God's moral education of men, each truth revealed, each step taken, points forward to something beyond, to a new truth or a new step. The new can, however, be apprehended only as men have understood and applied the old. Knowing the present by discerning and fulfilling God's purpose in it, we see its higher bearings and issues. Thus the covenant with David, the choice of his family to rule under Jehovah, pointed to the Messiah and His kingdom; but a true apprehension of His place and dignity could grow up only as that covenant was rightly observed, and its blessings were realized. The idea of the perfect kingdom under its last Ruler, could spring up and become general only as steady approach was made towards it in the reigns of His predecessors.

If, therefore, the true end of this covenant was not for a time seen; if there is little mention of the Messiah for several generations after David, and there was little expectation or hope of such a prosperous and holy Kingdom, — we need not be surprised at it: the history of the time sufficiently accounts for it. But it would be an error to conclude that there were none who early saw more in the future than a prolonged dynasty of sinful and mortal men. This will appear when we examine the Psalms as the expression of Messianic hopes, and especially the Psalms of David. In all the generations after the promise was given to David, there must have been in the more reflecting and spiritually-minded the perception that the redemption of men from sin and its evils — which was the purpose of the Theocracy — demanded higher manifestations and operations of God than could be put forth under the rule of princes corruptible and weak, such as his natural successors must be. The Davidic kingdom as it existed could not be the realization of that redemption for which they were longing, of that revelation of God to His people, and of that communion with Him, which was their ardent aspiration. There must be something to come higher and better than this. Must there not be here, as in all God's actings, progress from the imperfect to the perfect? and will not the perfect King, He who in all things does God's will, be the Messiah, the last, the immortal One?

We can thus easily conceive that there might have been such steady progress in their religious development under wise and pious kings, such "following on to know the Lord," that they could have apprehended more and more the purpose of God in the Messiah, and have been so prepared for Him, that His kingdom would have come in a normal way, not preceded by a day of darkness and of severe judgment, but as the light of dawn that shines brighter and brighter till the sun rise; and been welcomed as a Kingdom of righteousness. But if, on the other hand, there was no such national progress, if the kings were rebellious and wicked, and the people became increasingly disobedient and immoral, then the contrast between the promises of God and their fulfillment must have led the thoughtful and reverent to look for a special judicial interposition of Jehovah.

In later years the expectation of the Messianic Kingdom, one far higher than the Davidic, must have arisen in the consciousness of many as the fruit of experience. The covenant had not been fulfilled. Time had shown the weakness and wickedness of the kings, the division of the kingdom, the failure of righteous rule in both divisions, contempt of Jehovah, and general immorality. The experience of this would, in all who trusted in God's promises, awaken the hope that a king would yet come who would fulfill them; through whom Jehovah would be honored, and the people be blest. (Ps. lxxxix. 36, 37.) And, looking forward to the future, they felt that Jehovah could not continue to dwell in His holy city with rebellious kings who defiled it, and dishonored Him: a day of judgment must come; a holy king must appear; Jehovah's people must be brought into their true position, or He must depart from them. But His covenant cannot fail, He will fulfill His purpose. Thus there was begotten, by the failures of the past and by the evils of the present, the hope of one greater than David, who would honor Jehovah, and whom Jehovah would honor, and in whose Kingdom there should be righteousness and holiness and peace without end.

CHAPTER VII.

ORIGIN AND ELEMENTS OF THE MESSIANIC BELIEF.

HOWEVER figurative in its terms, and vague in itself, is the promise that the Seed of the woman should bruise the serpent's head, it cannot well be doubted that all along from the earliest times, there existed among men the expectation not only of deliverance from sin and its evils, but also of a personal Deliverer. (Gen. iii. 15.) Probably all early peoples had through tradition some knowledge, always imperfect and often perverted, of this Deliverer to come. To make known His purpose in Him, and to prepare the way for Him, was henceforth the chief end of all God's actings. Of this deliverance, or, as expressed by the apostle, of "the times of restitution of all things, God hath spoken by the mouth of all His holy prophets since the world began." (Acts iii. 21.) How far this purpose in the Deliverer was understood in the earliest times, by those to whom it was known, it is not necessary for us to inquire. In the special promises made to Abraham this primitive promise was confirmed and made more definite, so that the patriarch saw with the eye of faith "the day of Christ," the day of redemption and of the Redeemer. (John viii. 56.) Isaac and Jacob, "heirs of the same promise," looked forward to the same day. (Heb. xi.) And in foresight of Him Jacob declared, "The sceptre shall not depart from Judah, nor a Lawgiver from between his feet, until Shiloh come; and unto Him shall the gathering of the people be." (Gen. xlix. 10.) Of Him and His rule did the Gentile prophet Balaam speak: "There shall come a Star out of Jacob, and a Sceptre shall rise out of Israel. . . . Out of Jacob shall come He that shall have dominion." (Num. xxiv. 17, 19.) And as the time drew near, when kings were to reign under Jehovah over His people, Hannah spake in prophetic inspiration: "The Lord shall judge the ends of the earth; and He shall give strength unto His king, and exalt the horn of His Anointed." (1 Sam. ii. 10.)

Through the covenant with David, a great step onward was made in the way of Messianic revelation, and this in two important points. The promised One is to come of David's line, and His place is defined as that of the Ruler of the elect nation under Jehovah.

It has been already shown, that the covenant with David involved in it the promise of the perfect King and the perfected kingdom. If Jehovah would rule His people through a man chosen of Him, His King, it must be that in due time He would raise up One who would in all points fulfill His purpose, and administer His kingdom in perfect righteousness; and then would be realized all the hopes of the patriarchs, and of all later generations, who had looked forward to redemption. This King would be "the Seed of the woman," "the Star out of Jacob," Jehovah's Son and Anointed One.

Thus, from this time the thought of the Redeemer was inseparably connected in the minds of all who had any knowledge of the redemptive purpose, with the theocratic kingship in the family of David. He was presented to the elect people as One to be their King, and His kingdom not as one wholly new and distinct, but as the continuation and development of the theocratic. In both is Jehovah the Supreme Ruler, and the covenant relations remain the same. It was, therefore, a most important step in Messianic revelation when the monarchy was set up, and the people saw the government administered by a man as the servant of Jehovah. From David, it was easy to pass in imagination to His greater Son; from the Davidic kingdom to the more glorious kingdom which this Son should administer. Thus from the present they could look forward to the future: the real, however imperfect, served as the basis of the ideal. This conception of the Messianic Kingdom as like the Davidic, and yet something far higher and holier, once obtained, was never lost. It was present to the popular imagination as a bright vision, indistinct in outline, and far off, but never ceasing to be to the faithful and believing an object of earnest expectation and hope.

The chief elements that entered into this conception of the future Kingdom may be thus distinguished: First, its universality. A period would come when Jehovah would rule all nations in righteousness, and all dwellers on earth would serve and worship Him. Second, the place of the Jews as His own people in this universal kingdom. Through their instrumentality should it be set up, and in it should they be the first among the nations. Third, this kingdom would be administered by one of the seed of Abraham and family of David, the promised Messiah.

It is only to the last of these elements that the term Messianic, strictly speaking, can be applied; for a great enlargement of the theocratic government — an universal Kingdom under Jehovah — could be conceived of without the existence of the Messiah as its Head; and, also, that without Him as their King, the Jews might have in it the highest place.

Let us now note each of these three elements.

1. The belief in an universal kingdom of righteousness. This stood intimately connected with the conception of God as a supreme, righteous, moral Governor. All sin, all disorder, are in their very nature offensive to Him, and, if tolerated for a time, must ultimately be suppressed. Among the gods of the nations was there none like unto Jehovah, and before Him would all nations come and worship. (Ps. lxxxvi. 8, 9.) Thus it was easy for the Jews to look forward to a time when the rebellious and evil would be cut off from the earth, and only the obedient and good be left. (Ps. ix. 15-20.) And this was more than a matter of inference: it had been promised by God. At Sinai He had said, "All the earth is mine." And to Moses, "As truly as I live, all the earth shall be filled with the glory of the Lord." (Num. xiv. 21.)

2. The belief that the Jews would have the place nearest to God, and so be the first among the nations. This followed from their special covenant relation to Him. He had chosen them that He might first reveal Himself to them, and then through them to the world, "that all the peoples of the earth might know that the Lord is God, and none else." (1 Kings viii. 60.) Their special relation to Him was not a transient one, but to continue even when all the nations had become obedient to Him.

3. The belief that one of their race and of the family of David would be at the head of this universal kingdom, administering it under Jehovah. This rested on the promises made to Abraham and to David. But it was not till the actual establishment of the monarchy, that the conception of the future Messianic Kingdom and of its King, in their relations to Jehovah, could take definite outline. As under the Theocracy David ruled

the elect people, a true king, but in entire subordination to Jehovah, administering the government under His direction and for His ends, so would it be in the greater Kingdom to come. By the mouth of the prophet God had promised David that He would set his family to be the royal family, as in the present, so in the future kingdom. "I will settle him in my house and in my kingdom for ever." (1 Chron. xvii. 14.) When this kingdom should assume its universal form, it would be one of this family who must be His King. As the nation was Jehovah's people, — the elect among the nations, — so their earthly head was His King.

It was from this period, the reign of David, that the three distinctive elements just mentioned began to enter into the popular conception of the future. But all these elements, though inseparable in the purpose of God, were by no means equally, and at all times, present in the popular consciousness, or prominent in the prophetic utterances. That Jehovah would in due time make manifest His authority over all nations, and that the Jews would continue to be His chosen people, it was easy for them to believe, because of His own natural supremacy, and of their existing covenant relations. But it was not so easy for them to believe the promises respecting the person and lordship of the Messiah, the Son of David, as universal Ruler. In regard to His person, many perplexing questions must early have arisen in the minds of the thoughtful. Would He be a man like David, one prepared by God, and specially endowed by His Spirit, or more than man? And as to the Kingdom, would it be for a limited time, or forever? And if forever, or without any visible end, would His life be supernaturally prolonged by Divine favor, or would He be by birth immortal? Would all the people be holy? And would the law of death be set aside, wholly or in part? How could He administer an universal kingdom? Would it be extended over the nations by voluntary submission, or by force? and what would be their spiritual relations to Him? These questions find no answer in the covenant itself. Nor did the prophets, as we shall soon see, in their revelations, answer them with distinctness. Indeed, some of them say nothing of the Messiah at all; and the language of others who speak of Him, might be understood as referring to a dynasty rather than to an individual. Only in comparatively few is the Messiah clearly set forth in His personality and special offices.

It is not to be denied, that for many years after David the future Messianic Kingdom was not clearly discriminated from the existing theocratic: it was Jehovah, not the promised King of David's line, that filled the horizon of the prophetic future; and this may be readily understood when we remember how prone were the people to lower the spiritual claims of Jehovah upon them, and to substitute a human for a Divine administration. But whether Jehovah alone be mentioned as the King ruling the world in righteousness, or the Messiah, also, as reigning under Him, still there is ample proof that an extension of the theocratic rule to embrace all nations, with corresponding increase of honor and blessing to the chosen people, was continually before the eye of the prophets, and more or less a living element in the faith of the nation.

Regarded as a new and higher stage of redemption, what additional spiritual blessings did the Jews expect for themselves in the Messianic Kingdom? And how was Messiah to be Jehovah's instrument for their communication? Upon these points, little light was at first given. But it was plain to the more discerning, that since both the Theocracy, and the Messianic Kingdom to follow it, were means for the blessing of His people, there would be in the latter some new manifestation of Jehovah, whereby they might have a larger knowledge of Him in His Divine attributes, and be brought into closer communion with Him, and so attain to greater moral purity and blessedness. The great spiritual distinction of the Messianic Kingdom above the Theocracy would be in a higher revelation of Jehovah to His people, whereby the evils of sin both in man and nature would be in higher degree overcome, and the people made obedient and faithful and holy. And among the nations oppression and misery would cease, the righteous would be exalted, and all the world walk in His light. And He by whom Jehovah would bestow all these blessings would be the Messiah. As David had been His instrument in building His temple and blessing His people, and, also, His instrument in subduing His enemies, so, but in far higher degree, should be David's greater Son. As Jehovah's King all would obey Him, and His sceptre be a sceptre of righteousness, and all nations rejoice in His rule. (Ps. lxxii.)

The features of the Messianic period as involved in the covenants at Sinai and with David, may be thus summed up: Then will the rule of Jehovah be extended over all nations. Everywhere He will be acknowledged and worshipped as the One Supreme and Holy God. The Jews will continue to be His elect people, and be admitted to higher communion with Him; and, dwelling in their own land, and walking in all holy obedience, will have the first and central place in the universal Kingdom. A man to spring from the family of David will administer the Divine government under Jehovah, and be King over all the earth; and the seat of His rule will be Jerusalem, where will be some special manifestation of Jehovah's Presence, making it to all the world the centre of authority and worship. And this kingdom, administered in perfect righteousness, will endure forever, or for a period without any definite limit.

The Messianic Kingdom was thus presented before the covenant people as an object of hope, because in it they would be blest with far larger measures of blessing, both in things spiritual and temporal. Its chief characteristic was a new revelation of Jehovah through the Messiah, when " Mount Zion should be the joy of the whole earth ; " a revelation in which all nations should behold His glory, and bow down before Him and worship. Whether in their visions of the future the prophets look beyond the Messianic Kingdom, or whether it is to them the culmination of God's redemptive work, will be a matter for later consideration. It need scarcely be said that the conceptions of this kingdom were various as the spiritual condition of individuals, — some looking upon it as bringing with it full deliverance from sin, and close communion with God; some as showing forth God's righteousness in the overthrow of His enemies some as a time of national exaltation ; and some, doubtless, as a means only of greater earthly honor and happiness. The dividing line between the existing theocratic and the future Messianic Kingdom is the coming of the Messiah. But in both is Jehovah the One Supreme Lord, from whom all blessing comes.

CHAPTER VIII.

THE PREPARATION OF THE THEOCRATIC PEOPLE FOR THE MESSIANIC KINGDOM.

UNDER the Theocracy the Jews were put in training for a higher stage of God's gracious revelation. The covenant relation established at Sinai was not the end, but a means to the end, — a preparatory step in the spiritual education of the people. When through the law, with its sacrificial and cleansing rites, they had come to a deeper knowledge of sin, and ardent longings had been awakened in them for higher degrees of holiness; when through the teaching of God they had learned in some measure His purpose in redemption, and were taught to render Him due obedience, — then they were prepared for a new revelation of Himself to be made in the Messianic Kingdom. Thus the Theocracy and the Messianic Kingdom stood to one another in very close moral relations. If the former failed of its purpose, if those under the law were not convinced of sin, if they were not taught obedience, if they were not made holy in heart and righteous in life, then could there be no true desire for the larger spiritual blessings which the latter would bring. Only those faithful under the Theocracy could be ready for the Messianic Kingdom; only as having the end of their calling in view, — that God might be sanctified through them in the eyes of all nations, — would they press on to reach it; only to the faithful could it be an object of hope.

We are to note that this preparation under the Theocracy must be a national preparation. The covenant was with the nation as such, and the end to be attained could be attained only through a nation. If the people, represented in their heads and rulers, sinned against Jehovah, and did not keep His statutes, His judgments upon them were not individual, but national, their end being to effect national repentance. If this was not effected, and individuals only were made repentant, it would not avail, since it was not as a ruler over individuals, but as seated on David's throne, and ruling over a holy people, that the Messiah could manifest Himself to the nations.

Thus the Jews as a people were put on trial whether they would or would not go on with God in His purpose, step by step, as He revealed it to them; and be found a people prepared when the appointed time of the Messianic Kingdom should come. The end for which God had chosen them was set before them, — to be "a kingdom of priests and a holy nation," — and it was their duty to press on from the lower to the higher, that His purpose in their calling might be accomplished.

As every new step which God takes in the execution of His work in redemption is a fresh test of the faith and obedience of His children who are workers together with Him, so was it in the Messianic covenant with David. Through this His people were put in a new position, and brought under new obligations. He would have the Messianic kingdom to be distinctly set before them, and its vision to inspire them to the more diligent discharge of present duties. Faithful use of all existing means of preparation alone could make them ready for the Messiah. It has been already noted, that for a long period after David there was little apprehension of His purpose in the election of the kingly family. Some there doubtless were in every generation who discerned that purpose, who saw clearly the relation of the present to the future, and knew that the new Kingdom could not come without greater faith and obedience and holiness. It was impossible for the people to stand still: they must go forward or backward. Whether they would go on to fulfill Jehovah's purpose in their election, or sink down from one stage of spiritual declension to another, and end in general apostasy, was to be determined by their own free action.

As the nation was on trial through the election of the house of David, so also was the royal family. Since the Messiah was to come of the Davidic line, a special responsibility lay upon its members ever to remember their high calling, and to keep themselves holy unto the Lord. As the high-priestly house of Aaron was to be most zealous and diligent in fulfilling His will in its sphere of worship, so was it to be with the kingly house of David in its sphere of rule. If its heads — the kings and princes — failed to recognize their relations to Jehovah as His servants; if they were not obedient to Him; if they abused their office, and were selfish, oppressive, cruel; and, above all, if they permitted or encouraged idolatry, — then would they most effectually oppose and hinder the Divine purpose, and expose themselves and the people to severest judgments. But if they were faithful in their place, trusting in Jehovah and serving Him, examples of obedience to the people, then would they be efficient helpers in preparing the way for His coming, whom God would set on His holy hill of Zion.

Thus with the Davidic covenant, the Jews, headed up in their king, entered upon a new stage, civil and religious, of their history. For this God had prepared them by a wonderful revival of spiritual life in the time of the prophet Samuel. Never had there been in the nation such energy and fullness of prophetic utterance, in which the kings themselves participated. All external circumstances were favorable to make the reign of David the starting-point of a new and glorious development. The conquest of Canaan, begun under Joshua, was now finished; the people had taken full possession of the land; and there were no enemies, far or near, to molest or make them afraid. And within the nation there was peace. Through the building of the temple, worship was celebrated in its completest and noblest forms. Jerusalem had become the holy city, where Jehovah dwelt and manifested His glory, and by the mouth of many prophets He declared His will.

It only remained that both king and people should walk in all the commandments and ordinances of the Lord blameless and await in hope the coming of the Messiah. That David himself felt the responsibility of his position and its high dignity, is shown in his history, and especially by his words in Psalm ci., which is generally ascribed to him: "I will behave myself wisely in a perfect way. . . . Mine eyes shall be upon the faithful of the land, that they may dwell with me."

CHAPTER IX.

HISTORY OF THE KINGDOM FROM DAVID TO ITS DIVISION.

THE question from which tribe the king should be taken was one that naturally excited, from the first, some tribal jealousy. Judah and Ephraim had long been the leading tribes, and each was unwilling that the other should be exalted by the possession of the royal dignity. In the case of Saul of Benjamin, little jealousy was felt; but when David was taken from Judah, and the city of Jerusalem became the capital, and seat of the temple, some discontent was awakened, which several times found expression during David's reign. But the heroic qualities of the king drew all hearts to him; and although the last years of his life were embittered by domestic dissensions, yet was he able to preserve the tribes in unity, and to transmit a firmly established throne to his son. And the secret strength of this unity was not in his civil organization, nor in the disciplined army he had formed, but in the newly awakened religious feeling of the people. So long as this was strong, the bonds that bound the tribes to Jerusalem and the temple could not be broken. Where Jehovah dwelt and was worshipped, was the centre of national unity; and the house of David was recognized by all as the house He had chosen to rule the people under Him. It would be an error to suppose that because David was in his general spirit of obedience a man after God's own heart, he did not often err, both in his private life and in his public acts. Nor did his administration of the theocratic government in any true way realize the fullness of the Messianic promises. In two things especially he sinned, and brought upon himself and his posterity and people the Divine judgments. The first was the matter of Bathsheba, when God said to him, "Behold, I will raise up evil against thee out of thine own house;" the second, that of numbering the people, when seventy thousand died of the pestilence. It is probable that David was moved to number the people through a desire to increase the army, and to place the kingdom before the world as a great military power; so little did he, familiar with war, understand what was the real defence of Israel, and what its true place as Jehovah's witness among the nations.

Solomon, David's successor, was a man of great intellectual gifts, but who was never ready fully to accept his position as a theocratic king. David knew that the first requisite in the ruler who should sit on the theocratic throne, was obedience to Jehovah, and that "the fear of Him was the beginning of wisdom." Solomon had asked for wisdom and knowledge, but not for "a perfect heart to keep Jehovah's commandments." This very reputation for wisdom and knowledge, which extended through all the nations, became a snare to him. His temptation was the same as that of David, though under a different form and in a higher degree, to make the Theocracy one of the powers of this world, and to exalt himself, rather than Jehovah, as the ruler. His government became more and more that of an earthly king, whose trust is in armies and fortresses, in wealth and political alliances. He sought to develop commerce, and sent his ships to distant ports: riches flowed in, and with them luxury and ostentation. The simplicity of national life was corrupted, and the customs of the heathen around found rapid entrance.

But it was in the religious spirit of Solomon and of the people that the greatest change took place. It is to be noted, that, so far as recorded, he had no prophets as his counsellors, as Nathan and Gad had been counsellors to David, — a clear sign that he did not feel the need of them, and trusted to his own judgment. He took many wives of the heathen peoples around him, contrary to the Divine command; and through them he was led into the toleration of idolatry, building high places and chapels where his wives could burn incense and offer sacrifice to their several gods. It is not improbable that he thought every form of religion to have some truth in it, which in this manner he was willing to recognize. This toleration of idolatry God would not endure; and because of it He would rend the kingdom from him in the days of his son, except the tribe of Judah, and give it to another. This was speedily fulfilled after his death, through the agency of political causes. The people had been greatly burdened with taxation, the result of Solomon's costly buildings and the great magnificence of his court; and the feeling of dissatisfaction was strong, especially in the northern tribes. When Solomon died, the people desired of his son, Rehoboam, that the taxes should be lightened: his foolish and insulting answer led to immediate revolt, and to permanent political division. The strong empire of David gave place to two weak and hostile kingdoms.

This disruption could not so suddenly and quickly have taken place, unless the way had been prepared by a decay of the religious life in the nation at large. The worldly — perhaps we may say sceptical — spirit of Solomon had infected many. The temple of Jehovah lost in some measure its sacredness, His worship, though the chief, was not the sole worship. To other gods a degree of honor might be paid; sacrifice in high places was tolerated in Jerusalem, and probably elsewhere in the land. Thus the strong bonds binding the tribes into religious unity had become relaxed, and were swiftly sundered under the pressure of pecuniary burdens and tribal jealousies.

Thus the house of David, called to so high dignity as to administer the government under Jehovah, and placed under the most favorable circumstances to enable it to fulfill its calling, failed early in the trial. Through its sin and folly the kingdom was speedily rent in twain. The covenant of God with David could not, indeed, fail; but its fulfillment in the Messianic Kingdom, which had seemed so near, receded into the distant future. The necessary moral conditions for its establishment were wanting on the part both of king and people; and long and stern years of discipline were needed ere the true preparation of heart could be found, even in a remnant.

CHAPTER X.

HISTORY OF THE TWO KINGDOMS AFTER THE DIVISION.

NATIONAL unity was essential to the accomplishment of the Divine purpose in the chosen people. As Jehovah was the one God, so in all His appointments, civil and ecclesiastical, should a witness be borne to His unity before the world. In one place only would He dwell: there was one Holy City, one Temple, one Altar, one High Priest, and one King. To this unity the formation of two rival and hostile kingdoms was, as it proved, a fatal blow. If two kingdoms, then two Kings, two Capitals, and, following speedily, two Altars and two Priesthoods. It was, indeed, possible that the political division might have taken place, and yet the people have remained ecclesiastically united, the people of the Northern kingdom continuing to worship at Jerusalem. And it was counted as the special sin of Jeroboam, that he did not permit his people "to go up and do sacrifice in the house of the Lord at Jerusalem." (1 Kings xii. 26, etc.) But neither he, nor any subsequent king, was willing that the ten tribes should do this; and, to guard against it, altars were set up at Bethel and Dan, the two extremities of the kingdom; and new priests, not of the house of Aaron, ministered at them. The interests of the two kingdoms became more and more antagonistic, and the chasm between them broader and deeper. Often they were at open war, and though for political ends there were occasional treaties of amity, and attempts at reconciliation, these were but transient. That God would have overruled the evil consequences of division, and restored unity under a king of the house of David, had there been a true spirit of repentance, we may believe; but there was no such repentance, and all expectation of the restoration of national unity under the Davidic family soon passed away.

The position of each of the two kingdoms had its peculiar features. The kings of Israel, not being of the house of David, had no covenant right to the throne, and should have looked upon themselves as holding it at the Divine pleasure; God using them as His instruments to punish the sins of that house. But this position they did not accept. They desired to make the national division permanent, and thus establish the permanence of their own thrones; and, therefore, put every obstacle possible in the way of a re-union. There was not for a time an open denial of Jehovah as the theocratic Ruler by the Northern tribes, nor was His worship wholly set aside, yet His authority was practically denied. The ecclesiastical was entirely subordinated to the civil: the priesthood was made by the State, and used for political ends. (1 Kings xiii. 33.)

That the ten tribes would become more and more alienated from the Theocracy, was almost inevitable. We may note two stages of their decline: the first was the institution of the worship of the golden calves by Jeroboam. We may believe, that, as in the case of the calf made by Aaron, these were symbols of Jehovah taken from the Cherubim of old; but the thing was greatly offensive to Jehovah, both as contrary to His commands, and as opening the way to all idolatrous practices. Second, the introduction of the worship of the Phœnician deities, Baal and Ashtaroth, under Ahab and Jezebel, in union with the worship of Jehovah. This king built a temple for Baal at Samaria, his new capital, and his queen a chapel for Ashtaroth at her palace in Jezreel. There were, as we are told, of the prophets of Baal, four hundred and fifty; and of the prophets of the grove, four hundred. With this open establishment of idolatry was joined the persecution and slaughter of the prophets of Jehovah. The efforts of Elijah, and afterwards of Elisha, checked for a little while this idolatrous tendency; but the heart of the people was corrupted, and a few only retained their integrity. Elijah thought himself the sole witness to the Lord in Israel, but was assured by God that there were seven thousand that had not bowed the knee to Baal. (1 Kings xix. 18.)

Thus, so far as the acts of the rulers could effect it, and not without the assent of a large part of the people (1 Kings xix. 10), the ten tribes were put without the pale of the covenant; and it is to be noticed, that they are never called by the prophets God's people. Idolatry had taken such deep root, that even the sanguinary measures of Jehu wrought but a transient and imperfect reformation. The spirit of heathenism had penetrated so deeply into the national life, that it could not be purged out by judgments. (2 Kings x. 20–31.)

The situation of the Southern kingdom was unlike that of the Northern in two most important particulars: it was ruled over by the house of David, and within its borders were the Holy City and the Temple. It was, therefore, not disturbed by dynastic changes, no ambitious chiefs of other families daring to claim the throne; and the established worship was supported by a strong body of priests and Levites, both those within its borders at the time of the division, and those who left the North-

ern kingdom to dwell in Judæa. It was thus saved from
the corruption of public morals which civil dissension
inevitably brings with it, and also from those temptations to idolatry to which the worship of the calves at
Bethel and Dan opened the way. But Judah, nevertheless, was not faithful to Jehovah. Solomon and Rehoboam his son permitted their wives to offer idolatrous
worship, and tolerated the building of pillars to Baal,
and consecration of groves to Ashtaroth. (1 Kings xii.,
xiv.) The punishment quickly came. Jehovah gave
Jerusalem into the hands of Shishak, king of Egypt,
who "took away the treasures of the house of the Lord,
and the treasures of the king's house; he even took away
all." (1 Kings xiv. 25, 26.) How soon was the temple
builded by Solomon, and at its dedication filled with
the glory of the Lord, pillaged and desecrated by
heathen hands! But this was not for destruction: it
was to show the people that Jehovah was their true
King, and that all transgressions against Him would be
punished. (2 Chron. xii. 5-12.) It is impossible to follow the history of the kingdom of Judah in detail. It
is sufficient to say, that at no time during its continuance, or from the time of the division to its overthrow
(975-586 B.C.), was there a full and faithful keeping of
the covenant. There were able and pious kings who
attempted, and in a measure effected, religious reforms,
and under whom there was prosperity at home, and
honor abroad; but the general religious tendency was
steadily downward. Attempts were early made to establish friendly relations between the two kingdoms, as
by the inter-marriage of the royal families of Jehoshaphat and Ahab; but these relations were not permanent.
Each kingdom looked upon the other as an enemy,
and was ready to enter into alliances with the heathen
nations around it to gratify its hate. Neither God's

heavy judgments upon Judah, nor His wonderful acts of deliverance, brought the people to repentance and to obedience. None of David's descendants had an equal measure of faith, and with like zeal kept the Divine commandments: none of them realized that the fear of the Lord was their true protection. Even the best of the kings trusted more in their armies and confederacies, and in the help of the heathen, than in the arm of Jehovah.

The introduction of idolatry into Israel, and its open establishment by Ahab and Jezebel, may probably be regarded as the turning-point in the destiny of that kingdom. It was the sin unto national death. And perhaps the same significance may be ascribed to the reign of Jehoram in Judah, of whom it is said, "He walked in the way of the kings of Israel, like as did the house of Ahab; for he had the daughter of Ahab to wife: and he wrought that which was evil in the eyes of the Lord." (2 Chron. xxi. 6.) Not only did he make high places in the mountains of Judah, and compel the inhabitants of Judah to commit fornication, but built, also, in Jerusalem a temple to Baal with altars and images, where worship was carried on. Of Jehoram it is said, also, that he marked his accession to the throne by the murder of his brothers. The Divine punishment speedily came. Jehoram perished miserably of sickness, and was unhonored in his burial. Athaliah his wife, daughter of Jezebel, seating herself on the throne, attempted to "destroy all the seed royal,"—all of the house of David (2 Kings xi. 1); and, like her mother, she made use of her power to establish idolatry; she dared not, indeed, wholly shut up the temple of Jehovah, but she did all that was possible to break up the house of God, and to bestow upon Baalim all the dedicated things of the house of the Lord. (2 Chron. xxiv. 7.) Her rule continued six years; and it seemed for a time as if Jehovah were to be banished from His own city, the family of David to be rooted out, and the heathen to triumph in Judah as in Israel.

From this miserable apostasy and fall there was, as we shall see in its place, no real recovery. We may look upon the inter-marriage of the house of David, followed by the establishment of idolatry in Judah, the reign of Athaliah, and the almost total extirpation of David's line, as a turning-point in its history. The idolatrous worship then publicly set up, never afterwards lost its hold upon a large part both of the chiefs and people. A strong heathen party enters now as a permanent element into all its history. It is to be noted as a sign of the times, that the two kings following Athaliah — Joash and Amaziah — both died by the hands of conspirators, showing how little reverence was felt for them regarded as Jehovah's kings, His representatives.

CHAPTER XI.

THE MESSIANIC HOPE FROM THE DIVISION OF THE KINGDOM TO THE TIME OF WRITTEN PROPHECY.

It has often been noticed as remarkable, that none of the prophets in Judah or Israel, from the time of Solomon down to the time when the prophets began to write their prophecies, or for near two centuries, made any mention, so far as recorded, of the Messiah or the Messianic kingdom. Why was this? Why was not this kingdom held up as an object of hope to encourage the hearts of the people in those dark and troubled days? To this it may be answered, that by no means all the utterances of the prophets during this period are preserved: they may have spoken of the Messiah and His kingdom to the faithful, though their words are not reported.

But there is another answer: our brief historical survey shows us that at no time after the division of the kingdom could the coming of the Messiah have been to the nation at large an object of true spiritual desire or hope. The moral conditions were wanting. The promises respecting Him appealed to faith, and His kingdom in its higher characteristics could not be an object of mere intellectual apprehension. It has been already observed, that only as the people were faithfully fulfilling their duties to Jehovah as the theocratic King, could they understand the nature of the higher blessings of the future kingdom, and truly desire them. That in a time of general unfaithfulness, affecting both king and people, there should have been no true expectation of the Messianic Kingdom, and no mention of it by the prophets, need not, therefore, surprise us. The prophets could not speak of future spiritual blessings to those who had no ear to hear. It was their immediate duty to make the people see their unfaithfulness in their present relations to Jehovah, to convince them of their sins, and, if possible, to bring them to repentance. God sent by their lips many messages to His people, but they had special reference to present transgressions and perils and judgments. In the Northern kingdom, Elijah and Elisha and their companions warned the wicked princes and people of God's anger, and in some cases inflicted by His command severe punishments, but were silent as to Him that was to come. How, indeed, could they speak of Him as the representative of Jehovah, and the Son of David, to those who were openly worshipping Baal, and fighting against the house of David! The first step was to repent, and return to Jehovah, and walk in His ways, and thus be brought into that spiritual condition in which they could hear with joy of the holy Kingdom He had promised.

In the kingdom of Judah, also, the prophets of this period may have been silent as to the Messiah, and, if so, probably from the same cause. Obedience under the Theocracy was the indispensable condition of preparation for the Messianic Kingdom; and this obedience was not simply of individuals, but of the nation headed up in its kings. As the sin had been national, so must be the repentance. Idolatry from the first was tolerated, and afterward sanctioned by royal authority, and thus found entrance into the hearts of the people. (2 Chron.

xii. 1.) The images of idols and their impure rites defiled Jerusalem, the city of the great King. In the palace of David was not found that pure and holy atmosphere in which could be nurtured Jehovah's promised Deliverer, the Righteous One; oppression, greed, luxury, were seen everywhere in the land; and the efforts of the occasional faithful kings to stay the flood of evil were unavailing.

Thus it was that to neither kingdom from the time of the division was the promise of God respecting the Messiah as His righteous and holy King, an object of hope, and, therefore, could not be made a subject of prophetic exhortation. The higher stage of Divine revelation and of holiness could not be desired by those who were unfaithful in the lower. That there were individuals who discerned its purport, and ardently desired its fulfillment, we may well believe; and the witness which the Psalms bear to the Messianic hopes of this time will be later considered.

CHAPTER XII.

WRITTEN PROPHECY: ITS PLACE AND SIGNIFICANCE.

So familiar are we with the fact of written prophecy as forming a large part of the Old-Testament Scriptures, that we scarcely think to ask ourselves why prophecy should be written. But a little reflection shows us that prophecy written down and preserved for a future generation or age, was not in accordance with the spirit of the Theocracy, and that its first appearance marked an epoch in God's dealings with His people. His Presence among them assured them of the continual communications of His will as there might be need. (Exod. xxv. 22.) One of the appointed channels of such communication was the prophet. (Deut. xviii. 18–22.) How often He made use of the prophets, especially after the time of Samuel, declaring His will day by day as He saw fit, the sacred histories abundantly attest. But none of their words were for many years written down, except as embodied in the historic narratives, as, for example, the words of Elijah and Elisha in the history of Israel. Their utterances were for their own day and generation; nor was there any necessity that a prophet of one generation should write down his words for the guidance of the next. Jehovah, ever personally present among the people, could at no time fail to find organs to make known His will, speaking by them as He saw occasion to speak.

In considering the work and place of the Hebrew prophets, we must remember that these were defined by the relation of the people to Jehovah as the theocratic King. The prophet was the chief organ of His utterance; and, therefore, the range of the prophetic word was large and varied, embracing every thing necessary to be made known in the administration of the Theocratic State. Prediction of future events was but a small part of his office. The great outlines of God's purpose in His people were already known to them through the covenants with Abraham, and with the people at Sinai, and the promises connected with them, and through the law which was written down for perpetual remembrance. (Josh. viii. 32–35.) Through the covenant with David the goal was set before them, the universal Kingdom of Jehovah under the Messiah: the matter of practical interest was how they should reach this goal. As an army on its march surrounded with enemies needs daily guidance under the new circumstances of peril in which it is placed, so with the elect people. Jehovah was their leader; and the prophet was present to give them His commands, to point out their pathway, and to show them the dangers to which they were exposed, both from within and without. In the life of David we have an example how often Jehovah declared His will by His prophets in all matters pertaining to the duties of the king and the welfare of the people.

Thus, under the Theocracy, prophecy was designed primarily for the immediate present. The prophet spake for his own time; his words were fitted to meet the exigencies of the day; they were pre-eminently practical. The word spoken, whether to the king or people, was to enable them to fulfill present duty, not to discern in detail the remote future. There was no need, therefore, that it should be written down, except as it became a part of history. The prophets come and go each with his message; but Jehovah who gives the word, abides ever with His people, able to make daily such new revelations of His will for their guidance in the present, and to open the future, as shall please Him.

Thus prophecy under the Theocracy, according to its true intent, was spoken and not written. Most significant, therefore, is the change that meets us when written prophecy appears, and the transient spoken word takes upon itself a permanent form. Now the prophet is seen speaking not merely to his own generation, but to indefinite generations following. What does this indicate? It indicates two things: first, a future withdrawal of Jehovah's Presence from His people, and a consequent cessation of prophetic utterance; second, a delay, longer or shorter, in the fulfillment of the Divine purpose respecting the Messiah and His Kingdom. Each of these is to be considered.

First, So long as Jehovah continued to dwell among His people, and to commune with them, they could never want such light respecting the future as might be necessary for the discharge of present duties. "Surely the Lord God will do nothing, but he revealeth His secret unto His servants the prophets." (Amos iii. 7.) That a prophet should write down his prophecies by Divine direction, pointed forward to a time when Jehovah would no longer be with them, to speak to them by prophets as He had done. (Amos viii. 11, 12; Lam. ii. 9.) It implied a period of silence: it was the storing up of bread for coming years of famine.

These two things, the cessation of prophecy and the withdrawal of the Divine Presence from the people, stood in the most intimate moral relations. If their King, He must dwell among them, and make known to them His will. When His people through their sin became obstinate in their rejection of His words, and would not listen or obey, He would cease to speak to them by His prophets. Nor could He continue to dwell among them, and yet have no communion with them, — a King, but unable to declare His will; a silent God, dumb because they have no ears to hear. When, therefore, He began by His Spirit to move the prophets to write down their words for the instruction of future generations, it foretold that the time was coming when He would cease to speak to His people by the living voice, He would depart from them, and they would be left to the guidance of the written word.

Second, The fact of written prophecy indicated, also, that there was to be no speedy fulfillment of the Divine purpose in the Messiah. His Kingdom was not near, but after "many days;" and the word, therefore, must be preserved for the instruction of future generations; and the cause of this delay was the moral unpreparedness of the people, as shown in the refusal to hear the prophets, and obey their words. As of old, when marching from Egypt to the promised land, and near the border, the people yielded to unbelief, and so were compelled to wander up and down in the Wilderness for long years till a new generation had arisen, so must it be again. Through the covenant with David, they had been placed as on the border of the Messianic Kingdom. Jehovah was among them, to speak to them by His prophets, and to lead them steadily onward; but they had not hearkened to them, and pressed forward: and now many weary years must elapse, and generations pass away, before they would behold its glories. They would bear with them in their wanderings the prophetic scroll, but hear no more the living voice of their King and God.

This transition, therefore, from spoken to written prophecy marks an epoch in the history of the elect people. It is generally agreed that the earliest written prophecies may be placed about the middle or in the latter part of the ninth century (B.C.). If we ask what there was in the character of that time when the prophets began to write down their prophecies, to account for this change, we find in history a ready answer. We have already noted the period when both kingdoms, under the leadership of their respective kings, Ahab of Israel, and Jehoram of Judah, gave themselves up to idolatry, and which period may be regarded as a decisive turning-point in their history. From this beginning of national apostasy, although followed by a violent re-action for a time, there was never any real and permanent recovery. Both kingdoms, though with unequal steps, went steadily onward in their downward path. It can cause us no surprise that the same time which was a turning-point in the spiritual relations of the elect people to Jehovah, was such, also, in their political relations to the heathen states around them. As the ninth century saw the beginning of prophecy written down in the Divine foresight of their apostasy, it saw also the origin, or rather the revival, of the Assyrian monarchy appointed by Him to be a chief instrument for their chastisement. At this time (about 850 B.C.) the small and independent kingdoms on the banks of the Euphrates and Tigris became subject to an Assyrian monarch, who extended his conquests over Lebanon to the Mediterranean coast. Tyre and Sidon, and later Damascus and Syria, were conquered; and it is probable that Israel under Jehu was forced to pay tribute (825 B.C.). A few years later, Ahaz, king of Judah, alarmed by the confederacy against him of Syria and Israel, became the vassal of

Tiglath-pileser. (2 Kings xvi. 7.) The kingdom of Israel was soon overthrown by the Assyrians (722 B.C.); and Judah, like the corn between the upper and nether millstones, was kept in continual alarm and perplexity by the conflicting powers of Assyria and Egypt. To the north the prophets continually pointed the eyes of the people as the real source of danger: "I will bring evil from the north, and a great destruction." (Jer. iv. 6.) The fear of Assyria, and afterwards of Babylonia, lay as a heavy burden on the hearts of all who feared God, and hearkened to the warning words of His prophets.

It was thus at a time when both the kingdoms, Israel and Judah, had, by flagrant acts of idolatry under the leadership of their several kings, broken their covenant with Jehovah, rejected His authority, and dishonored His name; and when by His providence He had so ordered events that Assyria was becoming the ruling power of the East, ready to be His instrument, "the rod of His anger," in the infliction of His just judgments, that written prophecy began. It was a most momentous time, and full of the gravest issues, not only for the elect people, but for all the nations; not only for that generation, but for many generations. The sin of His people was not, indeed, final; there was still scope for repentance; the anger of God might yet be turned away. But, if they did not hearken to the prophetic warnings, before them was set the fearful threatening of national overthrow and exile.

Thus to the prophets of this time was given a twofold commission, — to speak God's word for the immediate present, and to write it down for the remote future. They spoke first to the living, to rebuke, warn, instruct, and comfort, if so be that by true repentance God's threatened judgments might be turned away. And then, when the words spoken had been proved unavailing, He moved them to make such a summary of them as might be useful for the coming generations, and write them down to be read during the long years of exile and dispersion.

Written prophecy has its peculiar character, because written down in the Divine foresight of the rejection of the people by Jehovah, of His departure from them, and of their overthrow and dispersion in the earth. A chief distinctive feature in it is that it announces, more or less clearly, a great day of judgment as at hand, and as its chief elements the coming overthrow, the expulsion from the land, and their scattering among the nations; and as the ground of this judgment it makes prominent the present sinful condition of the people. The prophets assume that the teachings of Moses as to the judgments of God upon them for continued disobedience, were known. (Lev. xxvi.; Deut. xxviii.) The people were not ignorant that their national existence was dependent upon the faithful keeping of the covenant, and that the penalty of expulsion from their land was foretold as the final chastisement. The prophets, therefore, in announcing that God was about to inflict this final chastisement, do not reveal any thing new as to the Divine purpose in the punishment of His people if persistently disobedient, but announce that the time for the fulfillment of His threatened judgment is approaching. That Jehovah could not continue to rule over a sinful people, but would cut them off from His land, had been declared of old: the peculiarity of the prophetic word now is, that it declares their sinfulness to be already so great that it is in the purpose of God to inflict this last judgment. Yet in their predictions the prophets are not declaring the decrees of a fate, but the purpose of a merciful God who loves and would save His people.

Even to the very last, they call to repentance if haply His righteous anger may be turned away; but only national repentance can avail, for it is national apostasy that has provoked His righteous anger.

Thus, true to its practical intent, prophecy which we now possess in its written form, was first spoken. The prophets speak each to his own generation, and their words all revolve about these three points: first, the blessings temporal and spiritual given by God to His covenant people if faithful; second, the judgments that will come upon them if unfaithful; third, His renewed grace to them when repentant. It was common to the prophets that they had special discernment, through the Spirit, of the purpose of God in the election of the people, and saw the goal to be reached; and they had also discernment of their present spiritual condition, and, therefore, could judge aright the present time, and see its bearing on the future. They discerned when the people were walking on in the path appointed them, and when they were turning aside from it, or were going backward. As those thus enlightened, the prophets have a lively sense of the sins and evils of their own times; and a large part of their utterances are outbursts of sorrow over the general apostasy, mingled with severe rebukes, warnings, and threatenings. (Isa. xxii. 4; Jer. ix. 1, etc.) They see in the distance the coming national overthrow, because of persistent national transgressions; and they strive in every possible way to awaken the nation to a sense of its danger, and to persuade it to repent.

We may take the words of the earliest prophet who wrote, Joel (about 850 B.C.), as an illustration. The kingdom of Judah is suffering under Divine judgments, — drought, locusts, and famine; the neighboring tribes have invaded the land, and carried away some of the people, and sold them as slaves. It is their sin that has brought on them these calamities, and, therefore, the prophet earnestly calls them to national repentance. Let all — elders, priests, and people — assemble, and sanctify a fast; and, if they repent not, he points forward to heavier judgments to come. He speaks of "the day of the Lord," with its clouds and darkness; not a day of blessing and salvation, but a "day of destruction from the Almighty." He foresees the final chastisement when the people will be taken captive, and the land divided among its invaders. But God's purpose does not fail: out of the national overthrow a remnant will be saved, and through that remnant there will be deliverance. Jehovah will return, and dwell again in Zion. Jerusalem will be holy: He will gather the nations to judgment, and all that have oppressed His people shall be made desolate. He will then reign in righteousness over all the earth.

Thus Joel strikes the keynote for all the prophets that were to follow. His prophetic vision embraces the future in its chief phases down to the establishment of the universal Kingdom. He gives in few words the general outline which the later prophets fill up in detail. In them all is distinctly and repeatedly set forth the present sinfulness of the people, each prophet speaking according to his discernment of the moral condition in his day; and emphatic warnings are given of the approaching judgment in the national overthrow and captivity. They also point forward to the ultimate deliverance of the repentant, and the national restoration and reconstitution under the Son of David, and the fulfillment of all the covenant promises. "After many days" the purpose of God in His elect people will be accomplished, and through them all nations be blessed.

To sum up what has been said, the normal place of the prophet is under Jehovah as the King, to speak to His people day by day such words as He may give, and on all matters temporal and spiritual as He may please. To write down their words pointed to the cessation of prophecy, and to the departure of Jehovah from them: they are to be left to the guidance of the written word. But this guidance is no real substitute for Jehovah's personal word through His prophets, since no people judging itself by a book can know its own spiritual state, and whether it is or is not fulfilling the Divine purpose. Nor is this to deny the place of the priests as public teachers. Jehovah ceasing to guide them by His prophets, the nation is left to follow blind guides, to hearken to prophets who speak out of their own hearts, and to do what seems to itself good. Therefore the last prophet of God, Malachi, who declares the functions of the priest, foretells one who is to come before "the great and dreadful day of the Lord," and who shall "turn the heart of the fathers to the children, and the heart of the children to their fathers." (ii. 7, iv. 5.) Though the voice of prophecy should be long unheard, yet at last it is through a prophet sent of God, and illumined by His Spirit, that they must be taught what He would have them do to prepare the way of the Lord.

As bearing on the future, and opening the purpose of God to the end, written prophecy had a wide field before it. It looked forward to acts of God necessarily demanding considerable periods of time. The two great points in the near future are the approaching captivity and dispersion, and the subsequent return of a remnant. The nation, if it heed not the prophetic warnings, is to be overthrown, the people carried away captive, a time of severe discipline is to follow, the salvation of a remnant, the national reconstitution of this remnant, and finally the fulfillment of the Divine promises in the establishment of the Messianic Kingdom. The prophetic vision extends far beyond the narrow territorial limits of Judah and Israel. The elect people is to be cast forth into "the sea of the nations." All lands shall thus know of their holy calling, of their transgressions and their punishment; and finally all peoples will be made partakers of the Messianic blessings at their restoration.

Though the prophets knew it not, their words, written down, were to be read by Jehovah's scattered children for many centuries, and in lands remote of which they had never even heard. As records of the past, of the sins of their fathers, and of God's dealings with them, and as embracing His purpose to its consummation, the prophetic writings were in the Divine intention for their light and guidance and warning till the consummation should come. The prophets wrote, as declared by the apostle, for the learning of all that should come after, that, through the patience and comfort of their words, all generations, down to the day of their fulfillment in the Messianic Kingdom, might have hope. (Rom. xv. 4.)

But written prophecy embraces, also, God's words addressed to many heathen peoples: these words could not in the nature of the case have been spoken to them, and they have long since ceased to exist as peoples. Why, then, written down and preserved? Not simply that we of these latter days may see their fulfillment, and thus have our faith confirmed, for this fulfillment cannot in many cases be proved because of our historical ignorance. They were written rather because the purpose of God in the Jews as a people, both as wanderers and when restored and dwelling in their own land, brings them into continued relations to other peoples, and especially to those dwelling immediately around them; and although the earlier peoples, as Edom and Moab, Syria and Egypt, may cease to exist, yet other peoples arise, and the same relations in substance continue. As His own chosen nation, through whom He will reveal Himself to the nations, the Jews hold through all historical time an official position, and have a sacred character, and in the day of their restoration and of the judgment of the nations, the great question will be, how far have the other nations regarded them as His people, and so treated them.

The words, therefore, addressed of old to heathen peoples, and written down by the prophets, though having special significance for the time when written, have significance also for all the peoples that may be brought into relation with the elect nation; and especially at the time when Jehovah shall regather them, and set them again in their land as the head of the nations. Then His purpose in them will be revealed in the eyes of all. (Deut. xxvi. 19.) The judgment of the nations as nations at the establishment of the Messianic Kingdom, will be based on their treatment of those whom God had set apart as His own, and whom He then attests in a special manner to be His by His wonderful dealings with them in their restoration.

CHAPTER XIII.

HISTORY OF THE TWO KINGDOMS TO THEIR OVERTHROW.

WE have seen that the reigns of Ahab and Jezebel in Israel, and of Jehoram and Athaliah in Judah (918-880 B.C.), may be regarded as turning-points in the histories of their respective kingdoms. Heathen gods were worshipped by royal authority in both capitals, in Samaria and in Jerusalem; heathen priests and prophets were protected and honored; the priests and prophets of Jehovah were neglected and despised, and in some instances were persecuted and put to death. This was a crime against the majesty of Jehovah, both as their God and their King, which He did not pardon. From this national apostasy there was not, in either kingdom, any real recovery. There were in Judah some pious kings who did their utmost to purge the nation from idolatry, and bring the people to repentance and obedience, but without lasting success. The leaven of idolatry had too thoroughly penetrated the popular mind. There were ebbs and flows in the tide, but the general tendency was steadily downward.

It is not necessary to go into historical details, except to show how far the prophetic utterances were affected by the national unbelief. As the years went on, both kings and peoples were more unwilling to hear the Divine rebukes and warnings. In Judah, several prophets were at different times put to death, and Amos was forbidden to prophesy in Israel. To be a prophet, and to declare God's will, became increasingly dangerous, and demanded supernatural firmness and courage. Upon the unwilling Ahaz Isaiah must force his words (Isa. vii.); and the tradition is, that he perished by violence under Manasseh. God said to Jeremiah, who shrank from his mission, "I have made thee a defenced city, and an iron pillar, and brazen walls against the whole land, against the kings of Judah, against the princes thereof, against the priests thereof, and against the people of the land. And they shall fight against thee." It is thought by many that this prophet, also, died by violent hands. To Ezekiel God said, "Be not afraid of them; . . . behold, I have made thy face strong against their faces, and thy forehead strong against their foreheads. As an adamant harder than flint have I made thy forehead: fear them not, neither be dismayed at their looks." And what was true of these greater prophets, was true, doubtless, of the lesser: it was at the peril of their lives that they declared the will of God to His rebellious people.

Notwithstanding all the stubbornness and perversity of His children, Jehovah still remained a covenant-keeping God, and unwearied in His reproofs and warnings. His words to His prophets were, "Go, speak unto them, and tell them, thus saith the Lord God, whether they will hear, or whether they will forbear." Nor did the prophets cease to declare that God would be merciful and forgive if they repented and returned to Him: "As I live, saith the Lord God, I have no pleasure in the death of the wicked, but that the wicked turn from his way, and live." "Return, thou backsliding Israel, saith the Lord; and I will not cause mine anger to fall upon you: for I am merciful, saith the

Lord." But there was no deep or lasting national repentance. A few, doubtless, here and there hearkened to the words of the prophets, and humbled themselves before God; but the great body continued as rebellious as before. With disobedience and idolatry came every form of immorality. How severe are the words of Hosea and Amos addressed to the people of the Northern kingdom: "The Lord hath a controversy with the inhabitants of the land, because there is no truth, nor mercy, nor knowledge of God in the land." (Hos. iv. 1.) Amos declares that God had sent many punishments upon them, but they had sinned more and more. At Bethel and Gilgal they worshipped idols, the poor were oppressed, the rich lived in selfish luxury. Judges were bribed, the Sabbath was desecrated, and the whole land polluted.

In a few years after these two prophets had witnessed in vain to the Northern kingdom, its destruction came (722 B.C). A little before its overthrow there was a gleam of outward prosperity under Jeroboam, who was a wise and able ruler. He freed his people from the yoke of the Syrians, restored the kingdom to its former bounds, and made it strong in the eyes of men. But it was, as seen by prophetic eyes, inwardly full of evil and corruption. Great political confusion and discord followed his death, and the throne became the prey of the most daring and unscrupulous aspirant. In the space of two hundred and fifty years after the division of the kingdom, there were nine dynasties and nineteen kings, and two short periods of anarchy. It was natural that the help of Assyria, now the dominant power, should be called in by rival claimants; and when Hoshea, the king, refused to pay tribute, the Assyrians conquered the land, and carried a great part of the people into captivity. Such was the end of the kingdom of Israel.

In the kingdom of Judah, there was not the same rapid decay. The Davidic succession to the throne was not disputed; and several of the kings were zealous for the honor of Jehovah, and were able to effect salutary though transient reformations. But idolatry could not be rooted out, nor was there any true reliance upon the power of Jehovah to defend them from their enemies. Nor did the destruction of the kingdom of Israel warn them, and bring them to genuine confession. On the contrary, as the prophets became more and more definite in their utterances respecting the anger of Jehovah and the approaching overthrow, the pride of the people and their stubbornness increased. Without faith in Divine help, the rulers essayed to secure their safety by appealing, now to Egypt, and now to Assyria. And even after the time of the end had come, and the king Jehoiachin and his princes had been carried to Babylon (598 B.C.), those that remained behind in Judah, in complacent blindness fancied that all danger of further invasion was passed. For twelve years under Zedekiah time was given for repentance, but without effect. We read that " Zedekiah did that which was evil in the sight of the Lord." This last opportunity to repent not being rightly used, the destruction of the kingdom of Judah soon came. The servants of Nebuchadnezzar " burnt the house of the Lord, and the king's house, and all the houses of Jerusalem, . . . and brake down the walls of Jerusalem round about." The words of God by the mouth of His prophets were fulfilled; the time of the captivity had come.

CHAPTER XIV.

MESSIANIC BELIEF IN THE PROPHETS DOWN TO THE EXILE.

WE may find in a recent landscape-painting an illustration of what meets the eye as we open the pages of written prophecy. In this painting we have before us in the foreground a highway with its passers-by and its various activities, and beyond this and low down in a broad valley, a lake lying in deep shadow; and still beyond, a range of hills, their highest points shining in the sun. Thus, in the prophetic picture, in the foreground is the active present, — the events political and religious which occupy national attention; and more remote, and dimly seen in the future, is the time of captivity and exile; and still beyond this, and far distant, is the glory of the Messianic Kingdom. The prophetic eye does not, indeed, look upon a lifeless canvas, upon moveless figures; the present is ever changing; each prophet has his own distinctive point of view, and the time of the exile is ever drawing nearer. But the great features of the prophetic landscape remain unchanged; only, as the day of overthrow approaches, the present becomes more full of movement and of historic detail, as is seen in Isaiah and Jeremiah, and the prophet's word becomes more circumstantial and minute. We see before us the tumult of peoples, the marching of armies, the siege of cities: all is excitement and turmoil, anxiety and alarm. Over the sky the clouds are gathering; but through the deepening darkness the Spirit of God in the prophets points ever to the promised Kingdom, that the faithful may be saved by hope.

As was to be expected, there is great variety in the details. What is distinct and full in one prophet, is often indistinct and partial in another. This has its explanation in part from their differing mental constitutions and spiritual endowments, and in part from the differing circumstances of their times, and consequent varying points of view; the future always, in prophetic utterance, being presented in a certain correspondence to the present. As the day of national overthrow draws nearer, the utterances are more express and minute, both as to the nation by which it is to be effected, the extent of the dispersion, its duration, and other matters necessary to be known by those who have part in them.

Let us first sum up the chief points of agreement in their presentation of the future by the prophets of this period.

1. The day of God as impending, — a day of righteous retribution, in which He will manifest His holiness and justice in the punishment of the evil; but the end of which is to bring to repentance, and to prepare the way for His universal Kingdom. His judgments affect, first and chiefly His own people in their overthrow and captivity; then the heathen nations also, not only those in immediate relation to His people, but all on the earth.

2. The regathering of the tribes, the restoration of a remnant purified by Jehovah's discipline, their reconstitution, and His return to dwell among them at Jerusalem, and the blessings spiritual and temporal that follow.

3. The universal Kingdom of Jehovah. Those persistently rebellious among the nations are cut off: the residue become obedient, and are taught of the Lord, and partake of the blessings of His rule. The mention by these prophets of the Son of David as the universal King, will be considered later.

Let us now briefly pass in review the prophets of this period, in chronological order, noting the particulars just mentioned. Of Joel, the earliest (850 B.C.), we have already spoken in part. He sees in the present judgments of God upon the people the signs that "the day of the Lord" is approaching, — "a great and terrible day:" the people will go into captivity, and their land be possessed by their enemies. (iii. 1, etc.) There will be a time of universal war; Jehovah will sit in judgment on the nations, for their oppression of His people; "the harvest is ripe," "their wickedness is great." (iii. 13, etc.) The sun, moon, and stars will be darkened, the heavens and the earth will shake. But the Lord will be the hope and strength of His people: a remnant will be delivered, and upon them will He pour out His Spirit, and through them there will be deliverance to all who shall call on His name. (ii. 28, etc.) Then will Jehovah dwell in Zion, and His holy city no more be defiled by strangers, and to spiritual He will add all forms of temporal blessings. (iii. 17, etc.)

In Amos (about 800 B.C.) the utterances are clear as to the judgments to come on the people, the more severe because of their greater sin as His chosen. (iii. 1, etc.) His chastisements had not availed to bring them to repentance; therefore, He has punished them. (iv. 6-12.) But sorer punishments are to come; they shall go into captivity beyond Damascus (v. 27); He will scatter them among all nations. (ix. 9.) But His purpose will not fail, only the sinners among them shall be cut off. He will bring again the captivity of His people, and plant them upon their land, and bless them with all temporal blessings. (ix. 11-15.)

Hosea (about 780 B.C.) repeats the same declarations in substance, but adds that the captivity is for "many days;" in "the latter days" they shall return. (iii. 4, 5.) They shall be greatly increased in number, and shall be called "the sons of the living God," and God will betroth them unto Him forever, and they shall know the Lord. (ii. 19.) Nothing is said by this prophet of the judgment of the nations, and but little of outward and temporal blessings. (ii. 18, etc., xiv. 5-7.)

Micah (about 750 B.C.) announces the coming of Jehovah to judgment. "The mountains shall be molten under Him, and the valleys shall be cleft. . . . For the transgression of Jacob is all this, and for the sins of the house of Israel." (i. 4, 5.) He will not spare His own city and holy hill. Zion shall be ploughed as a field, and Jerusalem shall become heaps, and the people shall be carried to Babylon. (iii. 12.) But this desolation is not to continue. "I will surely assemble, O Jacob, all of thee; I will surely gather the remnant of Israel." They shall come up out of all countries, and Jehovah will show marvellous things as at the coming up from Egypt. "The nations shall see and be confounded, . . . they shall be afraid of the Lord our God, and shall fear because of Thee." (vii. 15-17.) Here, as often in the prophets, there is a twofold presentation of the relation of the nations to His returning people, first as hostile, but afterwards, when through Divine judgments the nations are humbled, all submit to Jehovah's rule, and there is peace. Thus we read that "many nations are gathered against the daughter of Zion, saying, Let her be defiled, and let our eye look upon Zion." But

God shall gather them as the sheaves into the floor. "Arise and thresh, O daughter of Zion. . . . Thou shalt beat in pieces many people. (iv. 11-13.) "The remnant of Jacob shall be among the Gentiles in the midst of many people as a lion among the beasts of the forest." "I will execute vengeance in anger and fury upon the heathen, such as they have not heard." (v. 8, 15.) It is through this manifestation of His severity that the residue of the nations are brought into submission to His holy rule. Then shall there be universal peace, and "every man shall sit under his vine and under his fig tree." (iv. 4.) Jerusalem will be the religious and political centre of the world.

The prophecies of Isaiah, extending through a long period (759 to 698), are often divided into two parts, the last chapters (xl.-lxvi.) being ascribed to a prophet living during the exile. Without accepting or denying this division, it will be convenient to speak here chiefly of the first part. (Chaps. i.-xxxix.) It was given to this prophet to announce a series of judgments not to end till the holy seed was found, the purified remnant; and it was declared to him by God, that all the words he might speak to the people would but harden them. In one point of view, it may be regarded as pronouncing upon them a sentence of judicial blindness. (vi. 9-13.) As this commission was given him in the year that king Uzziah died (758 B.C.), and so at the very beginning of his ministry, it must have greatly affected the character of all his utterances. That "the day of the Lord" was rapidly approaching as a day of punishment, and the captivity about to come because of the sins of the people, were to him most assured. No words of warning or rebuke that he could utter would bring them to repentance. The captivity must come, Jehovah using Babylon as His instrument. But, if this punishment failed to bring to repentance and to obedience, still another and another must follow. The prophet's eye, therefore, overlooks the whole period of penal blindness and its judgments, down to the end, though without seeing how remote that end may be. Like all the prophets, he speaks primarily to his own generation, and present events fill the foreground. But he is looking far beyond these to the greater things to come; and thus there is in his words such a frequency and rapidity of transition from the immediate present to the remote future, as is found in no other prophet. As Moses, in the record of the forty years of wandering in the wilderness, speaks only of the events at its beginning and its close, so is it with Isaiah of the period of the exile. He sees only the beginning and the end, the entry into the captivity and the exit from it. He passes at a bound from the Assyrian to the Messiah, from the ruins of Babylon to the rebuilding of Jerusalem, from the desolate land of Israel to the new heavens and earth.

In so far-reaching a vision, it is a matter of prophetic necessity that present relations and events be used as symbols of those in the distant future. Egypt and Assyria and Babylon, Edom and Moab, realities of the present, become names descriptive of like hostile powers in the future, with which the elect people will then be brought into relation; and therefore there is in this prophet such largeness of expression, such an absence of local and temporal particulars, both as regards events now present and those yet to come. Jehovah's people abide His people, and the law of retribution is the same and unchangeable; but the instruments by whom He inflicts His judgments are new, and one may be named as a type of all.

This character of universality appears in all Isaiah's

words. He speaks as one who stands at the end, when the purpose of God in His people is about to be made known to all the nations. He calls on the heavens and the earth to hear what God had done for them, and how they had repaid Him. And now will He judge them; but His judgments affect also all the world. The day of the Lord is upon all the pride and glory of the earth. (ii. 10–22.) Not in one land only, but throughout all lands, are His people to be scattered; not Babylon only, but all nations are to be His instruments to execute His judgments on them, and from the four corners of the earth will He gather them. (xi. 11, 12.) And at the end, when He shall "rise to shake terribly the earth," and to humble the loftiness of man, the disorder and confusion will have become universal. All the bonds that bind society together will have been dissolved. No land, no people, no class, will in that day escape His judgments. "The earth is utterly broken down, the earth is clean dissolved, the earth is moved exceedingly." Then will "He punish the host of the high ones that are on high, and the kings of the earth upon the earth." And this is the day in which He alone will be exalted. "Then the moon shall be confounded, and the sun ashamed, when the Lord of hosts shall reign in Mount Zion, and before His ancients gloriously." (Chaps. xxiv.–xxvii.)

Thus through His mighty actings in righteousness the whole earth is brought at last to know Jehovah, to know Him as the One Supreme and Holy God. "The glory of the Lord shall be revealed, and all flesh shall see it together." And in this revelation of Himself before the nations, His elect people bear a most important part as His helpers. First, the time of penal blindness comes to its end, the veil is taken from their hearts. "The eyes of the blind shall be opened, and the ears of the deaf shall be unstopped." They will see His hand, they will hear His words, and cry unto Him; "and the rebuke of His people will He take away from off all the earth." Again at Jerusalem will He manifest His Presence by visible symbols as of old. "The Lord will create upon every dwelling-place of Mount Zion, and upon her assemblies, a cloud and smoke by day, and the shining of a flaming fire by night: for upon all the glory shall be a defence." (iv. 5.) And not only in that day will the living be gathered to Him, "the ransomed return and come to Zion, with songs and everlasting joy upon their heads:" He will gather, also, the faithful departed. "Thy dead shall live, my dead body shall they arise." Having thus perfected His purpose in His own, He will "destroy the veil that is spread over all nations." Then will they see His glory revealed in Zion, and go up to worship, and to be taught His will. "And many peoples shall go and say, Let us go up to the mountain of the Lord, to the house of the God of Jacob, and He will teach us of His ways, and we will walk in His paths." "Then the earth shall be full of the knowledge of the glory of the Lord, as the waters cover the sea."

In the prophet Jeremiah (630 B.C.), who addresses himself chiefly to the events of his own day, in which he bore so active a part, continual mention is made of the coming captivity in Babylon which is now at the very door; and he alone defines its length as seventy years. (xxv. 11.) As living at the time of the captivity, and seeing the general distress and despair, he comforts the believing by reminding them of the faithfulness of God. They are His covenant people, and they will assuredly return. As the ordinances of day and night are unchangeable, so is His covenant with His people. "If these ordinances depart from before me, saith the

Lord, then the seed of Israel also shall cease from being a nation before me forever." "From their iniquities will He cleanse them, and pardon all their sins, and He will write His law in their hearts, and will be their God, and they His people." "Yea, I will rejoice over them to do them good, and I will plant them in this land assuredly with my whole heart and with my whole soul. . . . And it shall be to me a name of joy, a praise and an honour before all the nations of the earth." All that has been said of the universal Kingdom, and of their place in it, will then be fulfilled. "At that time they shall call Jerusalem the throne of the Lord; and all the nations shall be gathered unto it." (iii. 17.)

We have still to ask what the prophets of this period say of the house of David, and of the Messiah. That during the exile and dispersion of the people the royal family must share the national fate, needed no special declaration: the throne must fall with the city and the temple. But, with the restoration of the nation, it will be restored. The Divine purpose is unchangeable, that, so long as the people remain His people, so long one of the house of David shall be His king.

Among the minor prophets Joel says nothing of the family of David: it is Jehovah who gathers all nations and judges them, and delivers and restores His people, and dwells among them in Zion, His holy mountain.

Obadiah speaks of "the day of the Lord as near upon all the heathen," of "the saviours upon Mount Zion," of the restoration of the possessions of Jacob, and of the kingdom as the Lord's; but he does not speak of David's house. Neither Nahum nor Habakkuk makes any mention of the Son of David. Zephaniah speaks of the restoration of the people, and of Jehovah as the King of Israel, but not of David's house.

Amos declares that God will bring again the captivity

of His people, and set them in their own land for ever, and then will He "raise up the tabernacle of David that is fallen, . . . and build it as in the days of old." (ix. 11–15.)

Hosea makes mention of the family of David: "For many days Israel shall abide without a king, and without a prince, and without a sacrifice," a subject and scattered people; but "afterwards they shall return, and seek the Lord their God, and David their king; and shall fear the Lord and His goodness in the latter days." (iii. 4, 5.) Here is plainly meant, not the literal David, but the promised One of his line. And under Him Judah and Israel will be reconciled, and become one people. "Then shall the children of Judah and the children of Israel be gathered together, and appoint themselves one head, and they shall come up out of the land." (i. 11.)

Micah prophesies that Jehovah will bring back the people whom He had driven out and afflicted, and reign over them in Mount Zion forever. (iv. 1–7.) And as the universal Kingdom is then established, so the Ruler of the house of David also appears. "But thou, Bethlehem Ephratah, . . . out of thee shall He come forth unto me that is to be Ruler in Israel; whose goings forth have been from of old, from everlasting." Not out of the royal city, but out of little Bethlehem should He come, as did David, thus pointing both to the obscurity into which the family had fallen, and to the fact that in Him a new founder would appear, and a new age begin. Till He come, the people must remain in their bondage: "Therefore will He give them up, until the time that she which travaileth hath brought forth: then the remnant of His brethren shall return unto the children of Israel. And He shall stand and feed " — rule — "in the strength of the Lord, in the majesty of the name of the Lord His God; and they shall abide: for now shall He be great unto the ends of the earth." (v. 2-4.) When the people are restored to the Divine favor, and the universal Kingdom is set up, He takes His place as Jehovah's King.

In the prophet Isaiah, mention is made of the birth of a child to sit upon the throne of David: "Unto us a Child is born, unto us a Son is given: and the government shall be upon His shoulder. . . . Of the increase of His government and peace there shall be no end, upon the throne of David, and upon his kingdom, to order it, and to establish it with judgment and with justice from henceforth even for ever." (ix. 6, 7.) Although it is not here said that He is a Son of David, yet no one can doubt who is meant. Again it is said, "There shall come forth a rod out of the stem of Jesse, and a Branch shall grow out of his roots." The house of Jesse is here likened to a tree that has been cut down of which only the stump remains, but there is still life in it. During all the years following the overthrow by the Babylonians, the family of David remains hidden. Except for a brief period, in the person of Zerubbabel, the throne is not re-established. But when the time comes for the reconstitution of the kingdom, then appears the Branch, — Jehovah's King and that which marks Him above all is His endowment with the Spirit, by which He is qualified to be the Ruler and the Judge. To Him thus endowed all power is given: "With righteousness shall He judge the poor, and reprove with equity for the meek of the earth; and He shall smite the earth with the rod of His mouth, and with the breath of His lips shall He slay the wicked." "In that day there shall be a root of Jesse which shall stand for an ensign of the people; to it shall the Gentiles seek; and His rest shall be glorious." (xi. 1-10.)

Of the promise of the Immanuel, it is not necessary to speak here in detail. (vii. 14.)

If we now consider this prophet's words respecting this King, we see that the conception of a man extraordinarily endowed with the gifts of the Spirit does not exhaust their meaning: "His name shall be called Wonderful, Counsellor, The Mighty God, The Everlasting Father, The Prince of Peace." (ix. 6.)

Without entering into the question how far these, and other like terms in the Old Testament, teach the fact of the Incarnation, one thing cannot well be doubted, — that they ascribe to Him a superhuman nature. Applied to a mere man, however richly endowed with natural and spiritual gifts, all feel them to be grossly exaggerated. He is not merely one in the line of David's successors, — greater, indeed, than any before Him, but with difference only of degree. He is not to be classed with them: He is the Wonderful, like none other; Immanuel, — God with us. And His government is not like theirs, temporary: "Of the increase of His government and peace there shall be no end." Immortal, He is the last of the Davidic kings.

To other words of this prophet, and the terms "Branch of the Lord," and "Fruit of the earth" (iv. 2), we must content ourselves with simple reference. But it is not to be overlooked, that it was given him to see the Lord in vision sitting as King in His temple; and we are told by the evangelist, that it was a vision of the Messiah: "These things said Esaias when he saw His glory, and spake of Him." (John xii. 38-41.) As in the case of the apostles on the Mount of Transfiguration, and of Paul on his way to Damascus, an indelible impression must have been made on the mind of the prophet. Beholding the heavenly majesty, the holiness, the angelic ministries, he was prepared to understand how great was this Son of David, and how glorious His kingdom. Well might he say, that when He should "reign in Mount Zion, and before His elders in glory, the moon would be confounded, and the sun ashamed." (xxiv. 23.)

The power of the Messiah, and His supernatural character, are less emphasized by Jeremiah than by Isaiah; but the permanence of the covenant with David is often and strongly expressed: "Thus saith the Lord; If ye can break my covenant of the day, and my covenant of the night, and that there should not be day and night in their season; then may also my covenant be broken with David my servant, that he should not have a son to reign upon his throne." (xxxiii. 20–26.) It is as enduring as His covenant with the people. In due time, therefore, when the nation should be restored, the throne of David must be re-established: "I will raise unto David a righteous Branch, and a King shall reign and prosper, and shall execute judgment and justice in the earth. In His days Judah shall be saved, and Israel shall dwell safely." (xxiii. 5.) "Alas! for that day is great, so that none is like it: it is even the time of Jacob's trouble; but he shall be saved out of it. . . . They shall serve the Lord their God, and David their king, whom I will raise up unto them." (xxx. 7, 9.) "In those days, and at that time, will I cause the Branch of righteousness to grow up unto David, and He shall execute judgment and righteousness in the land. In those days shall Judah be saved, and Jerusalem shall dwell safely." (xxxiii. 15, 16.)

Thus we find in all these prophets, not only the expectation of the restoration of His elect people, and of the future universal Kingdom of Jehovah, but also, in most of them, distinct mention that a Son of David will be the ruler under Him. In the prophetic future He stands under Jehovah the chief and central figure. No vision of the restoration is complete that does not behold Him sitting upon His throne, and His majesty corresponds to the majesty of the kingdom. (Mic. v. 4.)

CHAPTER XV.

THE NATIONAL OVERTHROW AND THE REMNANT.

THAT a time might come, when, through unfaithfulness to their covenant, the Jews would cease to exist as a nation, and be scattered over the earth, was distinctly spoken of by Moses. There was a point in national transgression beyond which Divine forbearance would not go. After threatening many heavy chastisements, God says, " And if ye will not for all this hearken unto me, but walk contrary unto me; then I will walk contrary unto you in fury. . . . And I will scatter you among the heathen, and will draw out a sword after you: and your land shall be desolate, and your cities waste." " And ye shall be left few in number, whereas ye were as the stars of heaven for multitude." " The Lord God shall scatter you among the nations, and ye shall be left few in number among the heathen." (Lev. xxvi.; Deut. xxviii.)

It was very hard for the elect people, who knew not the greatness of their sins, and whose pride in their election increased as the years passed by, to believe that God would thus give them up into the hands of their enemies, and scatter them among the nations. He would, therefore, have this His last judgment upon them repeatedly and distinctly announced by the prophets, that they might know whither their disobedience was leading them. Long before the time of actual captivity came, prophetic warnings began to be given. But in these, as in all announcements of coming judgments, there are increasing fullness and distinctness of utterance as the time draws near.

In Joel, the earliest of the prophets whose prophecies were committed to writing (870–850 B.C.), we find the national captivity foretold, but in indirect terms. Here we meet for the first time the phrase to "bring again the captivity of Judah and Jerusalem." The fact of such captivity is implied, also, in the words that follow: "I will also gather all nations; . . . and will plead with them there for my people and for my heritage Israel, whom they have scattered among the nations, and parted my land." (iii. 1, 2.) In this is foretold the national dispersion and the distribution of their land to heathen inhabitants, words which cannot be applied to a temporary invasion. We have thus in the very beginning of written prophecy, and probably more than two centuries before its fulfillment, a prediction of national overthrow.

In Amos and Hosea, the prophets next in chronological order (800–725 B.C.), and whose mission was chiefly to the Northern kingdom, there are many distinct and positive declarations of the coming overthrow and captivity. In Hosea: "I will cause to cease the kingdom of the house of Israel. . . . I will no more have mercy upon the house of Israel; but I will utterly take them away." (i. 4, 6.) "The children of Israel shall abide many days without a king, and without a prince." (iii. 4.) "My God will cast them away, . . . and they shall be wanderers among the nations." (ix. 17.) In Amos: "I will cause you to go into captivity beyond Damascus." (v. 27.) "The high places of Isaac shall be desolate, and the sanctuaries of Israel shall be laid waste." (vii. 9.) "Israel shall surely go into captivity forth of his land." (vii. 17.) " The eyes of the Lord are upon the sinful kingdom, and I will destroy it from off the face of the earth." (ix. 8.)

Both these prophets refer also to Judah as ultimately to be punished in like manner as Israel, but as spared for the present. Hosea: " Israel and Ephraim shall fall in their iniquity; Judah also shall fall with them." (v. 5.) Amos: " I will send a fire upon Judah, and it shall devour the palaces of Jerusalem." (ii. 5.)

It is not necessary to cite from the later prophets. In most express terms by Micah and Isaiah and Jeremiah, and all the prophets before the exile, did God foretell that His last and heaviest chastisement was about to come upon His people in both their kingdoms. Both would be overthrown, and all the tribes go into captivity.

It is necessary that we carefully consider here the elements that enter into the conception of " the captivity " as God's last and highest act of judgment. Primarily it refers to the deportation of the people from their land, and their subjection to the heathen nations. But the term has a larger meaning. It has already been stated, that, in establishing the Theocracy Jehovah entered into two new relations: first, that of King to the people; second, that of Proprietor to the land; and as consequent upon them, and subordinate to them, was established the relation of the people to the land as His tenants. The first two of these relations were co-existent: so long as He was their King, He dwelt in the land as His own, and His Presence was their national preservation. Even if, for a time, He permitted their enemies to invade the land, and overcome them, it was for their punishment and reformation. But to permit His people to be carried away captive to another land, and His temple to be destroyed, and His worship to cease, this was not compatible with His honor as their King, dwelling among them. When the sins of His people had reached that degree that He must cast them out from their land, and put them under the yoke of the heathen, and give up His temple to be burned, He Himself must first depart: the land, so long as hallowed by His Presence, could not be defiled by heathen possession.

The chief and essential element in the conception of the captivity, is, therefore, the cessation for a time of the theocratic relation, the sign of which was the withdrawal of Jehovah from the holy city and temple. Before the destruction by the Babylonians, when Jerusalem was taken, and the temple burned, and all the holy vessels taken away to Babylon, the prophet Ezekiel, an earlier exile, saw in vision the departure of "The Glory," the symbol of Jehovah's Presence, first from the temple to the midst of the city, and then from the midst of the city to the Mount of Olives. (Ezek. x. xi.) His habitation among them had been the crowning proof of His love: "I will walk among you, and I will be your God." "I the Lord dwell among the children of Israel." When the temple was dedicated, Solomon said: "I have surely built Thee an house to dwell in, a settled place for Thee to abide in for ever." It was His Presence that consecrated the land, and made it holy; and it could not be given up to the heathen to dwell in till He had departed from it.

This departure of Jehovah from His temple and land was the determining condition of the captivity, since it marked a change in His theocratic relation to His people, — a change that continues even to this day. They did not cease to be His covenant people. (Lev. xxvi. 44.) His purpose in them was still unfulfilled, His promises respecting the Messiah and His kingdom were not withdrawn, and He continued to accept their worship. But He Himself was no more reigning at Jerusalem; the Visible Glory no more dwelt between the Cherubim; the ark was not in the Most Holy Place; the holy fire no longer burned upon the brazen altar; there was no response by Urim and Thummim. The people might return, as they did from Babylon, the temple be rebuilt, the worship again set up; yet there was a change. They came back from their first exile and dispersion, but no more to be an independent nation. To their original standing as the theocratic people under His immediate rule, they were not restored. In the land their God had given them that they might freely serve Him without fear, the heathen ruled over them, the throne of David was not restored. For a brief period under the Maccabees there was an assertion of freedom, an hour of independence; but the eagles of Rome were already hovering over Jerusalem, and failing to discern their Messiah the Jews ceased to be a people among the peoples of the earth.

It is thus plain that the return of a part from the Babylonian exile, and their resettlement in their land, was not the end of the captivity, nor in any full sense a restoration. This cannot be till the Lord their God again dwells among them, and rules them through His King of the house of David, in truth and righteousness. The whole period from the overthrow by the Babylonians down to the present hour is, in the larger and truer sense, a period of captivity. When it shall end, they will come up from their bondage and dispersion as they came from Egypt: "the Lord their God will be with them, and the shout of a king be among them." (Num. xxiii. 21.)

The Jews must be cast out of their land because, like the Canaanites, they had defiled it. (Ezek. xxxvi.

17.) But their exile was not for destruction, it was for chastisement and purgation. After a time a remnant would return. It is therefore in the prophetic word respecting this remnant that the chief interest of written prophecy is centred.

It had been declared by God through Moses, that however great the sins of His people, and severe His punishments, He would not utterly destroy them, nor break His covenant with them. (Lev. xxvi. 44.) Although the nation, as a nation, should fail to respond to its calling, some repentant and faithful ones would be at last found whom He could reconstitute as a nation, and to whom His promises could be fulfilled. To this remnant, as the time of the captivity draws nigh, and its signs multiply, the eyes of the prophets searching the future are constantly turned: it is the hope that saves from national despair. So anxious was Isaiah that the people in his day, a century and a half before Jerusalem's overthrow, should know this gracious purpose of God, that he gives his son the name of Shearjashub, "the remnant shall return," a sign to them, that although the nation must be cast out of their land, it would not be utterly destroyed.

As regards this remnant, two questions present themselves: first, what was the purpose of God in its preservation? second, what were the moral conditions of its deliverance? As to the first, it was preserved, as appears from what has been already said, that He might by it reconstitute the nation, establish the Messianic Kingdom, and manifest Himself as God through His Son, the Messiah, to all the peoples of the earth. To this end were all His dealings with His people from the call of Abraham; to this end were all the words of the prophets.

But, besides this great and ultimate end, there was

another to be effected through the remnant,— the bringing of His Son into the world by His birth of a virgin. In the Holy Land, of a Jewish mother, and under the ordinances of the law, must He be born and nurtured; and at Jerusalem must He present Himself to the priests and rulers as the promised Messiah. There must be, therefore, at least a partial restoration of the people and of their Mosaic polity, before His birth. If, at His coming, they received Him, and were cleansed by Him, and filled with His Spirit, then would He gather them under His wings, and fulfill in them the great end of God in their election. But rejecting Him, and thus proving themselves unworthy of God's grace, they must again be visited with chastisement, and the last worse than the first. If continuing unfaithful, the bonds that yet bound them to the land must be wholly broken, and they cease to have a possession in it, but be scattered among all nations, till there should be found at last that remnant which should cry, "Blessed is He that cometh in the name of the Lord." (Matt. xxiii. 39.)

In due time the purpose of God as to the birth of His Son was accomplished. But His people did not discern Him as the Messiah when He presented Himself to them, but crucified Him; and a second more fearful overthrow and dispersion followed. Some were gathered into the Christian Church, but the larger part still remains dispersed over the earth. It is from these that the remnant is to be gathered — the remnant of the last days — by whom He will fulfill His promise, and glorify Himself in the eyes of all nations.

The second question has respect to the moral conditions of the deliverance of this remnant. These were clearly marked out in the same prophecy that foretold the captivity. (Lev. xxvi. 40.) The captives will not be delivered from their captivity till they shall confess their iniquity, and the iniquity of their fathers, and humble their uncircumcised hearts, and accept the punishment of their iniquity. Repentance, confession, humility, obedience, are the indispensable conditions of their restoration to God's favor, and of their return.

This purpose of God in regard to the remnant, it is very important to note. Having found the nation as such unfaithful, He will purge it with judgment; and the process of purgation must continue till He finds those able to discern, and ready to do His will. It is not a question of time, but of moral preparation.

In none of the prophets are God's dealings with His people in reference to this remnant so clearly brought out as in Isaiah. He begins his prophecy by showing that all the blessings God had bestowed upon His elect people had not made them faithful: "I have nourished and brought up children, and they have rebelled against me." Many sore judgments He had brought upon them, but in vain. "Why should ye be stricken any more? ye will revolt more and more." The time for the sorest chastisement was near at hand. His vineyard, notwithstanding all the care He had bestowed upon it, had brought forth wild-grapes; and now He will take away the hedge, and break down the wall, and lay it waste. But how long should this chastisement continue? Till its end was reached. It was not a transient punishment, like drought or pestilence or an invasion, but a permanent punitive condition, not to come to an end till through its discipline there should come forth an humble, purified, and obedient remnant. There might be from time to time alleviations of its severity, for during its whole period would God bless them as they showed themselves prepared to receive blessing; but there could be no restoration to the fullness of His grace, no entering into the Messianic Kingdom, till a radical moral transformation had been wrought.

It was given to Isaiah to pronounce upon the people a sentence of judicial blindness, an act which from its very nature must have formed a most important epoch in their history. God said to him, "Go, and tell this people, Hear ye indeed, but understand not; and see ye indeed, but perceive not. Make the heart of this people fat, and make their ears heavy, and shut their eyes." And when he asked how long this blindness will continue, he was told, "Until the cities be wasted without inhabitant, and the houses without man, and the land be utterly desolate, and the Lord have removed men far away, and there be a great forsaking in the midst of the land." (vi. 9-13.) With the purely doctrinal aspect of this commission, we are not here concerned. The prophet is assured that his words will not be understood by the people, but that their effect will be to blind and harden them. They had, by their disobedience in the past, brought themselves into such spiritual condition that they had no ears to hear, or eyes to see, what God would speak and do. (xxix. 10-14.) Therefore, He was about to bring His judgments upon them,—judgments far more severe than any yet inflicted. He would not cast them wholly away, but there should be stroke upon stroke till they should be brought unto an humble and penitent mind. "Then the eyes of the blind shall be opened, and the ears of the deaf shall be unstopped." (xxxv. 5.) "In that day shall the deaf hear the words of the book, and the eyes of the blind shall see out of obscurity, and out of darkness. The meek also shall increase their joy in the Lord, and the poor among men shall rejoice in the Holy One of Israel." (xxix. 18, 19.)

The first and immediate fulfillment of the prophet's words foretelling the captivity, was in the Babylonian conquest; but they reached beyond this conquest. There shall " be a great forsaking in the midst of the land. But yet in it shall be a tenth, and it shall return, and shall be eaten." (In Rev. Ver., "And if there be yet a tenth in it, it shall again be eaten up.") "As a teil tree, and as an oak, whose substance is in them when they cast their leaves: so the holy seed shall be the substance thereof." (vi. 13.) The meaning of these words is thus given by Professor Alexander: "However frequently the people may seem to be destroyed, there will be a surviving remnant; and however frequently the remnant may appear to perish, there will still be a remnant of the remnant left. And this indestructible residue shall be the holy seed." From the exile in Babylon a remnant will return. But if "the holy seed" be not found, this remnant will be judged and purged; and this process of discipline and purgation will continue till at last God finds His tenth, His portion, His holy seed, which He will plant in the land to be no more rooted out.

Other prophets speak in like manner. Ezekiel, a prophet during the exile, thus speaks of the third part of the people: "A third part thou shalt scatter in the wind; and I will draw out a sword after them. Thou shalt also take thereof a few in number, and bind them in thy skirts. Then take of them again, and cast them into the midst of the fire, and burn them in the fire; for thereof shall a fire come forth into all the house of Israel." (v. 2–4.) Upon these words Hengstenberg thus remarks: "The third part given to the wind consists of the fugitives. . . . God's sword — His vengeance — follows them even in the dispersion. . . . The binding of the few remaining hairs in the skirt denotes the tender care that the Lord takes of the remnant, and that He will gather them from their dispersion, and restore them to their home. To take of them again and cast them into the fire, presupposes that even among the remnant that were come to a better mind, corruption will afterward break out, so that God's judgment will once more manifest itself in a fearful manner."

It is impossible to quote here the many passages in the prophets that refer to this remnant, and to God's dealings with its members to prepare them for their future place: to cite a few is sufficient. In Isaiah we read: "Zion shall be redeemed with judgment, and they that return of her with righteousness." (i. 27.) "And it shall come to pass, that he that is left in Zion, and he that remaineth in Jerusalem, shall be called holy, even every one that is written among the living in Jerusalem: when the Lord shall have washed away the filth of the daughters of Zion, and shall have purged the blood of Jerusalem from the midst thereof by the spirit of judgment, and by the spirit of burning." (iv. 3, 4.) In the prophet Amos: "I will sift the house of Israel among all nations, like as corn is sifted in a sieve, yet shall not the least grain fall upon the earth. All the sinners of my people shall die by the sword." (ix. 9, 10.) In Zephaniah: "I will also leave in the midst of thee an afflicted and poor people, and they shall trust in the name of the Lord. The remnant of Israel shall not do iniquity, nor speak lies." (iii. 12.) In Jeremiah: "I will gather the remnant of my flock out of all countries whither I have driven them, and will bring them again to their folds. . . . And I will set up shepherds over them which shall feed them: and they shall fear no more, nor be dismayed." (xxiii. 3, 4.) "Turn, O backsliding children, . . . for I am married unto you:

and I will take you one of a city, and two of a family, and I will bring you to Zion." (iii. 14.) In Obadiah: "Upon Mount Zion shall be they that escape, and it shall be holy." (17.)

When God shall have completed His work of purgation, and established the purified ones in their own land, then will He again dwell among them in Jerusalem and Mount Zion, manifesting His Presence by symbols as of old: "So shall ye know that I am the Lord your God dwelling in Zion, my holy mountain: then shall Jerusalem be holy." (Joel iii. 17.) "I will make her that halteth a remnant, and her that was cast far off a strong nation: and the Lord shall reign over them in Mount Zion from henceforth, even for ever." (Mic. iv. 7.) "Then the moon shall be confounded, and the sun ashamed, when the Lord of Hosts shall reign in Mount Zion, and in Jerusalem, and before His ancients gloriously." (Isa. xxiv. 23.) "And the Lord will create upon every dwelling place of Mount Zion, and upon her assemblies, a cloud and smoke by day, and the shining of a flaming fire by night: for upon all the glory shall be a defence." (Isa. iv. 5.) "The King of Israel, even the Lord, is in the midst of thee: thou shalt not see evil any more." (Zeph. iii. 15.) "And the Redeemer shall come to Zion, and unto them that turn from transgression in Jacob." (Isa. lix. 20.) "I will take you one of a city, and two of a family, and I will bring you to Zion. . . . At that time they shall call Jerusalem the throne of the Lord. . . . In those days the house of Judah shall walk with the house of Israel, and they shall come together out of the land of the north to the land that I have given for an inheritance unto your fathers." (Jer. iii. 14–18.)

Two points are left undecided by the prophets, because depending on the moral effect of God's dealing with the people, — the length of the captivity, and the number that should constitute the remnant. In general, the prophets speak of the return of the remnant as "after many days;" or, in "the latter days;" or, "last days." This uncertainty as to time of fulfillment marks all prophecy, for the moral element ever overrules the chronological. God scrupulously respects the free will of men; and though His purpose is sure to be accomplished, and that at exact times known to Him, it is through His people's voluntary co-operation. It was not revealed to the prophets how long this disciplinary period of the captivity would continue, but they knew it must continue till there was wrought a true repentance, and an humble submission to the will of Jehovah. Nor was it revealed to them in how many this repentance and submission would at last be found: this only the issue could make known. Probably the prophets hoped and believed that God's judgments would bring the greater number to repentance, and prepare them to return.

It is probable, also, that some of the prophets before the captivity looked for the establishment of the Messianic Kingdom immediately after the return from the Babylonian exile, which return Jeremiah defines as at the end of seventy years. But prophetic language under the guidance of the Holy Spirit is general, and the conditional element in fulfillment is always recognized. The captivity must continue till its purifying end is reached. The remnant that should be gathered under the Messiah, and constitute the foundation of the Messianic Kingdom, must be "a holy seed," for the kingdom is holy. "The remnant of Israel shall not do iniquity, nor speak lies." Whether to those returning from the captivity in Babylon the Divine promises in the Messiah could be fulfilled, it was not given to the prophets before that captivity to foresee. Even Isaiah did not, we may believe, know when his words respecting their judicial blindness would have had their fulfillment. It might be, that proving unfaithful they would be again scattered, and only a remnant of that remnant be finally gathered under their Messiah. The prophets knew that God's purging process must continue till the dross is consumed, and only the pure silver and gold remain.

With the deliverance and restoration of this remnant, the salvation of the heathen nations is closely connected. The original purpose of the Theocracy can now be carried out, and Jehovah, dwelling among a holy and obedient people, can manifest Himself through them as the Lord of the whole earth. Thus this remnant, when itself delivered, becomes a means of deliverance also to others. "And it shall come to pass, that whosoever shall call on the name of the Lord shall be delivered: for in Mount Zion and in Jerusalem shall be deliverance, and in the remnant whom the Lord shall call." (Joel ii. 32.) "The remnant of Jacob shall be in the midst of many peoples as a dew from the Lord, as the showers upon the grass." (Mic. v. 7.) "Many nations shall come, and say, Come, and let us go up to the mountain of the Lord, and to the house of the God of Jacob; and He will teach us of His ways, and we will walk in His paths: for the law shall go forth of Zion, and the word of the Lord from Jerusalem." (Mic. iv. 2.) "I will make you a name and a praise among all people of the earth, when I turn back your captivity before your eyes, saith the Lord." (Zeph. iii. 20.) "The sons of the stranger, . . . even them will I bring to my holy mountain, and make them joyful in my house of prayer: . . . for mine house shall be called an house of prayer for all people." (Isa. lvi. 6, 7.) "At that time they shall call Jerusalem the throne of the Lord; and all the nations shall be gathered unto it." (Jer. iii. 17.) "The heathen shall know that I am the Lord, when I shall be sanctified in you before their eyes." (Ezek. xxxvi. 23.)

Thus in the prophetic future three points were clearly outlined: the gathering of the purified remnant, — the holy seed; the appearing of the Messiah and the establishment of the Messianic Kingdom; and the conversion of the nations.

CHAPTER XVI.

MESSIANIC PROPHECIES DURING THE EXILE.

THE prophets of the exile were Ezekiel and Daniel; and, according to some, the latter portion of Isaiah is to be ascribed to this period. (Chaps. xl.-lxvi.)

The utterances of Ezekiel, who was carried into captivity eleven years before Jerusalem's destruction by Nebuchadnezzar, and who began to prophesy in Mesopotamia to those captive with him (594 B.C.), have special interest as recording the departure of the Visible Glory from the temple and Jerusalem before their destruction; as showing the spiritual condition of the exiles; and as foretelling the return of the remnant, the invasion of Gog, a new division of the land, the re-establishment of worship in a new temple, the return of Jehovah to dwell in it, and the reconstitution of the Jewish State.

Among those who were carried captive with Ezekiel, there were many who did not believe that Jerusalem would be destroyed by the Babylonians, and cease to be the holy city, the dwelling-place of Jehovah. They expected soon to return to it, and see the kingdom restored to independence and prosperity. (Jer. xxix. 8-10.) It was, therefore, necessary for the prophet to show them how unfounded their expectations, and that because of their sins God was about to depart from His people, and to give up His holy temple to be defiled and destroyed by the hands of the heathen. In vision the prophet beholds the departure of the Visible Glory from the temple and the city before its overthrow. (Ezek. ix. 3, x. 4, 18, xi. 22.) The Glory was the symbol of Jehovah's Presence, as on Mount Sinai; and where it abode, there was His dwelling-place. When the Jews had made Him "a sanctuary that He might dwell among them," the Glory of the Lord filled the tabernacle. (Exod. xl. 34.) And there He continued to manifest Himself from between the Cherubim till the temple was built. At its dedication, we read that "the cloud filled the house of the Lord, so that the priests could not stand to minister because of the cloud: for the Glory of the Lord had filled the house of the Lord." (1 Kings viii. 10.) Notwithstanding all their subsequent idolatry and wickedness, Jehovah continued to dwell among them in His temple down to this time. But now that He is about to forsake them, and to give up His temple to be profaned and destroyed, the prophetic eye of Ezekiel beholds "the Glory of the God of Israel go up from the cherub, whereupon He was," to the threshold of the house, and then it departs from off the threshold of the house, and stands over the Cherubim at the door of the east gate; and at last, went up from the midst of the city, and stood upon the Mount of Olives. It was the sign that Jehovah no more dwelt among them.

This departure of the symbol of Jehovah's Presence from the holy city made it certain to Ezekiel that the hopes of the exiles were vain. A great change was about to take place in the relation of Jehovah to the nation. He would not interfere to save the city. "Mine eye shall not spare, neither will I have pity." He left the holy mount He had chosen, no more to return to it till they were prepared to be in truth a holy and obedient people.

Of the religious condition of the exiles in Babylon, we learn much from this prophet. Judging by the character of those carried away with Jehoiachin (2 Kings xxiv. 8–12), and from the words of God to Ezekiel when calling him to his prophetic work (Ezek. ii. 3, xiv. 1, etc.), His dealings with them in the overthrow of the kingdom had produced little salutary fruit. Unchastened by captivity, they were unwilling to hearken to the prophet's reproofs and warnings. "The house of Israel will not hearken unto thee, for they will not hearken unto me." His words are often very severe against the princes and chiefs, those who should have been the shepherds of His flock, now "scattered upon all the face of the earth." "Woe to the shepherds that do feed themselves. . . . Ye eat the fat, and ye clothe you with the wool; ye kill them that are fed, but ye feed not the flock." (Chap. xxxiv.)

It is plain that upon the larger part of the exiles, their captivity produced no good effect. With the most there seems to have been little regard for the Mosaic institutions, and little desire for their restoration. The evil influences around them infected them; and if they were repelled from idolatry in the grosser forms, yet their faith in their own covenant standing, and in the promises of Jehovah, was weakened. Seen from the walls of Babylon beneath which flowed the broad Euphrates, Jerusalem was an insignificant city, the Jordan a mountain brook. How poor appeared the narrow territory of Judæa and its steep and barren hills, in contrast with the wide and fertile plains of Chaldæa! Even the holy temple, compared with those of Babylonian deities, was architecturally mean and unworthy. What could the few warriors of Israel do against armies gathered from a hundred subject peoples? Every thing was fitted to make the exiles feel their relative insignificance, and that their hope of a great national future was visionary. It is most likely that a large proportion of them during the many years of expatriation, had become so wonted to the life of those around them, and penetrated by its spirit, as to be indifferent to their covenant relation, and to the claim of Jehovah upon them as His own people.

But, in contrast with this indifference of the many, the zeal of the few appeared the more marked. Whether the more earnest and devoted among them suffered religious persecution, is not clear, but the example of Daniel and his brethren shows that this might have been the case; and some expressions in the prophets Jeremiah and Ezekiel lead to this conclusion. These kept, so far as possible, the Mosaic laws, and valued more highly the religious privileges of which they were deprived. Of the feelings of such faithful ones, the one hundred and thirty-seventh psalm is a true expression: "Let my tongue cleave to the roof of my mouth, if I prefer not Jerusalem above my chief joy."

It was the intent of God that His people, scattered among the heathen, should bear a witness unto His name; but this the Babylonian exiles did not do. As the house of Israel had dishonored their God in their own land, so in the land of their captivity did they dishonor Him. "When they entered unto the heathen, whither they went, they profaned my holy name." (Ezek. xxxvi. 20.) As captives scattered through the land, and brought into close relations with the inhabitants, it was an opportunity for them to testify to Jehovah as the One, Holy, and Supreme God, a witness like that borne by Daniel and his companions in the capital city. (Dan. iii. 12.) This they did not do; and the burden of the prophetic message to them was, "Turn ye, turn ye from your evil ways; for why will ye die, O house of Israel?" (Ezek. xxxiii. 11.)

A people thus unrepentant under His judgments, Jehovah could not bless and take again into favor. Yet He would not wholly cast them off, nor suffer His purpose to fail. There were some repentant and faithful among the captives, and these He would bring back to their land. Before the destruction of Jerusalem He had shown to Ezekiel that there was an election that should be saved. He sees in vision "a man clothed with linen, with a writer's ink-horn by his side," who is commanded to go "through the midst of Jerusalem, and set a mark upon the foreheads of the men that sigh and that cry for all the abominations that be done in the midst thereof." (ix. 4.) It was men of this spirit whom God would deliver, the remnant that He would bring forth from captivity, and by them rebuild His temple and city. (vi. 8–10, xiv. 22.)

It is plain, however, that the words of this prophet looked beyond the return of the little company of Babylonian exiles under Joshua and Zerubbabel, and embraced that final remnant, "the holy seed" of Isaiah, in whom the Messianic Kingdom is to be set up, and God's purposes fully realized. A holy and obedient people will at last be found. God will dwell among them. The waste cities will be rebuilded, the desolate land will be tilled, and be as the garden of Eden, and they shall possess it forever. In that day, the old unity of the nation will be restored, and Judah and Israel will be one: "I will make them one in the land; ... and they shall be no more two nations, neither shall they be divided any more into two kingdoms at all." (xxxvii. 22.) At the head of this united kingdom is one of the house of David: "And David my servant shall be king over them, and they shall all have one shepherd." "I the Lord will be their God, and my servant David a prince among them." (xxxiv. 24.) And under His administration are fulfilled all the promises of material prosperity. "The tree of the field shall yield her fruit, and the earth shall yield her increase. . . . They shall dwell safely, and none shall make them afraid." This blessed condition is followed by no apostasy: "I will make a covenant of peace with them; it shall be an everlasting covenant with them. . . . I will set my sanctuary in the midst of them for evermore, and the heathen shall know that I the Lord do sanctify Israel." (xxxvii. 26.) Through His holy nation will He then be honored in the eyes of all the nations.

Whilst all the prophets speak of the return of the remnant, and of the glory and blessedness of the Messianic Kingdom, Ezekiel alone describes in detail the new order to be established. (Chaps. xl.–xlvii.) He was bidden to show to the people the pattern of a new temple and of its ritual. Of its details, and of the new division of the land among the tribes, we have no need here to speak. These concern the future, and can be at best but very imperfectly understood till the time of fulfillment comes. But a point to be noticed is, that as the prophet saw the departure of the Visible Glory from the first temple, so he sees its return to this, the last. "Behold, the Glory of the God of Israel came from the way of the east: and His voice was like a noise of many waters: and the earth shined with His Glory. . . . And the Glory of the Lord came into the house; . . . and, behold, the Glory of the Lord filled the house. . . . And He said unto me, the place of my throne, and the place of the soles of my feet, where I will dwell in the midst of the children of Israel for ever, and my holy name, shall the house of Israel no more defile." (xliii.

2–7.) It is to be noted that at this return it is said "the earth shined with His Glory." The Divine manifestation is no more confined to the limits of the Most Holy Place, nor of the temple, nor of the city, but the whole land is radiant with the heavenly light.

It is clear that Ezekiel did not expect that this new order would be established immediately after the return of the exiles from Babylon, but believed that this consummation would not be reached till other and sorer judgments had come upon them. Reference has already been made in another place to His words respecting "the third part," that "it should be scattered in the wind, and that God would draw out His sword after it:" teaching as Isaiah had done, that upon those who are delivered from one judgment another will come, and that this process will continue till the purified remnant is found. (v. 2, 4.)

The predictions of Ezekiel respecting Gog present many difficulties; but one thing we may at least say, that they have not yet been fulfilled. (Chaps. xxxviii., xxxix.) They look forward to the time when the last great effort shall be made by hostile nations to destroy the Jewish people, and which seems to be immediately preceding the Messianic Kingdom. But this prophecy has this peculiarity, that it supposes the Jews to have been restored to their land, and to be dwelling in it at peace at the time when Gog and his hosts come up against them. For this reason, some would put this invasion at the end of the Messianic Kingdom. To this there are very strong objections; and it is easier to believe that there will be a partial restoration of the Jews before the final one, a restoration brought about perhaps for political ends. The founding of a Jewish state in Palestine under the protectorate of Christian nations, is not now incredible; but this would not be the kingdom under their Messiah. There are several intimations in the prophets of such partial return of the people before the last overthrow, as in Zech. xii. 2-8, xiv. 1-3. Whether by Gog we are to understand an enemy distinct from the Antichrist who wars against the Church, or that the Antichrist is here described in his special relations to the Jewish people, it is impossible to say; but the manner of his destruction, and the national blessedness that follow it, seem to point to one and the same chief and last enemy.

Whether the last part of Isaiah (chaps. xl.-lxvi.) was written by some unknown prophet, and during the Babylonian exile, as held by many, or by Isaiah himself, is of no great importance in our inquiry, since the point of view, whether historic or prophetic, is that of the captivity; and we may consider it here. The writer looks upon the people as already under God's judgment, and in bondage. (xlii. 24, xliii. 28, xlviii. 20.) But the allusions to Babylon as the instrument of their punishment and the place of their exile are few and general. There are references to a deliverance, and express mention of Cyrus as a deliverer; but it is not the complete and final deliverance. There are many declarations that point to another and a wider dispersion, and to a regathering from many lands. (xliii. 5, 6; xlix. 12.) Babylonia is only one of the lands of exile: the return of a few from it is not the perfect deliverance. Hence, there is a largeness and generality in these prophecies, that allows their application to all the phases of the captivity, in the larger sense of that term, down to the end, and which cannot be narrowed down to the very partial return under Cyrus, and to the imperfect and dependent kingdom then established.

To work repentance in His people, and to bring them

to humility and confession, did Jehovah send them into captivity; and not till they were thus contrite and humbled, could He comfort them. (xii. 1. See Zech. xii. 10.) It is the sign that His discipline had produced its intended effect when He calls upon His prophets to cry: "Comfort ye, comfort ye my people." (xl. 1, 2. See lxi. 3.) Now her warfare is accomplished, and her iniquity is pardoned, and now can He return to them to dwell among them; but His way must be prepared, and then "the glory of the Lord will be revealed, and all flesh shall see it together." Doubtless there were some of penitent spirit, who could be comforted at the return from Babylon; and in them there was an inchoate fulfillment. But the eye of the prophet was directed to the end of the captivity, the end of their wanderings and their chastisement, and to that return when the purpose of God could be fully accomplished. And in all the later and larger part of these prophecies there is no allusion to Babylon, or to the partial deliverance from the exile there. It is perfectly consistent with this that there is given a description of Babylon's overthrow. (Isa. xlvii. 8.) As the power by which was inflicted God's first great act of chastisement, we have in its overthrow a prophetic foreshadowing of the greater enemy to come, and of his final destruction.

It is this vision of the remote future, and of the great fulfillment of all prophecy in the Messianic Kingdom, that leads this prophet to speak so often of the power of God to foretell what is to come, and which none but He can do. (xlv. 21.) When His purpose is fulfilled in His people, and "the times of restitution" come of which He had spoken by all His prophets from the beginning of the world, "declaring the end from the beginning," then will it be known that His purpose will stand, and all His pleasure will He perform. (xli. 26, xlvi. 10, xlviii. 16.)

In none of the prophetic utterances is the glory of the Messianic Kingdom so vividly set forth as here, and in none is the place of Israel as " a kingdom of priests and a holy nation " more clearly stated. " Arise, shine, for thy light is come, and the glory of the Lord is risen upon thee; . . . and the Gentiles shall come to thy light, and kings to the brightness of thy rising. . . . The sons of strangers shall build up thy walls, their kings shall minister unto thee; . . . the nation and kingdom that will not serve thee shall perish; . . . ye shall be named the priests of the Lord, men shall call you the ministers of our God." (lx., lxi.) Then does Israel fulfill its calling as the medium of God's revelation of Himself to the nations: " The Gentiles shall see thy righteousness, and all kings thy glory." " Behold, I create Jerusalem a rejoicing, and her people a joy." " I will gather all nations and tongues, and they shall come and see my glory." Now begins a time of national prosperity and peace, of righteousness and blessedness, that is to have no end. The perfect is not, indeed, yet come; the people are still subject to death. (lxv. 20.) But the foundation is already laid in their risen King for the new heaven and new earth; for He that "poured out His soul unto death " would live again, and " the pleasure of the Lord shall prosper in His hand." (liii. 10–12.) And from this time onward no fresh apostasy shall come in to hinder the fulfillment of the Divine purpose.

Although there is no express mention of the Messiah as ruling under Jehovah, yet that it is He who is spoken of as " The Redeemer," " The Salvation," " He that cometh from Edom," cannot be doubted by any one who believes that one Spirit speaks by all the prophets.

Isaiah saw Him upon His throne (vi. 1), and now He appears to take the kingdom. "The Redeemer" — Goel — "shall come to Zion, and unto them that turn from transgression in Jacob," — the purified remnant. "Say ye to the daughter of Zion, Behold, thy Salvation cometh; behold, His reward is with Him, and His work before Him." And a part of His work is to redeem His own from their enemies. "Who is this that cometh from Edom, with dyed garments from Bozrah? . . . I have trodden the wine-press alone. . . . I will tread them in mine anger, and trample them in my fury. . . . For the day of vengeance is in mine heart, and the year of my redeemed is come." (lxiii.) Here, as everywhere in the prophets, a day of sore judgments upon the nations precedes the day of salvation. (Ps. cx. 5, 7; ii. 8, 9.) But not as an earthly warrior does He subdue His enemies. His battle shall be "with burning and fuel of fire." "Behold, the Lord will come with fire, . . . to render His anger with fury, and His rebuke with flames of fire." But when He has punished His enemies, and purified His people, then shall the name of Jehovah be honored throughout all the earth. "And it shall come to pass that from one new moon to another, and from one Sabbath to another, shall all flesh come to worship before me, saith the Lord." (Chap. lxvi.)

It was the prophet Daniel whose prophecies most influenced the popular mind, and gave more definite form to their Messianic conceptions. This prophet was the first who set forth the Messianic Kingdom in its temporal relations to the successive great kingdoms of the world. The earlier prophets had repeatedly spoken of the relations of the Jews to the smaller states around them, but by Daniel they were taught the place which the monarchy of the Messiah held in the series of the great world monarchies. Four should precede it, and it should constitute the fifth and last. It was symbolized under the figure of a stone which was cut out without hands, and which should become a great mountain, and fill the whole earth. The time of its appearance was in the last stage of the last monarchy, in the time of the feet and toes of the image, and of the little horn of the fourth wild beast. (ii. 44, vii. 8–11.)

In another vision was revealed to Daniel who the head of this last kingdom should be: "Behold, one like the Son of Man came with the clouds of heaven, and came to the Ancient of Days, and they brought Him near before Him. And there was given Him dominion, and glory, and a kingdom, that all peoples, nations, and languages, should serve Him: His dominion is an everlasting dominion, which shall not pass away, and His kingdom that which shall not be destroyed."

Although no explanation is given as to this Son of Man, yet no doubt existed in the Jewish mind that it was their expected Messiah. In the interpretation of the vision, the prophet was told that the ruling power of the fifth kingdom, or that of the stone, was the saints of the Most High. "The saints of the Most High shall take the kingdom, and possess the kingdom for ever, even for ever and ever." As the elect of God, a holy nation, to the Jews must this pre-eminence belong; the kingdom could, therefore, be only the Messianic Kingdom, and the Son of David the King. He possesses the kingdom, and they possess it with Him.

In two important particulars do these visions of Daniel — for into the more obscure words respecting the seventy weeks we need not here enter — give fresh light respecting the Divine purpose. First, that the Messianic Kingdom could not be established till the counsel of God respecting the four world monarchies had been accomplished; until that time the theocratic people must take a position of subjection. The establishment of the Messianic Kingdom could not, then, be at the return of the exiles from Babylon. They would not regain their independence, but must remain a subject people till the times of heathen dominion, "the times of the Gentiles," were fulfilled. Not till then could there be a restoration of the theocratic kingdom. Second, with their national deliverance was inseparably connected the coming of the Messiah; till He came they would be exposed to great oppression and affliction from the successive monarchies impressively set forth under the symbol of fierce wild beasts. This revelation respecting the future, its perils and sufferings, should have taught them how great their sins before Jehovah that He should thus give them up into the hands of such enemies; and also have greatly increased their longing for the coming King. In point of fact, however, it was perverted to increase their pride; for they now felt assured that in due time all their enemies would be overthrown, and universal dominion be given into their hands. Understanding this dominion in a fleshly way, the Messianic Kingdom lost in good measure its high and holy character, and became but one in the series of the world monarchies.

Yet, on the other hand, it is probable, that, among the more spiritually-minded of the Jews, the conception of the person of the Messiah was elevated through the vision of Daniel. He appears coming in great majesty with the clouds of heaven before the Ancient of Days; and they could not but ask, Is not this more than a descendant of David? Is He not a superhuman and heavenly Being? There is no proof that any thought of the Incarnation as taught in these visions; but they who meditated upon the words of the earlier prophets, could scarcely have failed to see that there was to be a revelation of the power and glory of Jehovah in the Messiah, such as had never been before; and that the place assigned Him and the honor given Him in Daniel could not be bestowed upon a frail and mortal man.

CHAPTER XVII.

THE RETURN FROM THE BABYLONIAN EXILE, AND THE PROPHETS AFTER THE RETURN.

THE captivity in Babylon did not bring the Jews to national repentance, and so lead to national restoration. When God had prepared the way by the establishment of the new Persian kingdom under Cyrus, and had moved this ruler to give permission to such of the captives as desired it to go up to Jerusalem to rebuild the house of the Lord, but few availed themselves of it (536 B.C.). Only forty and two thousand went up. A considerable number of these were priests, and some Levites; but, for the most part, they seem to have been of the poorer and humbler class. The proclamation of Cyrus speaks of building the temple, not the city and its walls; and to this work did the returned exiles first address themselves. (Ez. iii.) Having erected the altar of burnt offering, they proceeded to lay the foundation of the temple; this was done in the second year after their return, but for a considerable period their work on the temple was hindered by the opposition of their heathen and Samaritan enemies (534–516 B.C.). But it is plain that this external hostility was not the sole cause of the delay; it was rather the slothfulness and indifference of the colonists themselves. To arouse and quicken them, God sent the prophets Haggai and Zechariah; and at last the temple was completed. (Ez. v. 1, vi. 15.)

After the rebuilding of the temple, a period of more than fifty years passed (515-458 B.C.), of which we know very little. Then came Ezra the scribe from Babylon, followed after some years by Nehemiah (445 B.C.). By the latter the walls of the city were rebuilt; and by his efforts and those of Ezra many abuses were corrected, and the Mosaic laws enforced with more strictness. The last of the prophets was Malachi (432 B.C.). A brief survey of the condition of the Jews after the return from exile will enable us better to understand the words of these last prophets.

At no time after the conquest by the Babylonians did the Jews regain their political independence, except for a very short period under the Hasmoneans. They dwelt in their own land as a subject people. If not oppressed by their Persian rulers, still they were by their local position much exposed to spoliation and suffering through the wars which Persia waged with other states, especially with Egypt. At first they occupied but a very small part of their old territory, but were scattered through it, chiefly in the northern and central parts. Being so few in number, it was for a time a question whether they could be preserved as a distinct people, or would be merged in the peoples around them. Two things were especially on the hearts of their leaders, — to keep them separate from the heathen by strict prohibition of intermarriage, and to re-establish the rites of worship. The first step was to rebuild the temple, for this alone could be a centre of unity to the returning exiles. In their condition of political subjection to heathen governors, the only rule possible under Mosaic institutions was that of the priests in ecclesiastical matters; and, as the office of high priest was hereditary and permanent, it soon became the chief and most influential.

The Jews who returned from Babylon were probably those least tainted with idolatry, and their dislike of their heathen rulers naturally intensified their aversion to heathen deities. But for a considerable period after the return the intermarriages with the heathen, which their rulers vainly attempted to repress, exposed them to temptation; and there are indications that some yielded to it, and fell into idolatry. (Ez. ix. 1, etc.) Gradually, however, they became more and more strictly monotheistic, and looked with increasing abhorrence upon idols and idolatrous worship. Their reverence for Jehovah did not, indeed, lead them to obey His commands, or to make great sacrifices for His honor, as is shown in the complaint of the prophet Haggai that they were more eager to build their own houses than His house.

It must be borne clearly in mind, that this return under Zerubbabel and Joshua was not a national restoration, nor was it a re-establishment of the original theocratic relation. Jehovah was no longer their King as of old; He did not return to dwell among them. He could not dwell in a land over which heathen princes ruled, — in a city in which His will was not supreme. When He returned, it must be to assert His high prerogatives over both people and land, to separate the good from the evil, to judge the heathen nations, to exalt and bless His chosen ones, and fulfill all that the Theocracy was originally designed to accomplish.

The return of a remnant to remain in subjection to heathen rulers was, therefore, primarily for the preservation of the people till the hour of the Messiah should come. It was a continuation of national existence under the law of Moses, but on a lower plane. Yet was this remnant itself on trial; for by faithful obedience to such Mosaic laws as were applicable, it might hasten

the return of Jehovah to dwell again in Jerusalem,
and the establishment of the Messianic Kingdom. Before the exile, and while Jehovah was dwelling among
them, this Kingdom was presented as the completion and
exaltation of the existing Theocracy; but after the exile,
when Jehovah had ceased to dwell among them, the
restoration of the Theocracy, and the establishment of
the Messianic Kingdom, were presented as to be contemporaneous and identical. The return and dwelling
of Jehovah in Jerusalem, and the appearing of the Messiah, were thus to take place at one and the same time;
and both alike were the object of hope.

In immediate connection with this trial of the returned remnant, whether it would by its moral preparation regain what it had lost, or fall still lower, two
things are to be noted: first, that the returning exiles
had at their head a prince of the house of David —
Zerubbabel — and the high priest Joshua; second, that
prophets were given to help these leaders in the execution of their work. The means were thus in the hands
of the remnant to prepare the way for the fulfillment
of God's promises, — means both for the right order of
worship under the Aaronic priesthood, and for the revival of the Davidic dynasty, — and the prophetic voice
also was there to warn and to guide. Much was wanting in the second temple that had been found in the
first; but faithfulness to their covenant might restore
what was lacking, and the day quickly come when Jehovah would return, the Messiah appear, and all that
the earlier prophets had spoken be fulfilled. But, because the people were not faithful in that which was
left them, all these means of preparation were given in
vain. Zerubbabel was the last prince of the house of
David, and the royal family sank speedily into obscurity.
The High Priesthood continued for a time, indeed, in

the line of Joshua, but passed at last into the line of strangers; and the spirit of prophecy, quenched by disobedience, was silent for centuries.

Let us now turn to the utterances of the three prophets after the exile, — Haggai, Zechariah, and Malachi. These took their distinctive character from the changed relation in which the returned remnant stood to Jehovah as the theocratic King. They all recognized the fact that He had departed from the holy city and temple, that He was still absent, and that with His return the true prosperity and blessedness of the nation would begin. "Lo, I come, and I will dwell in the midst of thee, saith the Lord. And many nations shall be joined to the Lord in that day. . . . And the Lord shall inherit Judah His portion in the holy land." (Zech. ii. 10-12.) "The Lord, whom ye seek, shall suddenly come to His temple. . . . He shall purify the sons of Levi, and purge them as gold and silver. . . . Then shall the offering of Judah and Jerusalem be pleasant unto the Lord, as in the days of old. . . . And all nations shall call you blessed." (Mal. iii. 1, etc. See Hag. ii. 6-9.)

We may note the following chief points of agreement in these prophets as to the present and future of the people: —

1. All recognize the fact that the mere return from Babylon to the land, and the rebuilding of the temple, did not restore the theocratic relation existing before the exile. The covenant is not abrogated, but Jehovah is no more present with them as their King. His return to dwell among them is still future.

2. The day of Jehovah's return to dwell again at Jerusalem is "the day of the Lord," "that day," the time when He "will shake the heavens and the earth," and "destroy the strength of the kingdom of

the heathen." "And the Lord shall be King over all the earth: in that day shall there be one Lord, and His name One."

3. He will then deliver and sanctify His people, and dwell among them. In that day "Jerusalem shall be called a city of truth, and the mountain of the Lord of Hosts the holy mountain." At the dedication of the temple they offered "a sin-offering for all Israel, — twelve he-goats, according to the number of the tribes of Israel." "I will save my people from the east country and from the west country, and I will bring them, and they shall dwell in the midst of Jerusalem; and they shall be my people, and I will be their God in truth and in righteousness."

4. In that day, the nations, humbled by His judgments, "will come to seek the Lord of Hosts in Jerusalem, and to pray before the Lord."

5. This return of Jehovah to His people, and the setting up of the Messianic Kingdom, are contemporaneous events; Jehovah being revealed to men through "The Branch," who shall "build the temple of the Lord, and sit and rule upon His throne."

Let us now consider the individual utterances of these prophets, — first, of Haggai and Zechariah, who prophesied during the time of Zerubbabel and Joshua.

The words of Haggai (520 B.C.) were, for the most part, of a practical character, reproving the people for their remissness in not building the temple, exhorting them to diligence and to firmness of faith, and encouraging them by promises of Divine assistance. Their covenant with Jehovah is still in force: "I am with you," "My Spirit remaineth among you;" therefore they are not to fear. There is no direct mention of the Messiah, yet there are not wanting allusions to Him and to the future Messianic Kingdom. The prophet speaks of a day when Jehovah will "shake the heavens and the earth, the sea and the dry land, and all nations, and will make the glory of the latter house greater than of the former," (or, as some prefer to render it, "the latter glory of the house greater than the former glory.") That this did not have its fulfillment in the successive overthrows of the Persian and Greek kingdoms, or in any accessions of proselytes, is obvious: the prophecy has a larger scope, and looks forward to "the great day of the Lord," of which all the prophets before him had spoken. "In this place will I give peace, saith the Lord of Hosts," — words to be fulfilled under the Messiah, when He shall judge all nations, and establish universal peace. "In His days shall the righteous flourish, and abundance of peace so long as the moon endureth." (Ps. lxxii.)

Divine promises of this character are, as we have already seen, both absolute and conditional: absolute, as declaring the unchangeable purpose of God; and conditional, as to the time of their fulfillment. They can be fulfilled only when the people are spiritually prepared. "And this shall come to pass, if ye will diligently obey the voice of the Lord your God." But there was no such preparation among the returned people down to the time of the coming of His Son. To that temple which they builded the long-promised One came. He was among His people, the Messianic King, to speak peace; but they received Him not: and at the close of His ministry He declared of that temple that it should be destroyed, and not one stone be left upon another. But the prophecy, though so long delayed in its fulfillment through the unpreparedness of the people, remains in force, as we are taught in the Epistle to the Hebrews. (xii. 26.) It is at the return of the Risen King from heaven to seat Himself upon the throne of His glory, that "every thing that can be shaken will be shaken; and only those things which cannot be shaken," because good in the sight of God, "will remain."

The words addressed to Zerubbabel — "In that day I will take thee, and will make thee as a signet, for I have chosen thee" — are plainly spoken of him as the representative of the Davidic family, and type of the true David to come. He was the chief of that family, and this promise to him was an assurance that God remembered His covenant with David; and in the day when He should shake the heavens and the earth, the Messiah to come of David's lineage would be to him as a signet.

The prophecies of Zechariah, like those of Haggai, had an immediate practical purpose, yet were far more of a symbolic character, and of a larger prophetical scope. We find in general the declaration of Jehovah that He had not cast off His people: "He that toucheth you, toucheth the apple of mine eye." He was still "jealous for Jerusalem and Zion," and in due time would return and dwell in them as of old. But ere this there must be a great moral change: "Turn ye unto me, saith the Lord of Hosts, and I will return unto you." Under the figure of Joshua, the high priest, the official representative of the priesthood, whose filthy garments were removed and clean raiment given him, was set forth the cleansing of the priesthood; and this must be before He could bring forth " His servant, The Branch." (Zech. iii. 3.) At another time the prophet was bidden to take silver and gold and make crowns, and set them on the head of Joshua, and say to him, "Behold, the man whose name is 'The Branch.' He shall grow up out of His place, and He shall build the temple of the Lord. . . . And He shall bear the glory, and shall sit and rule upon His throne, and He shall be a Priest upon His throne, and the counsel of peace shall be between them both." Here are set forth the regal and priestly offices of the Messiah, who will be the true builder of the temple of Jehovah. Of Him both Zerubbabel and Joshua are types.

Thus in the visions of Zechariah is the glorious future of Israel immediately connected with the Messiah. Under Jehovah He administers the government, and bears the glory, and brings peace to His people: "The counsel of peace shall be between them both." All that is done by Zerubbabel and Joshua is only preparatory to this, the preservation of a people from whom the Messiah shall spring, and whom as their Prince and Priest He will exalt and bless. Not till He comes can there be a full gathering of the scattered nation. When thus regathered, and restored to Divine favor, "many peoples and strong nations will come to seek the Lord of hosts in Jerusalem, and to pray before the Lord." There will be such a revelation of His glory, that "ten men out of all languages of the nations will take hold of the skirt of him that is a Jew, saying, We will go with you, for we have heard that God is with you." It is Jehovah who is presented as the Supreme Lord, and chief object of worship, but with Him is His King: "Behold, thy King cometh unto thee: He is just, and having salvation; lowly, and riding upon an ass, and upon a colt the foal of an ass. . . . He shall speak peace unto the heathen: and His dominion shall be from sea even to sea, and from the river even to the ends of the earth." (ix. 9, 10.)

But there are clear intimations in this prophet, that many dark days were before the people ere Jehovah would reign in righteousness. He appears when all nations are gathered against Jerusalem to battle.

"Then shall the Lord go forth, and fight against those nations, as when He fought in the day of battle. And His feet shall stand in that day upon the Mount of Olives, . . . and the Lord my God shall come, and all the saints with thee." (xiv. 1-5.) This is their final deliverance; now is the universal Kingdom set up. "And the Lord shall be King over all the earth: in that day shall there be one Lord, and His name one." Then will He inflict terrible judgments upon those that had fought against His people: some will perish by a plague, others by mutual slaughter. But a residue will be left; and it is said of them that they "shall go up from year to year to worship the King, the Lord of hosts, and to keep the feast of tabernacles." Then will take place those physical changes in the neighborhood of Jerusalem, which shall prepare the city to be the fitting capital of the theocratic kingdom, the city of the Great King. (xiv. 9, etc.)

The last of the post-exilian prophets was Malachi, the exact time of whose prophecy is uncertain, but probably about ninety years after the first return from exile. Let us note the changes that had taken place during this period, that we may the better understand his words.

Under Ezra the scribe a new body of the exiles returned (458 B.C.). Upon his arrival he found that through intermarriages with the people of the land, the colonists were in danger of becoming heathenized. (Ez. ix.) He therefore gathered them together, and so wrought upon them by his words as to bring them to a confession of their sin, and to obtain from them a promise of amendment, which promise for a time seems to have been kept. (Ez. x.) Some twelve years later came Nehemiah with authority from the Persian king to rebuild the walls of the city. But, although these were rebuilded, the internal condition of affairs was very unsatisfactory. The poor complained greatly of the evils brought on them by their poverty, and of the oppression of their wealthier brethren; and in this there was effected a partial reformation. The efforts of both Ezra and Nehemiah were now directed to the awakening of a higher consciousness of their standing as the covenant people. A solemn fast was appointed; and the people entered into a covenant to walk in God's laws given by Moses, and in all His judgments and statutes, and especially not to intermarry with the heathen, to observe the Sabbath days and the Sabbath years, and to pay the tax appointed for the temple service, and the tithes and first-fruits.

After some years passed at Jerusalem as Persian governor, Nehemiah returned to Persia. How long he was absent, we are not told; but on coming again to Jerusalem he found the old abuses revived, — intermarriages with the heathen, desecration of the temple, taxes unpaid, and tithes and offerings neglected, the Sabbath profaned by traffic, and the house of God forsaken. (Neh. xiii. 7, etc.) Nehemiah seems to have used with vigor his authority as governor to put away these abuses, but of the result of his labors we have no information.

It is probable that Malachi prophesied either during the absence of Nehemiah in Persia, or after his return; he spake to meet the evils of the times, and his words are, for the most part, of rebuke and warning. The character of his utterances shows us a people in whom there was an outward observance of the law, but without any true zeal for God, or genuine obedience. The rites of worship were maintained, but the general feeling was that of irreverence and indifference. Many years had now elapsed since their return, and yet the colony — for it was no more — was weak and oppressed.

They were Jehovah's people, yet His promises of blessing had not been fulfilled, their expectations had been disappointed; they were without courage or hope; even their worship was a weariness. The priests are addressed as those that despise God's name; they are mercenary, and so avaricious that they will not render God the smallest service without reward. By their conduct they had caused many to stumble at the law. With their connivance the people offered Him polluted bread, the blind and sick and lame were sacrificed, they robbed God in tithes and offerings. They had taken heathen wives, and put away the wives of the covenant. Even God's moral government over men was hardly recognized; for they said, "It is vain to serve God, and what profit is it that we have kept His ordinances? Every one that doeth evil is good in the sight of the Lord. . . . And where is the God of judgment?"

These words of the prophet indicate a people profoundly discouraged and helpless. Their sore experiences since their return had not awakened in them any real sense of their sin. On the contrary, they justified themselves, and charged God with unfaithfulness. "Your words have been stout against me." "They wearied the Lord with their words." The prophet speaks to meet this despairing and irreligious spirit, and strives to arouse them to a strict observance of the law. (iv. 4.) "Remember ye the law of Moses my servant." He saw that their salvation consisted in making the line of religious separation between them and the peoples around them broad and high.

But the law alone could not prepare them for the kingdom of the Messiah. For this a living messenger was needed: only one sent of God, and speaking in the light and power of His Spirit, could show unto the people their sins under the law; and such an one was promised. This promise of a forerunner to prepare His way was a testimony to them, that under the institutions then remaining they could not be prepared. Having lost the original means of preparation, God must send to them a special messenger. Such a promise was not wholly new; for Isaiah had spoken of the voice of one crying in the wilderness, "Prepare ye the way of the Lord." To this earlier utterance Malachi doubtless refers, but he gives it greater definiteness: "Behold, I will send you Elijah the prophet before the coming of the great and dreadful day of the Lord." From this time the expectation of a herald, and of special preparation, was closely connected with the coming of the Messiah.

The declaration that "the name of Jehovah should be great among the Gentiles, and that in every place incense should be offered unto His name, and a pure offering," looks forward to the universal Kingdom so often spoken of, and is not to be understood as foretelling that His special relation to the Jews should cease, or Jerusalem cease to be the appointed centre of worship. On the contrary, when they should "bring unto Him an offering in righteousness," then would it be "pleasant to Him as in the days of old;" and if they obeyed and honored Him, then "All nations shall call you blessed; for ye shall be a delightsome land."

There is no direct reference to the Messiah in this prophet except in the prediction, "Behold, I will send my messenger, and he shall prepare the way before me: and the Lord whom ye seek, shall suddenly come to His temple, even the Messenger of the covenant, whom ye delight in: behold, He shall come, saith the Lord of hosts." Are there two persons mentioned here, or three? If but two, these are Jehovah and the messenger whom He sends to prepare the way before Him. He who is designated as "the Lord,"—Adon,—and as "the Messenger of the covenant," must be identified with Jehovah, or with the messenger who prepares His way. If three persons are mentioned, — Jehovah, the messenger, and the Lord and Messenger of the covenant, — then the last must be the Messiah. And the change in the words made by the Saviour in His application of it to the Baptist, leaves no room for doubt as to its Messianic meaning. "For this" — the Baptist — "is he of whom it is written, Behold, I send my messenger before thy face, which shall prepare thy way before thee." He who sends is Jehovah, the messenger is the Baptist, and He that comes to His temple is the Messiah.

This prediction is from the Old-Testament point of view; distinguishing the comings of Jehovah and of the Messiah, yet making them to be contemporaneous. As seen before the Incarnation, the Messiah comes with Jehovah; as seen after it, Jehovah comes in the Messiah. The messenger will prepare the way before Jehovah, that He may re-establish the old theocratic relation; but the re-establishing of this relation demands that His king of the house of David also be restored. And the preparation for the one is the preparation for the other. We have already seen, that, so long as He dwelt at Jerusalem, the Davidic throne continued to stand; when He departed, it fell. So long as He continues absent, it is not set up again; when He shall return, His king will sit anew on the throne. He comes to His temple, — the palace temple. (See Isa. vi. 1; Ps. xlv. 8, 15.) And the day of His coming is the great and the terrible day of the Lord, when He will purge and refine His own, and spare them, and gather them as His jewels; but the wicked and the proud shall be stubble, and perish.

CHAPTER XVIII.

MESSIANIC BELIEFS IN THE PSALMS. — MESSIAH AS KING.

THE Psalms are distinguished from the prophetic utterances, amongst other points, in this: that they were not spoken to the people, not messages sent of God, but the spontaneous, though inspired, expressions of individual feeling. Probably, if we could trace their origin we should find it for the most part in some special outward event affecting the heart of the Psalmist, and awakening emotion which sought expression in song. Extending over a period of probably more than five hundred years, counting from the earliest to the latest, and therefore widely differing in manner and matter, there is yet a fundamental unity, — a unity having its root in the covenant relation of the people to Jehovah, and which manifests itself in common beliefs, hopes, fears, joys, and sorrows. If it were not for this community of sentiment of which the Psalms are the utterances, they could not have been used in common worship: as purely individual utterances, they must have perished with their writers. But this fundamental unity does not exclude, both in form and contents, much diversity. As having many authors, living under widely dissimilar circumstances, and differing in degrees of spiritual knowledge and literary power of expression, we may expect to see in them a variety of conception and of statement as regards both the character of God and His purpose in His people. It is not impossible that some of the Psalmists may surpass the prophets in their deep insight into the Divine character, in their spiritual understanding of His purpose, and in their steadfast faith. Personal communion with Him may give such sense of His holiness and of human sinfulness, such apprehension of the way of salvation through the Messiah, that truths are seen by them which cannot yet be revealed by Him to the people at large, and promises dark to others are to them full of light.

We are here concerned with the Psalms only as regards the one point, — how far the Messianic beliefs of which we are speaking are found in them; and we may designate as Messianic Psalms all those that distinctly mention either of the three elements already spoken of as entering into the Messianic conception of the Jews. Their references to a suffering Messiah will be considered elsewhere.

1. The kingdom of Jehovah as now established in Israel, and to be established over all the earth. That Jehovah is the King of Israel, and will judge and rule all nations, is often declared in the Psalms. "The Lord is King for ever and ever." (x. 16.) "The kingdom is the Lord's, and He is the Governor among the nations." (xxii. 28.) "The Lord sitteth King for ever." (xxix. 10, xxiv. 7-10, cxlv. 13.) "He hath prepared His throne for judgment, and He shall judge the world in righteousness. . . . The wicked shall be turned into hell, and all nations that forget God." (ix. 17.) In several Psalms, mention is made of His coming to judge the earth. "For He cometh, He cometh to judge the earth." (xcvi. 13.) "A fire goeth before Him, and burneth up His enemies round about. . . . The hills melted like wax at the Presence of the

Lord, at the Presence of the Lord of the whole earth." (xcvii. 3, 5; xcviii. 9; lxxxii. 8.) Thus through His acts in judgment His universal Kingdom is established. "All the ends of the world shall remember, and turn unto the Lord; and all the kindreds of the nations shall worship before thee." (Ps. xxii. 27, cii. 15, cxxxviii. 4.)

2. In this Kingdom, His elect people will have the highest place; they are "His inheritance," they are "the people of His pasture and the sheep of His hand." It is among them that He dwells, and through them that He manifests Himself to the nations. To them it belongs "to declare His glory among the heathen, His wonders among all people." In the land which He had given them, upon Mount Zion, will He dwell, and from thence will He show forth His righteousness in the eyes of all nations. "The Lord hath chosen Zion; He hath desired it for His habitation. This is my rest for ever: here will I dwell." (cxxxii. 13, 14.) "Beautiful for situation, the joy of the whole earth, is Mount Zion, on the sides of the north, the city of the Great King." (xlviii. 2.) "When the Lord shall build up Zion, He shall appear in His glory." "From heaven did the Lord behold the earth, . . . to declare the name of the Lord in Zion, and His praise in Jerusalem, when the people are gathered together, and the kingdoms, to serve the Lord." (cii. 16–22.)

3. In this kingdom there is a King under Jehovah, of the house of David. There are several allusions to the Davidic covenant: "The Lord hath sworn in truth unto David: He will not turn from it." (cxxxii. 11, 12, 17.) "He chose David His servant, and took him from the sheep-folds. . . . He brought him to feed Jacob His people, and Israel His inheritance." (lxxviii. 70.) "I have made a covenant with my chosen, I have sworn

unto David my servant, thy seed will I establish for ever, and build up thy throne to all generations." (lxxxix. 3, 4; xviii. 50, etc.)

Mention is also made in several Psalms of a King, an Anointed One, but nothing is said of His name or lineage. In Psalm ii. such a King is spoken of whom Jehovah has set upon His holy hill of Zion, and to whom He will "give the heathen for His inheritance, and the uttermost parts of the earth for His possession." In Psalm xx. prayers are offered for a King going forth to battle, and who is called His Anointed: "Now know I that the Lord saveth His Anointed." In the Psalm following (xxi.), thanksgiving is offered for His victorious return. In Psalm xlv. mention is made of the marriage of a King, who wins great victories, and of whom it is said, "I will make thy name to be remembered in all generations: therefore shall the peoples praise thee for ever and ever." In Psalm lxxii. prayers are offered to God for a "king's Son," that He may rule the world in righteousness, and under whose rule all nations are blessed. In Psalm cx. Jehovah says to One whom the Psalmist calls his Lord, "Sit thou at my right hand. . . . Thou art a Priest for ever after the order of Melchizedek;" and to whom He gives the promise of victory over all His enemies.

Who is this King? Is one and the same person meant in all these Psalms? or did their writers refer each to some king of his own day? To answer this, we must consider them in the light of the Davidic covenant.

We have seen in our examination of this covenant, that in the promises made to David special mention is made of his house and of his kingdom as to abide forever, but not of any individual king: "Thine house and thy kingdom shall be established for ever before thee;" "thy throne shall be established for ever." (2

Sam. vii. 12, etc.) How did David understand this promise? That he applied it to himself, was not possible. Did he look for a succession of kings without end? or did he believe that one would come in due time in whom the promise could find its perfect and final realization, — one who would not die like all before him, but abide the eternal king, and administer an universal kingdom? Let us ask what light the Psalms give us on these points.

We can easily believe that David, as a man specially endowed by the Spirit, had an insight into the meaning of the promises made him respecting his Son deeper than any of his contemporaries or royal successors. (2 Sam. xxiii. 2.) It is plain from the Psalms generally admitted to be his, that he knew and felt the dignity of his place as Jehovah's king, His anointed, and had a just sense of the duties it involved. (Ps. xviii., ci.) But it was his chief honor to be the father of the Anointed One to come. Wherever, therefore, in any Psalm he speaks of a king in terms far surpassing any that could be justly applied to himself, we must suppose that he looks forward to his greater Son. There was, indeed, much which all his successors as theocratic kings must have in common, springing from a like relation to Jehovah. (Ps. lxxxix. 18, Rev. Ver.) Each might be called "His son;" "His king, seated on His holy hill;" "His anointed;" and, if faithful, each had the promise of His help to overcome all his enemies. And of David, as the first in the line of these kings, might all this be said in a pre-eminent degree; but not of himself, and of no successor except One, could it be said that he had an universal and eternal Kingdom.

If we now examine the Psalms generally ascribed to David in which mention is made of such a king, we shall see that his words can be fully understood only as applied to the Messiah. In Psalm ii. mention is made of a great assemblage of nations and peoples to cast off the rule of Jehovah and of His Anointed. Such rebellion, in a limited degree, might have occurred in the life of David, or of any one of his successors; but the language here clearly intimates that it is an universal and final attempt of the nations to free themselves from their subjection to the Lord and His King. The promise, "Ask of me, and I shall give thee the heathen"— the nations— "for thine inheritance, and the uttermost parts of the earth for thy possession: thou shalt break them with a rod of iron; thou shalt dash them in pieces like a potter's vessel," points to a full and absolute investiture of power, and to a last and complete victory over all enemies. Thus He by whom this is effected is marked out among the successors of David as the highest and the last. He is in such sense as none other "The Son of God," "The King," "The Anointed."

In Psalm xx., generally regarded as David's,— a prayer to be offered on his behalf when going forth to war,— there is nothing asked that might not have been fulfilled to him; but in Psalm xxi., also his, and a commemoration of a victory, there is a largeness of expression which makes its exclusive application to him difficult. "He asked life of thee, and thou gavest it Him, even length of days for ever and ever." "For thou hast made Him most blessed for ever." This length of days and eternal blessing belong much more to the Messiah than to David. (2 Sam. vii. 13; 1 Chron. xvii. 14.)

In Psalm cx. the writer, whom we cannot doubt to be David, clearly distinguishes between himself and another whom he calls his Lord: "The Lord said unto my Lord, Sit thou at my right hand." That these words were not spoken by David of himself, need scarcely be said. The writer in spirit sees one who is not only a king exalted to God's right hand, but a priest: "The Lord hath sworn, and will not repent, Thou art a priest for ever after the order of Melchizedek;" i.e., a priest sitting on a throne. This prerogative of priesthood did not belong to the sons of David as heirs of the throne, but is given to Him of whom the Psalmist speaks; and by this He is distinguished from all before Him. And this priesthood is given to Him as a personal prerogative, and secured to Him forever by Jehovah's oath.

It is this Royal Priest who is to be the instrument for executing Jehovah's judgments upon His enemies. "Jehovah will send the rod of thy strength out of Zion, rule thou in the midst of thine enemies." Then will His foes be made His footstool. Here is marked a new stage of Jehovah's actings, beginning in judgment upon the nations, and ending in their submission. Under His Royal Priest His universal Kingdom begins.

Let us now turn to those Psalms not written by David, which are generally regarded as Messianic, — the forty-fifth and seventy-second. The former seems to have been written on the occasion of a royal marriage. Who is this king? That he was of David's line may be assumed. Was he a king of the writer's own day? Of all the historical circumstances, except so far as the Psalm itself declares them, we are ignorant. That this king was regarded as a type of the Messiah, the Psalm as Messianic, both by the Jews and in the Church, is well known; and in the Epistle to the Hebrews it is quoted as having direct reference to the Son. "But unto the Son He saith, Thy throne, O God, is for ever and ever." Let it be admitted that the term Elohim — God — is here used, as in some other places, in a secondary sense, or that the words may be rendered, as by some, "Thy throne is God's throne," and so are in themselves applicable to every successive theocratic king, still the other expressions used by him point to One pre-eminent among the sons of David. He is One loving righteousness and hating iniquity, and who is anointed with the oil of gladness above His fellows. His children shall be made princes in all the earth, His name shall be remembered in all generations, and be praised by the peoples for ever and ever.

But what significance, as applied to the Messiah, has the marriage relation? By the queen cannot be meant the Jewish people, since she is bidden to forget her own people and her father's house, which plainly implies that she is of foreign lineage. If it be prophetically spoken of Christ and the Church, the words find an easy application. The queen is the type of the Church, the Lamb's wife, gathered from all nations. (Eph. v. 32; Rev. xix. 7.) It is of the children of the Church, the sons of God, that He will set princes in the earth. But it must be acknowledged that this mention of the new election, and of its special relation to the Messiah, is such as is not found elsewhere in the Old Testament.

In the seventy-second Psalm we find mention made of One, a king's Son, and in the order of royal succession, to whom is given a kingdom of righteousness and peace without end. "All kings shall fall down before Him, all nations shall serve Him. . . . They shall fear thee as long as the sun and moon endure, throughout all generations. . . . His name shall endure for ever." In this Psalm a King appears under whom there are such righteousness and peace in the earth as never before. Nor is His rule one of force, though no enemies can stand before Him, and "He breaks in pieces the oppressor." The establishment of the kingdom is not here described, as in Psalms ii. and cx., but its order and prosperity and universality when established. And the King under whom this is done is thus clearly distinguished from all those before Him, whose rule had been so partial in extent and imperfect in character.

Thus our examination shows us that while, to all the successors of David as Jehovah's kings certain promises are made, all if faithful are to be upheld by Him, and their people, under their righteous rule, will have internal prosperity and peace, and strength to overcome all enemies from without; yet there are certain points in which one King and His reign are distinguished in all these Psalms from all kings and reigns before Him. It is an universal Kingdom; the whole earth is His inheritance; all nations are subject to Him, and under His sway righteousness and peace everywhere prevail. It is a kingdom without end; the kingdom now attains its permanent form. Jehovah has found One who can be in the highest sense His King and His Priest, and thus His purpose in His people can be accomplished. Now He is known and obeyed and worshipped in all the earth, by all peoples; and He by whom He acts, in all His works, both of judgment and of blessing, is a Son of David. This King is thus lifted up above all of His predecessors.

In certain Psalms of uncertain date (xcvi.-xcix.) mention is made of the coming of Jehovah to judge the earth, and to establish His kingdom; and yet nothing is said of the Messiah, or of any one of David's line. How is this to be explained? It is said by some that these Psalms were written after the Babylonian exile, and at the time of the rebuilding of the temple, when the house of David no longer sat on the throne. If it be so, we may understand how the desire for Jehovah's return to His holy city to reign again over them, might put out of mind the remembrance of the promised One of the house of David; for not till the old theocratic relation, broken at the national overthrow, was re-established, and Jehovah dwell again on His holy hill of Zion, could His King administer the government under Him. To Him, therefore, rather than to the Ruler under Him, were the eyes of the Psalmist turned, as even now we call on God to arise in judgment, although we know that all judgment is given to the Son. (John v. 22.) Or it may be, that in the mind of the Psalmist the two were inseparably associated, — the revelation of Jehovah to judge the world in righteousness, and the appearing of Him of the house of David, to whom He would give the rule over the nations. That this coming of Jehovah was not merely for the restoration of the old order, — the state of things before the exile, — is plain from its terms. He appears in terrible majesty; "a fire goeth before Him, and burneth up His enemies round about, His lightnings enlightened the world, the earth saw and trembled, the hills melted like wax at the Presence of the Lord." In this day not only does "He remember His mercy and His truth toward the house of Israel," but "all the ends of the earth see the salvation of God," all the earth is called upon to make a joyful noise unto the Lord, to rejoice and sing praise. "He hath done marvellous things, His right hand and His holy arm hath gotten Him the victory." It is plain that this day is the same as that spoken of in the other Psalms, in which Jehovah acts in judgment through His Anointed King, and by Him rules over all the nations.

We thus find, in some of the Psalms, clear proof that their writers looked forward to the universal kingdom of Jehovah, to be administered by a Son of David; and that this Son was to be distinguished from all His predecessors. The impossibility of arranging the Psalms in a defined chronological order renders it impossible to trace in them the growth of Messianic beliefs; nor can we say how general at any period was the knowledge among the people of the purpose of the Davidic covenant as fulfilled in the Messiah, or expectation of its speedy fulfillment. If their hopes reached only to a renewal of the prosperity and glory of the kingdom in the days of David and Solomon, then each successive occupant of the throne may have been looked upon as one who might do this. As all the kings of this family had in virtue of the Davidic covenant a kind of Messianic character, there is no reason why a Psalm may not have been written of any one of them, in which desires are expressed and prayers offered for the fulfillment of all the promises to David.

But if such hopes were early cherished, and find expression in some Psalms, the national experience soon showed how sadly the house of David failed to respond to its high calling. Of the great disappointment of the national hope, Psalm lxxxix. is an expression, and also an appeal to God to remember His faithfulness, and fulfill His oath to David. It is plain that this Psalmist, who may have lived at the time of the exile, looked for the restoration of David's house, and in the person of One in whom the covenant promises would have their complete and final fulfillment.

CHAPTER XIX.

THE PRESENTATION IN THE LAW AND PROPHETS AND PSALMS OF A SUFFERING MESSIAH.

THE knowledge which the Jews could have had of a suffering Messiah, one who should die for the sins of the world, could have been drawn from three sources only: first, from patriarchal traditions, resting on earlier Divine revelations; second, from the rites and teachings of the law; third, from the words of inspired men, — prophets and psalmists. But as the conception of a suffering Messiah cannot be separated from the consciousness of sin, and to develop this consciousness was a chief end in the spiritual education of men, thus to prepare them to receive the promised Redeemer; of this development we must first speak. And we may mark three stages: that before the law, that under the law, and that since Pentecost under the Spirit. It is with the first two of these stages that we are here concerned; the last will be considered later.

But, before these points are historically considered, we may note the distinction between the consciousness of personal sin and the knowledge of the corruption of human nature as a form of being originally good, but become evil, and so rejected of God. In all times and among all peoples there have been the consciousness of personal sin, the sense of guilt and fear of Divine punishment; and these have entered as essential elements into all religions. But knowledge of the evil condition into which our humanity was brought by the sin of Adam, making it incapable of answering the end of its creation, and that there must be a second Adam to restore what had been lost, could not be given, at least in its full measure, till the Incarnate Son came in "the likeness of sinful flesh," and died and rose again. Then was it revealed, that only through "the law of the Spirit of life in Him" could men be set free from the law of sin and of death.

1. We may now inquire as to the degree of consciousness of sin before the time of the law, and what knowledge was then given of a Redeemer, and of His expiatory work. The general character of the antediluvian, or patriarchal, period has already been spoken of. It was the period of infancy; the capacities of humanity had not yet been proved, nor its dormant propensities to evil been quickened into full activity. It was not possible that men in the earliest times should have known the full power of sin, what depths of evil were in it, its many forms of hostility to God, and its destructive energies: these could be revealed only in the experience of the race. But we may believe that from the first there was in fallen man the consciousness that he was fallen, and morally unclean, and deserving of punishment. He knew that he was separated from God, banished from His Presence, and brought under the law of death; the ground had been cursed because of his disobedience, and his earthly life made one of toil and weariness. And we may believe that the consciousness of sin was deeper and more active in the earliest fathers than in the later antediluvian generations, as the memory of their intercourse with God in Eden was yet fresh, and their conceptions of Him, as there revealed, more distinct and vivid. That there was early

in patriarchal history a loss of the sense of sin is clearly implied in the biblical narrative. That this primitive and deeper consciousness of separation from God involved in it, as a necessary element, a belief in a Mediator, — one to stand between the sinful and God, and through whom alone Divine forgiveness could be obtained, — we do not say. But it served as a basis for the revelation of such a Mediator to come, " the Seed of the woman that should bruise the serpent's head;" and also as a basis for the institution of the rite of animal sacrifice.

In the promise of the Seed of the woman, the first victory of good over evil was assured. But by whom was it to be won? Was it then understood as the promise of a personal Deliverer? We can scarce doubt this, and that it continued during the antediluvian period to be the hope of the faithful. But the victory was not to be won without a struggle; the heel of the victor should be bruised: and it may be that under the figure of "the bruising of the heel," the first patriarchs saw some form of personal suffering predicted; possibly His death. But, as with many words of God respecting the future, the truth wrapped up in them was of slow growth; for promises that embrace ages can be but partially understood by those to whom they are spoken.

What knowledge of the mode of redemption, or of the person of the Redeemer, was gained through the rite of animal sacrifice, it is not easy to say; but of its meaning Adam and his children must have had some apprehension. They saw the special calling of the priest as a mediator, and that without an offering for sin — the shedding of blood — there was no acceptable approach to God; and the idea of mediation must have become familiar to them, and in some degree that of substitution. Every father was in a measure a priestly mediator. (Job i. 5.) More light may have been given them, both as regards sacrifices and the purpose of God in the Deliverer, than is recorded in the very brief biblical narrative; but, even if so, it is not probable that there was at so early a period such consciousness of sin, and such knowledge of the corruption of human nature, that the full meaning of sacrifice as to be realized in the Lamb of God was seen, or that need was felt of One who should die and rise again — the Just for the unjust — to bring men to God.

2. The consciousness of sin under the law, and the knowledge then given of the Redeemer and His work. Leaving it, as we must, undefined what knowledge respecting a suffering Redeemer was handed down from the early patriarchs to Abraham and his children, new light was given them through the Mosaic appointments. As they were the elect people, and as the promised Seed of the woman was to be of the seed of Abraham, the discernment of His work among them as one of redemption from sin depended on their consciousness of sin; and this, therefore, must be enlarged and deepened. In a twofold way was this done under the Theocracy: on the one side God manifested Himself to His people as the Holy One, and on the other the law He gave brought to light the evil in their hearts. By admitting His people into immediate intercourse with Himself, Divine Holiness was brought into direct contrast to human sinfulness. To all other peoples He was a God afar off; but He dwelt among them, and the place of His habitation was holy. "I am the Lord your God; ye shall therefore sanctify yourselves; and ye shall be holy, for I am holy." And, on the other side, by the law was given the knowledge of sin. (Rom. iii. 20.) "I had not known sin but by the law," says the apostle.

Now was disclosed, as never before, the power of the rebellious will, how strong the lusts of the flesh, and the tendencies to idol-worship, and how great the enmity of the carnal mind to God's holy rule. Thus through the law there was brought into clearer consciousness man's alienation from God, and his obstinate opposition to His will. Testing themselves by His righteous commands, the faithful among His people learned to know themselves as sinful, and this more and more in each successive generation. And that there was more than the consciousness of personal sins, that there was, at least in some, the knowledge of the corruption of human nature, appears from the Psalms. (li. 5, lviii. 3.)

As God dwelling among the people was manifested to them as the Holy One, and His righteousness revealed through the law, and their sinfulness was thus brought into clearer light, the necessity of redemption was more deeply felt. But by whom should this redemption be effected? Who could stand between them and God? Must there not be a High Priest to come, holier than those of Aaron's line? Through the sacrifices of the law, so sharply discriminated and carefully set in order, each with its own special purpose and typical meaning, and especially through the greater sin-offering, were their eyes directed forward to One who should make an atonement for them, that would need no repetition. It may be that a few in all generations, made through the law deeply conscious of personal transgressions, and of the evil in their hearts, and specially illumined by the Spirit, saw that the blood of animal sacrifices could not take away sin, and that these must be typical of a sacrifice to be offered more truly redemptive. And to such the primal promise of the Seed of the woman would have new and higher meaning.

But was this Seed of the woman to be identified with their Messiah? Was the Son of David to bruise the serpent's head, and His heel to be bruised? Was He typified in the sacrifices of the law, and His blood to be shed for the sin of His people? If a definite belief of a vicarious sacrifice to be offered by the Messiah, and of atonement through His blood, was in fact attained to by any through the types of the law, it was by very few only. It was through the prophets, therefore, that the Messiah must be set forth as one to suffer and die. And we must ask what were the conditions that determined these prophetic revelations.

In general, it is to be kept in mind that the words of the prophets were determined, first of all, by the covenant relations of the people to whom they spake; and, second, by the circumstances of the times. As there was progress to a definite end in the history of this people, so there was progress in the revelations to them of God's truth. His purpose in the Messiah embraced all men in its results. He was to be the Redeemer of all, — "the Lamb of God to take away the sin of the world." (John i. 29.) As made to the first parents of the race, the promise of the Seed of the woman was made to all their children; but the higher truths respecting Him, His person and His work, could be spoken only to that one people which God had chosen, and prepared to hear by His previous training. As the nations at large knew nothing of the Son of David, who under Jehovah should rule over all the earth, so they knew nothing of Him as one who should save them from sin by His sacrifice upon the cross. God's revelations by His prophets of the Messianic salvation were not made to them, for they could not have understood them.

Hence it was, as will be seen, that in the presentation of a suffering Messiah, the prophets speak of Him primarily in His relations to the elect people. He suffers to restore them to God's favor. Of the bearings of His sacrifice on other nations who stand in no covenant relations to Him, they do not speak. In due time it would be made known to them that His redemptive work embraced all the children of Adam, both the living and the dead: but the words of the prophets were to the children of Abraham; and the revelation to the nations of His purpose in His Son must be through them when fully instructed in His ways and made ready for His kingdom.

Of the threefold work of the Messiah to be fulfilled in redemption according to the Divine purpose, as the Sacrifice on the cross, as the High Priest in heaven, and as the theocratic King and Judge, the last was first set forth by the earlier prophets. It could not, in the nature of the case, have been otherwise, each new revelation of the Divine purpose in Him resting upon the preceding; and it was God's promise to David of the Son to sit on his throne, that gave definite form to the Messianic expectation. This is not to deny that the great lessons of the law were Sacrifice and Atonement; no promise of a King could supersede them, for they lie at the basis of redemption. But the prophetic presentation of the Redeemer is primarily as the Ruler under Jehovah of the elect people. To the Jews abiding faithful to their covenant, the only intelligible presentation that could be made of their Messiah of the royal house of David, was that of a King who should reign in righteousness, and whose coming is an object of hope. As He comes to administer the kingdom under Jehovah, if the people were walking at His coming in obedience to Jehovah, they would welcome Him and His holy rule. A voluntary rejection of Him would not be possible. It was not, therefore, consistent with their position as His faithful elect, that the prophet should announce a Messiah whom they would reject and crucify, and so bring on themselves Jehovah's terrible judgments. And yet His sacrifice on the cross for all men must precede His work as their King. How, then, could a knowledge of a suffering Messiah be brought to His people in a manner consistent with their moral trial? It is plain that only in view of a change in their original relations to Jehovah, could such an announcement be made. And this change took place at the time of the Babylonian exile.

In the Messianic conception springing from the covenant with David, the Messiah is one who succeeds to the throne in virtue of His royal descent. He is the rightful heir. And coming as a King, there must be an independent nation over which He can reign. He is not one who must be the Redeemer of His people before He can reign over them, for this presupposes some condition of national bondage out of which they are to be redeemed. Jehovah had redeemed them when he brought them up out of Egypt. (Deut. vii. 8.) And this position of national independence they should have preserved; but coming again into bondage, they must be again delivered. The Son of David, therefore, must restore them to freedom before He can reign over them.

We now see why the Messiah could not have been presented by the prophets as the Redeemer of Israel, till the Babylonian captivity was near in the prophetic vision. A change was approaching in the relation of the nation to Jehovah. Because of its persistent violations of the covenant, He was about to forsake His holy city, and scatter the people among the nations. Nor would He spare the royal family. The Messiah, therefore, could not succeed to the throne in regular succession as all the kings before Him had done; He must first restore the nation and rebuild the throne. Thus, as they saw the captivity approaching, they were able to understand that the Messianic Kingdom must be preceded by a work of national deliverance.

We may now inquire as to the nature of this deliverance. And we must first note the nature of the new captivity. It was not like that in Egypt. From Egypt Jehovah had brought them forth that He might make them His people, and constitute them a nation. Their special covenant relation to Him was not formed till He had brought them to Sinai. (Exod. xix. 5.) But their captivity in Babylon, and in all its subsequent stages, was a punishment inflicted by their covenant God because of its violations. Although His own people, He brought them under the bondage of the heathen as the expression of His righteous anger against them. As the greatness of their sin, so the severity of their chastisement.

This evil condition into which they had fallen necessarily presented a new aspect of the Messiah's work. He could not now come as a King to a people obedient, and waiting in joyful hope for His appearing, but to a people rebellious and apostate, and suffering under sore judgments. How could He deliver them? What were the elements of the deliverance to be wrought? We may speak of them as threefold: first, the turning away of God's anger, and the remission of their sins; second, their repentance and confession; third, their liberation from the hand of their enemies, and their restoration to their own land and to their place. All these must be done before the Messianic Kingdom could be set up.

The first and great step in this work of deliverance

was to turn away the just anger of Jehovah, and to restore His people to His favor. Even if there were seen on their part genuine repentance and true confession, yet a sense of sin and its confession were not sufficient in themselves to obtain its remission. Through the law they had been taught that "without shedding of blood there is no remission" of sin. The guilty cannot make atonement for themselves; there is need of a Mediator, and forgiveness must rest upon the ground of a special sacrifice. Even in the case of individual transgressors, a sacrifice must be offered, a victim slain, and its blood sprinkled by the priest. (Lev. iv.) So must it be for the sins of the nation; there must be a like work of priestly mediation, an atonement must be made for the people, that they might be cleansed from their sins before the Lord. (Lev. xvi.) After this had been done, they could be restored to their original standing as Jehovah's people, and receive the fulfillment of His promises.

To sum up what has been said: By His prophets God made known to His people that because of their sins a day of judgment was approaching; they must be cast out of their land, and be scattered abroad till "they accept the punishment of their iniquity;" then should their sins be forgiven, and they be restored. But this forgiveness must rest on the basis of a sacrifice offered for them, like that offered for the expiation of national sins on the Day of Atonement. And who should offer this sacrifice? It must be the Son of David, who should not only be a King, but also a Priest. (Ps. cx.)

In all this there was nothing that a spiritually-minded Jew might not have apprehended. Kingship and priesthood were familiar in their practical exercise, and both might have their highest representation in the Messiah. But was this all? Was the sacrifice by which their sins were to obtain remission, only a repetition of the sacrifices offered at Sinai? Was it the blood of bullocks and of goats that was again to be sprinkled upon the people? (Exod. xxiv. 8.) This involved no suffering on the part of the Messiah, it was simply the fulfillment of His priestly functions.

How, then, was the fact to be made known, that the Messiah must offer Himself as an expiatory sacrifice? He must be the Victim as well as the Priest. But how could this fact be made known? Could the mystery of His Person be then revealed, and the people be taught that the Son of God should become man, and so become the propitiation for the sins of the whole world? This was not then possible; for the knowledge of this mystery presupposed the knowledge of many truths respecting the nature of the Godhead, and of the Divine purpose in man, which they could not in this stage of spiritual culture understand. That God would "send His own Son in the likeness of sinful flesh, and for sin, to condemn sin in the flesh," was not apprehended till He came and died and rose again. Yet, on the other hand, if they saw in Him only a man, a partaker like other men of a corrupt nature, how could He offer Himself as a sacrifice for sin? Or was His suffering for His own people only, and in kind like that of any just man who gives up himself for the good of his country?

Thus it is obvious, that to make known the true nature of the Messiah's sacrifice as the Incarnate Son before He came, was intrinsically impossible; yet, if He were believed to be a mere man, false notions of that sacrifice were inevitable. But a partial revelation was possible, — one preparatory to a higher to follow. He could be presented to the people in terms that indicated at least a superhuman character, — one more than man; and those who meditated earnestly and reverently on the prophetic words must have had some anticipations, if vague, of His exceeding dignity and greatness. To their eye, He appeared as a dim but majestic form filling the future. As in the vision of the prophet, they saw "the likeness of a throne, and upon the likeness of the throne was the likeness as the appearance of a man above upon it." In this was shown to them that the fulfillment of the Divine promises respecting the universal kingdom could be only through One far higher than any of the sons of men. And such an One, not only a King, but "a Priest for ever after the order of Melchizedek," might offer a sacrifice for the remission of their sins, and in some way, not clearly understood, bear their iniquities. What the apostle says of us all even in this present higher stage of revelation, that we "see through a glass darkly," was far more applicable to them. As the resurrection life and the new heaven and earth are still mysteries to us, so to them were the sufferings of the Messiah and the glory that should follow.

We may now inquire what God was pleased to reveal by His prophets respecting the sacrifice of the Messiah.

It was by the prophet Isaiah that He made the fullest and clearest revelation. And why by this prophet and in his time? Such questions can be at best but partially answered. We see, however, a fitness that Isaiah, to whom it was given, as we have already seen, to reveal the purpose of God in some new and most important particulars, and who was permitted to behold in vision the Messiah on His throne, and was thus capable of speaking in the most exalted terms of His glory, should also speak most distinctly of His humiliation and sufferings. And the time during which he prophesied was one of great moment to the world, and especially to the elect nation. The king of Assyria — the founder of the Second Empire — had already made his power felt by both Judah and Israel, and every year beheld him a more threatening and dangerous enemy. And still obscure but visible to the prophet's anointed eye was the rising Empire of Babylon, the instrument of God to punish with overthrow and exile His disobedient people. (Isa. xxxviii. 6.) The dark shadows of coming judgments fell athwart the land. By timely repentance, they might be averted; but the prophet knew that they would not hearken to his words. He had heard the seraphim cry, "Holy, holy, holy;" and he was filled with a sense of his own uncleanness, and that of his people. So far had they fallen from their covenant standing, that God must address their rulers as "the rulers of Sodom," and the people as "the people of Gomorrah." (i. 10.)

Thus the time of this prophet was one of great national peril, whether viewed from without or within. Upon all who had any true apprehension of the love of Jehovah to them as shown in their election, of His continued goodness, and of their unthankfulness and persistent transgressions, and who believed the prophetic announcements of the punishment about to come on them, the present evils must have rested as a heavy burden. They saw that the anger of God was kindled against His people; and how should His anger be turned away? It was, therefore, a fitting time to declare to such that their Messiah would stand up for them; that He would offer Himself as a sacrifice, "the Just for the unjust, to bring them to God." It is true that the real nature of that sacrifice to be offered for them could not then have been understood, even by the more spiritual; but they could understand that only through this sacrifice could God's anger be turned away, and their sins be forgiven them. And they could understand, also, that the sufferings of the Messiah must precede His glory.

No prophet has given so high a presentation of the Messiah's person as Isaiah. He is "Wonderful, Counsellor, The mighty God, The everlasting Father, The Prince of Peace. Of the increase of His government and peace there shall be no end, upon the throne of David, and upon His kingdom." This presentation of Him as King precedes the mention of Him as the suffering servant, for the greatness of His person makes more conceivable the thought of Him as the sacrifice for the sin of His people. (Isa. ix. 6, 7.)

It is in his later prophecies that Isaiah presents the figure of the suffering Messiah. Upon the peculiar character of these, we have already had occasion to remark. He speaks as one standing at the end of the long captivity,— that period of rejection and desolation of which he himself had spoken (vi. 11-13), and of which the Babylonian exile was only the first stage, — when the discipline of God had done its intended work, and that remnant, long sought for, had been found to whom He could speak comfort, because conscious of their sins and truly penitent. "Blessed are they that mourn : for they shall be comforted." As the poor in spirit, the meek, the broken-hearted, they are prepared to say : "O Lord, I will praise thee : though thou wast angry with me, thine anger is turned away, and thou comfortedst me." (xii. 1.) And then can He give command to His prophets : "Comfort ye, comfort ye my people. Speak ye comfortably to Jerusalem, and cry unto her, that her warfare is accomplished, and her punishment is accepted." (xl. 1, etc., Rev. Ver.) Being now truly penitent, He can fulfill to them all His promises. "The glory of the Lord shall be revealed, and all flesh shall see it together." "Then will the Lord be unto thee an everlasting light, and the days of thy mourning shall be ended." Thus "the remnant shall return unto the mighty God." "A little one shall become a thousand, and the small one a strong nation."

Thus, at the end of the days, through God's dealings with them, are wrought in a remnant a deep consciousness of sin, and true sorrow and penitence; and they will rejoice in the fulfillment of the promise of the suffering Messiah. And to such, of the prophet's own day, and of all the years down to the end, in whom a like spirit was found, the knowledge that on Him the Lord would lay the iniquities of the people, gave the assurance of their future redemption, and filled their hearts with hope. (Luke ii. 38.)

It is this prophet who gives special emphasis also to the fact that the people must be holy, to have communion with God in His kingdom. He often calls Him by the name of "the Holy One of Israel."

This name is almost peculiar to Isaiah, being found rarely elsewhere, and only in writings of a late date. Its use by this prophet is in harmony with his place as the one who discerned most clearly the sinfulness of the people, and the spiritual demands of Jehovah upon them. As separated unto Him, they were holy: "I the Lord am holy, and have severed you from other peoples, that ye should be mine." (Lev. xx. 26.) But now because of their unholiness they will soon cease to be severed, they will be scattered among the nations. It is necessary, therefore, that they be often reminded, in the prophecies which look forward to the restoration, that Jehovah is "the Holy One of Israel, whom they have provoked unto anger." (i. 4.) They cannot remain in their unholiness; if restored, it must be as "the holy seed," — "the remnant that shall stay upon the Lord, the Holy One of Israel, in truth." (x. 20.) And then Zion shall be called "the Zion of the Holy One of Israel." This designation thus becomes most emphatic, as pointing to the future and showing what is demanded of the people before they can be restored.

We may note, also, the use of the term "Redeemer" — Goel — in this prophet. This term, in the family relations of the Hebrews, denoted one who, as nearest of kin, was "the avenger of blood," and the redeemer of the enslaved poor, and of the lost inheritance. (Num. xxxvi. 12; Lev. xxv. 25.) God had redeemed the people from their bondage in Egypt, and been their avenger upon their oppressors. "I will redeem you with a stretched out arm, and with great judgments." (Exod. vi. 6.) "Thou hast led forth thy people which thou hast redeemed." (xv. 13.) Thus Jehovah was their Goel. But this term could not be used of Him again except with reference to a new captivity and a new redemption. Having forfeited their land, to Him it belongs to redeem it, — to restore the old landmarks that had been removed. (Ps. lxxiv. 2; Prov. xxiii. 10, 11.) And as this redemption, embracing both the land and its enslaved possessors, is especially the burden of Isaiah's later prophecies, it is in these prophecies that Jehovah is presented as the Redeemer, — Goel, — and the people as "the redeemed." In most cases the Redeemer is also designated as the "Holy One of Israel:" "Thy Redeemer is the Holy One of Israel." (xli. 14.) "Thus saith the Lord, your Redeemer, the Holy One of Israel." (xliii. 14.) "Thus saith the Lord, the King of Israel and his Redeemer;" "Thus saith the Lord, the Redeemer of Israel, and his Holy One." It is the King of Israel, the Holy One of Israel, who must be the Redeemer of Israel. Thus these elements, all having Messianic significance, are united in the presentation of the Deliverer to come. How far, through these terms, the people may have understood that the promised King of David's line was the Holy One of Israel, and their Redeemer, — Goel, — it is not possible to say. Isaiah at least, to whom the vision of the Messiah was given, may probably have known that one and the same Person was meant, and have seen in "the Redeemer that should come to Zion," "the Virgin's Son," "the Branch out of the roots of Jesse," of whom the Spirit had spoken by him. But the law as to the redemption wrought by a kinsman, would naturally direct the thoughts of all to Him as one of their own kin, to whom such an office would properly belong, and yet One able to avenge and redeem.

It is true that the office of the Goel does not necessarily involve any personal suffering on his part; but the name, whether used of Jehovah or the Messiah, brings out clearly the condition of those to be redeemed, and so taught the Jews into what bondage their sins had brought them, and the need of a Redeemer. (Isa. lxiii. 1–6.)

But the name that points most distinctly to the suffering Messiah is that of "The Servant of Jehovah," which is found in the latter part of Isaiah. (xl.–lxvi.) To understand the application of this term to Him, we must consider its general usage in this prophet. The people as such had been chosen by God to serve and honor Him. "This people have I found for myself: they shall show forth my praise." "Remember these, O Jacob and Israel, for thou art my servant. I have formed thee; thou art my servant." (xliv. 21.) But the service He sought they had not rendered. "Thou hast made me to serve with thy sins; thou hast wearied me with thine iniquities." But although His people as such had failed to serve Him, the obedient servant, if but a remnant, must be found among them; and, from the nature of the case, this obedience would demand the highest degree of self-sacrifice and of devotion to Jehovah. At the head of this remnant should He stand who is the Servant, and who is obedient even unto death.

It is not easy, indeed, to determine in all cases the exact application of the term, "servant of Jehovah," as used in Isaiah, — whether to the whole elect people as such; or to the faithful few among them in the prophet's day; or to the last remnant, — the Holy Seed; or to Him who is such in an especial manner, — the obedient One, the Messiah. But there are some passages which cannot well be referred to any but Him, since there is such contrast between the people and this Servant that by the latter an individual is clearly meant. (Isa. xlii. 1–5, xlix. 5–7.) As to the nature of this service, in all the Messiah does He is acting for Jehovah, — One raised up to declare His will and to fulfill His purpose; and the term "Servant" is therefore applicable to Him in all the offices He fills, even the highest. But there is one work in which the term finds its fullest application, as showing the highest measure of self-renunciation and obedience: it is in the offering up of Himself for the sins of His people. He must take their iniquities upon Him, He must humble Himself, and suffer in their stead, and be obedient even unto death, that He may thus reconcile them to God. To do this, it is necessary that He put aside the royal honor that belongs to Him as David's Son and Heir, and take the lowest place, — a place of suffering and shame. And this work is one in which none can aid Him; it is purely personal.

The first intimation of this lowest form of service is found in Isaiah: "Thus saith the Lord, . . . to Him whom man despiseth, to Him whom the nation abhorreth, to a Servant of rulers." (xlix. 7.) But the fullest declaration is to be found in chapters lii. and liii. It is unnecessary to cite words so familiar, or to say more than that One is here to us presented who is despised and rejected of men, and stricken, smitten of God, and afflicted. But His sufferings were not for Himself; upon Him the Lord laid the iniquity of all. "He was wounded for our transgressions, bruised for our iniquities: the chastisement of our peace was upon Him, and with His stripes we are healed." Because of the transgression of His people was He cut off out of the land of the living, but He was to rise again from the dead. "He shall see His seed, He shall prolong His days, and the pleasure of the Lord shall prosper in His hand. . . . I will divide Him a portion with the great, and He shall divide the spoil with the strong."

We have here One presented who is rejected by His people under circumstances of special ignominy and reproach. "He pours out His soul unto death, and is numbered with the transgressors." But He suffers and dies for others; He is stricken for the transgressions of His people; on Him the Lord laid the iniquity of all. But He does not continue in the realms of the dead. He rises again, He is exalted, and made very high. He becomes an Intercessor. He shall sprinkle many nations, He shall see His seed, and shall justify many. Who can be meant here but the Messiah? To whom beside was it possible for the Jews to apply them? Why, then, it may be asked, did not the Jews in general so understand them? Two reasons may be given: 1. The lack of such apprehension of their sins against their covenant, and of God's anger with them, that the need of such a sacrifice could be felt. They could not see that the first work of the Messiah must be to make an atonement for them and cleanse them. In their subjection to their heathen masters, and feeling keenly their servitude, their natural thought was of One who by a strong arm should set them free, and bring back the glory of the Davidic reign. Thus the national bondage, which should have been a continual reminder of the transgressions which had brought it upon them, and have awakened in them a profound sense of sin and earnest desire for the coming of the suffering One, who should stand in their stead, and by whose stripes they should be healed, was looked upon rather as a wrong done by the heathen to Jehovah in their person, and which it belonged to Him to avenge. 2. The high place given after the exile to the law, and the great value set upon its literal observance as making righteous. The tendency of this was to make the thought of any sacrifice to be offered by the Messiah for their sins incredible because unnecessary. This point will be more fully spoken of in another place.

It may be said that the Messiah is here presented as suffering, not for the sin of the world, but for the sins of the Jewish people; and for their sins as a people, rather than for the sins of individuals. Upon the first point some remarks have already been made. It is in His special relation to the covenant people that Isaiah here presents the Messiah. "For the transgression of my people was He stricken." The bearing of that sacrifice upon other nations and upon all men, as the "propitiation for the sins of the whole world," could not be made clearly known to them till it had been accomplished.

As to the second point, that the sacrifice of the Messiah is presented as offered rather for the sin of the nation as such than for the sins of individuals, much light is cast upon it by the rites of the Day of Atonement. The appointment of this day as a yearly fast was to the end that an atonement might be made, first for the priesthood, and then for all the people, having especial reference to their worship as defiled by their sins. Upon this day every individual was called upon to afflict his soul: "For whatsoever soul it be that shall not be afflicted in that same day, he shall be cut off from among his people." (Lev. xxiii. 29.) After atonement had been made for the priests, the high priest kills "the goat of the sin offering that is for the people," and sprinkles its blood, "because of the uncleanness of the children of Israel, and because of their transgressions, even of all their sins." "This shall be an everlasting statute unto you, to make an atonement for the children of Israel because of all their sins, once in the year." (Lev. xvi. 15-24.)

Thus the sacrifices of this day had both an individual and a national application. No Jew thought of himself as separated from his people, and obtaining a blessedness which was purely personal; he must share in the common good or evil. The spheres of individual and of national life were so closely united in the Jewish mind that they could not be separated. The sense of national sin, bringing with it the loss of God's favor and the hiding of His face, could not but deepen in each heart the sense of its own sin and loss; and, on the other hand, the consciousness of personal sin must deepen the sense of God's anger against national sin. He who felt the guilt of his own transgression, would feel most strongly the guilt of the national transgressions. As the sacrifice to be offered by the Messiah was for the whole people, so was it for every individual member, but under the condition that each one "afflict his soul." To one not thus afflicted it had no cleansing efficacy, but he should be cut off from among his people. He would have no part in the Messianic salvation.

Clear as the meaning of the prophet's words is to us, the Jews at no period seemed to have had any clear apprehension of it. That one should die for all, and that He should become the Source of a new and higher life through resurrection, were truths that could be rightly known only as the time of their fulfillment came.

In the prophet Zechariah, after the exile, we find additional particulars respecting a suffering Messiah. (Chaps. xi.–xiii.) A commission is given to one to feed the flock, because their own shepherds failed to do this. But this Divinely appointed Shepherd is rejected and despised by the unthankful flock. And when He says to them, "If ye think good, give me my hire," they weighed for His hire thirty pieces of silver, — the price of a slave. This ingratitude of His people, shown in their treatment of Jehovah's Shepherd, found its highest expression in the reward given to Judas for the betrayal of the Lord, — a pitiful sum, but enough in the eyes of the rulers for the life of "the Prophet of Galilee," and, although they knew it not, "the Good Shepherd who giveth His life for the sheep." (xi. 4, etc.)

Again, mention is made of one whom His people have pierced, or slain, and for whom they shall repent and mourn. "They shall look upon me whom they have pierced, and they shall mourn for Him." (xii. 10.) In these words, as applied by the apostle, reference is made by the prophetic spirit to Jesus as the Incarnate Son, — very God and very Man. (John xix. 34, Rev. i. 7.) "They shall look upon me — they shall mourn for Him." In Isaiah mention is made of His death, but not by whom He is slain; here it is ascribed to His own people. Even if the words refer, as claimed by some, to a true prophet of that day, slain by the people as a false prophet, they would still have their highest fulfillment in Him who was sent of God, and rejected and slain.

"Awake, O sword, against my shepherd, and against

the man that is my fellow, saith the Lord of hosts."
(xiii. 7.) Who is this shepherd and fellow of Jehovah?
It might perhaps be any one who helps Him in the care
of His flock. But the Lord's words applying it to
Himself show that, as in the earlier passages just cited,
it has its especial fulfillment in Him. (Matt. xxvi. 81.)
He is the rejected Shepherd, He is the Man, the Fellow
of God.

Let us now turn to the Psalms, to see what indications we may find in them of a suffering Messiah. We have already seen that a king is presented in several Psalms, in terms that could not have been realized in any king that sat on David's throne. So in others we find a sufferer, whose sufferings are not only extraordinary, but stand in a special relation to the setting up of the Messianic Kingdom. The most noticeable of these Psalms is the twenty-second, which we must briefly consider. The whole tenor of this Psalm shows that it is a personal one, the record of personal experiences. There is much in it that might have happened to a faithful servant of Jehovah in an evil time, as for example to Jeremiah, to whom some ascribe it. The Psalmist is "forsaken of God," "a reproach of men, and despised of the people;" he is in great bodily affliction; "all my bones are out of joint, . . . my tongue cleaveth to my jaws, and Thou hast brought me into the dust of death." "The assembly of the wicked have enclosed me, they pierced my hands and my feet." If the piercing of his hands and feet refers to crucifixion, it can scarcely be historical, for such punishment was not then inflicted; but according to many it should be rendered "they bound," rather than "they pierced." (Rev. Ver., margin.) It is most probable that the Lord's hands and feet were both bound and pierced.

But granting that much said in this Psalm of persecution and personal outrage might have been realized in the experience of the writer, yet there are clear indications that the Spirit of God looked beyond the present to a greater Sufferer. The person so afflicted is evidently one of great eminence, whose deliverance is a matter of national interest, and a proof to all the people that Jehovah hears the cry of the afflicted. (Verse 23.) This might indeed have been true of David or of Jeremiah; but it could not be said of them, as is said here, that their personal sufferings stood in any direct relations to the setting up of the Messianic Kingdom. "The meek shall eat and be satisfied: . . . all the ends of the world shall remember and turn unto the Lord: and all the kindreds of the nations shall worship before Thee. For the kingdom is the Lord's." Only of some very extraordinary one could it be said that his deliverance was of such moment that all the nations should be brought thereby to the worship of God. In the Messiah only could it be said that this Psalm has its complete fulfillment, both as to the sufferings and the glory that should follow. (Isa. liii. 12.)

There is also in this Psalm a clear prophetic reference to the remnant. "A seed shall serve Him, it shall be counted unto the Lord for His generation." (Rev. Ver., margin.) Or, as rendered by some, "He shall be accounted as Lord to that generation." (Verse 30.) A people is to be born, and this people is identical with the "seed," or "generation of the future,"—the remnant spoken of by the prophets. As was said by Isaiah, "He shall see His seed." (Ps. cii. 18; Isa. liii. 10.)

A like Psalm is the sixty-ninth. Here, as before, the writer is in deep distress. "I sink in deep mire, where there is no standing: I am come into deep waters, where the floods overflow me." . . . "They that hate me without a cause are more than the hairs of mine head." And they hate and persecute him because of his faithfulness to Jehovah. "The zeal of thine house hath eaten me up, and the reproaches of them that reproached Thee are fallen upon me." But this Psalm differs from the earlier one in the confession of personal sin (verse 5) ,and in imprecations upon his enemies. (Verse 22, etc.) There is nothing in this Psalm that may not have been in some measure in the experience of any faithful servant of God in a time of apostasy. Here also there is, though not so distinctly expressed, a connection between the writer's sufferings and the salvation of Zion. (xxxiv.-xxxvi.) Both of these Psalms were quoted and applied by the Lord to Himself.

In many other Psalms there is confession of sin, sometimes national, sometimes personal; and there is in some a remarkable blending of the two. In Psalm li. the Psalmist, whether David or another, makes confession of his sin, and asks forgiveness, and then by a sudden transition passes from himself to the people and its distress. "Do good in Thy good pleasure unto Zion, build Thou the walls of Jerusalem."

Thus we find in the Prophets and the Psalms an ideal — not imaginary — Sufferer; One in whom the idea of suffering is fulfilled. He stands as Mediator between the sinful people and their offended God, and bears the punishment of their iniquity. To His sufferings, which had been foreshadowed in the law, and foretold by the prophets, the Psalmists give personal expression. It was not consistent with the moral trial of the people and their free action that the Sufferer should be distinctly mentioned; nor could the true nature of His Sacrifice, or its bearing upon all men, be known till the Incarnate Son died and rose again. Yet so much light was given to the chosen people that the Lord could say to them: "O fools, and slow of heart to believe all that the prophets have spoken: ought not Christ to have suffered these things, and to enter into His glory?" (Luke xxiv. 25, 26; 44-46.)

CHAPTER XX.

THE DEAD UNDER THE THEOCRACY.

ASIDE from the existence of God and His relations to the living, there is no question so important as the state of the dead and their relations to Him. All knowledge here must come through revelation, for none return from the dead to teach the living. What revelation concerning this did God make to men at the first? Our inquiries involve two points: first, the fact of the existence of the soul after its separation from the body; second, the mode of its existence. As to the first, it may perhaps be said that the belief that the soul continues to exist after death, is innate in man, a primary belief, necessary and universal. Whether this is so, or whether that existence was made known by immediate revelation when the sentence of death was spoken, it is undoubted that this belief appears in the very beginning of man's history, and was very influential in moulding the religious systems of the most ancient peoples. If the Hebrews were ignorant that the soul exists after death, their position was a very exceptional one; and it is much harder to explain their ignorance than to believe their knowledge. That the early patriarchs so believed, clearly appears from the Scriptures, and being now generally admitted, needs not to be here discussed.

But as to the second point, the mode of its existence,

the Scriptures contain no distinct revelation. Why was this silence? Why was the invisible realm of the departed, which holds so important a place in all heathen religions, left in the Old-Testament records, with which we are now particularly concerned, almost wholly unnoticed? Two answers may be given: the first, derived from the inability of the human mind to conceive aright of the modes of disembodied existence, and from the limitations of human speech; the second, from the moral nature of death. Let us briefly consider each of these.

First, while the human mind is able to apprehend truths and facts of which it has no clear conception, as of God's self-existence and man's immortality; while we can apprehend the fact of disembodied existence, — of the soul as living separated from the body, — we cannot have any definite ideas as to the manner of its life. We can, indeed, give play to the imagination, and make mental pictures of the invisible world; but, if we do this, the imagination necessarily uses such means of representation as are familiar to it. It has no power to make wholly new presentations; it can only recombine the old under new forms; and the result is the picture of a shadowy land peopled with ghosts, differing only from the living by being divested of a certain gross materiality, — visible forms without solidity; and this is the picture of the realm of the dead presented in all the ancient religions. This inability truly to image departed souls, and to conceive their modes of existence, is not removed by mental culture. The wisest of to-day are no more able to do this than were the earliest patriarchs. And were men capable of understanding the details of disembodied life, it is difficult to see how, through words taken mainly from sensible things, any accurate knowledge could be conveyed.

We may thus on this ground understand why the Old Testament is so silent. Let us suppose that the Hebrews at the time of the exodus had only the general heathen conceptions of disembodied life. That souls continue to exist, that they are gathered into some undefined place (in Hebrew, "sheol"), and that they have some manner of communion with one another, so much was known to them. (Gen. xxv. 8, xxxvii. 35.) Let it be admitted that beyond this God's revelation to His people at first did not go; in this silence there was nothing to impugn His goodness. That He would give to the living so much light as would serve to their good, both present and future, and to His purpose in them, need not be said. But knowledge for which they were not prepared, and that could not be a healthful factor in their spiritual education, He would not give. And His silence is to be interpreted as in accordance with His uniform rule in His dealings with men, to teach them such things as they are able to hear. If St. Paul many centuries later could say of the vision to him of paradise, that he there heard "unspeakable words,"— words that it was not lawful for a man to utter (2 Cor. xii. 4),— we may well understand why the Old Testament speaks with such reserve of the invisible world of the dead, of angels, and of evil spirits.

The second reason for the silence of the Scriptures is found in the moral nature of death. As to this point they are in perfect harmony with themselves from beginning to end, and in strongest contrast with all other sacred books. Death is everywhere presented in them as an evil condition, the penalty of sin. Adam transgressed the command of God, and so came under "the law of sin and death." The body is an essential element in our humanity. The separation of soul and body, as destroying the integrity of man's being, and so marring its perfection, is an unnatural condition. It is obvious, therefore, that it could not be the will of God that the state of death, which is in its nature punitive, " the wages of sin," should be regarded as in itself something desirable, something better than life; and the separated soul as brought into a higher stage of being through its separation from the body. On the contrary, the fear of death was so stamped upon man's nature that no familiarity with it takes away its terror; which is a fact inexplicable were death natural to man, a mere transition from a lower stage of being to a higher. Nor would God have the dead exalted into objects of worship, demi-gods, the arbiters of human destiny; or invoked as teachers and guides of the living. Into these errors all the early peoples fell, and the pernicious results were manifest in many superstitious and idolatrous rites. Under the severest penalties Jehovah forbade to His people all necromancy, all attempts to call up the departed, either to learn the secrets of their abode or to ask their counsel.

This, then, was the first great truth in regard to death, to be established in the hearts of His elect people, that the separation of soul and body is the fruit of sin and an evil. This was done by the laws respecting the ceremonial impurity contracted by the touching of the dead body. " He that toucheth the dead body of any man shall be unclean seven days. . . . Whosoever toucheth a dead body, and purifieth not himself, defileth the tabernacle of the Lord; and that soul shall be cut off from Israel." So strict was this law, that if one died in a tent, " all that come into the tent, and all that is in the tent, shall be unclean seven days." Thus in a most expressive way were the Jews taught that death was a penalty of sin, a condition offensive to God, into which men came by disobedience. By meditating upon this, and seeing that for the purifying of such uncleanness the unclean must be sprinkled with "the water of separation," they would come gradually to understand the nature of death, and be kept from the error that it is an event made necessary by man's original constitution, and so without any moral significance.

This first truth having been established, that death is the penalty of sin, it was an obvious inference that the disembodied soul is in a relatively imperfect condition; for if by its separation from the body its capacities of knowledge and action and blessedness were enlarged, and it was brought nearer to God, then death would be no punishment. This point it is necessary to consider with some fullness, for a misapprehension of the teachings of the Old Testament upon it brings confusion into all our conceptions of the Messiah's work as the Redeemer from sin and death.

The fundamental facts stated in the beginning of the biblical history respecting human life as the unity of soul and body, of their separation by death as the fruit of sin, and the necessary inference that the disembodied state is one of weakness and imperfection, were the norm with which all the later precepts of the law and the utterances of the prophets are in entire harmony. Nowhere in the prophetic books or psalms is the state of death spoken of as other than an evil condition. This is seen in all the descriptions given of "sheol" as the place of the departed. It is set forth as the common receptacle of all the dead, without distinction of moral character; a place of gloom and privation; it is not in its depths that God reveals Himself, and is worshipped and praised. The life of the dead is not one of activity and joy. "In death there is no remembrance of thee: in sheol who shall give thee thanks?" (Ps. vi. 5.) "Shall the dust praise thee? shall it declare thy truth?" (xxx. 9.) "Wilt thou show wonders to the dead? shall the dead arise and praise thee? shall thy lovingkindness be declared in the grave? or thy faithfulness in destruction?" (lxxxviii. 10.) "Sheol cannot praise thee, death cannot celebrate thee: they that go down into the pit cannot hope for thy truth." (Isa. xxxviii. 18.)

Thus the Jews were taught that the disembodied state was not one in which God had pleasure, but a consequence of sin. To die was not passing from a lower to a higher degree of life, an ascent in individual progress, a drawing nearer to God. It was among the living that God dwelt, and to them did He reveal Himself. It was in the earth that His truth and faithfulness were to be manifested. "The living, the living, he shall praise thee, as I do this day."

It deserves to be attentively noted that no mention is made in the Old Testament of individual judgment and retribution at death. All alike go down to sheol, but nothing is said of a separation there of the good and the evil. This silence is most striking when put in contrast with the teaching of the heathen religions, all of which make judgment immediately after death one of their most prominent features. In sheol Jehovah does not sit, like Osiris or Minos, as judge of the dead. Why was this? Not that death placed all upon a moral equality in the eyes of Jehovah, or that He regarded all the departed, good and bad, with equal favor; for all His commandments to His people showed Him to be a God of holiness and justice, who would not spare the guilty. Why, then, did He not at each one's death judge him and reward him according to his works? Because His awards can be made to those only who stand before Him in the integrity of their being,—soul and body; and because His purpose in the Messiah demanded that there be a day of general judgment, in which the Messiah should sit as Judge. Individual judgment at death involves immediate separation and reward, a place of blessedness and a place of punishment. And these having been assigned them by God, and the eternal destiny of each decided, a future general judgment would be useless and idle, and the Messianic Kingdom lose its significance.

It is not at all inconsistent with this fact that the judgment of the dead is not at their death, that in the disembodied state God recognizes the distinction of good and evil. That the disembodied soul continued to stand in moral relations to Him, was too obvious to escape even the heathen mind. Its mode of existence did not affect its obligations to obey and honor Him according to the measure of its knowledge and of its capacities. Death, therefore, was no termination of moral responsibility. Wherever the soul might be, it was still under the eye of God, and subject to His will. Nor could God regard the evil in sheol with favor any more than the evil upon the earth. But that immediately after death each was judged, and eternal awards assigned, is nowhere affirmed in the Old Testament. From the hour of death, a veil hangs over all that takes place in the realm of the departed.

Nor is it inconsistent with the conception of sheol as a place of safe-keeping for all the dead, that a belief in a twofold division of it, and so of retribution already begun, should have arisen later in the Jewish mind, and become general; and have been adopted by our Lord in the parable of the rich man and Lazarus. The spiritual division of the good and the evil would easily pass, in popular apprehension, into a local division; and the soul, conscious of God's love and favor, be truly deemed blessed, as the soul, conscious of its sin and of

His anger, be deemed miserable. The term Gehenna, as a name for the place of punishment, had come in general use, and was employed by the Lord. Such later development of belief, in itself legitimate, is not forbidden by the silence of the law and the prophets.

It is in this matter of resurrection as preceding the judgment, and their connection with the Messianic Kingdom, that the Old-Testament teaching, as contrasted with the teachings of other religions, shows some of its most peculiar features. A day of general judgment preceded by resurrection was a conception unknown to the heathen mind. All judgment was individual, and took place at death: and resurrection, as the re-union of body and soul, had no place in their creeds; for the belief of some of the Oriental peoples, that there are cycles of indefinite duration, during each of which successive generations come and go, followed by an universal decay, and an absorption of all things into Deity, offers no analogy to the biblical doctrine. Nor does the belief of the Stoics, which is in substance the same, that at the end of a great cosmical period there is a general conflagration, and that the soul, which is in itself perishable, does not survive it; and then a new period begins, to end in like manner. Nor does the Persian dualism, if, indeed, it knew any thing of resurrection as a redemptive act, know of the true relations of resurrection to a day of judgment, as ushering in a Kingdom of righteousness. It was with the Persians as with the Egyptians, — every soul was judged at death, and entered at once upon its higher life of happiness, or lower life of misery.

Remembering the purpose of Jehovah to teach His elect people, first of all, the evil nature of death; and also to awaken belief in a future deliverance from it through the Messiah; and to make known the time and manner of this deliverance, so far as they were able to receive it; we proceed to consider the order of the revelations He made them, more in detail.

That sheol was not to be the eternal abode of the departed, that from it there should be deliverance, and that each class, the good and the evil, should ultimately go to its own place, was part of the Divine purpose; and gradual revelations were made, as we shall see, both as to the time and manner of this deliverance. First, as to its time. This was declared to be at the setting up of the Messianic Kingdom. The bringing up of the dead from sheol could not be an isolated event; it must be one in a series of Divine acts; and be determined as to its time by its special relations to God's purpose, which embraced both living and dead. As that purpose was more and more clearly revealed, the Messianic Kingdom became more conspicuous, and its importance more fully seen. Thus prophecy began early to connect deliverance from sheol with the setting up of the Messianic Kingdom. When the King Messiah came, then should the dead arise.

But would sheol then give up all its dead, both the good and the evil, and be from henceforth empty? At first this, like many other points, was left in obscurity; but it was gradually seen, that with the coming of the Messiah there was connected the deliverance of the faithful only from sheol. Not all the dead without distinction would then come forth to partake of the blessedness of this Kingdom, but such only as God should judge worthy.

Second, the mode of deliverance. This was to be through resurrection. The soul would return to earth, and be united to the body, no more to be separated from it; and then would the Messiah give to every man reward according to his works. When all were raised and judged, sheol, as the place of separate spirits, would be no longer needed.

Let us now trace the several steps of Divine revelation upon these points. How much knowledge the patriarchs before Abraham may have had respecting deliverance from death through resurrection, it is not necessary here to ask; but in the promises to Abraham was laid a foundation for further knowledge, since in their fulfillment the facts of the Messianic Kingdom and of the resurrection were necessarily involved. This patriarch did not refuse to offer up Isaac, his only begotten son, although the heir of the promises; for he "accounted that God was able to raise him up, even from the dead." (Heb. xi. 17, 19.) And the Lord's words: "Your father Abraham rejoiced to see my day, and he saw it, and was glad," show that he both foresaw the glory of the kingdom of the Messiah, and was assured that he should have part in it. Of the later patriarchs we are told that "they did not receive the fulfillment of the promises, but saw them afar off, and were persuaded of them, and embraced them, and confessed that they were strangers and pilgrims on the earth." (Heb. xi. 13.) Death and the disembodied state was not the goal to which they looked forward. This goal was "the land of promise" and "the heavenly city," in which God should dwell, and the Messiah should reign.

The covenant at Sinai brought still more clearly before the elect people the purpose of God in their redemption from death. By giving them possession of a land in which Jehovah would dwell, and reveal Himself as their God, He taught them that life in the body, holy and blessed, is the true condition of humanity; and the covenant with David confirmed this, since His Son, the Messiah, should sit on his throne. On the earth and in their own land must His people fulfill their calling as a kingdom of priests and a holy nation, and there the Messiah would reign in heavenly blessedness. If Abraham, Isaac, and Jacob, and Moses and Joshua, and Samuel and David, should partake of the blessedness of His kingdom, they must be brought up from the grave, and stand again among the living.

Thus in the covenants with Abraham, and with the people at Sinai; in the possession of the land in which Jehovah would dwell; and in the promise of the Messiah and of His kingdom; was embraced the pledge of a resurrection. Let us now turn to the utterances of the psalmists and the prophets, to see how far we can trace in them the growing consciousness of such future deliverance from the power of death.

In Psalms generally ascribed to David, there is a distinct reference to a deliverance from sheol. The apostle Peter quotes from Psalm xvi., and applies it to the resurrection of Christ: "He seeing this before spake of the resurrection of Christ." (Acts ii. 31.) The words, "I will behold thy face in righteousness: I shall be satisfied, when I awake, with thy likeness" (Ps. xvii.), cannot well be understood of any thing to be realized on the earth in this life, or in the disembodied state. The psalmist looks beyond this state to the time when he shall awake from the sleep of death. The likeness or form of God in which man was originally created, will be restored, and then will he "be satisfied;" for this implies a communion with Him, such as was given to Adam in Eden. Such expressions as "the path of life" may mean earthly life and prosperity, but if applied to the dead must imply resurrection; and the similar expressions, "the Presence of God in which is fullness of joy," and "at His right hand where are pleasures for evermore," must mean His manifestation in the earth, and among the living, and so involve a promise of the resurrection. The words, "God will redeem my soul from the power of sheol" (Ps. xlix. 15), taken with the context, clearly show that, after the night in sheol, the upright will be redeemed in the morning,—the morning of the Messianic Kingdom,—while the wicked will remain like sheep folded or imprisoned in it. "Death shall be their shepherd."

If we turn to the prophets, we find mention by Isaiah of the resurrection of certain righteous ones in contrast with the non-resurrection of certain wicked; and that a bodily resurrection is meant is now generally admitted. "The dead,"—the idolatrous Jews, or the heathen oppressors of the nation,—"they shall not live, the deceased, they shall not rise; . . . Thy dead shall live, my dead body shall they arise." (Rev. Ver., "My dead bodies shall arise," Isa. xxvi. 14, 19.) The wicked will abide in death, the righteous will live again; and the time when this shall be is the day of "His indignation," when "Jehovah cometh out of His place to punish the inhabitants of the earth for their iniquity;" the day when He shall "punish leviathan, the crooked serpent, and slay the dragon that is in the sea;" and when "Israel shall blossom and bud, and fill the face of the world with fruit." (xxvii. 1-6.) That this refers to the judicial acts attendant on the establishment of the Messianic Kingdom, and to the blessings that follow, is apparent. In Hosea it is said, "I will ransom them from the power of the grave,"— sheol,—"I will redeem them from death: O death, I will be thy plagues; O sheol, I will be thy destruction!" (xiii. 14.) This is far more than preservation from death; it is deliverance from it through resurrection. (1 Cor. xv. 54.)

In the vision given to the prophet Ezekiel of "the

valley of dry bones," and of their re-arrangement into bodies, — "bone to his bone," — and of their revivification, — "and they lived, and stood up upon their feet," — most commentators have found proof that the thought of bodily resurrection had at this time become familiar to the Jews, since, whether used here as a literal prediction, or as a symbol of the political restoration of the nation, such resurrection must at least have been regarded as a possible event. But others have drawn exactly the opposite inference, that the prophet would exalt the power of God in their political restoration by setting it forth as a work as utterly incredible in the eyes of men as that an army of the dead should live again. Taken in connection with the miracles wrought by Elijah and Elisha in bringing the dead to life, and the earlier words of the psalmists and prophets, we must, however, regard the former interpretation as most probable. (1 Kings xvii. 17, etc.; 2 Kings iv. 18, etc.)

In the prophet Daniel mention is made of a resurrection. (xii. 2.) "Many of them that sleep in the dust of the earth shall awake, some to everlasting life, and some to shame and everlasting contempt." This is clear as to the fact of a resurrection, partial in its extent; but it is here also a question of construction whether both classes of the just and unjust, in whole or in part, arise at the same time, one to life and one to shame, or the just only arise, and the unjust remain still in the invisible world. The latter agrees best with the language of Isaiah already quoted, where it is said of some, "dead, they shall not live," and of others, "thy dead shall live." But however construed, the resurrection is partial, and precedes the "everlasting life." Daniel connects this resurrection with "the time of trouble, such as never was since there was a nation, . . . and at that time thy people shall be delivered," which can scarcely be understood of any other period than that of "the great tribulation," of which our Lord speaks, and which was to precede the establishment of His kingdom. (Matt. xxiv. 21, etc.)

If the Jews at this time applied the words of Isaiah to the Messiah: "He was cut off out of the land of the living; ... He made His grave with the wicked and with the rich in His death," they must have believed in His resurrection, and this as preceding His kingdom, for His exaltation followed upon His death. Believing in His resurrection, they could easily believe that the righteous dead might also arise at His coming. But this point will be considered later.

It may be asked, Why were not the later revelations in the prophets respecting the disembodied state and the resurrection more full and clear? One answer may be found in the spiritual incapacity of the people to receive them. To know the real nature of death, it must be seen in its relations to sin; and therefore human sinfulness must be first realized as a fact of spiritual experience. Only as men feel themselves to be under the law of sin, can the desire of redemption be strong and active; and only as death is known to be the wages of sin, is it seen that the body is to be redeemed. The disembodied state, as a consequence of sin, cannot be eternal: life in sheol is not fullness of life; this fullness can be attained only in the Messianic Kingdom. But our survey of Jewish history shows that such consciousness of sin was awakened in few only, and the relation of sin to death was not seen, nor the nature of the higher life in the Messianic Kingdom; and therefore little could be said by the prophets respecting the part which the dead should have in it. The value of resurrection as an essential part of redemption could be understood only by those who saw in death the expression of the anger of God against sin.

But there were some in all generations, having a deep consciousness of sin on the one hand, and of the grace of God on the other, to whom death appeared in its true nature; but who through their close communion with Him attained to the assurance that death could not destroy that communion. Separation of soul and body would not bring separation from the living God. This feeling often finds utterance in the Psalms. "I am continually with thee." "Whom have I in heaven but thee? and there is none on earth that I desire besides thee." "My flesh and my heart faileth, but God is the strength of my heart, and my portion for ever." However weak in themselves, in the everlasting God was their strength. Because He lived, they would also live. (Ps. xxiii. 4, 6.) In their present communion with God was the pledge that He would not leave them among the dead, He would not leave them in the darkness of sheol, but make them to rejoice evermore in the light of His countenance. The more clearly bodily death was seen to be the consequence of sin, the more clearly was it seen that the purpose of God in redemption called for the re-union of soul and body; and thus the thought of resurrection as a redemptive act gradually took a firm lodgement in the more spiritually-minded of the people.

But there is another answer to this question. As the Incarnation is the key to all the actings of God, both in man's creation and in his redemption, it was not possible that the full significance of death in its relations to sin, could be known by any till His Son came, and "was made in the likeness of sinful flesh," and died and rose again. The Redeemer must Himself die, and through death destroy death. "Forasmuch as the children are partakers of flesh and blood, He also Himself likewise took part of the same; that through death He might destroy him that had the power of death." Rising from the dead, He is "made after the power of an endless life," One over whom death hath no more dominion. Thus out of death comes life, out of the mortal the immortal. " I was dead; and, behold, I am alive for evermore." (Rev. i. 18.) And through His resurrection only could men learn the true nature of the re-union of soul and body. His resurrection was not a mere re-union, but one under new conditions, and without possibility of further separation. "Christ being raised from the dead, dieth no more; death hath no more dominion over Him." (Rom. vi. 9.) "The second man is the Lord from heaven." To all who shall rise in His likeness, it is the entry upon a new stage of being, upon a higher, an immortal and heavenly life, in which all elements of man's nature, the material and the spiritual, are brought into perfectly adjusted and eternal relations.

Thus, not till the death and resurrection of the Incarnate Son, was it possible for men to know the full meaning of death, or its place in the economy of redemption; or the real nature of resurrection, and of the higher condition of being into which man was to be then exalted. Till He should die and rise again, "the Resurrection and the Life," darkness must hang over the realm of the dead, — a darkness which only His actings in His Son could dispel. It was not God's will that His children should attempt to penetrate this darkness, and to learn the mode of disembodied existence. In His own time and way, and as they were able to receive, He would give them light; and, relying upon His promises respecting the Messiah, they must walk by faith till His hour for action came. The resurrection is one in a series of connected events, an act not to be separated from God's other acts in the work of redemption, and having its own defined place in the series. None could rise out of death till the purpose of God in the Messianic King was perfected. He was to be "the first-born from the dead,"— "the author of life," — and in His likeness were the holy dead to rise. When He should come to establish His kingdom, and sit as Judge, then all whom God thought worthy to partake of its blessedness, would be raised together, and be gathered to Him. Therefore God would have His people to look forward in faith to the coming of the promised Redeemer, and in patience to wait through Him their redemption from death.

It is not without interest to note in several points the effect of this teaching respecting death, the disembodied state, and the resurrection, on the Jewish mind.

1. It brought before the people the great truth that the purpose of God in man was to be wrought out in the earth, and among the living. Although the multitude of the dead continually increased, yet not unto them were the mighty interests of humanity intrusted, not by them was redemption to be effected, not in sheol was the Messianic Kingdom to be set up. The victory over sin and death was to be won on the earth, and by the Incarnate Son, who could say: "I was dead, and, behold, I am alive for evermore; and have the keys of hell and of death;" and on earth should the glory of His kingdom be revealed. Thus the error was guarded against which prevailed everywhere amongst the heathen, that the dead constituted a company so separated from the living that God's actings in the earth had no longer importance for them. On the contrary, all His people were taught that the state of death is merely provisional; that sheol is only a

place of safe-keeping, not a permanent habitation; and that when God's time comes, He will re-unite the divided bands of His children, not by the death of the living, but by bringing the dead to life.

2. The condition of the dead being thus presented as one of rest, not of action, God finding His servants and helpers among the living, His people were kept from the adoration and invocation of the departed. While no form of worship among the early peoples was more ancient and widely spread than that of the dead, the Hebrews never deified or worshipped their departed chiefs and heroes. Neither Abraham nor Moses nor David, nor any hero or prophet, was invoked, or made an object of Divine honors. Nor from them was help sought. The noblest dead were not pictured as mighty and majestic spirits able to assist the living, but as the "Rephaim," weak, powerless shades. (Isa. xxvi. 19.)

3. Another effect was the close association in order of time between the resurrection and the setting up of the Messianic Kingdom. That the Messianic King should be Himself a man raised from the dead, though declared by the prophet, was certainly never a matter of popular belief. But it was possible for all to see an order in redemption, and that the dead could not rise till the Messiah came. And this was seen and declared by the prophets, so that the two events became closely associated in the popular mind, many proofs of which are given in the Gospels. (Luke xiv. 14, 15.)

4. Another effect was to keep the people from subordinating the purpose of God to individual happiness. It was in the very nature of the covenant relation that it embraced the people as a whole, and could not be realized in individuals; and that the highest individual happiness could be attained only as His work attained its completion in the Messianic Kingdom. It was not

for any one person to anticipate the time of the Kingdom, and to demand of God at death the blessedness which should be his in its due order. By His silence respecting any judgment and reward before the Messiah came, God not only taught all to wait His pleasure, but kept them from that indifference to the accomplishment of His purpose which necessarily finds place where individual salvation is made the chief end of hope and action. It may be said that no true Hebrew before the exile ever thought of entering at his death into the fullness of heavenly bliss; and that through death he attained the great end of life.

It has already been noticed that the belief in resurrection could not have been borrowed from any of the heathen nations with whom the Jews were in contact after the exile. If it were true that there were some among them who on religious or philosophical ground held some form of material body to be an indispensable organ of the soul, and so looked for a series of embodiments, yet they knew nothing of the moral nature of death, or of resurrection as a redemptive act. Of a life in the risen body, no longer under the law of sin and death, perfect and without end, they had no conception. The re-union of soul and body, if any believed in this, was only a passing event in the endless cycle of change, — life and death, death and life. But the general belief of antiquity was, that no re-union of body and soul after their separation was possible; and the prevalent philosophy of later times that matter and spirit are so essentially antagonistic, and spirit so much defiled and hindered by any contact with matter, that their separation through death is a great gain to the soul, made resurrection a doctrine offensive, and even absurd, to cultured heathenism.

It may be well here to make a brief statement of the

essential distinctions between heathen and biblical eschatologies; as the former is set forth in its philosophers, and the latter in the Old Testament.

1. In the former, sin is not placed in any direct causal relation to death; death is a natural event, and without moral significance. In the latter, death is the penalty of sin, the expression of Divine anger; through his disobedience man came under the law of death.

2. In the former, death, as the separation of soul and body, brings no loss; the disembodied soul enters rather into a higher sphere of being. Any re-union is, therefore, unnecessary, and the doctrine of the resurrection unknown or rejected. In the latter, all disembodied existence is necessarily imperfect because a destruction of man's original constitution; and resurrection of the body and re-union are thus essential to its perfection.

3. In the former, retribution follows at death, each soul as good or evil then receives its reward, there is no day of general judgment. In the latter, there is no retribution at death, other than the continued consciousness of the Divine favor or displeasure; but all wait for a day of general judgment.

4. In the former, there is no redemptive purpose underlying human history, and, therefore, there is no progress to a higher and perfect order, no eternal kingdom of righteousness as the goal. In the latter, there is continued and definite movement to an end, which is fullness of life in communion with God in the Kingdom of His Son; and to this end resurrection is an essential step.

5. In the former, there is no conception of any existence hereafter higher than that of man developed in his natural faculties. In the latter, there is the conception of a far higher condition of being, the supernatural,

the basis of which is the Incarnation; and whose consummation is in the holy and glorified humanity — the likeness of the risen Lord.

We thus see how widely differing are the heathen and biblical ideas of the future of man. Properly speaking, heathenism knows nothing of perfect and eternal life: it knows only of the disembodied and, therefore, imperfect state, and of the happiness or misery of the soul in its various transmigrations. But in biblical revelation the future of man is inseparably connected with the purpose of God in the Messiah; and as He entered into His perfected condition by resurrection, so must all who attain to highest blessedness. Through resurrection only is fullness and permanence of life. Hence, resurrection of the body after the likeness of Christ, is the cardinal fact in biblical eschatology.

CHAPTER XXI.

THE SCRIBES AS SUCCESSORS OF THE PROPHETS, AND THE MESSIANIC HOPE.

WE have already seen in what important particulars the position of the elect people after the return from the Babylonian exile differed from their position before the exile. Four things are enumerated by the Rabbis as wanting in the second temple, — the Shechinah or Visible Glory, the Ark, the Holy Fire on the Altar, and the Urim and Thummim. But the Holy Spirit, the spirit of prophecy, remained; and thus there was still an immediate revelation of Jehovah's will. With Malachi prophecy ceased; henceforth there was no one to say to them, "Thus saith the Lord." All that was now possible was to gather up the words that the prophets had spoken, with the law of Moses, and inspired songs, and apply them, as they were best able, to the regulation of their civil and religious life in the new circumstances in which they were placed. To preserve all the revelations of God, by whomsoever spoken; to interpret them, and enforce them, so far as of a practical character, was their present duty.

But by whom should this be done? It was an abnormal condition of affairs, one for which God had made no provision. Naturally the matter would fall into the hands of the priests, "for the priest's lips should keep knowledge, and they should seek the law at his mouth."

(Mal. ii. 7.) And this may have been the case at first, for Ezra was a priest; but a distinct class of men soon arose, into whose hands this work came. When through the cessation of prophecy the sacred books were looked on as the sole source of knowledge as to God's will, copies of them must be prepared, and those who prepared them must be students of the past. These soon came to constitute a special class, and they were far more than copyists; they were also interpreters, and in a manner lawgivers, since their interpretations became by degrees authoritative. New circumstances made, also, new applications of existing laws necessary. Probably Ezra took some measures to train up those who could be his successors. (Ez. vii. 6, 10.)

Thus a body of men arose, unknown to the original constitution of the theocratic state, having no official position, but very powerful in moulding the religious life of the people. The reading and explanation of the sacred books became an important part of the religious services on the feast and holy days. The scribes were able to bring gradually all classes under the observance of the law as they interpreted it, and through its provisions entering into the minute details of daily duty, to infold them as fish in the meshes of a net. Those who most strictly applied the teachings of the scribes to every-day life, were known as the Pharisees. These kept the law rigorously in all its details; they were by eminence the legalists, where all were legal. It naturally followed that they became the religious leaders of the people, recognized and honored as those in whom the legal spirit of the time found its fullest expression.

With the growth of the scribes and their adherents, the influence of the priesthood in some degree diminished. It was stripped of part of its influence as the teaching body, and the rise of synagogue worship tended in some degree to depreciate in popular esteem the temple service. The Holy of Holies empty, the fire from heaven upon the altar extinguished, this service lost in a measure its high and supernatural character; and became mechanical in its spirit, and monotonous in its routine. On the other hand, the reading of the sacred books in the synagogue, and the opportunity for comment on them, and the prayers there offered, opened a way for religious instruction and for the expression of devotional feeling, which met the spiritual needs of many; and which gave the scribes large scope to mould the opinions of the worshippers.

But if we now ask, how this changed relation of things following upon the cessation of prophecy bore upon the matter of the Messianic hope, we must answer, that it was detrimental. And this in two ways: First, through the exaltation of the law the work of the Messiah as the Redeemer from sin became subordinate, and comparatively unimportant. By the observance of the legal precepts the people were made righteous, and obtained the Divine favor. No special work of reconciliation to God was to be wrought by the Messiah, no expiatory sacrifice was needed. The one thing all-necessary and all-sufficient was to keep the law. Second, it was believed that the Messiah Himself would be subject to the law, and honor it by His perfect observance of all its precepts. The way in which He would bless the people in spiritual things would not be through any atonement offered by Him, but through His prayers based on His perfect legal righteousness, and so accepted of God. And He would enforce the law upon all nations.

It is to be noted, also, that this exaltation of the law affected in many minds the desire of national deliverance. As the legal precepts could be kept in some measure by the nation when under heathen rule, and even by those dwelling apart in heathen lands, a restoration to independence and national unity, as it should be realized under the Messiah, was of less moment. To obey the law wherever they might be, was to recognize the supremacy of Jehovah as their King. Hence, we see why many of the scribes and Pharisees were unwilling to rebel against the yoke of their heathen oppressors, and often counselled submission. The law was in a degree a substitute both for the Messiah and the Messianic Kingdom.

It was inevitable that the study of the sacred books, as carried on by the scribes, should tend to foster a spirit of intellectual pride fatal to all true spiritual self-knowledge. The scribe could not take the place of the prophet as a true guide, he could not discern the sins of the people, nor warn them of their dangers; out of the high-minded Pharisees the repentant and humble remnant could not come. The cessation of prophecy in Malachi left the people without the means of knowing their own spiritual condition, and their unpreparedness for the Messianic Kingdom. Testing themselves by a written law, they were their own judges; and the standard of their judgment was their own discernment of its meaning. In its application they naturally justified themselves, and a legal self-righteousness was the necessary result. They became vain in their own conceits, and made void the law by their traditions, which expressed their interpretation and application of it. The teachers, like the unjust steward, diminished the claims of God upon the people; where He demanded a hundred measures, they wrote down fifty. Out of this delusion of their self-righteousness, there was no one able to deliver them. No scribe could call the people to repentance; only a prophet illumined by the Spirit, and having a message from God, could discern what the sins of the people were, and declare to them His righteous anger. The Jews without a prophet easily deluded themselves into the belief that they were acceptable to God, the just who needed no repentance, a people ready for the Messiah. And no severity of judgment availed to bring them to a true knowledge of themselves, since they misinterpreted the very judgments.

It was not possible that the Messianic Kingdom could be rightly apprehended as to its spiritual character by those who thought themselves sufficiently prepared for it by an external observance of the law; and who wholly failed to understand the sacrificial ritual as intended to convince them of sin, and prepare them for its true expiation. Ignorant of their own hearts, they said of the Mosaic precepts, like the young ruler, "All these things have I kept from my youth up: what lack I yet?" As those thinking themselves prepared for His Kingdom by keeping the law, they could not see that it was needful that the Messiah should do any work for their spiritual deliverance at His coming. His work must be one of national deliverance, to free them from their enemies, and to restore their independence. This accomplished, they were ready for the fulfillment of all the promises of God to Abraham and to David. And as their conceptions of the Kingdom were low, so also their conception of the Messiah. He was to be a Scribe of the scribes, a Pharisee of the Pharisees. A great part of His office was to exalt the law, and make the people to obey it. That the Messiah was to suffer for their sins, to redeem them by His expiatory death, was something contrary to all their modes of thought; and the most express words of the prophets respecting His sufferings were easily explained away.

Thus neither the priesthood nor the scribes could

prepare the people for the Lord; but God, who always brings good out of evil, did through them preserve a religious unity, and so kept the people from being swallowed up by the heathen around them. The numerous legal prescriptions of the scribes served as so many barriers to keep them distinct; and the excess of their self-righteousness, their pharisaic pride, which made them odious to all peoples, was as a separating wall of fire. Yet we cannot doubt that there were many in this long period, who, like Zacharias and Elisabeth, "walked in all the statutes and ordinances of the Lord blameless;" and who, with the outward observance of the law, knew something also of its deeper meaning; and who looked for the Messiah, both as the Redeemer from sin, and as the King of Israel. (Luke ii. 38.)

Of the three great religious parties which grew up after the exile, one, the Essenes, had so greatly departed from the sphere of Old-Testament revelations, and of the Messianic hope, as not to be once mentioned in the Gospels. Of the Pharisees we have spoken as those most diligent to keep the law in the letter, but full of self-righteousness, and feeling no need of a Messiah who should be more than a political redeemer and chief. The Sadducees were men of the world, who had no faith in any special covenant relation of the nation to God, or in any thing supernatural. They were eager politicians, who expected to bring about their worldly ends by worldly means; and their denial of the resurrection of the dead followed from their general religious position. If they had any expectation of a Messiah, it was not of one sent immediately of God, and supernaturally endowed, but of one who by his own ability and force of will could place himself at the head of the nation, and achieve its independence.

CHAPTER XXII.

THE MESSIAH IN THE APOCRYPHAL AND APOCALYPTIC BOOKS.

WE are here interested in these books only so far as they cast light upon the Messianic belief of the Jews after the cessation of prophecy in the person of Malachi. They are of various kinds,—historical, prophetic, didactic, poetic, and fictitious. Probably most were composed during the Grecian and Maccabæan periods (332–105 B.C.), or a little later; but exact dates are not for us important.

It was impossible that there should not have been in the long period from Malachi to the birth of Christ (some four hundred years), some development of religious ideas among the people, both among those dwelling in Judæa, and those scattered in other lands. Many influences from without were acting upon them to modify their beliefs, both through their subjection to heathen masters, and the close intercourse into which they were brought with intelligent foreigners; and the repeated reading of the law and the prophets in the synagogues kept the fact of their Divine calling continually before them, and incited them to reflection upon the unfulfilled promises of God. Thus there were two processes going on in the popular mind,— the reception and assimilation of foreign ideas, and the doctrinal interpretation of their own scriptures; the latter being necessarily affected by the former, and by the historical progress of events. It is the interpretation only of their Messianic scriptures that here concerns us.

Turning to the Apocryphal books, we are at once struck with the fact, that of the three elements already spoken of as entering into the general Messianic conception, — the universal Kingdom under Jehovah, the place of the Jews in that kingdom as the ruling people, and the kingship of the Messiah, — there is frequent mention of the first two, but little or none of the last. All nations are to be subjected to Jehovah, and the Jews are to be restored to their own land, and to dwell in peace; but it is Jehovah, and not the Messiah, who reveals Himself in Jerusalem, and is Ruler and Judge. A brief examination of the Apocryphal books will clearly show this.

The Book of Sirach — Ecclesiasticus — speaks of the judgments to be inflicted on all nations, of the coming of Elijah, and of the gathering of all the tribes of Israel together to their own land. Mention is also made of the perpetuity of the Abrahamic covenant: "The days of Israel are without number." Earnest wishes are often expressed for deliverance from the sore evils of the times, both political and religious, and the hope of better days. (xxxvi. 12.) Although there is no mention of the personal Messiah, there is an allusion to the covenant with David as yet to be fulfilled in his descendants: "The Lord gave David a covenant respecting kings;" i.e., that his descendants should be kings. (xliv. 13, xlvii.)

The Book of Baruch expresses strong confidence, that as the nations around Zion had seen the captivity of the Jews, so they should shortly see their deliverance, which should come with great glory. (iv. 23.) The enemy that had persecuted Zion should be destroyed, and

Jerusalem be exalted forever. "The enemy hath persecuted thee, and shortly thou shalt see his destruction, and shalt tread upon his neck." "Miserable is she that received thy sons, O Jerusalem; for as she rejoiced at thy fall, so shall she be grieved over her own desolation." "Lo, thy sons come, . . . they come gathered from the east to the west by the word of the Holy One, rejoicing in the remembrance of God. . . . For God bringeth them unto thee, exalted with glory as the throne of a kingdom." "Set on thy head, O Jerusalem, the diadem of the glory everlasting, for God will shew thy brightness to every country under heaven. Thy name shall be called of God for ever, Peace of righteousness, and Glory of the fear of God." (iv. 37, v. 2, etc.)

The Book of Tobit foretells that Jerusalem will be rebuilt in great splendor, as the prophets declared, that God's tabernacle will again be set up in it, and that many nations will come from afar bringing gifts: "God is our Father for ever. He will have mercy again, and will gather us out of all nations, wherever we have been scattered among them. Many nations shall come from afar to the name of the Lord God, having gifts in their hands. . . . Jerusalem shall be built up with sapphires and emeralds, . . . and all her streets shall say, Alleluia." "All the heathen shall turn and fear the Lord God truly, and shall bury their idols; and all the heathen shall praise the Lord, and the Lord shall exalt His people." (xiii., xiv.)

The Book of Judith proclaims war to the nations that rise up against Israel: "The Lord will punish them in the day of judgment, putting fire and worms into their flesh, and they shall wail with pain for ever." (xvi. 17.)

In the First Book of Maccabees, there is a reference

to the covenant with David: "David through his piety possessed the throne of an everlasting kingdom." (ii. 57.) In the Second Book of Maccabees, there is mention of the restoration of Israel: "Plant thy people again in thy holy place, as Moses hath said." (i. 29.) "We hope truly in God that He will shortly have mercy upon us, and gather us together out of every land under heaven into the holy place." (ii. 17, 18.)

In the Wisdom of Solomon, probably of Jewish-Egyptian origin (B.C.), there is a passage wholly in the spirit of the prophets when describing the day of visitation and decision which ushers in the Messianic Kingdom: "The hope of the righteous is full of immortality, . . . and in the time of their visitation they shall blaze forth, and run to and fro like sparks among the stubble. They shall judge nations, and have dominion over peoples, and their king shall be the Lord for ever. (iii. 2, etc.) "The righteous live for evermore; their reward, also, is in the Lord. . . . Therefore shall they receive the kingdom of glory, and a crown of beauty from the Lord's hand." (v. 15.)

Thus the Jews, as represented in these books, still had firm faith in their covenant standing, and believed that in time all would be gathered together in their land, and that God would dwell among them as their King, and all nations would worship Him, and honor them as His chosen people. But how is the silence respecting the Messiah to be understood? Some explain it as showing that these writers had no belief that He was to come, but the allusions to the Davidic covenant show that this inference is too large. This much may be admitted, that with the decay of the house of David, and in the absence of any one of that line to whom their eyes could turn, they looked directly to Jehovah as their deliverer and ruler. It was easier to believe in a general fulfillment of the theocratic promises by Him acting providentially, than in the fulfillment of the more special ones to David in the person of his Son. There was strong faith in a great national future, but this would be rather through a glorious revival of the Theocracy than through the establishment of the Messianic Kingdom under one of the house of David; as in our own day there is a general belief among Christians in the ultimate triumph of Christianity, but this rather through spiritual agencies now in operation than through the coming of the Lord from heaven. The burden of present distress led the Jews to hope for speedy deliverance, and to seek it through any present instruments raised up by Jehovah, — warriors and princes and priests, as those of the Hasmonean family, — rather than to wait patiently for the Davidic Messiah.

It is probable that during the wars of the Maccabees, there was a partial revival of faith in the promises of God to David respecting his Son, but it would seem that there was no expectation of His speedy coming. This is plain from the action of the people in regard to Simon Maccabæus: "The Jews and priests were well pleased that Simon should be their prince and high priest for ever, until there arise a trustworthy prophet." It is not probable that by this prophet the Messiah was meant, but rather one who, after the way of the old prophets, should declare the mind of God.

As belonging to this period, the beliefs of the Alexandrian Jews as represented by Philo, may be mentioned. Although much disposed to spiritualize the Old-Testament prophecies, yet he seems to have looked for the regathering of his people into their own land, and that the waste cities should be rebuilded. And he apparently looked for supernatural blessings, — that its inhabitants would all be long-lived, that snakes and scorpions would cease to be poisonous, and wild beasts lose their fierceness, and fruitful harvests never fail. The Jewish victories over the heathen would be chiefly moral, the captives subduing their conquerors through the truth, converting not destroying them; yet he hoped that God would send a king to lead their armies, and bring the disobedient and wicked into subjection. (Num. xxiv. 7.) Whether he meant by this king the Messiah is in dispute; and also whether he identified the Messiah with the Logos, and so made Him pre-existent.

The Apocalyptic literature is generally regarded as having its origin in the Maccabæan struggle for freedom, and in the spirit of hope and expectation then enkindled. It is an attempt to bind together in a consistent whole, past and future, history and prophecy; and it is this which gives these writings their peculiar form. It is not easy to draw an exact line, so far as regards their general contents, between the Apocryphal and Apocalyptic books. But, as regards the Messiah, we may say that the Apocalyptic writers give Him much more prominence, and ascribe to Him a much more important part in the work of national redemption. As might have been expected, there were wide divergencies of belief as to details. We will briefly examine the most important of these books written before the time of Christ.

The Sibylline Oracles are of various authors and dates, but we are concerned with those only that are of Jewish origin, and pre-Christian. In these mention is made of a mighty king to be sent of God from heaven, who conquers all His enemies, gathers His people, rebuilds the temple, establishes upon earth universal peace, and makes the will of God to be everywhere obeyed. This king is of the family of David: heavy judgments will be inflicted on all the heathen nations, the object of which is not their destruction, but their conversion. There will then be but one temple; and Jehovah will manifest Himself gloriously in the holy city, and the kingdom be without end. There is no mention of the resurrection, but the earth will be melted and purified.

How far the Messianic parts of the several Books of Henoch may be cited as proofs of Jewish beliefs before Christ, is disputed; but the better authority assigns them a pre-Christian origin. The object of the book in general is, in opposition to Hellenic scepticism, to confirm the Jewish mind in the faith of the Old-Testament teaching respecting a future life, the promised Messiah and His kingdom, the resurrection and general judgment. The Messiah is thought of as pre-existent and supernatural. "Before the sun and the stars were created, His name was invoked in the presence of the Lord of spirits. . . . The elect and concealed one existed in His presence before the world was created, and for ever." " Then I beheld the Ancient of Days, . . . and with Him another whose countenance resembled that of man. . . . This is the Son of man to whom righteousness belongs. He shall punish kings and their dominions because they will not exalt and praise Him, nor humble themselves before Him. . . . All who dwell on earth shall fall down and worship before Him, and bring praise to the Lord of spirits. He is the judge of all concealed things, of all the works of the Holy One in heaven, of Satan and all his host. When He is revealed, there will be a resurrection; but of the righteous only. The earth will give up her dead, and hell — sheol — those in her. Then the earth will rejoice, the mountains skip as rams, the hills be as springs of water, and the righteous shall inherit it." This is the beginning of "the world to come," which endures forever.

Though the Messiah is spoken of as the judge of the earth and of all creatures, yet sometimes judgment is also ascribed to God. It is here, as often in the Old Testament, that judgment is now ascribed to Jehovah, and now to Messiah; the true thought to be expressed being that Jehovah is the ultimate source of all authority and judgment, but His authority is put forth through His chosen and Holy One.

In the "Psalms of Solomon" the writer confidently expects a king to be sent by God, of the house of David, and specially endowed by the Spirit, but not a supernatural being; and through Him all the promises made to the Jews will be fulfilled. He will gather together His people and purify Jerusalem, and no strangers will dwell in the land. The writer closely connects the theocracy of Jehovah and the rule of Messiah. The King is the Righteous One without sin, the "Anointed of the Lord." The nations are to be converted rather than destroyed, and will bring their gifts to Jerusalem. Mention is made of resurrection to life, but the inheritance of sinners is hell and darkness and destruction. That this kingdom is not thought of as eternal, but as temporal, may be inferred from the intimation that children will be born in that time to the holy people.

In the Book of Jubilees, said by some to be pre-Christian, but by most put later, it is declared that the Jews purified by God will again inherit their land, and rule over the nations forever. The lives of men will be prolonged even to a thousand years. Mention is made of the day of judgment, in which Jehovah will punish with sword and fire, but no mention is made of the Messiah or of the resurrection of the dead.

The Apocalypses of Baruch and Ezra being admitted to be after Christ, and probably later than the destruction of Jerusalem, are not of importance to us. Both regard the Messianic Kingdom as limited in time. Ezra says, it endures for four hundred years, and the Messiah then dies; and after it are the judgment and resurrection, both by Jehovah. Baruch seems to believe in a twofold form of the Messianic Kingdom: the first is of "this world;" and a second then begins, which is identical with "the world to come," and endures forever. At the end of the earthly kingdom is a general resurrection. All are raised in earthly bodies; and after judgment these are changed, some to glory, and some to shame; then the righteous behold the invisible world, and are made higher than the angels. During the first form of the kingdom Israel will be saved, and all nations be subject to the Messiah.

There are certain points in which there is entire agreement in all these books, Apocryphal and Apocalyptic. All believe that the Jews are God's chosen people; that they will return to their land; that the temple will be rebuilt, and worship restored; that all nations will acknowledge Jehovah, and keep His law; and, though not always affirmed, that one of the house of David will reign over them. But there was disagreement as to the person of the Messiah and His work. Some affirm that He will be man only, and mortal, not working any miracles, but a wise and able ruler; that His kingdom is of limited duration, and preparatory in its nature, and is to be followed by resurrection and judgment, and the eternal Kingdom of Jehovah. Others, holding, like the former, the Messiah to be mere man, ascribe to Him a more important part in the redemption of the people, and a higher place to the Messianic Kingdom. He is largely endowed with the Spirit of

God, He authenticates Himself by miracles, He conquers His enemies through supernatural judgments upon them; but His kingdom is of limited duration, and is followed by "the world to come," or Jehovah's eternal Kingdom. Others still, making Him to be more than man, the Son of God pre-existent and heavenly, give to Him the chief place in the work of national redemption. The administration of the kingdom is supernatural. He gathers the scattered nation, He raises the faithful dead, the new Jerusalem comes down from heaven, He judges the nations, casting the evil into Gehenna, all the nations love and honor Him, and His kingdom is without any assignable end.

It is in the first of these classes that the Apocryphal books may for the most part be placed. Their general spirit we may characterize as rationalistic. The Messianic prophecies are divested in great degree of their supernatural character: the Messiah is a man probably of David's house, God's instrument in their national restoration, as David was in the establishment of the kingdom. But his place is subordinate. It is Jehovah who will gather Israel out from among the nations, who will judge them and the heathen, and rebuild Jerusalem and the temple. And after the kingdom has thus been set up, the Son of David appears to reign; but His authority is very limited. His work is of chief importance as preparatory to that of Jehovah which is to follow. The Messianic Kingdom is a part of the present world, and serves to introduce the world to come; the resurrection and judgment follow it, not precede it. Thus the Messiah's kingdom is only a reproduction of the Davidic in an enlarged and higher form.

The conception of the Messiah in the Apocryphal books is also colored by the place given to the law at this period, and by the prevalent notions of legal righteousness. The law He may not change, nor alter any of the original theocratic institutions, but will restore them, and Himself be subject to them. As a diligent student of the law, a truly righteous man, His prayers for the people will be acceptable to God. It is thus only that He can make an atonement for them, obtaining grace from God through the merits of His perfect obedience. Through His prayers the sins of the people will be forgiven them. Thus He becomes their Saviour, obtaining the remission of their sins through His own personal righteousness, and not through any expiatory sacrifice. Being Himself a righteous man after the law, He teaches the people to obey it; and this law continues in force during the Messianic Kingdom.

But there were others who saw in the Messiah a supernatural being, and in His kingdom the beginning of a new and heavenly order, an order not of this world, but to be identified with the world to come. Therefore they thought of the resurrection and judgment to be by Him at His coming, and that He would abide forever. There is in the Apocalyptic books much diversity in the details, but we may say in general that they present a view of the Messiah and His kingdom much more conformable to the utterances of the prophets than that presented in the Apocryphal.

It is evident that the Jews as a people, during the centuries immediately before Christ, looked backward to the restoration of the theocratic rule of Jehovah, as the thing to be chiefly looked for, rather than forward to the Messianic Kingdom. Their sore punishment in the Babylonian captivity, and their oppression under the Persians and the Greeks, had made them realize in a higher degree than ever before that the rule of Jehovah over them was a reality; and the experience of His power and just severity awakened in their breasts a salutary fear of His judgments. They saw that to put the gods of other nations in comparison with Him, and to worship them, was an offence that He would not pardon. He was God alone. To this was also added a higher conception of His character through contrast with the heathen deities. Thus they became more and more strict monotheists, and His law demanded their exact obedience. This exaltation of Jehovah naturally brought with it the exaltation of His rule as distinguished from that of the Messiah.

CHAPTER XXIII.

THE RESURRECTION AND THE JUDGMENT. — THE MESSIANIC KINGDOM AND THE WORLD TO COME.

UPON no points were Jewish beliefs, as reflected in the Apocryphal and Apocalyptic books, more confused than upon the duration of the Messianic Kingdom, and the order of events that should precede and follow it; and especially upon the times of the resurrection and the judgment. It will be well to search out the grounds of this confusion to find, if possible, some data that may give definite and sure results.

As the starting-point of this inquiry, let us recur to the distinction made in the Introduction between the period of redemption and the ages that follow it. That redemption, from its very nature, must come to an end, is obvious. It is a work of God made necessary through man's sin, and has for its end his deliverance; and, when this end is attained as regards all who will be delivered, it ceases. There must come a time on the earth when all shall be obedient to God, and worship Him, and when "death, the last enemy," shall be destroyed; and a period of life and blessedness begin, to which there will be no end. That which distinguishes the redemptive age from that which follows it, lies in this, — that during the former there is moral probation; men are still under trial whether they will repent of sin and obey God or not. But when it is past, probation ceases: the moral state of all men, as good or evil, is fixed and unchangeable. When the work of redemption comes to its end, the final separation of the two classes is made; and they abide forever in the spiritual condition in which they are then found.

It is here, at the end of the redemptive period, that we must place the complete and final separation of the good and the evil. It is plain that it cannot have been before. So long as any are upon trial, God cannot pass sentence upon them determining their eternal destiny. The day of probation must be over before all can be judged. But the time of final judgment is also the time of final resurrection; since, as we are taught by the Lord, all who are in their graves must come forth to stand before Him in judgment. (John v. 28.)

We may now ask, to which of these periods — the redemptive or the post-redemptive — does the Messianic Kingdom belong? Most certainly to the former. As presented to us in the prophets, it is a continuation of the Theocracy under a higher form, but with the same end, — the revelation of God to men, and their salvation. The Messiah is the King under Jehovah, and during this Kingdom probation continues. He sits in David's throne, that He may bring all blessings to His own people, and salvation to the nations. Great as is the prosperity and happiness of the elect people under His rule, they are, however, never spoken of by the prophets as set wholly free from the law of sin and death. Even their most glowing descriptions do not present redemption as completed, death as abolished, and the law of eternal life as ruling in the earth. Men still remain mortal, and are under trial. It is the purpose of God to "create new heavens and earth," and to swallow up death in victory; and the Messianic Kingdom is the stage immediately preparatory to this, and prefiguring it; but, while the Kingdom continues, disobedience is still possible, and death. "There shall be no more thence an infant of days, nor an old man that hath not filled his days: for the child shall die an hundred years old; but the sinner being an hundred years old shall be accursed." (Isa. lxv. 20.) And as individuals may sin and be punished, so we are told that if any left of the nations at that time do not come up year by year to worship the King, the Lord of hosts, at Jerusalem, they shall be punished by the withholding of the rain. (Zech. xiv. 17.) The period of immortality and incorruption follows the Messianic age.

Regarded as redemptive, the Messianic Kingdom cannot be eternal; for this involves in it that the evils from which man is to be redeemed are eternal, and redemption is thus made a work without end; nor could it be followed by any resurrection or judgment. But, being redemptive, it comes to an end. How long it shall continue is determined by God, who sets the times and seasons, and who alone can give light as to the time or manner of its termination. And the question here arises, What light did He give by the Old-Testament prophets upon these points? Did He give them visions of the things to follow the Messianic Kingdom? Do they, in their predictions of the future, speak of the post-redemptive age, — of that eternal order into which all things are to be brought when the work of the Messiah as Redeemer is completed? Without presuming to say what might have been the mind of the Spirit in the prophetic utterances, yet taking them in their obvious meaning, we may doubt whether it was the Divine will that His people should then look beyond the Messianic Kingdom. Upon this would He have their attention fastened. So far as the prophetic vision extends, it beholds a world still in process of redemption. It sees in the future a new heaven and earth, as something to be ultimately realized, but only as begun, not completed. The heavenly and perfect and eternal order follows, in the Divine purpose, the Messianic Kingdom; but it is this Kingdom — the last stage of redemption — which is the great theme of prophecy, and which is ever held up to the people as the goal of their hope.

If we ask why this limitation of prophetic revelation, we may find it in the fact that here, as in all God's revelations respecting the future, He makes known only so much as is needful to show men their present duty, to fill them with hope, and prepare them to be workers together with Him. There is a limitation also in the spiritual capacity of man, which God regards in the revelations of His purpose. His children can know what perfected redemption is, only as they themselves advance toward it, and have part in it, one stage preparing them for the next. The heavenly and immortal order that follows redemption, and which is the consummation of all Divine manifestation, cannot be rightly conceived of till the last preceding stage — the Kingdom period — is reached. When His children have been made partakers of the glory of the Kingdom, then will they be able to apprehend the nature of the higher and eternal glory that shall follow. We may therefore say that the prophets do not divide the future, as then lying before them, into the two great periods, redemptive and post-redemptive; their division is that of pre-Messianic and Messianic, — the time before the Messianic Kingdom, and the Kingdom itself. The former continues till the Messiah appears as King to rule for Jehovah, and the end of the pre-Messianic time is defined by the setting up of the Messianic Kingdom; and to this Kingdom no end is assigned, for it was not God's will then to make known what should follow it.

As there is frequent mention of a resurrection and judgment in the Old-Testament prophets, we may here ask to what time in the order of the Divine actings they refer them? As has been said, the final resurrection and judgment must be at the end of redemption; and, as the Messianic Kingdom is redemptive, they cannot be till that kingdom comes to its end. The last separation of the good and the evil is not made till probation ceases. The resurrection and judgment of which the prophets speak, must therefore be placed at the beginning of the Kingdom; they are the initial acts of the Messiah in His administration of the theocratic rule, and must, from their relation to the Kingdom, be partial; universal resurrection and judgment cannot be till its close. But of such close the prophets make no mention. Their farthest vision beholds the children of Israel still enjoying the blessings of the Messianic Kingdom. (Isa. lx.; lxv. 18–23; Joel iii. 20; Amos ix. 14; Ps. lxxii; Ezek. xxxvii. 21–28.)

But it may be asked, if the prophets speak of the Kingdom of the Messiah as without end, how did some of the later Jews come to believe that it would be of limited, and as some said, of brief duration? As we have seen, the conception of the kingdom must be closely connected with the conception of the King. If the words of the prophets respecting Him were not understood, if He were not seen to be more than man, then His Kingdom must be essentially an earthly kingdom; and His administration, however righteous and full of blessing, come at some time to an end. It could not be the final and unchangeable period, but preparatory to it; beyond the Messianic Kingdom must be that of Jehovah. To Him as the eternal God belongs all rule, and His Kingdom must be without end. The real question, therefore, for the Jews was this: What is to be the relation of the Messiah to Jehovah? Is He to be forever His King, the Ruler for Him without end? Or is the relation temporary, as with all the kings before Him; and the Messianic administration after a time, perhaps a very long time, to cease?

We are now prepared to see clearly the difficulty which presented itself to the Jewish students of the prophets in the time preceding the Lord's advent. It was primarily as to the duration of the Messianic Kingdom. On the one hand, there is no prophetic mention of a post-Messianic period, no intimation that the kingdom of Messiah will end, but on the contrary, express declarations that it will be without end. (Isa. ix. 7, Dan. vii. 13–14.) Yet, on the other hand, it was obvious to the thoughtful that the Messianic Kingdom was a stage of redemption, and as such was not itself the final and perfect order, but preparatory to it, and therefore must be limited in time. And as to the person of the Messiah, if the kingdom was limited in time, was not also His life? Or, if not mortal, did not His special relation to Jehovah as His King cease? Those who had most spiritual discernment as to the Divine purpose, might well have been perplexed as they meditated upon these things; nor is it strange that the more rationalistic should have interpreted the predictions of the prophets respecting the Messianic Kingdom, as poetical descriptions never to be realized. Doubtless the time would come, it was said, when the nation would regain its independence, and a son of David sit on the throne, and a period of great prosperity follow. But this was all that the prophets had promised. Jehovah alone was the King, and His kingdom would never pass away.

Thus we may see how, upon the faith of many, the Messianic Kingdom as portrayed in the prophets lost its hold; and as the years went on, and the historic conditions became more and more unfavorable, the fulfillment of the Messianic predictions seemed more and more improbable. Gradually less and less importance was attached to the Messiah and His reign. The silence respecting Him in the Apocryphal books has been noticed; it is Jehovah who raises the dead, and who sits in judgment. Yet it is plain from the words of the people in our Lord's day, that the expectation of a Messiah who should abide forever was still general. "The people answered Him, We have heard out of the law that the Christ abideth for ever;" and this involved a like duration of His kingdom. We may probably say of the larger part of the Jews for many years before the Lord came, that their conceptions of the future were very indefinite, both as to the purpose and nature of the Messiah's reign, and as to its duration.

If the Messianic Kingdom, compared with the age to follow, was relatively of so little importance as some said, where then were the resurrection and judgment spoken of by the prophets to be placed? Would they precede or follow the Messianic Kingdom? The later Jewish writers who speak of a resurrection at all, accept the words of the prophets, and place it before the Kingdom; others are silent as to a resurrection, though they speak of "the day of God," and of national judgment. It was undoubtedly the popular belief, that there would be at the appearing of the Messiah a resurrection of the just, embracing the faithful departed of Israel, and probably also the earlier patriarchs; whether any of the wicked would then be raised for punishment was uncertain. In Daniel only is mention made, as his words are generally understood, of a resurrection of the wicked, but of a part only. (xii. 2.) It was not apparently ever a Jewish belief that there would be, either before or after the Messianic Kingdom, an universal resurrection embracing the dead of all ages and races, but rather that the wicked dead would remain in sheol: in what condition, whether of positive punishment or of semi-conscious misery, was not known; some seem to have thought of annihilation as possible.

With the Jewish conceptions of disembodied life, we are not here concerned. This life may be considered in itself as a mode of being either good or evil, or in its relation to the Messianic Kingdom. As regards the former, there was in the silence of the Scriptures room for great variety of speculation; and the terms Paradise, Gehenna, Eden, Abraham's bosom, designations of differing conditions of disembodied life, began to be familiarly used. But these were all provisional states or places, and were to cease, except perhaps Gehenna, at the resurrection.

Thus we find that before the Lord's advent, there had gradually grown up the conception of three distinct periods as embraced in the Divine actings, — the pre-Messianic, the Messianic, and the post-Messianic. At the end of the first, according to the more general belief, were the resurrection and judgment of the just; at the end of the second, the resurrection of the unjust, in whole or in part. But how the post-Messianic period differed from the Messianic, and what was the place of the Messiah in it, was all in obscurity. Nor was this obscurity removed till the purpose of God was made known by His actings in His Son.

It was reserved to the apostles, after the Lord had ascended to heaven, to give the simple solution of questions so perplexing to the Jews. When the fitting time had come, St. Paul brought clearly to light the distinction of the redemptive and post-redemptive periods. (1 Cor. xv. 24-28.) The Messiah must reign till He hath put all things under His feet, and then shall He give up the Kingdom to the Father. Having completed redemption, He gives up His office as Redeemer, and the heavenly and eternal order begins. Thus the Messianic Kingdom and the work of redemption end together. Now follows the post-redemptive or post-Messianic age.

But what place in the Divine economy has the Messiah after He has given up the Kingdom to the Father? This question the Jews could not answer. Until the dignity of His person as the Incarnate Son was known, it could not be known that He would continue forever Jehovah's King, the Lord over all. But this once declared, it was easy to see how His rule would have a twofold form, first as Messianic King, then as universal Lord. He must first be seated on the throne of His glory to carry on and complete redemption; and when all things are subdued under Him, and death, the last enemy, is destroyed, then a new period will begin, which is without end, when He will be the Ruler for God over all the creatures He has made. He gives up the Messianic, or redemptive, Kingdom to the Father because its purpose has been accomplished; but, having established the perfect and unchangeable order, He continues to act as Ruler for the Father forever.

Thus what was full of confusion to the Jews is, through our knowledge of the Incarnation and of the apostles' teaching, made plain to us. We see how there may be the three periods, the pre-Messianic, the Messianic, and the post-Messianic; and the relation of these to each other. The pre-Messianic and Messianic are both redemptive, and the Old-Testament prophets spake only of these. Beyond the Messianic Kingdom as the last stage of redemption it was not the will of God that His people should then look. The true nature of the post-Messianic age, when redemption had been consummated, could not be made known to them: nor even to the apostles who had seen the Lord after His resurrection, was He pleased to give knowledge of any details. St. Paul simply says that God will then "be all in all." It would be both presumptuous, and foreign to our purpose, to attempt to explain these words; but they seem to point to a closer unity with God, into which the redeemed are brought through Christ, and a higher manifestation of His life in them; a full realization of His prayer, "As thou, Father, art in me, and I in thee, that they also may be one in us. . . . I in them, and thou in me, that they may be made perfect in one."

It is now easy, also, to see the true place of the resurrection and judgment of which the Old-Testament prophets speak. Out of the Messianic Kingdom, "all things that offend, and them that do iniquity," must be gathered. There is first the separation of the good and the evil, and then their respective awards; and this is "the great day of the Lord." This is done when the kingdom is set up. Of the judgments then to be inflicted upon the disobedient people, and upon the nations, the prophets are full; and of these there will be mention in a later chapter. It is enough to say in general that the Psalmist's words will then be fulfilled: "The Lord hath made Himself known; He hath executed judgment. . . . The wicked shall return to sheol, even all the nations that forget God." (Ps. ix., Rev. Ver.) And as the wicked are then cut off from the earth, so will the Messiah, who is Himself a man raised from the dead, call from their graves all whom He will. Those who are His helpers in the administration of the kingdom — His kings and priests — must be like Him in immortality and incorruption. Thus is accomplished at the beginning of the Messianic age the partial resurrection and judgment spoken of by the prophets. At the end of the Kingdom, of which end they do not speak, when the last stage of redemption is completed, all who are in their graves come forth to judgment.

It is thus through the teaching of the apostles, resting on the dignity of the Messiah's person as the Incarnate Son, and on the immortality and glory into which He admits those whom He counts worthy, that the Messianic Kingdom is restored to the high place it occupied in the prophets. The Spirit of God in them did not exalt it beyond its due measure. It is indeed limited in time, because it is redemptive in its nature, and for the same reason it is not the perfect order; but it is a new revelation of God in Jesus Christ; for it shows forth in the resurrection of the faithful the first-fruits of the life of the Risen One. It is the time when the righteousness and the grace of God are manifested to all nations, and when all the earth is at rest and peace. We may not overestimate it nor disparage it, but give it the place it holds in the Divine order. In it the work of new creation, already begun in the Risen One, will be carried forward in those who shall be changed into His likeness; and foretastes be given of the glory to be revealed when all things are made new. (Rev. xx. i. 5.)

We have still to consider the terms, "this world," or "this age," and "the world to come," or "age to come." These terms are not prophetical, but came into use after the exile, and became very familiar to the later Jews. Says Lightfoot, "The distinction of this world and the world to come is found in almost every page of the Rabbins." The primary meaning of these terms was to designate the two successive forms of the Theocracy, the pre-Messianic and the Messianic. "This world" is the present condition of things, looked at especially on its evil side. The misery of the people during and after the exile gave to it the secondary meaning of suffering and injustice, a period of oppression and misery. Contrasted with this was the future Messianic Kingdom as foretold by the prophets, — a period of prosperity, of independence, of righteousness and peace. Thus the two worlds, or ages, are not only successive in time, but in strongest moral contrast. " This world," especially in its last days, is full of disorder and wickedness; but in "the world to come" will be obedience and holiness. Thus "the world to come" became the general designation for the Messianic Kingdom.

Gradually, however, these terms underwent a change of their meaning. As the Messianic Kingdom began to be thought of as of limited duration, and was divested of its supernatural features, and regarded as of comparative unimportance, it began to be spoken of as a part of "this world," — its closing period; and "the world to come," as the post-Messianic Age, or the eternal Kingdom of Jehovah. But there does not appear to have been any uniformity of usage among the Rabbins; the usage in the Gospels will be later considered. The expression, "the last days," or "afterhood" of the days, or "afterpart" of the days, is used in the prophets of the last period of the pre-Messianic time, or of "this world," — that immediately preceding the setting up of the Messianic Kingdom. At a later day, and probably not till after the Christian era, when the Messianic hope had almost failed among the Jews, and the blessed existence of the individual soul after death had become of chief importance to the scattered and desponding exiles, the phrase "the world to come" began to be applied to the disembodied state. It was that condition into which souls entered at death. This was a great departure from its original significance; for the division of the two worlds, or ages, is not one of transition in individual existence, — from the embodied to the disembodied, — but of periods of time in the historical actings of God which embrace all men alike. Neither by the Lord nor His apostles is the condition of the separated soul called "the world to come."

This phrase is used in its true meaning in the Nicene creed: "I look for the resurrection of the dead, and the life of the world to come." We attain to this life through resurrection. This is the order in our Lord's words: "I am the Resurrection and the Life."

CHAPTER XXIV.

MESSIANIC BELIEFS IN OUR LORD'S DAY AS SET FORTH IN THE GOSPELS.

LET us now inquire what were the Messianic beliefs current among the Jews in the time of our Lord's ministry, so far as they can be learned from the Gospels. And the inquiry embraces two points: first, their beliefs respecting the person of the Messiah; second, their beliefs respecting His work. A brief consideration of the names given Him will help us as to both these points.

It should first be noted that there was at this time a wide-spread expectation among all classes that the Messiah would soon come. It may be that this was awakened by the new relation into which the nation was brought by its subjection to the Romans, regarded as a fulfillment of Daniel's prophecy. And the appointment of Herod, an Edomite, to rule over them, naturally recalled to mind the promises respecting the Messiah. But we may rather refer this expectation to the working of the Spirit of God upon the national mind, preparing the people for the work He was about to do. Thus we are told that when the Baptist began his ministry, "the people were in expectation, and all men mused in their hearts of John, whether he were the Christ or not." (Luke iii. 15.)

The designations of the promised Redeemer as found in the Gospels, are, " The Messiah " or " The Christ,"—

both terms meaning "The Anointed,"—"The Son of David," "The King of the Jews," "The Son of God," "He that should come," or "The Coming One," "The Prophet," and "The Saviour of the world."

When the Jews sent the deputation of priests and Levites to ask the Baptist, "Who art thou?" he replied, "I am not the Christ." "Why baptizest thou, then, if thou art not the Christ?" Andrew said to his brother Peter, "We have found the Messias, which is, being interpreted, the Christ." At Peter's second confession he said, "Thou art the Christ, the Son of the living God." When Jesus was at Jerusalem at a feast, and taught, the people said, "Do the rulers know indeed that this is the very Christ? . . . When the Christ cometh, no man knoweth whence He is. . . . When the Christ cometh, will He do more miracles? . . . Others said, This is the Christ; but some said, Shall the Christ come out of Galilee? Hath not the Scripture said that the Christ cometh of the seed of David?" "The Jews had agreed that if any man did confess that He was the Christ, he should be put out of the synagogue." On one occasion they said, "If thou be the Christ, tell us plainly." Martha said, "I believe that thou art the Christ, the Son of God, which should come into the world." The Jews at Jerusalem said, "We have heard out of our law that the Christ abideth for ever." At the Lord's trial the high priest said, "I adjure thee by the living God, that thou tell us whether thou be the Christ, the Son of God." One of the points in the accusation before Pilate was, "that He said that He Himself is Christ, a King." The rulers deriding Him on the cross, said, "Let Him save Himself if He be the Christ, the chosen of God." In the same spirit, the malefactor says, "If thou be the Christ, save thyself and us."

Not only to the Jews was this title familiar, but to the Samaritans also. Thus the Samaritan woman said, "I know that Messias cometh, which is called Christ." (John iv. 25, also verse 29.) And the Samaritans said, "We know that this is indeed the Christ." This term was also used by those possessed of devils. "Devils came out of many, crying out and saying, "Thou art the Christ, the Son of God, . . . for they knew that He was the Christ."

Another title in common use was "The Son of David." On the healing of one possessed, the people were amazed, and said, "Is this the Son of David?" Thus was He addressed by the Syro-Phœnician woman: "O Lord, Son of David." And in like manner by the blind men: "Have mercy on us, O Lord, Son of David." The multitude on His entry into Jerusalem cried, "Hosanna to the Son of David." The Lord in a question to the Pharisees gives the two designations, — "How say they that the Christ is David's Son?"

Equally common was the title "Son of God." After a storm on the Sea of Galilee, His disciples said, "Of a truth, thou art the Son of God." When hanging on the cross, those that passed by said, "If thou be the Son of God, come down from the cross." The centurion said, "Truly this was the Son of God." Unclean spirits fell down before Him, and cried, saying, "Thou art the Son of God." In the wilderness He was so addressed by the tempter, "If thou be the Son of God." At His trial the judges asked, "Art thou the Son of God?" and demanded of Pilate His death, because "He made Himself the Son of God." This name is several times used in union with that of the Christ. Thus, in the adjuration of the high priest, "Tell us whether thou be the Christ, the Son of God." In the confession of Peter, "Thou art the Christ, the Son of the living God." In the confession of Martha, "I believe that thou art the Christ, the son of God."

The name "King of the Jews" is less frequently found. It was used by the Magi: "Where is He that is born King of the Jews?" And by Pilate: "Art thou the King of the Jews?" Pilate used it also in the inscription on the cross, "This is Jesus, the King of the Jews." At His entry into Jerusalem, some cried, saying, "Blessed be the King that cometh in the name of the Lord." The chief priests, mocking Him on the cross, said, "If He be the King of Israel, let Him come down from the cross." It is sometimes joined with other names. Nathaniel said, "Thou art the Son of God, thou art the King of Israel." The Jews accused Him before Pilate that He affirmed "Himself to be Christ, a King."

The name of "Son of man," though continually used by the Lord of Himself, was not used by others, and was strange to the popular ear. On one occasion the people said, "How sayest thou, the Son of man must be lifted up? Who is this Son of man?" The name "He that should come," or "the Coming One," was used by the Baptist: "Art thou He that should come?" And the Lord said, "Blessed is He that cometh in the name of the Lord." And the people said at the entry into Jerusalem, "Blessed is the King of Israel, that cometh in the name of the Lord."

Apparently it was believed that the Christ would be also a "Prophet;" but in some instances the two terms are contrasted. When the deputation to the Baptist asked Him "if he were the Christ, or Elias, or that prophet," they must have intended to make a distinction. When the Lord asked the disciples, "Whom do men say that I am?" they replied, "Some say, John the Baptist; some, Elias; others, Jeremias, or one of the prophets." (So Herod also, Matt. xiv. 2.) And in a discussion of the Jews respecting Him, some said, "This is the prophet; others said, This is the Christ." Yet in some cases the title prophet is clearly a Messianic designation. After the miracle of the feeding of the multitude, those present said, "This is of a truth that prophet that should come into the world;" and they desired "to take Him by force, and make Him a King." At the entry into Jerusalem, the multitude said, "This is Jesus the prophet of Nazareth of Galilee." The disciples at Emmaus spoke of "Jesus of Nazareth, which was a prophet mighty in word and deed before God, ... and we trusted that it had been He that should have redeemed Israel." The name of "Saviour of the world" was given Him only once, and, what is most remarkable, by a Samaritan woman. (John iv. 42.)

It is probable that these names were used with much indefiniteness, but some general conclusions can be drawn from them as to the current Messianic beliefs in regard to His person. That of "Son of God" may have indicated a Divine origin and a supernatural character, a Sonship in kind unlike all other; yet it may be questioned whether it had in fact more than a theocratic signification, indicating one who was pre-eminently the Son, the first and chief among the sons of God. In this sense it is equivalent to prince or ruler of His children.

The name "Anointed," — the Messiah, — the Christ, — applied both to the high priest and the king, pointed to Him as one who should receive the fullness of the Spirit in fulfillment of Isaiah, "And the Spirit of the Lord shall rest upon Him." (xi. 2.)

The name "Son of David" proves that faith in the Davidic covenant had not failed, and that one of Jesse's line was expected to re-establish the kingdom, and be King over Israel. The scribes and priests agreed in their answer to Herod, that He should be born at Bethlehem, David's city. The people when discussing His birthplace said, "Hath not the Scripture said, that the Christ cometh of the seed of David, and out of the town of Bethlehem, where David was?" It is not in contradiction to this belief that others said, "We know this man, whence he is; but when the Christ cometh, no man knoweth whence He is." In this declaration of ignorance as to the origin of the Messiah, we find an echo of the utterances of the Book of Enoch respecting Him as "the concealed One." This would not exclude His birth at Bethlehem, but merely affirmed that at His appearing as a deliverer, no one would know whence He came.

The name "Son of man" as used by the Lord of Himself, declared both the reality and the fullness of His humanity, One in whom all men found their representative, and who could be the Lord and Head over all. The name "Prophet" indicated One who should express the mind of God, and be the organ for the utterance of all His will, as was Moses of old. It was clearly the popular belief that the Christ would not only be king, but also prophet.

From all this we may draw the general conclusion that the Jews as represented in the Gospels were looking for one to come of the house of David, that He would be a man endowed with prophetic and miraculous powers, but not a supernatural being.

We note, second, the Jewish beliefs as to the work of the Messiah. It is said of Anna the prophetess, that "she spake of the child to all them who looked for redemption in Jerusalem." (Luke ii. 38.) And of the two disciples at Emmaus, that they "trusted that it had been He that should have redeemed Israel." (Luke xxiv. 21.) What were the elements that entered into the conception of this redemption?

It cannot be doubted that the first and most prominent element in the popular mind was national deliverance. As a people specially called to the service of God, freedom to do His will was an indispensable condition of such service. To be under the bondage of the heathen was wholly inconsistent with Jehovah's rule over them. And such deliverance had been continually held up by the prophets as a work to be effected by Jehovah or by the Messiah: "A King shall reign and prosper, and shall execute judgment and justice in the earth. In His days Judah shall be saved, and Israel shall dwell safely." (Jer. xxiii. 5, etc.)

But such deliverance from the yoke of their oppressors, and the restoration of national independence and unity, were not all that was embraced in the promised redemption: the higher element was salvation from sin. And all who had any spiritual perception of their covenant relations to Jehovah, knew that there must first be restoration to His favor; and that this could be only when the people manifested a spirit of repentance, and readiness to fulfill all the obligations imposed on them by the covenant. All who had eyes to see the departure of the people from God's ways, and the greatness of their transgressions, knew that they must be morally prepared for their deliverance: they must first be cleansed from the guilt of sin. But how this would be effected by the Messiah, they had very indistinct apprehensions. Others, and the larger part, who had no sense of the national transgressions, and of their own spiritual condition, and felt no need of cleansing, but trusted in the works of the law, thought only of political deliverance to be effected by some great acts of Divine power in the destruction of their enemies, — mighty judgments executed by the Son of David. As the people of the covenant, all were to be regarded as holy; and a separation by the Messiah of the evil from the good was apparently not thought of as necessary or possible.

We must distinguish here between the opinions of the people, and the knowledge given through the words of the angels and through the utterances of those inspired by the Spirit. The angel who announced to Zacharias the birth of a son, declared that he should "turn many of the children of Israel to the Lord;" and should fulfill what was spoken of Elias, "to turn the hearts of the fathers to the children, and the disobedient to the wisdom of the just, to make ready a people prepared for the Lord." The angel sent to the Virgin Mary declared that to her Son "the Lord would give the throne of His father David, and that He should reign over the house of Jacob for ever, and of His kingdom there should be no end." To Joseph an angel declared that the name of the Virgin's Son should "be called Jesus, for He shall save His people from their sins." To the shepherds the angel said, " Unto you is born in the city of David a Saviour, which is Christ the Lord." Additional light as to the Divine purpose in the Messiah was given also through the utterances of the Spirit. Mary refers to His birth as the beginning of the fulfillment of the promises to Israel: "He hath holpen His servant Israel in remembrance of His mercy, as He spake to our fathers, to Abraham, and to His seed for ever." Zacharias prophesied wholly in the manner of the Old-Testament prophets: "Blessed be the Lord God of Israel; for He hath visited and redeemed His people, and hath raised up an horn of salvation for us in the house of His servant David." This redemption was primarily a national one, as appears from what follows: "that we should be saved from our enemies, and from the hand of all that hate us, . . . that we, being delivered out of the hand of our enemies, might serve Him without fear." But as a condition of this deliverance was the remission of sins. The Baptist should go before Him and prepare His ways, "to give knowledge of salvation unto His people in the remission of their sins."

The words of the Baptist, "Behold the Lamb of God, which taketh away the sin of the world," were doubtless the special utterance of the Spirit, and not the expression of general belief; and showed the close spiritual relation of his own preparatory work of baptism to that to be wrought by Him who should bear the iniquities of all. How far the Baptist understood his own words, and foresaw the cross and the resurrection, we need not ask. (Matt. xi. 2, etc.)

CHAPTER XXV.

THE LORD'S OWN TEACHINGS RESPECTING HIS MESSIANIC WORK.

It is a point of deep interest to know how far the Lord in His own teachings confirmed or corrected the prevalent Messianic beliefs. A part of these were already verified in His person;. for He was of the house of David, and born in Bethlehem, and was recognized by the people as a prophet, and a worker of miracles. He had been preceded by one sent of God to prepare His way. He was, also, in a sense in which they knew it not, the Son of God. But how far did He in His teachings confirm the general beliefs respecting the Messianic Kingdom, and His own functions as the Messiah?

These teachings may be best arranged under distinct heads.

(*a*) That there was to be such a kingdom, He taught by His preaching "the gospel of the kingdom," and announcing that it was "at hand." "The time is fulfilled, and the kingdom of God is at hand." (Mark i. 15.)

(*b*) It was His kingdom, the Messianic Kingdom, that of the Son as distinguished from the Theocracy, or kingdom of the Father. "I appoint unto you a kingdom, as my Father hath appointed unto me; that ye may eat and drink at my table in my kingdom." (Luke xxii. 29, 30.) "My kingdom is not of this world. . . . Now is my kingdom not from hence." (John xviii. 36.)

But although His kingdom became administered by Him, yet was it the kingdom of God, He ruling in it with delegated authority. "All power" — authority — "is given unto me in heaven and in earth." (Matt. xxviii. 18.) He speaks of it as both His kingdom and that of the Father. (Matt. xiii. 41-43.)

(c) This kingdom was future, and not to be set up till the Lord should return from heaven. "When the Son of man shall come in His glory, and all the holy angels with Him, then shall He sit upon the throne of His glory." (Matt. xxv. 31.) He must depart, and go to the Father, and be invested with authority, and at His return He would establish His kingdom. "A certain nobleman went into a far country to receive for himself a kingdom, and to return. . . . And it came to pass that when he was returned, having received the kingdom." (Luke xix. 12. See Matt. xvi. 27.)

(d) He identifies His kingdom with "the world to come." His coming should be at the end of "this world," or age, and at the beginning of the new. During His absence, the tares and wheat were to grow together; the harvest would be at the end of the world. "The harvest is the end of the world. . . . As the tares are gathered and burned in the fire, so shall it be at the end of this world." (Matt. xiii. 39.) The same is taught also in the parable of the net. (Verse 49.) Hence His disciples asked Him, "What shall be the sign of thy coming, and of the end of the world?" (Matt. xxiv. 3.)

(e) During the whole period of His absence, there should be troubles and trials for His people. "If the world hate you, ye know that it hated me before it hated you. . . . Because ye are not of the world, but I have chosen you out of the world, therefore the world hateth you. . . . The servant is not greater than his lord. If they have persecuted me, they will also persecute you. . . . They shall put you out of the synagogues: yea, the time cometh, that whosoever killeth you will think that he doeth God service." (John xv. 18.) So, also, there would be disturbances in society, and convulsions in nature, wars and rumors of wars, and famines and pestilences and earthquakes. "All these are the beginning of sorrows,"—of the "birth-throes" of the Messianic Kingdom.

(*f*) Immediately before His coming should be a time of "great tribulation," marked by many physical signs in the sun, moon, and stars; "the powers of the heavens shall be shaken." (Matt. xxiv. 29.) Then shall be great distress and perplexity among the nations, and the Jews be sorely oppressed by their enemies, and tempted by false prophets and false Christs, and many shall be led away and perish. (Luke xxi. 24.) At this time should Elias be sent to prepare a people for the Lord. (Matt. xvii. 11.) "And the Son of man shall be seen coming in a cloud with power and great glory," to deliver His people, and to punish their enemies.

(*g*) At His coming He will enter upon His functions as the Judge, and will separate between the good and the evil, the tares and the wheat. "The Son of man shall come in the glory of His Father with His angels; and then He shall reward every man according to his works." (Matt. xiii. 41, 42; xvi. 27.) He will judge the nations according as they have treated His people. "Before Him shall be gathered all nations: and He shall separate them one from another, as a shepherd divideth his sheep from the goats." (Matt. xxv. 32.) Those who have rejected His rule will be destroyed. "Those mine enemies which would not that I should reign over them, bring hither, and slay them before me." (Luke xix. 27.) The unfaithful of the covenant people will be cast out. "The children of the kingdom shall be cast out into outer darkness." (Matt. viii. 12.)

(*h*) In His kingdom the believing Gentiles will have part. "Many shall come from the east and west, and shall sit down with Abraham, and Isaac, and Jacob, in the kingdom of heaven." (Matt. viii. 11.)

(*i*) Then will be the resurrection of the holy dead, or of the just. "This is the will of Him that sent me, that every one which seeth the Son, and believeth on Him, may have everlasting life: and I will raise him up at the last day." (John vi. 40.) This resurrection is at the end of this age, and those raised from the dead enter into the blessings of the world to come. "They which shall be accounted worthy to obtain that world, and the resurrection from the dead, . . . are the children of God, being the children of the resurrection." (Luke xx. 35.) This resurrection is partial, and embraces only those "accounted worthy" of such honor.

(*j*) After the resurrection follow the holiness and blessedness of the Messianic Kingdom. Then all the wicked are cast out, and only the righteous are left. "The Son of man shall send forth His angels, and they shall gather out of His kingdom all things that offend, and them which do iniquity, and shall cast them into a furnace of fire. . . . Then shall the righteous shine forth as the sun in the kingdom of their Father." Then these glorified saints, especially the apostles, will be helpers of the Messiah in the administration of His kingdom. "Ye which have followed me, in the regeneration," — restoration, when all things are to be delivered from their present bondage of corruption, — "when the Son of man shall sit in the throne of His glory, ye also shall sit upon twelve thrones, judging the twelve tribes of Israel." (Matt. xix. 28, xx. 23.) To the servants faithful during His absence, on His return and possession of the kingdom, He gives rewards; one to rule over ten, and another over five cities. (Luke xix. 15.) "I appoint unto you a kingdom, as my Father hath appointed unto me." (Luke xxii. 29, 30.)

Thus, in all these points, — the establishment of the Messianic Kingdom, its administration under one of the house of David, the coming of a forerunner, the judgments attending its introduction, the separation of the holy and unholy among the covenant people, the judgment of the nations and the rule of the Messiah over them, the resurrection of the pious dead, and the bringing in of a new age, "the world to come," — the Lord confirmed the general beliefs.

But although the Lord confirmed in these important points the current Jewish Messianic beliefs, He also in other points corrected them. There was, as we have seen, much doubt as to the official relations of the Messiah to Jehovah, and as to the work to be done by each at the establishment of the Messianic Kingdom, some affirming that the Messiah's part was of very little importance. The Lord early takes occasion to declare that it was given to Himself to do all that the Father would do. The Messiah — the Son — was Jehovah's instrument to work the whole work of redemption. (John v. 19, etc.) "What things soever the Father doeth, these also doeth the Son likewise." But He does all in virtue of authority derived from God. "The Son can do nothing of Himself, but what He seeth the Father do." The Lord illustrates this fullness of power given Him in two particulars, both of highest moment — resurrection and judgment — in regard to which the Jews were much perplexed whether to be done by Jehovah or the Messiah: "For as the Father raiseth up the dead, and quickeneth them; even so the Son quickeneth whom He will. For the Father judgeth no man, but hath committed all judgment unto the Son." And this authority to raise the dead and to execute judgment was without limitation: "All judgment" was committed unto Him. Not only would He raise the righteous dead, but the wicked also of all generations: "All that are in their graves shall hear His voice, and shall come forth." Thus the Lord corrected the unworthy notions of the office of the Messiah then prevalent, as if His place and work were of little importance; and taught them that He was to be honored even as Jehovah is honored. (Verse 23.) Nor does He anywhere give any intimation that His kingdom was to be limited in duration.

Another point was His relation to the law. Would He be subject to it and obey it, or would He change and annul it? His words were explicit: "Think not I am come to destroy the law. I am not come to destroy, but to fulfill." (Matt. v. 17.) Yet He asserts His authority to set aside all traditions that made it vain or violated its spirit. He said on one occasion, "The Son of man is Lord also of the Sabbath." (Mark ii. 28.) He claimed, also, the authority to forgive sins, which the scribes thought to be the prerogative of God alone, and accounted blasphemy. (Mark ii. 5.) The observance of the law could not bring them to God: "No man cometh to the Father but by me." "I am the Way and the Truth."

But the Lord opened to them a wholly new field of Messianic truth when He taught them of the mystery of His Person, and of the prerogative given Him to be the source of the new and eternal life: "For as the Father hath life in Himself, so hath He given to the Son to have life in Himself." To be the last Adam, and to give His life to men,—a new and higher form of life,—was His high dignity. Therefore He said of

Himself, "I am the Life. He that believeth on me hath eternal life." And the Author of this life must Himself nourish it. "I am the Bread of Life." "The Bread of God is He which cometh down from heaven, and giveth life unto the world." "I am the Resurrection and the Life." "He that believeth on me hath eternal life." "Whoso eateth my flesh, and drinketh my blood, hath eternal life; and I will raise him up at the last day."

Thus the Lord confirmed the Jewish beliefs respecting the Messiah and His work in some chief particulars, corrected them in others, and brought forth some distinctively new. Through the revelation of His Divine personality as the Incarnate Son, the whole Messianic conception was so enlarged and exalted that the most majestic predictions of the prophets fall far short of the reality of the glory of His Kingdom.

It will be observed that the Lord says little respecting the national restoration of the covenant people, and the re-union of the tribes, so often and emphatically declared by the prophets. But His words respecting the approaching destruction of Jerusalem, and its treading down, and the captivity of the people until "the times of the Gentiles are fulfilled," imply clearly that when they are fulfilled, it will be rebuilt and they re-gathered. And if His words respecting the rule of the apostles over the twelve tribes are to be taken in their literal sense, as is most probable, they are a confirmation of the prophetic promises. (Matt. xix. 28; Luke xxi. 20–28, xxii. 28.) But this comparative silence is easily explained from the relation in which He stood to them during His ministry among them. He came as their Messiah, and they were put on trial whether they would receive Him or reject Him. If they rejected Him, a new stage of Divine judgment must come upon them; a new destruction of their city and temple, and a new dispersion. It was not till they had clearly manifested their hatred to Him, and near the end of His ministry, that the Lord declared to them their impending overthrow, and that "their house should be left unto them desolate." But this desolation was not to be forever. The time would come when, brought to repentance, they should say, "Blessed is He that cometh in the name of the Lord." In foresight of their continued disobedience, and fresh punishment, He was about to found the Church, — a new Election gathered from both Jews and Gentiles, — and this should be His instrument during His absence of proclaiming and ministering the truth and grace of God to the world. As a nation they had rejected Him, and the punishment about to come upon them was national. What should be the future of the nation when it should repent, what further purpose of God was to be fulfilled by it, was fully declared in the Old-Testament prophets. Respecting this the Lord was silent, for there was no need that He should speak.

To explain the special position of His Church yet to be gathered, and its relation to the Jewish nation, and their respective places in His kingdom, was not a part of the Lord's teaching. When the Church had been established by the descent of the Holy Ghost at Pentecost, then the Jews that believed could understand, what they could not have understood before, that the purpose of God embraced another election taken from all nations; and that in it larger grace would be ministered to those believing than could be given under the institutions of Moses. To gather this election, to educate it, and prepare it for its high calling, was God's present work, — a work to be continued during the Messiah's absence. And this accomplished, — the fullness of the Gentiles being brought in, — then would "come the Deliverer out of Sion, and turn away ungodliness from Jacob." It was by the actings of God in their punishment and in the Christian election, that the Jews must come to the right apprehension of His purpose.

II.

THE REVELATIONS OF GOD TO MEN IN THE CHRISTIAN CHURCH.

CHAPTER I.

THE MESSIAH IN HEAVEN.

THE Messiah came as the prophets had foretold. He was of the house of David, son of a virgin, born at Bethlehem; but His people knew Him not. He was rejected and crucified; He rose from the dead and ascended into heaven. This departure from the earth, and continued existence in heaven, was something the Jews had not known or anticipated, although intimated in prophecy; but it was a fact of highest moment, and we must ask ourselves how it bore on the further work of redemption. How was this work now to be carried on? In what relation did He, thus absent, stand to the elect people, and how could He fulfill to them the promises respecting the Messianic Kingdom? How could He, invisible, reveal God unto the nations? How could He Himself be made known unto the world?

To answer these questions, we must consider the threefold relations into which the Messiah was brought at His ascension, — first, to Jehovah; second, to the Jewish people; third, to the nations.

First, His relation to Jehovah. He was the "Word with God" before the worlds were made; as "the Word made flesh" had He suffered on earth; but now as the Son of man, raised from the dead, immortal and glorified, He is seated at His right hand, and made Lord over all. As the Anointed One, — the Messiah, — the Christ, — in whom is the fullness of the Spirit, He is the perfect instrument for the further execution of the Divine purpose in the earth, both to the Jews and to the Gentiles. Made after the power of an endless life, He is prepared to fulfill the ministry of the Great High Priest, and to baptize with the Holy Ghost; and to Him all authority is given. (Acts ii. 33.) Now is fulfilled in Him what is prophetically written in the Psalms: "I have set my King on my holy hill of Sion." "Sit thou at my right hand till I have made thy foes thy footstool. . . . Thou art a Priest for ever after the order of Melchizedek." (Ps. ii., cx.; Heb. vii. 16, 17; viii. 1, etc.; Eph. i. 20.)

Thus anointed and glorified, He is prepared to fulfill the whole purpose of God in redemption. And this purpose now enters upon a new stage, the nature of which is to be carefully noted as determined by the relation into which He is brought, first to the Jews, second to the Gentiles.

Abraham was called, that in his seed all nations of the earth might be blessed. But when the promised Seed "came unto His own, His own received Him not." And after His ascension He was again rejected by them in the person of His apostles, to whom He had said, "He that receiveth you, receiveth me," and whose testimony to Him they refused to hear. (Acts xiii. 45, 46.) Their punishment came upon them speedily in the destruction of their city and temple by the Romans, and the dispersion of the people. Thus it became impossible that He could stand to them in the relation of their King, for they had no national existence, and could render to Him no national obedience. He could not manifest Himself to the nations as the Son of David, sitting upon Jehovah's throne, and ruling over them as a nation.

To understand the position of the Jews in this new dispersion, and their relations to the Messiah, we must note two things: First, That they did not cease to be the covenant people. Their position, after the destruction of Jerusalem by the Romans, was in its essential elements the same as after its destruction by the Babylonians, only that they were now dispersed among all nations; and that this dispersion was not for years, but for centuries. As the sin was greater, so the punishment was more severe. Second, As the Messiah had come, and had been rejected by them, their restoration to God's favor could not be till they had repented and confessed their grievous sin, and sought forgiveness in His name. (Zech. xii. 10, etc.) Only through Him could they have access to His Father, and He as the High Priest must cleanse them from their iniquities, and send down upon them His Spirit. Continuing unrepentant, they must abide in dispersion. But we must consider more particularly the purpose of God in this new dispersion of His people, and especially its bearing on the Gentiles. It is the apostle Paul who has spoken most fully on this point in his Epistle to the Romans, and we must therefore carefully note his reasonings and conclusions. (Chaps. ix., x., xi.)

The apostle declares that his "heart's desire and prayer to God for Israel is, that they might be saved." It is generally admitted that by Israel is meant the Jewish nation as such; and that by "salvation" is not meant merely the deliverance of individual souls from eternal death, it has its usual Messianic sense, the salvation of the nation. Whether individual Jews after Christ's rejection could be saved from God's wrath by faith in the cross, was not in question, for it was not doubted. The point before the apostle was, whether God had cast away His people, the covenant people, so that they no longer stood in any covenant relation to Him, nor had any claim to the fulfillment of the covenant promises under their King, — the Messiah? It is the fulfillment of these promises that he terms "their salvation," following in this the Old-Testament prophets who make this salvation to be realized in the setting up of the Messianic Kingdom. (Isa. xii. 2, etc.; xlix. 8; lii. 7, 10; Ps. xcviii. 3; Luke i. 69–75.) In the same sense it is used by Peter. (1 Pet. i. 5.) That through their rejection of the Messiah they had put away from them this salvation, and that God's heavy judgment was about to come upon them, are facts the apostle assumes. (Matt. xxiii. 37, etc.) He speaks of their "fall," of their "casting away," of their being "branches broken off." But more than this, he affirms that "through their fall salvation is come unto the Gentiles." What, then, is the connection between the fall of the Jews and the salvation of the Gentiles? How could the exclusion of His ancient people from the place He had given them, bring to the Gentiles any benefit?

We have already abundantly seen that the election of the Jews was to the end that through them all other nations might be brought to the knowledge of God, and be blessed in the Kingdom of His Son. And we cannot doubt that if they had continued in the grace of God, and received their Messiah, this end would have been effected. But from this grace they fell; "they stumbled at the Stone of stumbling." How does this their sin affect the Divine purpose? It but brings out in a more wonderful way God's mercy and wisdom. He so overrules it that "their fall becomes the riches of the world; and their diminishing, the riches of the Gentiles." Now is brought out that mystery "which in other ages was not made known unto the sons of men, . . . that the Gentiles should be fellow-heirs, and of the same body." To be "fellow-heirs" is much more than had been promised by God through the prophets to the nations in the Messianic Kingdom. To be of the same body, is to be lifted up into such relation to the Christ that they are made members of Him. The fall of the Jews as the elect people opened the way for a new election, which through Christ should be brought nearest to God, highest in honor, and be His chief instrument in the further stages of His work. Thus "the fall of the Jews was the riches of the world," because, they failing to answer the end of their election, the Messianic Kingdom was not set up then, and the Gentiles can now become His elect, and being made members of Christ, be partakers in the highest degree of spiritual blessings.

It may be said, to guard against possible misapprehension, that the apostle is not speaking here of the deliverance of individual Gentiles from God's eternal wrath. He does not affirm that if the Jews had not fallen, no Gentile could have escaped everlasting damnation. Because special grace had been given to the Jews, all grace had not been withdrawn from the Gentiles. Nor does He affirm that the Jews must be cast away in order that the Gospel might be preached to the Gentiles. It was the special calling of the Jews to make known their Messiah, and His salvation to all nations; and had they remained faithful, this calling they would have fulfilled, as they are still to fulfill it. (Zech. viii. 22.)

As we are now able to see how the failure of the first

or national election opened the way for the choice of a second — the church — taken from all peoples, we can, also, see how the restoration of the first to its covenant standing may be a source of fresh blessing to the nations, or to all not included in either of the two elections. The second election is but a part, comparatively few, out of the multitudes of the Gentiles, as the Jews were only one out of many nations; and when it is gathered and completed, — the Church made like her Head, — a new stage of Divine activity begins. Then the Jews in the repentant "remnant" are restored to their original relation as the theocratic nation, and God is able to fulfill through them His promises of blessing to all the world. This is the fulfillment of the apostle's words: "If the fall of them be the riches of the world, and the diminishing of them the riches of the Gentiles; how much more their fullness?" Now a part only of the Gentiles are made rich through their membership in the body of Christ; but when "the Deliverer shall come out of Sion, and turn away ungodliness from Jacob," then will all the ends of the earth see the salvation of God. The receiving of the Jews will be "as life from the dead."

Thus the apostle distinctly recognizes God's way of carrying on redemption by elections, first of a nation, then of a body of individuals from all nations, each chosen with reference to its special end. The Jews, though cast off for the time as a people, are still "beloved for the fathers' sake," and are yet to fulfill the purpose of God in them; "for the gifts and calling of God are without repentance." And the Church, made up of both Jews and Gentiles, gathered individually during the time of the Lord's absence through the preaching of the gospel, will also fulfill its functions as the body of Christ; and through both elections, in the day of the Kingdom, will God manifest Himself to all the world.

To the Jews as the covenant people it was due that the Gospel be first preached, and not till they refused to hear was it preached to the Gentiles. (Acts xiii. 46.) Through their persistent disobedience, "the Kingdom of God was now to be taken from them, and given" to others (Matt. xxi. 43), and the Lord's words fulfilled, "Ye shall not see me henceforth, till ye shall say, Blessed is He that cometh in the name of the Lord." But during His absence, all among them who believed on Him might have part in the new election; the Jew in this relation had no advantage over the Gentile. (Gal. iv. 28, etc.) Few comparatively in later generations have believed, the veil is still upon their hearts. They know not that their Messiah is risen and in heaven; but He will manifest Himself to them, and their unbelief, like that of Paul, will vanish away; and like Thomas they will cry, "My Lord and my God."

Having seen how the casting away of the Jews was for the benefit of the Gentiles, we are now to consider the new relation of the latter to the Messiah. In the prophets He had been presented in His special relation to the Jews as their Messiah, and only through them to the nations; but by His work on the cross, and His exaltation into heaven, He was now brought into direct relations with all men. First, by His atoning sacrifice as Son of man, He opened the way for the approach of all to God. Now the gospel of forgiveness could be everywhere preached, to the Gentiles as well as to the Jews, that all might believe and be saved. (Rom. iii. 22.) Thus His relation to men as their Saviour from sin through the cross, was universal. All might come unto Him, and through Him enter into the fullness of the grace of God. Second, as the Risen One, He became the fountain of a new and heavenly life of which all who believed in Him might be made partakers. "Thou art my Son, this day have I begotten thee," was interpreted by the apostles of His being begotten in resurrection. (Acts xiii. 33.) When He ascended and was glorified, He was made the second Adam. (1 Cor. xv. 45.) Humanity in Him then reached its highest condition; no more under the law of sin and of death, but able to receive the fullness of the Spirit, and to be glorified with the glory of God. "The first man is of the earth, earthy; the second Man is the Lord from heaven." As the second Adam, the quickening Spirit, He could give His heavenly life to all who came unto Him in faith. Believing, they were baptized into Him, made members of Him, branches in the Vine. In this gift of a new life there was no difference put between the Jew and the Gentile, bond or free, male or female. All the children of the first Adam might become the children of the Second.

Thus, both as the Crucified One and as the Second Adam, His relations to the world were universal. His sacrifice on the cross was for all. He was "the propitiation for the sins of the whole world." All who sought to be members of Him, were made in regeneration partakers of His life. "Go ye and make disciples of all the nations, baptizing them." And those thus made disciples, without distinction of race or of sex, constituted the new election, the Christian Church. The Messiah exalted into heaven, and thus set free from all local and national bonds, can now be presented to all on the earth as their Saviour and Lord. He died for all; the gospel can be preached unto all. He is the Son of David, but He is more; He is the Son of man.

CHAPTER II.

THE NEW ELECTION, AND ITS CALLING AS THE BODY OF CHRIST.

THE first act after the ascension of the Messiah was the sending of the Holy Ghost, that the Church might be gathered. This new election, taken from among all nations, was to the Jews a matter of great surprise. How far it had been foretold in the prophets, is a point into which we need not here enter. (Isa. lxv. 1.) But if foretold, it had not been comprehended by the elect people as a part of the Divine purpose. (Eph. iii. 6.) The subjection of all nations to the Messiah, and their blessedness under His rule, was one of the most familiar themes of prophecy; but an election from all nations to stand in closer relations to Him, and to be advanced to higher honor in His Kingdom, than themselves, was something as new to them as it was incredible. This subordinate position was more offensive than banishment from their land, and a temporary suspension of the theocratic relation; and is a stone of stumbling even to this day.

The purpose of God in this new election was in general the same as in the election of the Jews, that to its members He might first reveal Himself; and then through them, made like unto His Son, reveal Himself to the world. To this end, the gospel was to be preached to every creature, that whosoever believed might enter into this elect number. As thus individually gathered through the word preached to them, they were brought by regeneration into organic unity. They were made members of Christ, and so members one of another; one Body of which He is the Head.

The term "Body of Christ," so often applied by St. Paul to this election, needs careful consideration if we would understand the place of the Church in the Divine economy of redemption. The body of a man is that material organism through which he stands in relation to things external and material, by which he manifests himself to others, and puts forth his activity. It is a part of himself, and subject to his will. So is it with the Church, the body of Christ. It is composed of those who have been made partakers of His life, and thus are one with Him. They are by the appointment of God, and by the operation of the Spirit, so united and organized that through them the Head can put forth every form of activity, both to gather and to perfect those gathered; and by them to manifest Himself in His glory to all the world. As His body, a part of Himself, and obedient to His will, the instrument of His present actings, by which, though absent, He speaks and works, it testifies that He is living; and though in heaven is carrying forward on the earth the Divine purpose in redemption.

We thus see the peculiar place of the new election as the body of Christ. Its very existence is the proof that He now lives in heaven as its Head. Primarily, we know of His resurrection and ascension through the testimony of the apostles; but to this personal witness there is added that which the Church gives through its existence, its endowments of holiness and power, its ordinances, its teaching, its worship. Regarded merely as a system of abstract doctrine, of religious truth taught by one long since dead, and held only as an intellectual deposit, Christianity might be placed upon the same line as other religions. But the Church is an insoluble enigma. The facts which its history presents cannot be explained if we deny its connection with the Living Head. We have here to do not only with truth, but with life. The phenomena of Christian life everywhere meet us, and these can be explained only by the fact that the Head of the Church is the living Man, Christ Jesus; and that it is His life which is given through divinely appointed channels to its members.

It is here that we meet the great peculiarity of the Church. There is no other religion than the Christian which affirms that its Founder now lives, that its members are baptized into Him, and made partakers of His life. Mohammedanism does not affirm this of Mohammed, nor Buddhism of Buddh. It is indeed true in a figurative sense, that a teacher lives in his disciples, a truth lives in its votaries. But what Christianity affirms of Christ is, that He rose from the dead, and now lives a perfect man — body, soul, and spirit re-united, and no more capable of separation; that His life is conveyed in regeneration to believers; that they live by abiding in Him; and that all together constitute one body. There are many bonds by which men may be bound together, — common lineage, common belief, common worship, common interests; but in the Church it is the life of Christ which is the bond of unity. Regeneration is unknown to all heathen religions. They speak of a moral change, but Christianity of a new birth. It alone declares its Head to be an immortal and glorified Man, who died to make atonement for the sins of the world, and is now exalted to God's right hand, " the Beginning of the new creation."

It is in this vital relation of the Church to Christ, that its distinctive feature consists. It cannot exist separate from Him. It lives because it is His Body, and its life is the fruit of His life. If He is not, no one can be baptized into Him; if there be no vine, there can be no branches in the vine. Therefore, the Church living on earth is a continual witness to Him as living in heaven. "Because I live, ye shall live also." Every act of regeneration through the Spirit sent by Him, attests His resurrection. And every one regenerate can say with the apostle, "I live, yet not I, but Christ liveth in me."

Thus there appeared in the earth after Christ's ascension, a great religious community, such an one as had never been seen before. In it all distinctions of race, of sex, of age, of culture, of position, as conditions of membership, were set aside. Wherever the life of the first Adam was found, there might be given the life of the Second. The Spirit of life in Christ Jesus laid hold of the most diverse, the most estranged, the most hostile, and made them one, thus giving proof that His mission is universal. There is "one body, one Spirit, one Lord, one faith, one baptism, one God and Father of all."

Through this body perfectly constituted for its end, should the ascended Messiah carry on the work of redemption in the earth, and so give proof to the world of His resurrection and present activity. The appearing of the Church in the world was thus a clear and most wonderful manifestation of a new life that had entered into humanity. God in His Fatherhood had given a new Head to the race, the second Adam, the God-man. In Him, the supernatural in its highest sense began. The Church in its very existence as His body, is supernatural. "Ye are not of (out of) the world, even as I am not of the world." It is lifted up and seated with Him in the heavenlies; as partaking of His life, the life of the resurrection, it is not under the law of sin and death; as abiding in Him, the Holy One, it must be holy. He speaks and acts from heaven by the ministers whom He appoints; He preaches the Gospel to all nations, He guides and instructs and blesses His people. As the Great High Priest He leads their worship, and intercedes for them before the Father.

Thus did God in the Church, through the headship of His Son, bring men into closer relations with Himself than had been possible before; and make a higher revelation of Himself to the world. The way of approach to Him was now opened as it had not been before; and, cleansed by the blood of Jesus, the obedient worshippers had liberty of access into the holiest of all. Thus the two elements of revelation and of redemption, which mark every stage of God's purpose in man's salvation, were here seen in far higher measure than in earlier dispensations. God is revealed in the Incarnate Son, a revelation so surpassing any that had previously been made, that the Evangelist could say, "No man hath seen God at any time; the only-begotten Son, which is in the bosom of the Father, He hath declared Him." Although Himself in heaven, and invisible to men, the Risen Lord is manifested in those to whom He has given His own life, and has made partakers of His holiness and power. The Church abiding in Him is His witness to the world through her heavenly life, and teaching of truth, and supernatural works. As the Father invisible is revealed in the Incarnate Son, so the Son, now for a time invisible, is revealed through His body, the Church.

And as revelation, both of the Father and the Son, entered upon a new stage when the Church was formed and set to be "the light of the world," so did redemption. Now for the first time could men be delivered from the law of sin and death by the law of the Spirit of life in Christ Jesus. (Rom. viii. 2.) And as receiving His life, they could also receive a fullness of spiritual endowment not given before. (1 Cor. xii. 3, etc.) As they had a knowledge of God through the Son, of which all before the Incarnation were ignorant, so they had, as members of the Son, a closeness of union with God not given before to any. "As thou, Father, art in me, and I in thee, that they also may be one in us." And, on the other hand, there was through His sacrifice and priesthood, a consciousness of forgiveness, of cleansing, of peace; a liberty of access to the Father; a fullness of communion with Him, of which none who lived before the Son had died and risen again, and was glorified, and had sent down the Spirit, could be partakers.

CHAPTER III.

THE TWO ELECTIONS, JEWISH AND CHRISTIAN, COMPARED.

THE great and essential distinction between the Jewish people and the Christian Church, the old election and the new, has already been pointed out. It is found in the relation of the Church to the risen and glorified Lord as His Body. Its members have received His life in regeneration through the Holy Spirit sent by Him at Pentecost. This day was, therefore, the birthday of the Church. The new election began then to be gathered; and this gathering continues through the preaching of the gospel, till the full number is completed, and the way made ready for the next stage of redemption.

Starting from this fundamental distinction, let us compare in some of the more important points these two elections.

1. We notice that the Jewish election was of a nation; the Christian is from all nations. In placing Himself in the relation of King to one nation, Jehovah would manifest Himself to all the nations as the One Supreme and Righteous Ruler. This people under His government was to be His witness to all the world. There was no command given them to make proselytes, and they were not to invade the peoples living outside the borders of the land He had assigned them. It was

through this one nation, purified and obedient, that He would be made known and honored in the eyes of all nations.

This kingly relation was in its nature limited to one people, and could not be universal without destroying the end for which it was established. But the time had now come when Jehovah would manifest Himself to the world as the God and Father of all men, and the Messiah as the Saviour of all. Therefore, in this second election He no longer regarded the distinctions of races or of peoples. Wherever the children of Adam were found, there should the gospel of the cross and of the resurrection be preached, that all might partake of the life of the Risen One, the second Adam. As He had made atonement for the sins of the whole world, the Church was to be composed of all believers, without distinction of Jew or Gentile, bond or free.

Thus, this new election is God's witness to the world that He is the God and Father of all. He could not be revealed as Father till His Son became Incarnate, nor the Son be revealed as universal Saviour till He had been set as Head of the universal Church. A gospel preached to every creature is the proof that the love of God in sending His Son embraced all; that His Son died for all; and that all may by regeneration be made partakers of the new and heavenly life.

2. We notice that there is a higher knowledge of God, and therefore a deeper sense of sin, in the Christian than in the Jewish Church. The knowledge of sin, what it is, and its evil nature, must come through God's manifestation of Himself to men. As they learn to know Him in His holiness, and in all His Divine perfections, they become more and more sensible of their sinfulness and guilt. The Jews had a partial knowledge of Him through His special relations to them, His dwell-

ing among them, and through the law He gave them. (Lev. xi. 44; Rom. iii. 20.) What sense of sin was thus wrought in the hearts of the more faithful is shown in the confessions found in the Psalms and elsewhere. (Ps. xxxviii., li.; Job xl. 4, xlii. 5, 6.) But through the Incarnate Son, there was both a higher knowledge of God given than was possible before, and a clearer expression of His holiness. As being in Christ, and so having access to the Father, we learn to know ourselves as having a fallen and corrupt nature; to abhor all evil, and to seek remission and cleansing. They who lived before the holiness of God and His righteousness were revealed in Jesus Christ, could not know the full measure of the holiness and righteousness God demands of His children. (John xv. 24.) In Him — "God manifest in flesh" — could now be seen the perfectly pure and righteous and holy One. Therefore, that men may see sin as it is, its full guilt and pollution, they must know Christ and be in Him; and so come into communion with God. Thus, as those in Christ, Christians could have a deeper sense of sin, a higher apprehension of God's claims upon them, a clearer knowledge of the Divine purpose, and yield a truer obedience to His will, the obedience of love; than was possible to the Jews before Christ through the rites and precepts of the law.

3. We notice that the spiritual standing of the Church is far higher than that of the Jewish people; and, therefore, all its ordinances, its worship and priesthood have a far higher character. This follows from the fact that it is the body of Christ, and the temple of the Holy Ghost. We are told by the evangelist that "the Holy Ghost was not yet given, because Jesus was not yet glorified." (John vii. 39.) He must be glorified before He could receive and send down the Holy Ghost. (Acts ii. 33.) When, through resurrection and ascen-

sion, humanity had in Him attained its perfected condition, then did He begin to make men partakers of His life. To be "in Him," "branches in the Vine," through the regenerating power of the Spirit, is the highest spiritual condition possible, till the work of redemption is completed and the glory of the Kingdom is attained.

The ordinances and ministries of the two elections were correspondent to their differing spiritual conditions. The Jews had circumcision as the initial rite, which was a sign of the renunciation of the life of the flesh, a confession of the sinfulness of the natural man. (Col. ii. 11.) The Church has baptism into Christ, — into His death that we may die unto sin, into His resurrection that we may walk in newness of life. (Rom. vi.) The blood of bulls and goats for the purifying of the flesh, has given place to the blood of Christ that purifies the conscience from dead works to serve the living God. (Heb. ix. 12, etc.) The "bread of the presence" has given place to the "bread of life." The high priest who entered with incense once a year into the most holy, has given place to the risen and immortal Priest who has "gone into heaven itself, now to appear in the presence of God for us."

The Jews had the pattern of heavenly things, but the Church has the heavenly things themselves. Through the headship of the Son, and the sending of the Holy Ghost, the shadows of the law were made the realities of the body of Christ. Therefore it is that where before were but symbols and types, all pointing to the future, now are sacraments, — channels of present grace. Everywhere in the Church, in every ordinance and appointment of God, there is life; nothing is empty and formal. The Spirit of Christ is everywhere, quickening the word spoken, and making it effectual to whatever purpose it may be uttered, whether to convince of sin, to cleanse, to enlighten, to consecrate, or to bless. The worship of the Church is, therefore, "worship in Spirit and in truth,"— in the Spirit who came at Pentecost; in the truth, the perfect reality of which all Jewish rites were but types.

As the Sacrifice of Christ was for all, so is His present Priesthood. His Church is, therefore, a house of prayer for all in the earth. This was prophetically declared of the Jewish temple, and will have its fulfillment when the elect nation shall be brought into its right relations to the nations. (Isa. lvi. 7.) But in Him, the Great High Priest who has passed into the heavens, the sorrows and needs of universal humanity now find their perfect expression. As the Son of man, who knows all that is in the heart of man, and who through His own experience of suffering is "touched with the feeling of our infirmities," all men may go unto Him with assurance of pity and sympathy. And through the Holy Spirit sent by Him, and dwelling in the Church, He kindles in the hearts of His own children the same pity and sympathy for all, which find continual utterance in their prayers and intercessions. Thus, through His body by which He acts and speaks, is His Priesthood in the heavens carried on in the earth, and made real, universal, and never-ceasing. Hence, the Christian Church is called in higher degree than the Jewish, to continual prayer and worship. Not only is it to begin and end each day with holy services as did the Jews, but also to present before God continually the memorial of the sacrifice of His Son, which is the basis of all acceptable worship. Not upon one altar only, but in every place where believers are found, incense and a pure offering are to be offered in His name.

4. We notice the differing forms and degrees of miraculous powers under the Theocracy and in the Church.

Dealing with the Jews as a nation, under a national covenant, the miraculous interpositions of Jehovah were of a corresponding nature. The land chosen by Him for them was distinguished from other lands in that it was not to be subjected to those evils of drought, barrenness, earthquake, plague, and famine, to which other lands were exposed. If these took place, it was as penalties, inflictions of Divine justice upon its inhabitants because of their transgressions of the covenant. And they touched the whole people, not individuals merely. Of Divine interpositions for the blessing of individuals, special cases of healing, deliverances from danger, there are, indeed, scattered instances in their history; and there were also punishments upon individuals specially inflicted; and the sin of one might bring judgments upon all, as in the cases of Achan and David. But as Jehovah's relation to the Jews was national, so were the blessings promised them and the judgments threatened. He looked upon them in their corporate capacity, and dealt with them according to their corporate action.

Thus the holy land, as the land of His elect people, and hallowed by Jehovah's dwelling in it, was distinguished from other lands in its exemption from physical evils, and in the fullness of material blessings. By His power would He preserve the people from the invasion of their enemies when attending His feasts at Jerusalem, and at all times give them the victory when invaded. All the surrounding nations should thus know that it was His land, and honor Him who could thus defend and bless His people.

With the Church, on the contrary, made up of individuals dwelling in all lands, God can stand in no such national relation. Every nation made up of the baptized may be truly called a Christian nation, and its rulers owe allegiance to Him and to His Son; but as such it is no part of the Church, nor are its rulers rulers of the Church, nor its sins sins of the Church. But although not to be looked upon as a nation, yet is the Church capable in still higher degree of corporate action; for it is one through the unity of life, and therefore it may disobey and be punished, or obey and be blest. But these blessings and punishments must be spiritual, not material; such as may extend to the whole body, wherever its members may be found. And as the Church is made up of those individually regenerated, the dealings of God with them are individual as well as corporate. The life of the Vine is indeed the life of the branch, but each branch is dealt with according to its own spiritual condition. It may be purged to bring forth more fruit, or it may wither and be cast out.

Thus, in both the elections, Jewish and Christian, was the supernatural power of God to be continually put forth, to the end that He might be known in the earth as a God above nature; and as ruling over all for the blessing of His people, by putting forth His power in a manner corresponding to His purpose in each election.

5. We notice that in the Christian Church, a far higher measure of spiritual gifts and endowments is found than existed in the Jewish. As the body of Christ, its higher life was the basis of higher spiritual operations; it could be what the Jewish people was not, the temple of the Holy Ghost, in which He could manifest Himself in all forms of activity, and bestow upon His faithful ones all endowments of power and holiness, and all diversities of gifts. Although the gift of prophecy was common to both elections, yet among the Jews was it occasional, and to a certain degree exceptional; for there was no order of prophets, God raising them

up at intervals as He had need. But in the Church, the ministry of the prophet was constituent and permanent; since the Holy Ghost sent at Pentecost dwelt in it to make known the will of the Lord, and to show or declare the things to come. (Eph. iv. 11; John xvi. 13, etc.) The prophetic gift was one that all might possess, and which all were to covet earnestly. "He that prophesieth speaketh unto men to exhortation and edification and comfort." But the gift of tongues in the Church was the new and characteristic gift, since it especially marked the indwelling of the Spirit in men. "He that speaketh in a tongue speaketh not unto men, but unto God." (1 Cor. xiv. 1-24; Acts ii. 4.) And other gifts than those of utterance were given, each of which was a manifestation of the Spirit. (1 Cor. xii. 7, 10.) To show forth the power of Christ, His members were promised all forms of supernatural help. "In my name shall they cast out devils, they shall speak with new tongues; they shall take up serpents, and if they drink any deadly thing it shall not hurt them; they shall lay hands on the sick, and they shall recover." All these things were to be done in the name of Christ, and for a witness unto Him as the Saviour from sin and death. And, therefore, such a promise could not have been made till He was about to ascend and to be set Head over all things unto the Church. Such an ordinance also as that for the anointing of the sick did not exist under the law, and could have a place only amongst those made partakers of His life.

It is plain from this comparison that the Christian Church is no mere continuation and enlargement of the Jewish. This is common to them both that they are elections, some taken from the many, that through them when brought into their perfected condition, God may manifest Himself to the world. The great line of distinction between them is found in their relations to the Messiah. The Jews under their covenant looked forward to Him as their Deliverer, their King, who should fulfill all covenant promises; but Christians have in Him already come the fountain of their life; of His glorified humanity they are already made partakers. The body of Christ is, therefore, something essentially new; distinct both in life and constitution, in its gifts and powers, from the election that preceded it. And the end to be hereafter accomplished by it, when both elections are completed, is distinct. Each will then serve as a means of Divine revelation; but the Church as the Lamb's wife seated in the heavenlies, moves in a sphere into which none other can be exalted, and which is for the blessing both of the Jews and the nations.

CHAPTER IV.

THE CHURCH NOT THE MESSIANIC KINGDOM.

IT was natural that the Christian Church, brought into such close communion with the risen Lord, should have early begun to believe that He had already entered upon His work of rule as the Messianic King, and had called it to be ruler under Him. Since all authority in heaven and earth was given Him, and He was set at His Father's right hand "above all principality, power, might, and dominion," was He not in the fullest sense a King? Why was it necessary that He should come back to the earth to reign? As the Church was to be gathered from all nations, including the Jews, did it not show that this people had fulfilled its mission, and had no national place in the Messianic Kingdom? Why could He not reign from heaven through the Church, guided and inspired by the Spirit whom He had sent down?

Thus reasoning from the unquestioned facts, that the Risen One is Lord over all nations, and that the gospel is to be preached to all, and that the Church is His body through which He would execute His will; the conclusion was near at hand that He was seated at His ascension on the throne of His glory, and then began His reign; and had called the Church to be the administrator of His authority on the earth during His absence. This conclusion was early formulated in the phrase, "the

Church is the kingdom." All the promises of God in the Old Testament respecting the Messianic Kingdom, it was said, were to be fulfilled in it, and before the Lord's return. All the nations were to be subject to the Church, all the saved were to be gathered into it; and it only remained that at His return He should assign to all men their final rewards, and give up the Kingdom to His Father.

This belief respecting the high place and authority of the Church, involving the denial that the Jews as a people had any place in it, early found a ready reception in the congregations gathered from the Gentiles. They had little knowledge of the Jews, except as those who had rejected and crucified their Lord; and who still as a people hated and despised all who believed on Him. And as the repulsions between the Jews and Christians increased, and the Gentile element became predominant in the Church, this mode of thinking and feeling prevailed more and more. It contrasted its own universalism with the particularism of the Jewish people, its spiritual worship with their carnal ritual, its heavenly riches through its union with Christ and the presence of the Holy Ghost, with their poverty of knowledge and of gifts; and it asked, Will God go backward? Having reached a higher stage of His work, will He descend again to a lower? Why should the unfaithful nation be regathered and set anew in its land? Why should the Lord of all humble Himself to be the King of the Jews?

It was in vain that the Jews appealed to the promises made to their fathers, and to the declarations of the prophets respecting their place in the Messianic Kingdom as the children of Abraham and the covenant nation. It was not difficult to give to these promises another interpretation. It was said, that the true descendants of Abraham and heirs of the promises were those who received the Messiah when He came; and that the prophecies of future blessedness and honor under His rule belonged to them, and to all who believed His gospel, and not to the literal Jews. The nation as such had forfeited its right, and had no further place in the redemptive purpose of God. All that Joel and Isaiah and other prophets had said of a remnant to be saved, was to be fulfilled in those who entered the Church. As a people, the Jews were henceforth to Jehovah as one of the Gentile nations; they were to be saved individually through the gospel, not as a nation. The Old-Testament prophecies of the extension of the Kingdom and its glory, should have their fulfillment in the new election, made up both of Jews and Gentiles. Thus, it became in time the general, almost the universal, belief of Christians, that the Church is the Kingdom; and that all that is said in Old-Testament prophecy of the reign of the Messiah is fulfilled in it during His absence in heaven; and this belief continues to be very general to this day. Its effect has been very great in determining the history of the Church, both as to doctrine and polity; and it therefore demands our consideration.

There are certain elements here to be carefully distinguished; and, first, we ask in what sense Christ now rules in the Church, and in what sense He now rules over the nations? At His ascension, the Lord as glorified became the perfect instrument for the completion of the Father's purpose in man's redemption, and was clothed with all His authority. But redemption was still to be carried on, as we have seen, by means of an election; and it is the new election — the Church — that is the sphere in which He now exercises in full measure His authority. But it is as its Head that He rules over it, not as its King; for this latter title is never used of this relation. Nor is His rule over His Church legal and external, like that of an earthly king; or even like that of Jehovah over the Jews. The relation between Him, the Head, and the Church, His Body, is a living one, such as nowhere else exists, or can exist; His will is the law, not merely of its action, but of its life. Its members "are under the law to Christ," because they are first in Him. The Spirit whom He has sent and by whom He regenerates and purifies, works in them such discernment of His will that His commandments approve themselves to their spirits as just and holy and good, and they joyfully obey them. Thus it is that as the Head He rules in the Church through the law of a common life; and where this community of life is full, obedience is perfect.

We ask second, in what sense He now rules over the nations? Here we must distinguish between His immediate and His providential rule. As Jehovah was absolute ruler alway over all nations, and yet was not the theocratic King of any till the election of Israel, so the Lord Jesus became the "Prince of the kings of the earth" at His ascension, but does not yet stand in immediate kingly relations to any one people. His investiture with universal authority does not involve the instant possession and exercise of it. "I have set my King upon my holy hill of Zion. . . . Ask of me, and I shall give thee the heathen for thine inheritance." (Ps. ii. 6-9.) "Sit on my right hand, until I make thine enemies thy footstool." (Ps. cx.) "Thou hast put all things in subjection under His feet. . . . But now we see not yet all things put under Him." (Heb. ii. 8.) The kingly relation is a new and definite one, to be made by God's special act. As the sphere of Jehovah's theocratic action was the Jewish election, so that of Christ now is the Christian election. Providentially He reigns over all nations, executing the Father's will, raising up and casting down kings and magistrates that He may prepare the way for the universal Kingdom, which He is in due time to set up. But His actings are not seen as His except by the eye of faith. He reigns, but He is invisible, and the world at large knows it not; the nations pay Him no conscious obedience.

Thus, headship over the Church, and lordship over the nations, as established at the ascension, are two distinct and very unlike relations. In the one, His authority is immediate, and extends to all offices, to all ordinances, to all worship; no one can lawfully rule or teach, or fulfill any ministry in His Church, to whom He does not give commission. The body, if in its right condition, obeys in all things the will of its Head. In the other, His authority over the nations is not manifested in specific laws, in the direct appointment of rulers, in the punishment of offenders. He is not seen or known as exercising royal prerogatives.

Had it been the purpose of God to set the Son at His ascension as the King of the nations, He would in some way have made His kingship so plain that the nations could not have been ignorant of it, and of the duty of allegiance and homage. There must, also, have been in every land those publicly invested with His authority to act as His representatives, and with power to give commands and to compel obedience. But such an exercise of His kingly power would have anticipated the universal Kingdom; and would have been inconsistent with His action in the gathering of disciples out of the nations through the preaching of the gospel, and with the place given the Church as His witness during His absence. All nations, indeed, now owe to Christ obedience; and the principles of His gospel, as made known to them, should rule in their legislation, and guide public action, and He will help them and bless them through His Spirit; but He does not appoint their princes, nor dictate their laws, nor is His hand seen in judgment. Even if all the individuals of a nation are baptized, it is not, therefore, under Christ as its King, though as members of the Church they are under Him as its Head.

Admitting this distinction between the immediate rule of Christ in His Church and His providential rule over the nations, we easily see that the last is not the fulfillment of the Divine promises respecting the Messianic Kingdom. This fulfillment begins when the Father gives Him the nations as His inheritance, and He comes forth from His Presence; and then "the Gentiles shall see His righteousness, and all kings His glory." At the sounding of the seventh trumpet it is said, "the kingdoms of this world are become the kingdoms of our Lord and of His Christ," and He "takes His great power," and begins to reign. (Rev. xi. 15.)

The fundamental error in the assertion that the present dispensation is the period of the Kingdom, and that the Church is now reigning with Christ, is seen in the consideration of the following particulars: —

That it makes the Church, while being gathered and still imperfect, to fulfill the functions it can fulfill only after it has been gathered and perfected; that it sets aside God's purpose in the Jews; that it confuses Christ's two offices of High Priest and of King; that it makes the present, or Church period, the last period of redemption; and that it seats sinful and mortal men in the throne with the Risen and Glorified One.

1. To affirm that Christ now rules through the Church, is to confound means and end in the Divine purpose of redemption. The Church is an election,

some taken from many: but an election is never its own end; it looks forward to something to be done by it when it is completed. The elect are chosen by God and brought into special relations to Him, that they may be used by Him for the blessing of others not of the election; and this end is not effected, in the true sense, till the elect are completed in number, and prepared for their work. As those gathered at our National Military School cannot fulfill the end for which they have been chosen till their education has been completed, nor an army go to war till it has been organized and armed and disciplined; so is it with the elections of God, both Jewish and Christian. This is not to deny that membership in the election, in every stage of its history, is a great individual blessing; nor that, by those gathered from generation to generation, a partial witness is borne for God unto others, and a partial work done. The Church in every age has been His instrument to teach and bless the world. But it remains true that the larger and higher end of the election is not yet reached.

The processes of gathering and of training are only preparatory to future service. This is true of both elections, Jewish and Christian. The Jews must be brought into their true condition as a holy nation, and the Church into its true condition as the glorified body of Christ, ere they can fulfill that for which God has chosen them. Their high work and place are in the future, when, being brought into entire submission to Christ's will and filled with His Spirit, they can be in their respective places His fit instruments to carry on His work, as He in His perfected humanity is the perfect instrument of the Father. He did not receive power till He was risen and glorified; and His servants of both elections must likewise wait till He has prepared them for the respective works He has for them to do in the Messianic Kingdom. The Church must be completed in number, and glorified with the glory of her Head, ere she can be sharer in His dominion.

2. That it sets aside God's purpose in the Jews, His first election. The Jews were chosen that through them as a nation, made obedient and holy, and ruled by His Son, Jehovah might manifest Himself to the nations. And this their calling they have never fulfilled. This is not to deny that God has made them His instruments to enlighten and bless the world; and yet His purpose in them has not been accomplished. For many centuries they have been under His discipline, and scattered in all lands, and yet wonderfully kept by Him for the place they are to fill. To deny them their place in the Messianic Kingdom, is to say that God's purpose can be attained by other means than those He has chosen. But "His gifts and calling are without repentance," for He acts in infinite wisdom; one election cannot take the place of another, the Church cannot take the place of the Jewish nation. Each has its own sphere, and both are necessary for the full revelation of God and of Christ, and for the full accomplishment of the redemptive work.

3. That it confuses the two offices of the Lord, that of High Priest and that of King. These two offices are successive in their order as regards His work in redemption. Ascending, He entered within the veil to do a priestly work, "made an High Priest for ever after the order of Melchizedek." (Heb. vi. 20.) This work continues till He comes forth to take His great power, and to reign. (Rev. xi. 17.) During this period His Church is called to offer up on earth continual prayers and supplications for all men, and to preach everywhere "the gospel of the kingdom;" and it is able to do this only through the power of His intercessions and the

ministry of His Spirit. He now stands before the golden altar, and has not yet seated Himself on the throne of His glory. (Heb. iv. 14, viii. 1; Matt. xxv. 85.) This priestly work He continues till all His Church is gathered, and prepared in spirit to be made like Him in glory; and then He comes forth. So long as He abides in the Most Holy, the Church is to fulfill its priestly calling, to preach the gospel unto all men, and wait till He appears and seats it with Him in His throne.

4. That it makes the present, or Church period, the last period of redemption. If this be so, two results follow: first, that His return is for final judgment, and all probation must then cease; all found unrepentant must be cast out and perish. It is scarcely possible, therefore, that His immediate coming can be an object of hope, even to the few who are ready for Him, since the door of salvation to the race at large will then be suddenly and forever closed. To prolong the time of His absence to the uttermost and so to prolong the time of salvation, must be rather the prayer of the Church. And to this instinctive feeling must be, in part at least, ascribed the fact that in so few of the liturgies of the Church any prayers for Christ's speedy coming are found.

It needs but little reflection to see that the apostles could never have believed that the Lord's return would put an end to all probation, and bring in at once universal and eternal judgment. Had this been so they would not have thought it possible that His return could have been within their own lifetime; or have desired it, since the number that could hear and believe their Gospel must have been very small. How could all to be saved be gathered in the brief space of two or three generations? It is plain that the apostles looked upon the Church as an election, — how many in number they knew not; and that the completion of this election did not bring in the day of final judgment, but rather a day of larger redemption. Being itself completed and perfected, the Church would then become an instrument for the salvation of others. Therefore, the return of the Lord was to bring double blessing, first, as lifting the Church into a condition in which it could render higher service; and second, as opening a new stage of redemptive activity, in which, through the Church perfected, He would manifest His glory before the Jews and the nations.

Again, it affirms that the present dispensation, or Church period, being the last, is the time in which all promises of prosperity and blessing made by the Old-Testament prophets are to be fulfilled. This must be so, since these promises refer to the redemptive and not the post-redemptive age. If their fulfillment must, therefore, be in this dispensation, and before Christ's return, has it already taken place? Have the glorious descriptions of the universal Kingdom already been realized? This will scarcely be said by any. The history of the Church from Pentecost downward has not been such that we can see reflected in it the holiness and truth and peace, or the universal extension, of the Messianic reign. If, then, the fulfillment of the prophetic predictions is not found in the past of the Church, it must be in its future. And if so, the Church is warranted in looking forward to a time of ever-increasing prosperity; for as Christ now reigns through His Church ruling for Him on earth, He must continue thus to reign till all things are subdued under Him. The time, therefore, must come when the Church will rule all the world in the name of Christ, and the universal Kingdom be realized in His absence. When He returns, it will not be to set up the Kingdom, but to give it up to the Father.

But when we read the words of the Lord and of His apostles respecting the state of the world and of the Church during His absence, and at His return, we see that they do not correspond to the words of the prophets who describe the peaceful and glorious reign of the Messiah. He declared to His disciples that "as the world had hated Him, it would hate them;" that they would be subject to reproach and persecution and death. (John xv. 18-21.) He nowhere gives any promise of blessedness to the Church until His return. He speaks of wars and famines and pestilences and earthquakes as only "the beginning of sorrows," and of "the great tribulation" that is to precede His coming; and asks whether "the Son of man at His coming will find faith on the earth;" and the apostles speak of the lawlessness and wickedness that mark the last days, and of "the mystery of iniquity" as already working, and to work till "that Wicked be revealed." It is impossible to believe that the Old-Testament prophets on the one hand, and the Lord and the apostles on the other, speak of the same period of time. The former speak of the prosperity and glory that shall be in the world when the Messiah has set up His kingdom; the latter of the trials and tribulations through which the Church must pass during its time of preparation, and before it can be seated with Him in His throne; a type of which was seen in the Lord's own life.

5. That sinful and mortal men dwelling on earth now sit with Christ in the throne of His glory. He was not invested with universal authority till He rose from the dead, and ascended to God's right hand. (Eph. i. 20.) Must not those who are to be His kings be first made like Him? Must they not be prepared as He was prepared? Through men, mortal and frail, indeed, He now administers His government in the Church; His present

work being to gather it and to prepare it for His return in glory. But while helping to prepare others for their high calling, they are themselves in process of preparation; and the place of their present authority is in the Church, not in the world. To affirm that mortal and sinful men are already admitted to have part in His functions of universal rule, and are empowered by Him to govern the nations, is a proud and presumptuous ante-dating of the Kingdom. His kings must be first made like Him, immortal and incorruptible. When the earthly in them is changed into the heavenly, then can they exercise His heavenly authority.

If the living, still under the law of sin and death, are already reigning with Christ, and kings are by His will now subject to priests, the State to the Church, then there seems no reason why the dead may not also be partakers of His rule. They are, indeed, still under the law of death, and wait for the resurrection; but if the living, who are not yet perfected and glorified, may sit in their thrones, why not the dead saints, also; and if the dead are His kings and priests, why may not the baptized offer to them their petitions, and ask their help? To ask for the intercessions and for the aid of those, whether living or dead, who now reign with Christ, cannot be wrong and contrary to God's will. Thus, before the resurrection, the Church in its two great divisions of the living and the dead is invested with the authority which the Father gave to His Son only after He had exalted Him to His own right hand.

While in all the great divisions of the Christian Church the fundamental principle has been accepted, that the present dispensation is the period of the Kingdom, there is wide diversity as to the extent to which it has been practically carried out. The Church of

Rome accepts and defends its full logical results. The Church, it affirms, is a monarchy; it has its earthly head, Christ's one vicegerent; who, because the ruler of the Church, is also the ruler of the nations. The State, indeed, has its own sphere, and there are kings and princes; but as the soul rules the body, so the Church rules the State; and kings and princes are subject to Christ's vicar. To him all owe obedience; and if it be not voluntarily rendered, it must be enforced; and that not merely with spiritual censures, but also with civil penalties. It is right to silence heresy, to crush out error with inexorable rigor, to punish with imprisonment and death all who stubbornly refuse to submit to papal authority. Kings and magistrates, if they refuse to obey Christ's viceroy, may be rightly deposed. Not only is the Church on earth reigning, but the dead saints are also reigning. They may be invoked to help the living, and states and peoples may put themselves under their protection.

In the Greek Church there has not been the same logical boldness in carrying out the principle that the Church is the Kingdom, to its legitimate conclusions. In point of fact, that Church has always been in a position of submission to the State; and its claims have been practically little more than assertions that it alone has retained the doctrine, ministries, and practices of the primitive Church, pure and undefiled; and while using the arm of the civil ruler to put down heresy within the nations of its faith, it has never attempted to enforce its supremacy over others.

In the Reformation the same principle was retained, but under modified forms. Its chief leaders occupied themselves very little with the prophetic future of the Church, or with the purpose of God towards the Jews and the nations. The coming of the Lord was thought of as that of the Judge for final judgment; and there was little expectation of any great prosperity to the Church before that day, which was thought by most not to be far distant. It was not till later that the Reformers began to be dissatisfied with the eschatology inherited from Rome, and to ask whether the Scriptures did not promise to the Church a period of far higher prosperity than it had yet enjoyed. They could not say that its highest development was in the past, for this past was filled with the Roman Church, which they denounced as apostate; it must, therefore, be in the future. The Kingdom, indeed, was set up at Christ's ascension; but His people had been unfaithful, and the gospel hindered. Gradually, however, all the world would become subject to Him through the preaching of the pure gospel, and the nations everywhere become Christian.

Thus, while holding fast the dogma that the present dispensation is the kingdom period, and that all the saved must be gathered into the Church before the Lord's return, the later Reformers and their followers began to put the fulfillment of prophecy respecting the universal Kingdom in the future. A time is coming, it was said, whether within a few years or many centuries, when all the world will be converted to the truth, and acknowledge Christ as Saviour and Lord. Thus the history of the Church was divided by them into two great periods, — that down to the Reformation, one of progressive error and decline, and that following the Reformation, one of ever-increasing truth and prosperity. In both periods Christ seated in heaven was, indeed, reigning; but only in the last would the world believe on Him, and everywhere honor Him. Thus, the Kingdom is in fact in the future rather than in the past. But in the conception of His reign, almost all the features that mark a kingdom were gradually given up. Christ, it was said, is a King of truth; He rules through the truth; His Kingdom is extended as the truth is received; His kings are the teachers of truth. He subdues the world by the preaching of the Gospel. His Church is one, in that its members hold certain common beliefs, not through the existence of any central authority, or unity of administration; and this community of belief is consistent with manifold sects, with all forms of polity, and with the largest liberty of individual judgment and action.

Thus the reign of Christ is made in effect that of a teacher over his disciples. He rules them in so far as they accept the truth which they find in the Scriptures. If the time comes when the truth there revealed is universally received, then His reign is universal. Starting from these principles, a very natural and easy step onward, and one since taken by many, is to regard Christ's chief work as that of a teacher; and as the truth is more important than the personality of the teacher, so with Him. He ceases to be thought of as a king, a living ruler exercising authority, and soon to return to earth to execute judgment and righteousness; and Christianity separated from Him, takes upon itself the form of an ethical system, a moral force in the education of the world. His person and work have but a minor interest.

Thus the conception of the Messianic Kingdom as we have traced it in the Old Testament, early became radically changed. Of the three elements entering into this conception, the first only, that of the universal rule of Jehovah as to be ultimately realized, but under a spiritualized form, has been retained; the other two elements — the place of the Jews as the theocratic people dwelling in their own land; and of the Messiah as ruling over them, and thus ruling over the nations, and blessing them — were gradually lost from sight. The Jews were put aside, their mission having been fulfilled; and the Messiah need not therefore return to earth, but from heaven can rule the nations through the Church. The saints of the new election take the Kingdom and possess it, the King abiding in the heavens.

The belief that the Church is thus set to rule the world, has brought about results that appear at first directly contradictory. In the Roman communion it has furnished the ground for claims of absolute rule over the baptized, and of universal authority over the nations. Affirming its infallible guidance, and concentrating all power in the hands of a single chief, its history is the record of most strenuous and persistent attempts to make its domination a reality throughout the world. In the Protestant bodies, especially in those more advanced, the same belief has furnished the ground of republican or democratic forms of polity; all believers as having the Spirit of Christ being equal, the expression of His will is, therefore, to be found in the votes of majorities, rather than in the judgment of any official persons. As all elected rulers owe their election directly or indirectly to the popular will, this will as supreme takes upon itself, in a manner, the attribute of infallibility. But whether democratic or despotic in polity, all divisions agree that the work of redemption is to be effected by the Church during the Lord's absence; and that He returns only to gather all to His bar, dead and living, and to pronounce final sentence.

It is instructive to see how the Anabaptists of Germany during the Reformation, and the Fifth-monarchy men of England, starting from the same assumption that the Church is the Kingdom, should have been led in the general ferment of the time to attempt to make it a reality by violence. Their reasoning was simple and short: the kingdom is Christ's, it is administered by His saints, we are His saints, we will take it by force. To reign on earth during the absence of Christ and before the resurrection, has been the one point in which the Anabaptists and Roman Catholics, Greeks and Protestants, have for the most part agreed; the distinction has been as to the manner in which that reign is to be realized.

In our own time, two currents of opinion are distinctly visible: one, perhaps most noticeable in Protestant bodies, a return to the prophetic teaching respecting the Messianic Kingdom, — a growing belief that at the coming of the Lord, the Jews, restored to their land and to God's favor, will fulfill the purpose of their election under the Messiah, and that God will be sanctified through them in the eyes of all nations; the other, departing ever more widely from the prophetic teaching, and giving up all expectation of Christ's return, and even denying His present existence, believes in no supernatural future, but identifies the Kingdom with the general spread of civilization, and gradual improvement of humanity.

CHAPTER V.

THE ETERNAL LIFE, AND THE DEAD IN CHRIST.

WE have already seen that the Jews expected in the Messianic Kingdom a higher form of existence, a blessed life free from the evils of the present. This life was defined by the term "eternal." This phrase, eternal life, is first met with in the prophet Daniel (xii. 2), and later in the Maccabees, and other Apocryphal books. It was one in common use in the Lord's day, and is often found in the Gospels. The young ruler, as also a lawyer, asked the Lord "what he should do that he might have eternal life" (Matt. xix. 16, Luke x. 25); and the Lord Himself often employs it. We must, therefore, ask what were the elements of this conception of eternal life in the Jewish mind?

A chief difficulty in our inquiry is the vagueness of the terms, "life" and "death." We have only the one term life, to denote several distinct conditions of human existence. It is applied first, to that condition in which man was created, when God breathed into his nostrils the breath of life, and he became "a living soul." The life of man as thus created in God's image, and for communion with Him, was complete as to its elements, body and soul being united; and was capable of development. But by transgression man came under the law of sin and death. This was a lower and evil condition of humanity, in which, and before the actual separation of soul and body, there could not be fullness of life, either bodily or spiritual. After this separation man is said to be dead, yet the separated soul continues in a state of conscious existence. Thus it has a life in the body, its normal state; and a life without the body, its abnormal state. Death is both the act of separation of soul and body, and the condition of separation that follows it; the dead are the disembodied.

We have thus three distinct states of human existence: first, that of man as he was created, and not under the law of death; second, that after the fall, when he had come under the law of sin and death; third, that of the disembodied soul. To all these the term life is applied. To these we may add a fourth, the state after the resurrection, soul and body having been re-united. And of the disembodied we may make two classes, according to moral position, — the good and the evil; and of the risen, also, two like classes, each having its own special conditions of life.

To which of all these differing states of human life, embodied and disembodied, good and evil, is the term eternal to be applied, using it in the sense of "everlasting," or "without end"? With the first, that of Adam as created, we are not here concerned, since it no longer exists. Nor can it be applied to the second, that of Adam as fallen, for all the fallen are under the law of death, and eternal cannot be affirmed of life in mortal flesh. Can we apply it to the life of souls disembodied, whether righteous or unrighteous? This cannot be, since disembodied life ceases in this form at the resurrection. We can, then, only apply "eternal" to that form of life which begins at the resurrection, and which is, therefore, without end; and it may be applied to all who are raised from the dead, both just and unjust. Thus, regarding eternal life as a defined form of human

existence which continues without end, it must be the
life that follows the resurrection, — soul and body being
then re-united, — and not any that precedes it.

But eternal life thus defined may be good or evil,
blessed or miserable, since there is a resurrection both of
the just and the unjust; and we must take therefore into
account another element than simple duration, and this
element is a moral one. It is said by our Lord, "the
righteous shall go into life eternal." In its common
acceptation in the New Testament, it is a blessed life
without end; and the chief element in this blessedness
is full communion with God. We have, then, to ask to
which of the possible differing states of human existence the term eternal life in the sense of full communion with God without end, may be applied?

Upon this point the New-Testament Scriptures are
very emphatic; the term "eternal life," in the sense
just defined, cannot be applied to any condition but
that of the righteous after the resurrection, when they
are brought into their highest and permanent form of
being. There is, indeed, a life in communion with God
common to the faithful on the earth and to the righteous departed. Both live in the Divine favor, and are
spiritually blessed. But both are in a relatively imperfect condition, and one that is not permanent; the first
being under the law of sin and death, the second being
among the dead, — separated souls. There is in neither
of them fullness of life, according to the measure even
of their original constitution; and because of this their
communion with God is necessarily limited and imperfect. He who is in his original goodness, like a vessel
unbroken, can receive from God according to his full
measure; he who has fallen from it, like a vessel broken,
can receive only in part. Neither the soul in the mortal
body, nor the soul without a body, can enter into the

most Holy Place, into the very presence of the living God. Fullness of life, and, therefore, fullness of communion with God, is given to him alone, who stands before Him in the perfect integrity of his nature, wholly set free from the law of sin and death, and exalted in the resurrection to the highest form of human existence.

Having now before us the two elements of the conception of eternal life as the perfected and final condition of humanity, attained through resurrection, and admitting into fullest communion with God; we see that it was one that the Jews could not have had till Christ died and rose again. Their teaching under the law had been negative rather than positive. A chief point to be taught them was that the dead, even the most faithful, were not in full communion with God. Disembodied existence was never the Jewish ideal of human blessedness; sheol is never set forth as a place where God is revealed. He dwells among the living; and the dead must arise, and return to the light of day, and stand before Him in His holy hill, if they would behold His glory. As the highest manifestation of Himself was to be made in the coming Messianic Kingdom, it was life in this Kingdom that was the object of spiritual hope.

So deeply had this teaching respecting the imperfection of disembodied existence taken root in the Jewish mind, that it was not till the Grecian period (333–167 B.C.), and through the influence of Greek philosophy, that other beliefs began to find adherents. It was said, that the soul is a part of the Divine essence; that any union with matter as in the body, hinders and defiles it; that such union is, therefore, temporary; and that, when released from the body, it enters in virtue of its ethereal nature into its true and higher condition of being. It was under the influence of this philosophy that the disembodied state began to be regarded by some of the later Jews as the highest and most blessed state; and the resurrection of the body, and its re-union to the soul, as both unnecessary and unworthy. There is no reason, however, to believe that this philosophy, though it is reflected in some of the Apocryphal books, ever greatly influenced the popular mind. Its influence upon Christian doctrine through Origen and the Alexandrian school, it is not our place to examine.

We may, then, say that as regards the dead, the restoration of the integrity of man's nature — the re-union of soul and body in the resurrection — was a chief and indispensable element in the current Jewish conception of eternal life in our Lord's day. No Jew ever thought of the disembodied soul as to have part in the Messianic blessedness. It is, of course, to be remembered that this belief was modified in its details according to the spiritual discernment of individuals; and that in many minds there was, doubtless, great confusion, both as to the nature of the Messianic Kingdom, and of resurrection life, and very low conceptions of both.

We may now ask whether the Lord in His own teaching added any new element to the Jewish belief? Being Himself the promised Messiah, He claims the prerogatives that belong to Him as such; He alone has authority to admit to the Messianic Kingdom, and to participation of its blessed life. "Ye will not come unto me that ye might have life." (John v. 40.) "My sheep hear my voice, . . . and I give unto them eternal life." (John x. 27, 28.) "This is life eternal, that they might know thee, the only true God, and Jesus Christ whom thou hast sent." (John xvii. 3.) But He teaches more than this. He not only admits those who believe on Him to life in the Messianic Kingdom, but He Himself is the source of this life. The Father had given Him "to have life in Himself," and so to be a fountain of life to others. "I am the Life." "I am the Bread of life." "I am the Vine, ye are the branches." "Abide in me, and I in you."

Thus to the elements already existing in the Jewish conception of eternal life, a new and higher one was added by the Lord in His teaching, — life in Himself. Those who would become partakers of this life must be made members of Him, regenerate or new-born. (John iii. 3–6.) But of this new element the Jews in His day could have no right knowledge, since they knew not that He was the incarnate Son; nor that through resurrection He should enter into an estate of immortality and glory. During His own lifetime, therefore, He could only indirectly teach them that the eternal life was something more than a blessed existence in the Messianic Kingdom. Nor till after His resurrection could the truth be presented by the apostles, that the Risen One had become the second Adam, the Quickening Spirit; and that He gave His own heavenly life to those who believed on Him. "The second man is the Lord from heaven. . . . As we have borne the image of the earthy, we shall also bear the image of the heavenly." (1 Cor. xv. 47–49.) As life derived from Him who can die no more, it is no longer under the law of death; as the life of the glorified Son, it is the highest possible form of creature existence; and all partaking of it are capable of entering into the closest communion with God, and so of attaining the highest conceivable blessedness.

In reading the Lord's words spoken to the Jews of His day, we cannot be surprised that there are in them such depths of meaning that they failed to understand them. Faith in Him and His Messianic claims as a condition of entrance into His Kingdom, they could imperfectly understand; but what did He mean when He said, "The bread of God is He which cometh down from heaven, and giveth life unto the world. . . . If any man eat of this bread, he shall live for ever; and the bread which I will give is my flesh, which I will give for the life of the world." "As the living Father hath sent me, and I live by the Father, so he that eateth me, even he shall live by me"? These expressions and manifold others, speak of a communication of His life to all believing on Him, that was then incomprehensible. It was not till after the Day of Pentecost and the descent of the Spirit, that the apostles themselves knew the nature of the eternal life as life in Christ risen from the dead. It was not merely the cleansing and exaltation of the life received from Adam, but something distinctively new. To this they continually bear most emphatic witness. "The gift of God is eternal life in Christ Jesus our Lord." (Rom. vi. 23.) "This is the record, that God hath given us eternal life, and this life is in His Son." (1 John v. 11.)

The term "eternal life" had thus to the apostles and disciples a largeness and a depth of meaning which it could not have had to the Jews. Having its origin in the heavenly Man, this life was heavenly. "If any man be in Christ, he is a new creature." Abiding in Him, the sinless and holy One, holiness is its law. "He that abideth in Him, sinneth not." It is a life not subject to the law of death; for as the life of Him who is risen from the dead, it embraces both soul and body, and assures their future re-union if they shall be separated. But the possession of this life did not, indeed, assure against bodily death. "And if Christ be in you, the body is dead because of sin." (Rom. viii. 10.) It did give assurance of resurrection. "The body is for the Lord, and the Lord for the body. And God hath both raised up the Lord, and will also raise us up." To be in Him " who was dead, and is alive again for evermore," makes it certain that the body of our humiliation will in due time be fashioned like unto the body of His glory. (Phil. iii. 21.)

It was from not knowing that this new life in Christ is still subject to death as the dissolution of soul and body, till the number of His elect in the Church is completed, that the early Christians at Thessalonica were so troubled when some of their number died. How could they who had been made partakers of the life of the immortal One, go down, as all before had done, into the grave? Probably, as they expected the speedy return of the Lord, they thought that death must be a special judgment from God; and that those visited by it would be excluded from the Messianic Kingdom. This error the apostle Paul corrected, and taught the Church that the power of death would not be overcome till the Lord's return; and that those sleeping in Him would enter the Kingdom at the same time with the living. "We which are alive and remain unto the coming of the Lord shall not prevent them which are asleep." (1 Thess. iv. 15, etc.)

If a special vital relation with the Risen One is thus established in those regenerate through the Holy Spirit sent by Him, as symbolized by the Vine and the branches; we may find here the ground of distinction between the dead in Christ and those who died before He became the last Adam, the Quickening Spirit. Doubtless all in every generation before He came who died in faith, are blessed in their communion with God. But there seems good reason to believe that those made members of Christ since He ascended, continue in the invisible world to stand in a special relation to Him, and through Him to the Father. However this may be (and positive assertions would be presumptuous), it is obvious that the language of the apostles respecting them that "sleep in Jesus," is very unlike the language of the Old Testament respecting the departed. All who have been made partakers of His life continue to be one in Him. They do not through death cease to be branches in the Vine. The dead are separated in body from their brethren on earth, but they are not separated in spirit either from them, or from the Lord. Through the one Spirit there is community of life. Of the communion which the faithful departed have with Christ we cannot adequately speak, for it is spiritual; but it is of such a nature that the apostle could say, "For me to live is Christ, and to die is gain," and he is "in a strait" whether to choose to live or to die. But in view of the labors and sufferings before him, he says that "to depart and to be with Christ is far better." This language could never have been used of a state of unconsciousness, an error which, indeed, is refuted by the presence of the one Spirit in the one body, binding all, both those living in Christ and those sleeping in Him, into unity. It is impossible that a part of the members of the same body and having one life, can be in a state of consciousness, and a part in a state of unconsciousness.

Yet the apostle does not look upon the dead in Christ as having fullness of life, and so prepared to be His helpers either in His present work or in the future Kingdom. The goal to which he looks forward is the resurrection: "If by any means I might attain unto the resurrection of the dead;" or more literally, "from the dead." (Phil. iii. 11.) "Not for that we would be unclothed, but clothed upon, that mortality might be swallowed up of life." (2 Cor. v. 4.) Fullness of life can only be possessed by those who are made in resurrection like the risen Lord, immortal and incorruptible; and thus are they prepared for His service, as He at His resurrection became the perfect servant of the Father. Then may they be His kings and priests.

It is most remarkable that with the supreme importance given in the New Testament to the fact of resurrection, first of Christ and then of His members, it early began to be regarded by some in the Church as comparatively unimportant, although holding a prominent place in its creeds; and now by many the body is regarded as constituting no essential element of the eternal life. The disembodied saints are believed to be not only at rest and in peace, but already glorified, and even exalted to be rulers together with Christ. This point in some of its bearings has been elsewhere noticed. This premature exaltation of the faithful departed has not been confined to any part of the Church, though assuming somewhat different forms in the Roman-Catholic and Greek communions on the one side, and in the Protestant on the other. The latter have been contented to affirm that faithful souls do "enter at once into glory," but assign them no official place in heaven; the former, dividing them according to spiritual condition, make a part to be now reigning with the Lord, priests to whom intercessions may be addressed, and princes whose help may be implored. It is difficult to see how, if already glorified, and able to fulfill heavenly ministries, and to be now kings and priests unto God, any element of the full eternal life is wanting in them.

But high as the position of the dead in Christ may be, and great their blessedness, they are, nevertheless, the dead; in a condition the fruit of sin, and in which there is necessarily, therefore, imperfection and weakness. They rest from their labors. Their active service does not begin till He calls them to come forth from the invisible world, and, clothed in immortal and incorruptible bodies, to take part with Him in the administration of His kingdom. It was a true perception of their imperfect condition, and a right feeling that led the early Church to say in her worship, "May they rest in the peace of God." But we must note how inconsistent is this prayer with the actual exaltation of the dead to a place of rule and intercession. To complete the prayer we must add: "And may they awake to a joyful resurrection."

CHAPTER VI.

THE APOSTASY AND THE ANTICHRIST.

IT is to be noted that the apostle Paul, in what is generally believed to be one of the earliest of his Epistles, the second to the Thessalonians, speaks so distinctly of an "apostasy" or falling away; the beginnings of which he already discerned. That this falling away was not a mere local and temporary defection, but was existing in germ in all the churches, and that it would continue to increase down to the end, are apparent from the language he uses here and in his later Epistles. Its root was the loss of the first love (Rev. ii. 4), and the consequent alienation from God; but its characteristic, as here given by the apostle, was the spirit of lawlessness, which would become stronger and stronger till its last and highest exponent should appear, — "that wicked" or "lawless one," the "son of perdition." This lawless one is to "seat himself in the temple of God, showing himself that he is God;" whose "coming is to be after the working of Satan, with all power and signs and lying wonders;" and he is to be destroyed by the Lord Himself at His appearing. (2 Thess. ii. 1-10.)

This most remarkable announcement by the apostle of the Gentiles almost at the beginning of his ministry, is one that deserves the closest attention. Several times he recurs to the same topic, and warns the churches of the imminent danger. His words are like those of Moses when he foretells to his people their future, the sin of rebellion and its punishment. (Lev. xxvi.) They were intended to make the churches watchful against the beginnings of evil. (Acts xx. 28–31; 1 Tim. iv. 1; 2 Tim. iii. 1.)

The other apostles speak in like terms. The Apostle John warns against "the spirit of Antichrist, whereof ye have heard that it should come, and even now already is it in the world." "As ye have heard that Antichrist shall come, even now are there many Antichrists. . . He is the Antichrist that denieth the Father and the Son." (1 John ii. 18–22.) Antichrist is not only an opponent of Christ, but one who puts himself in the place of Christ; not one who pretends to be the historical Christ, and yet he presents himself as a substitute for Christ. The apostle Peter, in his Second Epistle, describes those in whom the same spirit is found, and which should especially manifest itself in the "scoffers of the last days;" but does not use the term Antichrist.

Turning to the Gospels, we find the Lord to have given like prophetic warnings. In the parable of the tares and wheat He foretells the sowing of tares among the wheat, and represents both as "growing together till the time of the harvest." He does not send forth His reapers to separate them till both are ripe. To the Antichrist He pointed when He said, "I am come in my Father's name, and ye receive me not: if another shall come in his own name, him ye will receive." (John v. 43; Luke xviii. 8.) To him, also, the Spirit of God points in the Book of the Revelation under the title of "the beast" who opens his mouth in blasphemy against God, and who is cast alive into the lake of fire. (Rev. xiii. 1, xix. 19, 20.)

This form of wickedness summed up in the Antichrist, differs from any that was manifest in pre-Christian times, or indeed that was possible, in that it takes the form of direct hostility to Christ as the Incarnate Son and Saviour. Its support is in human pride, denying the fall of man and the corruption of his nature; and in consequence, the necessity of an atonement. It rejects as something humiliating and unworthy of man's dignity, and as a reproach to the goodness of human nature, the truth that there is salvation only through the Sacrifice of Christ; and affirms that men can be saved without an Incarnate Son, and without the cross. So far from needing a Saviour, — One who shall reconcile him to God, and cleanse him from sin, — man has the elements of divinity in his own nature, and needs only scope for their full development to attain to Divine excellence.

Thus the spirit of Antichrist in its last embodiment, is the culmination of all hostility to the purpose of God in man's redemption. By affirming that man is not sinful, only imperfect, and capable of unlimited moral progress, it makes idle all that God has done in sending His Son to bear the sins of the world: proudly declaring that man is not fallen, and that no work of salvation is needed; and that in the race by natural development is God to be revealed, not in any one person by supernatural Incarnation; it leaves no place for Jesus Christ, either as the Saviour from sin or as the Revealer of God.

The appearing of the Antichrist, therefore, marks the highest form of human wickedness, since it not only shows the rejection of the grace of God as manifested in the gift of His Son, but is also the setting of a rival in His throne. And this wickedness appears in the Church, in the company of those whom God has called to be His own children. The Antichrist and his chief adherents come not from the heathen, nor from the Jews, but from among the baptized. (1 John ii. 19.) They are those who have been brought into vital relation to Christ, but have fallen away, and have become "withered branches" in the Vine; those who, "having known the way of righteousness, have turned from the holy commandment delivered unto them;" "twice dead;" "wandering stars." They have received the Holy Spirit, but have grieved and quenched Him, and can no more be renewed unto repentance. (Heb. vi. 6.) In them the apostasy reaches its fullest measure; their sin is the sin unto death. We may thus understand why it is that they are set forth as "cast alive into the lake of fire;" the first so punished, since it is later that the devil is cast into it. (Rev. xix. 20, xx. 10.) As the greatness of the sin, so the swiftness and terror of the punishment.

The Antichrist — the lawless one — is not an accident, nor a strange and unaccountable phenomenon, but the necessary result of a long preceding development; and this both in the Church and in the world. He is not the cause of the Christian apostasy, but its product. The spirit of lawlessness whose workings were seen at the beginning in the rejection of Christ's rule through His apostles sent immediately by Him, must come to the full, ere the lawless one can appear. (2 Cor. x. 8, etc.; 3 John ix.) That must be done in the Church which was done among the Jews, when they said, "We will not have this man to reign over us." And in the State, kings and statesmen having cast off the rule of Christ, their people no longer obey them; and out of the anarchy, the raging sea, comes forth the mighty one who can rule the nations. (Rev. xiii. 1, etc.) So, also, as the representative of worldly culture and human pride, he is its last and highest exponent. There is a steady process of self-exaltation as our race progresses in its knowledge of the material world, and in its control over it. At first, man, ignorant of the forces of nature, fears them, and deifies them, and worships them; but as knowledge increases, he learns to regard them as physical forces to be used by him for his own good. He exalts himself above nature, he is its lord to rule over it: and this not as a prerogative given him by God, but in his own right as his conquest. With this increase of power and knowledge is a gradual diminution of the sense of sin, and of dependence, and the growth of a spirit of self-deification. That which has been in the decay of paganism, takes place again in Christendom, — the apotheosis of man. Man cannot cease to be religious, to seek after the Divine; if God does not descend to men, men must ascend to God; there must be a point of union. If Christ be denied as the Incarnate Son, revealing God in flesh, and bringing us into communion with Him; then in the Antichrist will man be seen "sitting in the temple of God, showing himself that he is God." The craving for a perfected or Divine humanity cannot be stilled. If men are not made partakers of the Divine nature by regeneration, and perfected through resurrection, they aspire to be so by natural development. Thus, at the last day, the Antichrist becomes possible. With the loss of the sense of sin; with a growing consciousness of the great powers of humanity, and their possible unfoldings during the ages; the work of Christ as the Saviour from sin, and as the one Revealer of God, becomes more and more offensive." Man will be his own Saviour and Lord, and go unto God in his own name.

The Antichrist appears not only as Christ's antagonist in the Church, but as also claiming the rule of the world; and it is in this aspect that in the Revelation he is symbolized as "the beast that comes up out of the sea," and to whom "the dragon gives his power and his seat" (or throne), "and great authority." (Rev. xiii. 1, 2.) He is the vicegerent of Satan, whom the Lord called "the prince of this world." (John xiv. 30.) The dominion which Satan proffered, and the Lord refused, this man accepts. (Matt. iv. 8.) As Christ sits in the throne given Him by the Father, so the Antichrist in the throne given him by Satan. And as the Father is worshipped through the Christ, so Satan through the Antichrist. "And they worshipped the dragon, which gave authority to the beast." It need scarcely be said that the "great authority" of Satan is by God's sufferance, not self-derived. (Luke iv. 6.) "All this power will I give thee, . . . for that is delivered unto me; and to whomsoever I will, I give it." Power is given to the beast over the earth as a judgment by God upon the peoples and the nations at the end, as it was given of old to the Assyrian. (Isa. x. 5, 6.)

This close relation of the Antichrist to the god and prince of this world, is to be carefully noted. Not only does the former receive of the latter his great authority in the earth, but is endowed by him with superhuman powers. It is said of the man of sin that "his coming is after the working of Satan," or, according to the energy of Satan, "with all power and signs and lying wonders." (2 Thess. ii. 9; Rev. xiii.) There is such community of feeling and action between them in opposition to God and His Christ, that he can receive the fullest satanic endowments, and become the chief instrument of satanic hate. "There was given unto him a mouth speaking great things and blasphemies, . . . to blaspheme God's name, and His tabernacle, and them that dwell in heaven." He "makes war with the saints, and overcomes them," and "power is given him over all kindreds and tongues and nations." In him, fallen humanity reaches its highest development; he becomes its most powerful and magnificent exponent; he is "the leviathan" of the sea, "the king over all the children of pride." "All the world wondered after the beast; . . . they worshipped the beast, saying, Who is like unto the beast? who is able to make war with him?"

When it is said that power was given to the beast over all kindreds and tongues and nations, it is not probably to be understood as foretelling an absolutely universal kingdom, but as prophetic of a great world-monarchy still future, surpassing in extent all that has hitherto existed. And the possibility of this increases year by year, as the facilities of intercommunication become continually greater, and through general intercourse new and friendly relations among nations are established. The earth has already so become one that nothing can take place in any land that is not speedily known in, and that does not affect according to its importance, every other land. There is, also, a community of interest, of opinion, and of feeling, such as has never been before. Nations heretofore dwelling apart lose their isolation, and the great currents of national life run into one still greater, — the life of the race. Under all the differences of lineage and of language, of laws and of customs, there is already a broad, underlying unity which may serve as the basis for the structure of an universal government. Knowledge of what is taking place in the most remote lands is immediately attainable in all the chief centres of Christendom. It is now possible that a single dominant will may make itself obeyed in every important country of the earth, through the almost instantaneous transmission of its commands; thus giving to the ruler a certain omniscience and omnipresence. And the Scriptures in their description of the reign of Antichrist, do not speak of the fusion of all peoples into one, and the abolition of all national distinctions, but of "ten kings," heads of distinct states, who enter into a confederacy of which he is made the head. It is but an enlarged application of the principle of federative union. "These have one mind, and shall give their power and strength (authority) unto the beast." (Rev. xvii. 13.) Nor is this unity without God's special agency; for it is said, God "hath put in their hearts to fulfill his will, and to agree, and to give their kingdom unto the beast."

Thus he, who is the opponent of Christ, becomes a substitute for Him. He promises to the nations that unity and prosperity and peace, that harmony of interests, and reconciliation of antagonisms, of which the prophets spake as to be realized in the Kingdom of the Messiah, but which has never been realized in Christendom. And there are many everywhere saying in their hearts: the Christ of the Church has not fulfilled, and will never fulfill, the old prophetic dreams. We have waited long centuries for His Kingdom, and the confusion and misery continually increase. There must be a new departure: man must assert his own dignity, and freeing himself from superstitious fears and antiquated observances, which repress his energies and burden his spirit, build up on new foundations the Kingdom of Humanity. What the Christ has failed to do, the Antichrist will promise to perform, and the world will believe him.

III.

THE REVELATIONS OF GOD TO MEN IN THE MESSIANIC KINGDOM.

CHAPTER I.

THE MESSIANIC KINGDOM: ITS NATURE AND PURPOSE.

ALL prophecy, as we have abundantly seen, pointed forward to the universal Kingdom of Jehovah, administered by the promised Son of David. For this the world is to wait, in it all nations will be blessed: it is the consummation of prophetic hope. All His prior actings in redemption are to prepare the way for this, its last stage.

In considering the nature and purpose of this Kingdom, we are to note the two elements — revelation and redemption — that meet us in every stage in the execution of the Divine purpose, and go hand in hand till its end is reached. The more God manifests Himself to faithful men, the higher and purer is their conception of His character, and the more intimate the communion with Him into which they are admitted. In His light they see light, and this more and more as His purpose goes on. Jehovah manifested Himself to the patriarchs under visible symbols, and thus taught them of His will; and to the Jews in higher degree through His dwelling among them, and by the laws He gave them. But these forms of revelation were necessarily very imperfect; and were but preparatory to that to be made in the person of the Incarnate Son, and in His teachings and works. The glory of God now shines in the face of Jesus Christ, "in whom dwells all the fullness of the Godhead bodily." Yet in Him while on earth, there was not a full and complete manifestation of His glory, since His first work was one of humiliation. He emptied Himself, and took upon Him the form of a servant. " He was made in the likeness of sinful flesh, that He might condemn sin in the flesh." It was not till He rose from the dead that He entered into that condition of humanity in which He could be glorified, and become, in the fullest sense, the "Image of the invisible God." And in this glory He now abides in heaven, and is seen only by the eye of faith. It is not till He comes forth that men can know what glorified humanity is, and behold how God is revealed in Him.

The highest degree of Divine revelation that can be made till redemption is completed, is, therefore, when the Risen Lord appears in glory to establish His Kingdom. This is the coming of Jehovah of which the Old-Testament prophets so often speak, but of which the Jewish people could have had only the most inadequate conceptions; and the majesty of which even the Church, illumined by His Spirit, can but dimly discern. The Kingdom period, therefore, is pre-eminently the period of Divine revelation, because the Incarnate King comes from Heaven in the glory of the Father, and of the holy angels, to seat Himself on the throne of His glory.

As the revelation of God reaches its highest stage at the coming of the glorified Lord from heaven, and in the kingdom that follows, so also does redemption. Full redemption is not attained in the Church in this dispensation. The life of the Risen One has been given to His members, but is not yet perfected in them; death is not yet swallowed up in victory. The dead in Christ are still waiting for their bodies to be given them at the resurrection; and the living for the change to be wrought in them at the translation, when the mortal and corruptible will give place to the immortal and incorruptible. None of His members have yet attained to the perfect likeness of the Head; they have not entered into His glory, and are not yet " manifested as the sons of God." " We which have the first-fruits of the Spirit groan within ourselves, waiting for the adoption, to wit, the redemption of our body." (Rom. viii. 23.) This perfected redemption cannot be till God enter on a new stage of revelation. "When Christ our life shall appear, then shall ye also appear with Him in glory." When made like Him, in spirit and in body, redemption is perfected in His members. They now enter into the glory of the heavenly condition.

But this perfected redemption at the Lord's coming is only attained by the members of the body of Christ, and by those of the earlier dispensations whom He shall account worthy to attain to the resurrection from the dead. Of the living upon the earth other than the baptized, there remain the two classes, the Jews and the nations. To the Jews He is then revealed as their Messiah, the Son of David. "They will look upon Me whom they have pierced, and mourn for Him as one mourneth for his only son." (Zech. xii. 10.) The veil will be taken from their hearts, and they will understand the purpose of God in Him, as declared by their prophets. They will submit themselves to Him, and He will pour out upon them His Spirit, and make them His holy people. They are not, indeed, lifted up into the condition of immortality and incorruptibility to which the Church has attained, but are so cleansed, sanctified, and illumined, that they can be the fitting instrument to fulfill the purpose of God in their election; and through them Jehovah will be revealed to all the world. The nations will now see in them such manifestation of the righteousness and goodness of God under the holy rule of Christ, that they will seek to join themselves to them, and to have part in the blessings of His Kingdom. (Isa. ii. 3, lv. 5; Zech. viii. 20–23.)

It is thus, as the last and highest stage of the redemptive work, that the Kingdom is brought before us in the Scriptures. Of the judgments that precede it, and the successive steps of its establishment, there is occasion to speak in another place. Its great characteristics are these: first, it is the period when He, the glorified Lord, who is now invisible, fulfilling His ministry as the great High Priest in the most Holy Place, will come forth, and be manifested in the earth as the Judge and King, the Power and the Righteousness of God. Second, with this manifestation of God in Him, redemption is perfected in the members of His Body, to whom He is the Resurrection and the Life. They see Him, and are made like Him, and so prepared to co-work with Him. Third, He is manifested to the Jews. The children of Abraham so long rejecting Him, are convinced, like St. Paul, through His appearing to them, that He is indeed their Messiah, and become submissive and obedient. Finally, through them regathered and set in their place, will He be made known to all lands. The unbaptized nations, who are the great majority of all the inhabitants of the earth, and still under the power of false religions, will be brought to know Jehovah, and gladly receive instruction at the hands of His servants.

It would be presumptuous to speak in detail of the constitution of the Messianic Kingdom, and of its administration; but certain points are clearly indicated in the prophets.

It has already been said that the two elections — the Jewish nation and the Christian Church — cannot fulfill their purpose, each in its respective sphere, till they have been completed and perfected. The Church must be brought through the resurrection or translation of its members, into the same state of glorified humanity into which its Head has entered; and thus be fitted to do His work in the time of the Kingdom, and to be partaker of His authority. And the Jews restored and sanctified, and brought under the rule of the Son of David, and obediently serving Him, are then fitted to be His instruments to teach and guide and govern the nations.

Thus in the Kingdom, when fully established, we find three distinct elements: first, the Church as the Body of Christ, no more under the law of sin and death, but made like Him, and in perfect unity with Him; second, the Jewish nation, God's holy and righteous people, in their own land and under the immediate rule of His Son; third, the nations at peace, obeying and worshipping God. We have in this threefold division the counterpart of the threefold divisions of the tabernacle and the temple, — the most Holy Place, the Holy, and the Outer Court. Into the first, where God dwelt, the high priest alone entered; it was shut to all beside: into the second, only the priests: in the outer court the people worshipped. And so in the Kingdom, Christ the High Priest, and those with Him, His priests made like Him, holy and immortal, stand in the immediate Presence of God, to which none beside can approach. The Jewish people, with their rites of worship at Jerusalem, then fulfill before the world their calling as a kingdom of priests; the holy city becomes the place of Divine manifestation to the nations, — the great ecclesiastical centre of the earth; and to the temple all the nations come up, doubtless in their representatives, at appointed times to worship before the Lord of hosts. (Jer. iii. 17; Zech. xiv. 16.)

It is through the two elections, each perfected and acting in its own sphere, that Christ fulfills His twofold functions as Priest and King. To His brethren, as made like Him in resurrection, belongs the first place; not only as priests ever worshipping the Father in the Most Holy, and making intercession for all, but also as kings. "I appoint unto you a kingdom as my Father hath appointed unto me." This is not simply to share in the blessings of the kingdom as one of righteousness and peace, — for this both the Jews and the nations do, each in its degree, — but to be the rulers in it. This is the prerogative of those only who have entered into the power and glory of the resurrection. (Rev. xx. 6.) In what way their functions of rule are to be exercised, it is not possible to say; but it is clearly intimated that some special administration over the Jews is to be intrusted to the apostles. (Matt. xix. 28; Luke xxii. 29, 30.) That the Jews will have rule over the nations, and that this rule will be exercised, not arbitrarily or oppressively, but under the direction of Christ with righteousness and gentleness, is also clearly declared by the Old-Testament prophets. (Deut. xxvi. 19; Isa. lx. 12.)

Thus there is during the Kingdom period a well-ordered system of government, embracing the whole earth, administered by Christ through those whom He appoints; a system adapted to meet the needs of all its inhabitants in all their varied conditions and degrees of intellectual and spiritual development. Now is first seen the full power of the Divine institutions of the family and the state, when filled by His Spirit, to produce the purest and noblest fruits in individual life. Now is, also, seen the full development of national life, the solution of all social and political questions, and the true unity of nations. All that men have ever imagined of human progress in science and art, will fall far short of the attainments of those who will study God's works, not from personal ambition or vanity, but out of love of Him, delighting in every new discovery of His wisdom and goodness, and using all knowledge for the blessing of their fellow-men. And now will all the earth worship the Father through the Son; Christ Himself leading the worship in the heavenlies with His Church; the Jews under material forms and rites adapted to their end, commemorating His redemptive work; and the nations in their own lands, and in solemn processions to the Holy City, acknowledging Jehovah as the One Supreme God, and offering to Him their homage.

The Kingdom period will be the true golden age of the world, for which the lofty-minded and pure-hearted of all generations have longed; a time in which all that is noblest and holiest in man will be called forth, and all that is evil will be repressed. Now is brought into strongest contrast the two conditions of humanity, the natural (psychical) and the spiritual, the mortal and the immortal, the life of the first Adam and the life of the Second. Between the disembodied and those in the body God has set a gulf that we may not pass over, and a natural repulsion; but between those in the immortal body and those in the mortal, there is no gulf and no repulsion. Both co-exist in the Kingdom period; and those still in mortal bodies, seeing in Christ and the Church what the perfected condition of humanity is, are lifted up with the hope of attaining to the same condition of immortality.

CHAPTER II.

THE JUDICIAL ACTINGS OF CHRIST AS PREPARATORY TO THE KINGDOM AND THE DAY OF THE LORD.

THE apostle Paul says of the Son, that "He must reign till He hath put all enemies under His feet; the last enemy that shall be destroyed is death." (1 Cor. xv. 25.) In these words we are taught that the whole period of the Kingdom is a day in which the Son is engaged in putting all things under Him, that He may establish that order which is eternal, because perfect. The last enemy to be destroyed is death, and this is apparently the last act before giving up the kingdom to the Father. (Rev. xx. 11–14.) But if the whole period of the Kingdom has thus a judicial character, the Scriptures enable us to distinguish two chief acts,— one at its beginning, and one at its end; and between these there is a time of peaceful rule over all the earth, in which the redemptive promises of God to men will be fulfilled. We may, therefore, distinguish between this rule of Christ in His kingdom when established, and His judicial acts preparatory to its establishment. He Himself says, that at "the end of the world," or "consummation of the age," He " will send forth His angels, and they shall gather out of His kingdom all things that offend, and them which do iniquity, and shall cast them into a furnace of fire. . . . Then shall the righteous shine forth as the sun in the kingdom of their

Father." "The angels shall come forth, and sever the wicked from among the just." Let us now consider this process of judgment at the setting up of the Kingdom more in detail, first, as to its nature; second, as to its subjects. The final judgment at its close will be later considered.

First, As to its nature. The work of judgment as here described has two elements, — first, separation; second, reward. Separation must be made among those living at the Lord's return, since up to this time the good and evil are commingled, the tares and wheat grow together, the sheep and goats make one flock. There must be a division, and each go to its own place. Upon this separation, in itself a judicial process, follows the award of blessing or punishment. Then the faithful inherit the Kingdom, and the wicked are cast out. When this separation is fully accomplished, and the obedient only are left, the period follows when "the will of God is done in earth as in heaven."

It needs scarcely be said, that before this separation of good and evil at the Lord's coming, there is a process of spiritual division ever going on, men dividing themselves according to moral character. There is a true sense in which every man now "goes to his own place," self-moved: the evil gather to the evil, the good to the good. This which has always been the case in human history, will be so pre-eminently at the time of the end, when God in His providence will so arrange events, that, as in the case of the choice of the people between Christ and Barabbas, the thoughts of all hearts in regard to His Son will be revealed.

It has already been remarked, that the characteristic of the time immediately preceding the return of the Messiah, is lawlessness, the highest exponent of which is the lawless one, the Antichrist. Men strive to set themselves free from all bonds, human and Divine, that restrain freedom of action. The Divinely appointed relations of the Family, the State, and the Church, lose their cohesive power because emptied of Divine authority; and obedience to human rulers becomes a matter of interest or of compulsion. Nothing is allowed to stand which hinders the supremacy of the individual will. Thus there is a general dissolution of social, political, and ecclesiastical bonds. Christendom becomes "the city of confusion," or "city of chaos." Through this dissolving process, the way is prepared for men to gather together according to their affinities. The anarchy of absolute individualism cannot indeed be endured, and hence a multitude of societies, unions, confederacies, secret and open, of all kinds, and for all purposes; — "the gathering into bundles" of which the Lord speaks. The institutions of God being set aside as failures because they have not brought peace and prosperity to the earth, not even to Christendom, something must take their place; and hence there are many attempts at the reconstruction of society, the removal of present evils, and the restoration of social order. But men, being no longer bound together by common principles and beliefs, nor by faith in God, can rally only around men; hence the last days are, above all, the time for the development of great personalities, mighty men of action; pre-eminent among whom and chief, is the last of the antichrists.

Thus the days preceding the Messiah are to be looked at from a twofold point of view: first, as a time when men, casting off Divine bonds, are set free to reveal in word and act all that is in their hearts. God so orders events that every man must at last take his place with the Christ or with the Antichrist. As the time of the harvest draws nigh, both the tares and the wheat ripen.

As the summer heat quickens all germs into life, so in this time will the faculties of men be quickened into intense activity; and as the time of ripening brings out the special characteristics of the wheat and tares, their nature being seen in their fruits, so with the good and the evil in that day. Every opposition will be brought to light, every antagonism will be sharpened. Mediations and compromises will be no longer possible: none will be able ignorantly "to call evil good, or good evil." "The hail shall sweep away the refuges of lies." It is the day of decision, when God will have men say plainly, and with full consciousness, whether they will have His Son as their Saviour and King, or not.

Second, as a time when those who reject the appointments of God, seek to replace them by human appointments; and to reconstruct the Family and State and Church on other foundations, and according to other principles, than those He has set and declared. And as man builds, God tests his work. He shakes the heavens and the earth, that all that can be shaken — all that is of man — may be removed, and only what cannot be shaken — all that is of God — may remain. During this period, as never before, the words of the poet are proved true, "The world's history is the world's judgment."

Thus, through the freedom of individual action from the dissolution of all old bonds, and through the providential actings of God, bringing into clear light His purpose in His Son, and forcing men to act, the process of spiritual separation is effected; first in the Church, and then in the Jews, and finally among the nations. The instrumentality by which these separations are effected, is the testimony borne by faithful men to God's purpose in Christ, followed by acts of judgment on the disobedient. Thus, at last, all are brought into positions in which they cannot be neutral: they must choose to act with God, or against Him, and are self-judged. Upon this will follow those special judicial acts of Christ whereby those separated will be gathered to their respective places to receive their final rewards.

As to the subjects of this judgment. There will be on the earth at the time of the setting up of the Kingdom, three distinct classes, — the Church, or company of the baptized; the Jewish people scattered abroad; and the nations, the unbaptized, or heathen: and the dealings of God with them are to the intent that all in each of these classes who will believe, may be gathered out from the unrepentant and unbelieving. The first separation is to be made in the Church, as having the highest place in the purpose of God, and most capable of discerning His truth. To it, therefore, must the first testimony be borne; and here will begin the spiritual division, preparing the way for the judicial acts to follow. As there are degrees of spiritual discernment and of faithfulness among those truly Christ's, there may be several successive messages and successive acts of separation. (Matt. x. 40, 42.) There may be the fully ripe, the almost ripe, and the green ears; the first-fruits, the harvest, and the gleanings. Those most devoted and faithful, the quickest to hear the Lord's words, and to discern His will, may first be gathered; and the rest in several successive companies, according to their spiritual development, till His own, all in whom the least germ of faith is found, shall be brought to Him. (Rev. xiv.) Thus, at last, the wheat and the tares will be separated, and not one grain of wheat be lost. On the other hand, all the apostates, all in whom the invincible heart of unbelief is found, will be hardened by God's dealings with them, will reject every testimony borne by His witnesses, and finally will join themselves to the Antichrist, and will perish with him. (Rev. xix. 19, etc.)

The second class is the Jews. These are scattered among the nations, yet do not remain unaffected during the Lord's dealings with the Church. A like process of spiritual separation is going on, also, among them, — some turning to Christ as their Messiah, and others made more hostile and bitter against Him; but probably its consummation is not reached till the work in the Church is finished. Here, as among the baptized, the separation is made by the word of truth, the witness borne by God's servants to His Son. Such witnesses will He raise up from the Jews themselves, the believing testifying to the unbelieving; and we may believe that at some stage earlier or later of His dealings with them, the prophecy respecting Elijah will be fulfilled. (Mal. iv. 5.) And the word of witness will be confirmed by God's actings, as foretold by their prophets, so that all who will, may know the Divine purpose. Thus, through His word declared to them, and by His mighty acts, will God awaken faith in their hearts, that "whosoever will call on the name of the Lord, may be saved." None will be lost but such as stubbornly refuse to see and to hear. Those brought to repentance and to faith in their Messiah, — "the remnant," "the holy seed" of the prophets, — He will reconstitute as a nation; and His Son will reign over them, and fulfill to them all the words the prophets had spoken. Only the persistently unrepentant will be left, who, joining themselves to the Antichrist, perhaps receiving him as their Messiah, are cut off with him.

The third class is the nations, the unbaptized, or the heathen. These not having the Scriptures, nor knowing the purpose of God in Christ, are not reached so much by a witness to the truth, as by His great and terrible works in the earth. He is made known to them chiefly through the Jews, both through the knowledge of His wonderful actings toward them in their national deliverance, and through those whom He sends forth from them as His special witnesses. (Ezek. xxxvi. 36; Isa. lxvi. 19.) In this people so widely scattered, so long afflicted, so greatly despised, and now so wonderfully regathered, and so visibly blessed and honored by God, the heathen nations will see His hand, and admire His power and goodness. "It shall come to pass that ten men shall take hold, out of all languages of the nations, of the skirt of him that is a Jew, saying, We will go with you, for we have heard that God is with you." (Zech. viii. 23.) Then will He be sanctified in their eyes. "The heathen shall know that I am the Lord when I shall be sanctified in you before their eyes." (Ezek. xxxvi. 23.) Thus the regathering of the Jews from dispersion and their restoration, more marvellous in all its attendant circumstances than the deliverance from Egypt, and from so many lands, will make God and the Messiah known unto all peoples. The revelation of His glory at Jerusalem, the righteousness of the Messianic rule, the blessings given to all the obedient, cannot be hidden. "All that see them, shall acknowledge them that they are the seed which the Lord hath blessed;" and to the city of the Great King will they go up that they may be taught of His ways, and offer to Him their worship. Those who remain to the end disobedient, rejecting the Messiah's rule, will He cut off from the earth. (Ps. ix. 17.)

Such is a brief general outline of those judicial actings of God, which precede and accompany the setting up of the Messianic Kingdom. That which marks them is, that they are in intent for salvation, not for destruction; chastisements to bring to repentance. He first sends forth His witnesses to make known His purpose and declare

His righteousness, and this witness is followed by the punishment of those who refuse to listen. Successive messages of warning, and successive punishments upon those who do not heed them, are the means of separating all who are penitent and have faith, from the persistently obstinate and unrepentant. Thus, out of each of these three classes, — the baptized, the Jews, the heathen nations, — are all at last gathered who see the hand of God, and become submissive to His will.

It is this period immediately preceding the setting up of the Messianic Kingdom, to which the prophets so often refer as "the day of the Lord," "the great and terrible day." It is presented in many aspects, but its special characteristic is the manifestation of Jehovah as the Righteous and Supreme Lord. It is the time when He presents Himself as the Judge, both of His own people and of the nations; and, as a day of judgment, it has a twofold character; it is both "a day of destruction" and "a day of salvation." Then He reveals both His mercy and His justice as never before in the history of the world. "He makes bare His holy arm in the eyes of all the nations." None dwelling on the earth shall longer be ignorant that He is the Almighty and Righteous God, and that He has given all power and dominion to His Son; and all who array themselves against His purpose will He destroy from off the earth. "It is a day that burneth as an oven; and all the proud, yea, and all that do wickedly, shall be stubble." "The day of the Lord of hosts shall be upon every one that is proud and lofty, and upon every one that is lifted up, and he shall be brought low. . . . And the Lord alone shall be exalted in that day." "By fire and by His sword will the Lord plead with all flesh, and the slain of the Lord shall be many."

As the great and terrible day, a day of vengeance, of

destruction, it was associated in the Jewish mind with all forms of terror and distress. It was thought of as ushered in by many portents, both in nature and among men, — famines, earthquakes, tempests, wars, signs in sun, moon, and stars; persecutions of the faithful, outbreaks of wickedness, a general dissolution of all social and religious bonds. The hostility of man to Jehovah and to His purpose in His Son is brought out as never before; the spirit of proud disobedience now reaches its height. The long-suffering of Jehovah comes to its end. He will no longer suffer the ungodly to triumph; He will interpose to deliver His afflicted people. But while a day of vengeance, it is also a day of mercy; since the way is thus prepared for the Kingdom of His Son and the Messianic salvation.

It was the longing of many Jewish hearts, "Oh! that the salvation of Israel were come out of Zion." But this was more than the salvation of Israel. "All the ends of the earth shall see the salvation of our God." "The Lord hath made known His salvation, His righteousness hath He openly shewed in the sight of the heathen." Out of the night cometh the day; and out of anarchy and violence, and all the forms of wickedness of the last times, come the peace and order and holiness of the Messianic Kingdom.

We know from our Lord's own words that He acts for God in all this work preparatory to the Kingdom. "The Father judgeth no man, but hath committed all judgment unto the Son." (John v. 22.) And in the prophets this is often declared: "Behold, thy King cometh unto thee: He is just, and having salvation. . . . He shall speak peace unto the heathen, and His dominion shall be from sea to sea, and from the river to the ends of the earth." (Zech. ix. 9, etc.; Isa. xi. 4.) He will execute Jehovah's righteous judgments upon His enemies. Then will be "given Him the heathen for His inheritance, and the uttermost parts of the earth for His possession; and He will break them with a rod of iron, and dash them in pieces, like a potter's vessel." Then will "He strike through kings in the day of His wrath. . . . He shall fill the places with dead bodies." And in Him are fulfilled the words respecting the coming of Jehovah to judge the earth. "He cometh to judge the earth; He shall judge the world with righteousness, and the people with His truth." In the Revelation, He is presented as coming from heaven: "I saw heaven opened, and behold a white horse; and He that sat on Him was called Faithful and True, and in righteousness He doth judge and make war." (xix. 11.)

These predictions by the prophets of the fearful judgment of God by the Messiah upon all who should oppose Him at the setting up of the Messianic Kingdom, our Lord confirmed in His own teachings. He declared that, at the time of His return, there "shall be great tribulation, such as was not since the beginning of the world, no, nor ever shall be; and except those days should be shortened, there should no flesh be saved." (Matt. xxiv. 21.) There shall be "upon the earth distress of nations, with perplexity; the sea and the waves roaring" (or, "in perplexity for the roaring of the sea and the billows." Rev. Ver.); "men's hearts failing them for fear, and for looking after those things which are coming on the earth." (Luke xxi. 25, etc.) "For these be the days of vengeance, that all things which are written may be fulfilled." The apostles speak in like way: "The Lord Jesus shall be revealed from heaven with His mighty angels, in flaming fire taking vengeance on them that know not God, and that obey not the gospel of our Lord Jesus Christ; who shall be punished with everlasting destruction from the presence of the Lord, and from the glory of His power." (2 Thess. i. 7–10.)

In the Book of the Revelation, which has especial reference to the Church, an order is clearly set forth in those disciplinary judgments preceding the Lord's return. In the trumpets there is first a note of warning, followed by a chastisement upon those by whom the warning is unheard; then another warning and another chastisement, the chastisements increasing in severity as men rebel and blaspheme. (Chaps. viii., ix. 20, 21.) Upon the trumpets follow the vials "full of the wrath of God," "the seven last plagues, for in them is filled up the wrath of God." The merciful actings of God having failed to bring all to repentance, He visits the unrepentant in righteous anger. "The first angel went and poured out his vial, . . . and there fell a noisome and grievous sore upon the men which had the mark of the beast, and upon them which worshipped his image." (xvi. 2.) But the more his displeasure is manifested, the more the evil in them is revealed; "they blasphemed the name of God, . . . and they repented not to give Him glory." The end of all is, that the hardened and the incorrigible gather themselves to the beast and false prophet, that they may resist to the last the Messiah and His Kingdom. (Rev. xix. 19, etc.)

Thus, among the living on earth, when these successive separations have been completed, are left only the holy ones of the Church, the repentant and restored among the Jews, the obedient among the nations. All the rebellious, all who remain hostile to God and to His Son, neither moved by His goodness nor trembling at His justice, are cut off from the earth. Now, all hinderances being removed, "all things that offend being gathered out, and them which do iniquity," the true order of the Messianic Kingdom is seen; and the Messiah rules over a world at rest, and in peace. How long a period will be occupied in these processes of separation and reward, has not been made known, but must necessarily be of considerable duration.

The Scriptures mention many events as immediately preceding the establishment of the Kingdom, which must be referred to this period, but whose exact order is not known, — the persecution of the Jews by the Gentiles, the ripening of the apostasy in the Christian Church, the appearing of the Antichrist, the growth of his power, the great and last confederacy of kings and rulers against the Lord and His Anointed, the partial regathering of the Jews, a new and final assault of the nations against Jerusalem, the sufferings and death of the martyrs, and the overthrow of the Antichrist, — events which apparently must demand years for their accomplishment.

From these judicial actings of God with the living, we turn to the departed, and ask whether, as some in the Church on the earth are changed into Christ's likeness at His coming, and made immortal that they may reign with Him; it is so likewise with some of the departed? Is there a separation among the dead, some rising before the rest? That the resurrection spoken of by the Old-Testament prophets is a partial one, we have already seen. We are told by the apostle that "we which are alive, and remain unto the coming of the Lord, shall not prevent them which are asleep. . . . The dead in Christ shall rise first; then we, which are alive and remain, shall be caught up together with them in the clouds." The faithful living enter into His glory by translation, the faithful departed by resurrection. Thus, there is at His coming a separation among the dead; not all are then raised, only those whom the Lord counts worthy. (Luke xx. 35.) "The Son quickeneth whom He will." This is the first resurrection, that to which St. Paul strove to attain. (Phil. iii. 11.) How great the number that will attain to it, whether all those who sleep in Jesus, or the most faithful only, it is not for us to decide. "Blessed and holy is he that hath part in the first resurrection: on such the second death hath no power." This election from among the dead, the clothing of some with their immortal and incorruptible bodies before others, has its ground in His purpose of progressive redemption and revelation, first in Christ raised from the dead and glorified, then in the members of His body made like Him; and faithfulness in the present life is the measure of reward in the life to come. "To sit on my right hand and on my left, is not mine to give; but it shall be given to them for whom it has been prepared of my Father." (Matt. xx. 23.) "Thou shalt be recompensed at the resurrection of the just." (Luke xiv. 14.)

CHAPTER III.

THE MESSIANIC KINGDOM IN THE BOOK OF THE REVELATION.

IN the Old Testament there are many prophetic books; in the New but one, the Book of the Revelation. This is most remarkable when we consider the place of the Church in the purpose of God, and the long centuries of her history. But not less remarkable are the form and contents of this book. As written for Christians, no longer under the law but having the Spirit, we might anticipate a plain outline of the future, a simple and direct mode of speech, clear indications of the dangers to be avoided and announcements of the judgments threatened. On the contrary, the Revelation is pre-eminently a book of symbols; and upon the right understanding of these symbols our knowledge of its meaning must depend. And these symbols are all of Old-Testament origin; applications of the types of the law, — its rites and times and numbers, — and of the recorded actings of God, to the history of the Church. As His purpose is one from the beginning, the knowledge of these symbols in their bearing on the future, must rest on the right understanding of their use in the past, and of their prophetical significance. The Book of the Revelation is not to be looked at apart and by itself, but is the consummation and crown of all earlier revelations; and presupposes that these are seen in their true relations to Him, who is the "First and the Last."

As to its contents, this book is a revelation of Jesus Christ, — a revelation of which He is both Author and End, the Revealer and the Revealed; and which will be completed when He comes from heaven to seat Himself on the throne of His glory. It is not a history of the Church as a kingdom of this world, and in its relation to earthly powers; for the Church is an election out of all peoples, and stands in no political relations to any, as did the Jewish people. It is an outline of the spiritual work of the Lord, as the Bishop and High Priest in heaven, to free His members from all worldly bonds, and make them like Himself that they may enter into His glory. The great events affecting the destiny of the Church are internal, not external; they have reference to her own spiritual condition, and not to God's actings in the world without. As Bishop, Christ speaks to the Church in the Seven Epistles, warning of errors, of dangers, and of judgments. In opening the seals, He is seen delivering the Church from her bondage under the power of the world, and bringing her again into the full spiritual liberty which is her right as His body. In the trumpets, He gives successive warnings of the judgments that will come on the disobedient; and in the vials, He pours out the wrath of God upon the obstinate and incorrigible. His work as High Priest in the Most Holy being finished, He comes forth to do His work as the Judge and the King. He makes all things new; and then, the purpose of the Kingdom having been accomplished, the everlasting age begins.

Such are in general the contents of this book. Into any explanation of its symbols we are not here called to enter; we are concerned only with the light given us in it respecting the Messianic Kingdom. But it is necessary that one principle of symbolic interpretation be kept clearly in mind, — that the names, whether of persons or of peoples, or terms descriptive of historical events, are not to be understood literally. Thus, Babylon is not the literal Babylon, nor Egypt the literal Egypt; nor, what is to be specially observed, are the Jews literal Jews, or the tribes the literal tribes, or the Holy City the literal Jerusalem. This book is for the Church, — the new election, — in which the Jews as such have no distinctive place; as the old election, they have their own prophets, whose words reach down to the Messianic Kingdom. When mentioned here, it is only as symbols, that through God's dealings with them as recorded in the Old Testament, light may be given to the Church.

The preparation of the Church for the kingdom of Christ, or the Messianic Kingdom, is the theme of this book. That she would pass through sore trials, and yield to the power of temptation, both the Lord and the apostles foretold; and we find them here set forth under symbolical forms. The seals which bind the Lord's inheritance must be broken; His children, having come into the captivity of Babylon, must be delivered. The effect of all God's dealings with His people is the separation of the faithful, and their union with Christ under the figure of "the marriage of the Lamb." Then can the Kingdom be set up.

As the Messianic Kingdom is here seen in its immediate relations to the Church, — not to the Jews, for of their relations to it their own prophets have abundantly spoken, — it will be presented to us in certain new aspects. These are, —

First, As preceded by the marriage of the Lamb, or that mystical union set forth by the marriage relation. It is quite another relation than that of Messiah to the

Jews when they shall be reconstituted as a nation. To them He is a King; to the Church, "bone of His bone, and flesh of His flesh," He is the Husband; they are His people; she is His wife. (Eph. v. 29, 32.) Now can she sit with Him in His throne, and eat at His table, and be His helper in the administration of His rule. This is the fulfillment of her calling, the consummation of her history; and, therefore, it is said, "Let us be glad, and rejoice, and give honor to Him, for the marriage of the Lamb is come, and His wife hath made herself ready. . . . Blessed are they which are called unto the marriage supper of the Lamb." (xiv. 7, 9.)

Second, The binding of Satan. It was only after the appearing of the Son of God in flesh, that the great enemy appeared conspicuous in opposition to God, His antagonist in the redemptive work. Although he was at first the tempter of Adam, and the victor; and re-appears at intervals in the biblical records; it is not till the Deliverer enters on His personal work that he is presented distinctly in the fullness of his malignity and power. He dares to tempt the Lord Himself; and ever after in the history of the Church uses all his arts of falsehood and craft to lead astray and destroy. The names given him by the Lord, — "the murderer," "the father of lies," "the prince of this world;" and by the apostles, — "the god of this world," "the slanderer," "the accuser," — serve to show that the cessation of satanic hostility and the binding of "the power of darkness" is a most important element in preparing the way for the establishing of the order and peace and holiness of the Messianic Kingdom. And it is his loosing out of his prison that brings about the final apostasy of the nations. It may be that the mention of "the unclean spirit" in the prophecy of Zechariah — "I will cut off the names of the idols out of the land, . . . and also I will cause the prophets and the unclean spirit to pass out of the land"—is a prophecy of the binding of Satan, although expressed in terms fitted to the people of Israel.

Third, The duration of the Messianic Kingdom. This is defined as "a thousand years." Whether this number is to be taken literally or symbolically, may be questioned; most of the Apocalyptic numbers are of the latter kind. (ix. 16, xiii. 18.) It may be so taken here, ten being the symbol of the Kingdom, and one thousand its cube. As the most holy place in the tabernacle and the temple was a cube, and so the Holy City (xxi. 16), it is not improbably a symbolical expression of the fullness of holiness to be realized in the fullness of time. But mere duration is of itself unimportant: it is sufficient to know that the Kingdom will continue till its purpose is accomplished.

Fourth, The unbinding of Satan and the deceiving of the nations. (xx. 7.) Old-Testament prophecy did not, as we have seen, speak distinctly, if at all, of events to follow the Messianic Kingdom. But in this book we are told that, after Satan is unloosed, he will deceive the nations which are in the four quarters of the earth, — Gog and Magog, — and gather them to battle against the camp of the saints and the beloved city; and that God will devour them by fire from heaven. It is most probable that the terms Gog and Magog are to be taken here, as other like terms in this book, in their symbolical meaning. Of the significance of this final rebellion, we have elsewhere spoken.

Fifth, The last and universal resurrection and judgment. Although the Lord on earth had spoken of a resurrection that should embrace all, yet He gave no details. Here, its nature and circumstances are more fully given. Only the dead are mentioned, those who still remain in their graves. All these are not wicked, but in part those whose names are written in the Book of Life, and who were not partakers of the first resurrection. "Whosoever was not found written in the Book of Life, was cast into the lake of fire." (xx. 11–15.)

Common to Old-Testament prophecy and to this book is the first resurrection, only that in the latter it is brought into special relations to the members of Christ. Nothing is here said of the departed of the Jewish dispensation, as this book is concerned only with the Church. Certain classes of persons are mentioned, of whom it is said that "they lived and reigned with Christ a thousand years. . . . This is the first resurrection. Blessed and holy is he that hath part in the first resurrection: on such the second death hath no power, but they shall be priests of God and of Christ, and shall reign with Him a thousand years." We know, however, from our Lord's words, that such of all generations as He shall count worthy to be His kings, and to reign with Him during the Kingdom period, He will then call from their graves.

Whether the Antichrist, the beast of the Revelation, was presented by the Old-Testament prophets in his special relation to the Jews as the anti-Messias, is not wholly clear. The later Jews looked for such an enemy to appear, and interpreted of him several utterances of the prophets, as, for example, in Isaiah, "the wicked" whom the Messiah shall slay with the breath of His lips. (xi. 4.)

CHAPTER IV.

THE JEWS IN THE KINGDOM, AND THE NEW COVENANT.

THERE are several references in the prophets to a "new covenant" to be made with the Jews, and most distinct in Jeremiah. "Behold, the days come, that I will make a new covenant with the house of Israel, and with the house of Judah: not according to the covenant that I made with their fathers in the day that I took them by the hand to bring them out of the land of Egypt; which my covenant they brake." (xxxi. 31. See also xxxii. 40; Ezek. xxxvii. 26; Isa. lv. 3, lix. 21.) What is the nature of this covenant, and when is it to be established? As this point is one of some difficulty, it must be briefly considered.

First, let us trace the relation of both covenants, new and old, to the promises made to Abraham. These promises were both universal and special; some embrace all nations, some are for his own posterity only. "In thee shall all families of the earth be blessed." "In thy seed shall all the nations of the earth be blessed." "Unto thy seed will I give this land." "I will multiply thy seed as the stars of the heaven, and as the sand which is upon the seashore, and thy seed shall possess the gate of his enemies." (Gen. xii. 3, xxii. 17, etc.) A relation is here established between Abraham and his seed on the one side, and all nations on the other, of such a nature that through God's blessing upon the former, the latter would be blessed. When the special promises to Abraham's children are fulfilled, then will follow the fulfillment of the universal promises.

We may now ask, by whom these promises were to be fulfilled, and when? Not by Abraham, or in his day. "The Seed," as we are taught by the apostle, is not his posterity in general, but the Christ. (Gal. iii. 16.) He is the one Son of Abraham, who is the chosen of God to bless first His own people, and then the Gentiles. And when? In the Messianic Kingdom, when He sits on "the throne of David and upon His kingdom, to order it, and to establish it with judgment and with justice;" and when "all kings shall fall down before Him, all nations shall serve Him." Therefore, till He take His Kingdom, neither the special promises to Abraham and to his posterity, nor the universal to the nations, can be realized; and to this realization Abraham looked forward, when "he saw the day of Christ, and was glad."

As the special promises must be accomplished in the Messiah and His own before the accomplishment of the universal, God's first step was to set apart the descendants of Abraham by giving them possession of their land. He entered into a covenant with them at Sinai, when Moses "took the book of the covenant, and read in the audience of the people: and they said, All that the Lord hath said will we do, and be obedient. And Moses took the blood, and sprinkled it on the people, and said, Behold the blood of the covenant, which the Lord hath made with you." (Exod. xxiv. 7.) But this covenant, and the possession of the land which followed, was not a full realization of His promises to Abraham respecting his posterity, for this could not be till "the Seed had come to whom the promises were made;" but it was a preliminary step to that realization. This covenant at Sinai cannot be separated from the law then given, "added because of transgressions," and not as a condition of the original promise. (Gal. iii. 17.) This covenant at Sinai they did not keep: "They continued not in my covenant, and I regarded them not." Therefore, as the elect people failed to fulfill their calling, God could not fulfill to them the special promises He had made to Abraham; and could not therefore fulfill through them the promises respecting the blessing of all nations. Were, then, His special promises to them to be revoked? Was His gift of the land to be recalled, and they cease forever to be a nation? No, for the end which He had set before Him in their election, had not been reached. For the breaches of their covenant He would judge them; but His promises to Abraham, made long before the covenant at Sinai, were not revoked; these must continue in force till the special work which that people was to do for Him as a witness to His truth before all nations, was accomplished.

For their violations of the covenant, their punishment came in due time. The elect people were driven from His land into temporary exile, and continued to be a subject people ever after. When, at last, the promised Seed came, through whom they might have received the fulfillment of all God's promises made them, they rejected Him, and put Him to death; and thus they brought on themselves the judgment of a dispersion which continues to this day.

We may thus see that what was done at Sinai, — the covenant then made, and the law then given, — was a means to the fulfillment, but not the fulfillment, of the promises to Abraham, either special or universal. Nor when He came who was to fulfill all the promises, both to His own people and to the nations, were they fulfilled; for having offered His sacrifice, He ascended to God. This fulfillment cannot be through Him abiding in heaven as High Priest, but sitting as a King on David's throne. Therefore, He must return to rule first His own people, Abraham's children, in truth and righteousness, fulfilling to them the promises; and through them to rule over the nations, fulfilling all promises to them. At His ascension into heaven, was all power and authority given Him, and He was prepared to be the "Mediator of the New Covenant." The Sinaitic covenant had grown old, and was ready to vanish away; but its vanishing away does not affect the special promises to Abraham, on which it rests: these abide, and must be fulfilled; and when they are fulfilled, the universal promises can be fulfilled. And He who fulfills them is not only the Son of David, but the Son of Man. Moses could be the mediator of a single people only, but Christ the Mediator both of His own people and of all nations.

For clearness, we may thus classify the covenants now in question: first, that made with Abraham, "the Father of us all," which was both universal and special in its scope. (Gen. xvii. 4–8.) Second, that at Sinai with the nation, which was special, embracing the natural seed of Abraham. (Exod. xix. 5–8.) Third, that to be established with the Jews in the Messianic Kingdom, and which is not a mere repetition of the Sinaitic, but a fulfillment of that made with Abraham. This new covenant is in fact the old carried into effect by Him, the Seed of Abraham, who alone was able to fulfill it.

With the covenant which the Lord inaugurated at His ascension with the Church, His body, to be gathered from all nations without distinction of Jew or Gentile, sanctifying its members with His blood, and sending upon them His Spirit, we are not here concerned.

A new relation was then established with men, involving a new election, and of necessity a new covenant. The standing of the new election is not that of the old, though both rest upon the promises made to Abraham.

The new covenant — the old renewed with the children of Abraham — became necessary through the breach of the old, "which my covenant," said Jehovah, "they brake." But in foresight that His people would not keep His covenant at Sinai, and that it might cease to have effect, God made provision for its renewal. This provision is found in the rites of the Day of Atonement; "for on that day shall the priests make an atonement for you:" and but for this provision of mercy by which their sins were put away, and their covenant relation preserved, they must early have perished in their apostasy. (Lev. xvi.)

We have seen elsewhere that after the return from Babylon, no such full expiation for the sins of a broken covenant as He had appointed in the rites of that day, could be made because of the absence of the ark of the covenant, and of the mercy seat, from the Most Holy Place. But God continued to accept their worship in the second temple, imperfect as it was, till the last crowning act of disobedience in the rejection of His Son, first in His own person, and then in the ministry of apostles, moved Him to cast them wholly out of their land; and through the destruction of their temple, He made their worship to cease.

But the purpose of God in His covenant with the Jewish people had not been reached; therefore He did not utterly cast them off. The branches were broken off, but it was His will to graft them in again; and the prophets looking to the future declare that "the days will come when He will make with them a new covenant." The covenanting parties are not changed: they are the same as at Sinai, — Jehovah and Israel. It is not a new relation, but a re-establishing of the old, "a grafting in again." But the Mediator of this covenant is a new Mediator, one greater than Moses who led them from Egypt, one who "has redeemed them from the curse of the law, being made a curse for them." He bore their sins in His own body on the tree, and the new covenant is "the new covenant in His blood." By His sacrifice on the cross — the great Sin-offering — He obtained the remission of their sins. But as it belonged to the priest to sprinkle the blood of the sacrifice on the ark and the veil and the altar (Lev. xvi. 15), so is it with Christ exalted to be High Priest. He entered "into the Holy Place by His own blood," and can sprinkle and cleanse the defiled people. (Heb. ix. 14.) The rites of the Day of Atonement can now be fulfilled once for all, and the sins of the covenant people be put away forever. (Heb. xiii. 11, 12.) He is "exalted that He may give repentance to Israel, and forgiveness of sins." "Their sins and their iniquities will I remember no more." Thus in Him, first in His death, and then in His exaltation and ascension to be made High Priest, were the foundations of the new covenant laid.

Christ, as "the Seed" to whom the promises were made, becomes the fulfiller of them all, both of the special and the general. The children of Abraham through disobedience — the failure to keep their covenant — had forfeited all. He by His obedience became entitled to all. The land is His, and He will give it again to them. He will bestow upon them all that the Father had promised them. Thus they shall hold all from Him as the Goel, the Redeemer. But this involves the acceptance of Him whom they once rejected; they must humble themselves before Him, for He cannot cleanse the unrepentant. "The Redeemer shall come to Zion, and unto them that turn from transgression in Jacob." The prophets speak of a great day of atonement to come, in which "they shall afflict their souls," a day of national repentance and mourning. Then will be fulfilled the prophetic words: "I will pour upon the house of David, and upon the inhabitants of Jerusalem, the spirit of grace and of supplications. . . . In that day shall there be a great mourning in Jerusalem, . . . and the land shall mourn, every family apart." (Zech. xii. 10.) "They shall come with weeping, and with supplications will I lead them." (Jer. xxxi. 9.) "In those days, and in that time, the children of Israel shall come, they and the children of Judah together, going and weeping: they shall go, and seek the Lord their God," saying, "Come, and let us join ourselves to the Lord in a perpetual covenant that shall not be forgotten." (Jer. l. 4.) And the Mediator between them and their God will be their Messiah, the Royal Priest, who has gone into the Holy of Holies. "Their Governor shall proceed from the midst of them; and I will cause Him to draw near, and He shall approach unto me," to offer sacrifice; . . . "and ye shall be my people, and I will be your God." (Jer. xxx. 21.)

What are the new elements that meet us in this renewal of the covenant? They are these three: —

First, The forgiveness of sins, especially the sins of a broken covenant: "I will forgive their iniquities, and their sins will I remember no more." Forgiveness of sins was not unknown under the law. It was the end of the sacrificial institutions: "The priest shall make an atonement for them, and it shall be forgiven them." (Lev. iv. 20.) And this was done year by year. But now, through the merits of Christ's sacrifice, and through His priestly work of expiation, there is such cleansing of the conscience as was not possible before. At the time of their restoration He will fulfill the rites of the Day of Atonement, once for all, by the sprinkling of the people, all who through repentance and the confession of their sins, are prepared to receive final absolution and forgiveness.

Second, Perfect obedience to the law of God. The will of God, that had been presented to the people by Moses in an external written law, becomes an inward principle : " After those days I will put my law in their inward parts, and write it in their hearts." The will of God is supreme under the new covenant as under the old, but under the new only is it perfectly obeyed with the obedience of the heart. This obedience was, indeed, demanded from the first : " Thou shalt love the Lord thy God with all thy heart, and with all thy soul, and with all thy strength; and these words which I command thee this day, shall be in thine heart." This obedience of the heart they had not rendered ; but in the time to come, they would walk in His statutes, and keep His ordinances in the power of the Spirit : " I will put a new Spirit within you." (Ezek. xi. 19, 20.)

Third, All are taught to know the Lord, so that there will not be need that one teach another : " All shall know me, from the least to the greatest." The knowledge of Him will not be confined to a part; He will make such a revelation of Himself that none will remain ignorant : " Thy children shall all be taught of the Lord." (Isa. lvi. 13.) " They shall see eye to eye when the Lord will bring again Zion."

Thus, forgiven and cleansed, filled with the knowledge of the Lord, and delighting in His law and keeping it, the people are prepared to take their true place as His people, and He in the full sense will be their God. And it is a change wrought through the Spirit sent upon them by the Son, the ascended Messiah, who is, also, the Baptizer with the Holy Ghost: "Then will I sprinkle clean water upon you, and ye shall be clean. . . . A new heart will I give you, and a new spirit will I put within you, and cause you to walk in my statutes, and ye shall keep my judgments to do them." (Ezek. xxxvi. 25–27.) And these spiritual blessings are to abide: "I will pour my Spirit upon thy seed, and my blessing upon thine offspring." (Isa. xliv. 3.) "This is my covenant with them, saith the Lord: my Spirit that is upon thee, and my words which I have put in thy mouth, shall not depart out of thy mouth, nor out of the mouth of thy seed, nor out of the mouth of thy seed's seed, saith the Lord, from henceforth and for ever." (Isa. lix. 21.)

It would be an error to imagine that these new elements in the covenant are in any way inconsistent with the original calling of the people to dwell in their own land, and to be a nation among the nations. On the contrary, now for the first time are they able to fulfill that calling, and prepared to answer the end of their election. By Jeremiah Jehovah declares that He would "make an everlasting covenant with them," and adds, "yea, I will rejoice over them to do them good, and I will plant them in this land assuredly, with my whole heart and my whole soul." "If the ordinances of the sun and moon and stars depart from before me, then the seed of Israel, also, shall cease from being a nation before me for ever." "As I have sworn that the waters of Noah should no more go over the earth, so have I sworn that I would not be wroth with thee nor rebuke thee." "I will cause the captivity of Judah and the captivity of Israel to return, and will build them as at the first, and I will cleanse them from all iniquity, . . . and I will pardon all their iniquities." "I will put my Spirit within you, and cause you to walk in my statutes, . . .

and ye shall dwell in the land that I gave to your fathers. . . . In the day that I shall have cleansed you from all your iniquities, I will also cause you to dwell in the cities, and the wastes shall be builded." (Ezek. xxxvi.)

It is as thus forgiven and cleansed and enlightened through the work upon them of their High Priest, that the Jews are prepared as a nation to fulfill the purpose of their calling under Him as their King; and be Jehovah's instrument for the revelation of Himself unto all the nations. This realization of the larger promises to Abraham respecting the nations does not set aside the special covenant made with his own posterity at Sinai, but is made dependent upon its renewal. Men may stand in various relations to God through Christ. He is, indeed, the Saviour of all from sin by His death, and all must come unto God by Him; but He may stand in one relation to the Church, in another to the Jews, in a third to the nations. He may be the Head of the Church; the King of the Jews, sitting on David's throne; and the universal Lord. This is a matter of Divine order, not of human arrangement.

As thus brought under their King, and enjoying the blessings of the new covenant, all nations will have knowledge of God's purpose in them, and of its fulfillment through the children of Abraham of whom He said: "This people, whom I have formed for myself; they shall shew forth my praise." "All flesh shall know that I the Lord am thy Saviour, and thy Redeemer, the mighty One of Jacob." Then the blessing of Abraham will come upon the nations. "Nations that knew not thee, shall run unto thee, because of the Lord thy God, and for the Holy One of Israel; for He hath glorified thee." "The knowledge of the Lord will fill the earth as the waters cover the sea." "The Lord hath made bare His holy arm in the eyes of all the nations; and all the ends of the earth shall see the salvation of our God." "The sons of the stranger, that joined themselves to the Lord, . . . even them will I bring to my holy mountain, and make them joyful in my house of prayer; . . . for mine house shall be called a house of prayer for all people."

The reference to the new covenant in the Epistle to the Hebrews (viii. 8, etc.) presents nothing inconsistent with what has been said, but a special examination of the writer's scope and argument is not necessary here.

It is by keeping clearly in mind the co-existence of the glorified Church and the restored people under their respective covenants, during the Kingdom period, that we can see the full meaning of the words of the Scriptures in regard to their relations to one another, and to the nations. To the Jews belongs the earthly Jerusalem, to the Church the heavenly, — the holy city that comes down from God out of heaven, having the glory of God. (Rev. xxi. 2, 10.) That this is a symbol of the Church, the bride, the Lamb's wife, we are expressly told. Though it stands in close relations to the earth, for the nations walk in the light of it, and the kings of the earth bring their honor and glory into it; yet it is to the earthly Jerusalem that they come up to worship. Their special relations to the Messiah are through the children of Abraham.

CHAPTER V.

THE LAST APOSTASY AND FINAL JUDGMENT.

DURING all the period of the Kingdom, the Jews and the nations are under trial; for probation does not end till the Son gives up the Kingdom to the Father. We may affirm absolute indefectibility only of those who have entered into the state of immortality and incorruption. How far all will render to God perfect obedience, we know not; but disobedience, whether of the individual or of a people, we may believe to be the rare exception. (See Isa. lxv. 20; Zech. xiv. 17, 18.) We are not told of any transgression till near the end, when Satan is unloosed, and "goes out to deceive the nations which are in the four quarters of the earth." This implies that till this unloosing there was at least general obedience to God's will under the rule of the Messiah. Through Satan's temptation a great multitude are deceived, and "they compass the camp of the saints about, and the beloved city." This last outbreak of human wickedness is speedily suppressed. "Fire came down from God out of heaven, and devoured them." (Rev. xx. 1-10.)

It has seemed incredible to many that after the establishment of the Kingdom, and the wonderful manifestation of God in it through Christ, and the peace and blessing of all nations under His rule, there should be another outbreak of rebellion. But there is nothing in this that is not in perfect consistency with all that has preceded it in the record of man's apostasy. There is no salvation but by abiding in the redemptive grace of God, whatever be the measure of that grace. The nations here mentioned — those standing in the outer court, and most remote from God — do not so abide, but are tempted and fall. It is possible that it is anger at the higher position given the Jews, that is the irritating cause. But, whatever the cause, the series of apostasies is now complete. Adam in Eden fell through temptation; the world before the Flood corrupted its way, and perished; the Jews crucified their Lord; the Church has its apostasy and its conflict with Antichrist before it reaches the goal; and at last all the light and happiness of the Kingdom do not keep many of its subjects from rebellion when the Devil is unloosed. And we may note the suddenness of their destruction at the end. As the light given them has been great, so is their punishment.

Following immediately upon their destruction is the casting of Satan into "the lake of fire," the symbol of eternal punishment. Now has the Lord put all enemies under Him but one: "the last enemy that shall be destroyed is death." All that are holden of death must now come forth. The Lord seats Himself on the great white throne, and "the sea gives up the dead which are in it; and death and hell deliver up the dead which are in them: and they are judged every man according to their works." Only the dead are here mentioned as brought into judgment. As we have seen, the living had been judged at the beginning of the Kingdom, and the unfaithful then cut off from the earth; and "the beast and false prophet were cast alive into the lake of fire," and all with him slain by the sword of Him that sat upon the horse; and there had been also a partial resurrection of the dead, "the resurrection of the just." Now at the end of the Kingdom the Jews and the Gentiles — all that have remained faithful but have not received the body of incorruption, and all that remain under death — are to be judged. The former, doubtless, enter without tasting death into a higher condition of being, free from all effects of sin, and blessed forever; but whether they enter into the Most Holy, and all distinctions of degree among the saved are then removed, we may not say. The dead, also, are judged according to their works; and all not written in the Book of Life come under the power of the second death. This last act of judgment being accomplished, death and hell — the grave and the place of disembodied souls — are no more needed. All, both good and evil, enter in their bodies into their eternal rewards.

The redemptive work is thus finished: the Messiah has reigned till all things have been put under His feet, and the last enemy, death, has been brought to naught. All things having been subjected unto Him, the end has come when He must deliver up the Kingdom to God the Father. "When all things have been subjected unto Him, then shall the Son also Himself be subjected to Him that did subject all things unto Him, that God may be all in all." It is impossible for us to understand what may be the full meaning of these words; but it is plain that, evil being suppressed, and all being brought into obedience to God, there may now be such a revelation of His glory to His holy creatures as was not possible before, even in the Kingdom. That the Son as incarnate — the God-man — is ever the image of God to all creatures, and the Ruler over all His works, is involved in the very nature of the Incarnation, and is abundantly said by the prophets and apostles; and what He now gives up, is the special rule administered by

Him for his works of redemption and judgment. He ceases to be Redeemer because redemption is completed: His place as universal King belongs to Him as the Son of God and Son of man, a prerogative inseparably connected with His person.

As the Messianic Kingdom is a time of higher revelation of God than any preceding it, it is thus a preparation for the still higher revelation to be made when the redemptive gives place to the eternal age. Respecting this the Scriptures are silent. Whether all the redeemed, both Jews and the nations, will then be exalted into the same state of dignity and glory into which the Church has already been exalted, and all distinctions of relation and condition will then cease; or whether they will continue to stand in distinct relations to God through Christ, and will fulfill special functions in the actings of God, perhaps towards other creatures in other worlds, during the ages to come, has not been clearly revealed; but the past leads us to expect in the future differences of calling and positions and degrees of honor.

CHAPTER VI.

THE NEW HEAVENS AND NEW EARTH.

No truth is more clearly stated in the Old Testament than that God is the Creator and Lord of all that exists. "In the beginning, God created the heavens and the earth." From the very character of God as omniscient, it follows that they were made for an end, and were what He designed them to be. All worlds and all material things have their place and meaning as means of revealing their Creator, partly in themselves, their existence and qualities, as proofs of His power and wisdom; but chiefly we may believe in their subordination to His purpose in the intelligent and moral beings for whose inhabitation and use they were made. But this revelation of God in creation, vast and varied as it is, was necessarily imperfect; the perfect revelation could be made only through the Incarnate Son. It was "for Him that all things were made," and, therefore, are what they are. But this ultimate end could not be known till the Word was made flesh, and dwelt among men.

For man was the earth specially made, as a house is made for him who is to inhabit it, and was adapted in all its arrangements to his needs. And as the moral element is the highest in man, we may believe that God in the physical constitution of the earth had reference to its bearings upon his spiritual education, even more than upon his bodily well-being. Besides those external influences, obvious and universally recognized, that affect man in his intellectual and moral development, there was also established by God such a relation between him and his dwelling-place, that there should be a correspondence in their history and destiny. Thus we are expressly taught by St. Paul, that through the transgression of Adam the earth was made subject to bondage; and in Genesis we read that God said to Adam, "Cursed is the ground for thy sake." (iii. 17; Rom. viii. 20.) As we are ignorant of the processes of creation, we know not how this curse was effected, nor with what changes accompanied. As he was placed in his first estate of innocence in the garden in Eden, full of fruitfulness and beauty, the ground yielding its fruits with little labor, so in its fallen state it was to bring forth thorns and thistles; and in toil and sorrow, and sweat of his face, should he eat his daily bread, — words which have had a sorrowful fulfillment in all subsequent ages. (Gen. v. 29.)

If, then, God established at first such a bond of unity between man and the earth, that the moral condition of the former should determine to a certain degree the physical condition of the latter, — a fruitful, peaceful, blessed earth for man remaining good; barrenness, disorder, toil, suffering for man become evil, — it can cause no surprise when we are told that in the Messianic Kingdom, all things will be made new. As man's disobedience brought it into bondage, so through man's obedience shall it be delivered. In the Messianic Kingdom as a new and higher stage of redemption, the physical will correspond with the moral. With the righteousness of that Kingdom, and the obedience shown to God, there will be progressive changes in the material order, through which the evils of the disobedient past will be done away, and a world be prepared in which the righteous will dwell. (2 Pet. iii. 13.) Upon two distinct grounds we may believe that the earth will ultimately be made new: first, that having been brought under the bondage of corruption, not of its own will, but by the sin of man, it is embraced in the scope of redemption; it is to enter into "the liberty of the glory of the children of God." (Rom. viii. 21.) Second, that God having made man, body and soul, and appointed the body to be an essential element in humanity, He will so order the material world that it shall minister in the highest degree to all his needs. If the body be raised into a higher condition through resurrection, there must be a corresponding change in its material environments, — the new creation serving as a means to higher knowledge of God, and to the continual enlargement of man's conceptions of His power, wisdom, and goodness.

To say, then, that the earth will be made new, is to say only what the whole scope of the Scriptures in their teachings respecting creation and redemption has prepared us to expect. The relation of temporal blessings to obedience under the Theocracy is distinctly taught. Everywhere in the prophets it is said that when His people become obedient, and truly honor Him, God will minister to them richly in all outward blessings, and in richest measure in the Messianic Kingdom. Then "the ploughman shall overtake the reaper, and the treader of grapes him that soweth seed;" then "the mountains shall drop down new wine, and the hills shall flow with milk, and all the rivers of Judah shall flow with waters." (Amos ix. 13; Levit. xxvi. 4, etc.; Joel iii. 18.) And as during the Messianic Kingdom all nations will serve and worship the King, and be blessed in Him, we cannot suppose that the curse pronounced upon the ground — sterility, and devastating storms, drought, famines, and pestilences — is then to continue. (Rev. xxii. 3.)

But what are we to understand by the "new" earth? Plainly, not new in substance, but in qualities. It is that change which our Lord spoke of as "the regeneration," or "new birth." "Ye which have followed me, in the regeneration when the Son of man shall sit in the throne of His glory, ye also shall sit on twelve thrones." It is that change in the physical order which begins when He — "the Beginning of the new creation" — establishes His Kingdom. It is that change of which the apostle speaks, as to be in "the times of restitution of all things, which God hath spoken of by the mouth of all His holy prophets since the world began." (Acts iii. 21.) We are thus taught that this change from the old to the new is essentially a restoration, the bringing in again of that condition of goodness which had been lost through man's disobedience. Nor is this, rightly understood, inconsistent with any thing we know of the geological history of the earth. Yet is it more than the mere removing the effects of the curse, it is adding new qualities, such as were not found in the original creation; perhaps by the re-arrangement of the old elements, rather than by fresh creative acts. The basis of this new constitution lies in the new and heavenly Man, the second Adam, for whom it is remade, and in whom our humanity was reconstituted, made anew, when He rose from the dead. As the resurrection of the body is not an absolutely new creation, and yet not a mere restoration of the old, so is it with the new earth. And, as the second Adam is higher than the first, being the Incarnate Son glorified, so will His world be in like proportion more excellent and glorious.

In this change from lower to higher, there is nothing in contradiction with the past history of the earth.

Geology tells us of many transitions, from a fiery mass to its present state of fruitfulness and beauty. The nature of these changes no finite being could have foretold, but all were in the line of the Divine purpose. And that they have ceased, that the end has been reached, and that there will be absolute permanence of present condition, no one will venture to say. If future changes are expected, as all do expect them, the question is, in what direction are these to be? Has the earth already reached its highest stage? Will it fall back into chaos and darkness? or will it go on into a still higher stage? If we trace in the past a uniform line of upward improvement, this may continue in the future. And, viewing the earth in its relations to the Second Adam, the new earth becomes a certainty.

But it is not necessary to affirm that the change from the old to the new is instantaneous. Not only the analogy of all God's actings in creation, so far as we know them, and of His rule over nature, but also the words of Scripture, justify us in thinking that this change is to be gradual, step by step, till its consummation is reached. The two more marked epochs are, doubtless, those at the beginning and end of the Messianic Kingdom. In the Old Testament, the coming of Jehovah to establish His Kingdom over all the earth is always spoken of as accompanied by marked physical phenomena, of which fire is an essential element, and earthquakes a frequent attendant — as at His manifestation on Mount Sinai, when "the mount was altogether on a smoke, because the Lord descended upon it in fire, . . . and the whole mount quaked greatly." (Exod. xix. 18; Ps. xviii. 7, 8.) Thus Micah speaks: "Behold the Lord cometh forth out of His place, and will come down, and tread upon the high places of the earth; and the mountains shall be molten under Him, and the valleys shall be cleft as wax before the fire." (i. 4.) "The mountains quake at Him, and the hills melt; and the earth is upheaved at His presence." (Nah. i. 5.) Thus, the Psalmist: "A fire goeth before Him, and burneth up His enemies round about. His lightnings enlightened the world, the earth saw and trembled; the hills melted like wax at the presence of the Lord." Of the coming of the Lord Jesus it is said by an apostle, that "He will be revealed from heaven with His mighty angels in flaming fire, taking vengeance on them that know not God." (2 Thess. i. 7.)

There are passages that may seem, indeed, to indicate a sudden destruction of the old, and creation of the new, especially in St. Peter. (2 Pet. iii.) But in his language he evidently does not make discriminations of time. "The day of the Lord will come as a thief in the night; in the which the heavens shall pass away with a great noise, . . . and the earth also and the works that are therein shall be burned up." "The day of the Lord" we have already seen to be a period of considerable though indefinite duration. The words of the apostle take in the whole period, and look forward to the consummation, — new heavens and a new earth, — without discriminating the several steps by which it is reached. We know also from what is revealed as to the execution of God's purpose in man, that His redemption is by stages. The first to be exalted into the glory of the resurrection is Christ, the First-fruits; then they that are Christ's at His coming; then, the end, when He delivers up the Kingdom to the Father. (1 Cor. xv. 24.) If the change from the old to the new were instantaneous at the Lord's coming, such progressive resurrection would not be possible; nor would the Kingdom period be one in which He is engaged in "putting all enemies under His feet." The words of Isaiah, also, referring to the same events, are inconsistent with such an instantaneous change, since he speaks of those dwelling on the new earth, as still under the law of death (lxv. 20, etc.); as are also the words in the Revelation as to the coming up of Gog and Magog against the city of the saints, at the close of the heavenly Kingdom. The Scriptures are uniform in their teaching that the Messianic Kingdom is to be a period of redemption; and, therefore, no such physical change can take place at its establishment as would destroy the race, or make the earth unfit for a place of probation.

If this physical change in the earth from lower to higher is progressive, yet with marked stages, we may believe that it will begin with the land which God gave to His people, and which He had thus so greatly honored. As it was appointed to be the seat of the Messianic Kingdom, and Jerusalem the royal city, here would naturally be seen the first manifestation of the power that would ultimately make the whole earth new. And this is often intimated by the prophets. The words of Micah cannot be rightly understood of a purely spiritual exaltation: "In the last days it shall come to pass that the mountain of the house of the Lord shall be established in the top of the mountains, and it shall be exalted above the hills." (iv. 1.) Of the same prophecy given in Isaiah, it has been remarked by Cheyne: "Mount Zion is to be physically raised, and to become fixed at the head of the lower mountains, which radiate, as it were, in all directions from it." Zechariah speaks of the great earthquake that shall be when the feet of the Lord shall stand upon the Mount of Olives, and He shall fight with the nations: "The Mount of Olives shall cleave in the midst thereof toward the east and toward the west,—a very great valley.... All the land shall be turned as a plain from Geba to Rimmon, south of Jerusalem." (xiv. 4, etc.) These words cannot be understood of other than physical changes; and these will be of such a character as to make Jerusalem "beautiful for situation, the joy of the whole earth," worthy in its local positions and environs to be "the city of the Great King."

In several of the prophets mention is made of a fountain that shall flow forth from the house of the Lord: "In that day living waters shall go out from Jerusalem, half of them toward the former sea, and half of them toward the hinder sea." (Zech. xiv. 8; Joel iii. 18; Ezek. xlvii. 1, etc.) It is in perfect accordance with all previously said, if these words are literally to be fulfilled. Thus beholding in fulfillment before their eyes all that was said by Moses of the exemption of the land, if the people were obedient, from all forms of physical evil; the forces of nature co-operating harmoniously with the labors of men; all nations will "call its inhabitants blessed, and their land a delightsome land." (Mal. iii. 12.) It is a false spiritualism that makes an antagonism between the inward and outward, the soul and the body, the spiritual and the temporal gifts of God. Job, who may be regarded as a type of the Remnant, when his captivity was turned received from the Lord twice as much as he had before. So when Jehovah restores His people, all His promises of temporal good will be more than fulfilled.

Whether this change is of the earth only as man's dwelling-place, or embraces the other heavenly bodies also, is not made known to us. We may at least believe that as the earth is a member of a planetary system so closely bound together by physical forces that each member is dependent upon the other members, these changes in it will be accompanied by such changes in the system as God shall see meet for the accomplishment of His purpose in man. The comparatively inferior position of the earth, physically considered in this system, is of no importance, since in the light of the Incarnation it stands, as the birthplace of the Son of God, and the place of the spiritual education of His Church in a relation to God in which no other orb can stand. It is to be noted how often the Lord refers to the signs to be seen in heaven, in the sun, moon, and stars at His return; and though, doubtless, there may be a symbolical interpretation in some cases, yet there is much ground to expect that "the powers of the heavens" will be literally shaken; to be followed by a readjustment of present relations, so that a higher order will be established whose stability shall be no more disturbed.

That the earth will be delivered from "the bondage of corruption" into which it has been brought through man's sin, and will be made new; that the process of new creation will be gradual; that it will begin with marked changes in the present physical order at the time of the setting up of the kingdom; that these changes will be first seen in God's own land; that during the whole process of deliverance the material changes will be compatible with man's habitation, and be subordinated to his welfare; and that the perfected deliverance — "the regeneration" in its highest measure — will not be till God's redemptive work in man is completed; — are truths involved in all that is taught us in the Scriptures of God's purpose in the Incarnate Son, who is Himself the Beginning of the new creation. As he "who is in Him, is a new creature; old things are passed away, all things are become new;" so will it be at last with the earth. It is already brought under the law of the new creation. As we who have the firstfruits of the Spirit, groan within ourselves, waiting for the redemption of the body; so with the earth that has been subjected to vanity, it groaneth and travaileth in pain. (Rom. viii. 19-23.) With His return as King begins the process of transformation; it is then, in a measure, delivered from the bondage of corruption, virtually made new; but its perfected condition is not reached till death, the last enemy, is destroyed, and it is prepared to be inhabited by those no more under the law of sin and death. "He that sat on the throne said, Behold! I make all things new." This may refer primarily to the earth: but doubtless the law of new creation in the God-Man, will ultimately embrace the whole universe; for it is due to the Son, for whom all things were made, that they correspond to Him in all material excellence, and thereby show forth in a fitting manner the goodness, the wisdom, and the glory of God.

How far a false spiritualism has gone in casting dishonor on the material creation, may be seen by some extracts from Edwards's "History of Redemption," in regard to the future of the earth. "Then," after their resurrection, "the saints shall take their everlasting leave of this earth. . . . Thus Christ's Church shall forever leave this accursed world, to go unto the highest heavens, the paradise of God. . . . When they are gone this world shall be set on fire, and be turned into a great furnace wherein all the enemies of Christ and His Church shall be tormented for ever and ever. . . . The miserable company of the wicked being left behind to have their sentence executed upon them here, then this whole lower world shall be set on fire. . . . This world, which used to be the place of Satan's kingdom, shall now be the place of his complete punishment, and perfect and everlasting torment." Thus the earth, Christ's birthplace and redeemed by Him, instead of being made new, is turned into the hell of the damned.

CONCLUSION.

CHRISTIANITY AND OTHER RELIGIONS.

THE rapid historical survey now taken of the purpose of God as given us in the Scriptures, historic and prophetic, will, it is hoped, enable the reader to see clearly the high place which the Incarnation has in that purpose. It may justly be charged against much of the current biblical interpretation of the day, that, making light of the Incarnation, it fails to apprehend the full significance of the sacred records; and so brings down Christianity from its lofty vantage position, and places it too much on a level with other forms of religion. The Bible is, above all, historical, and can answer its end only as its historic character is maintained. Chief and central of its facts is the birth of the Incarnate Son, in whom all the actings of God have their beginning and end. Denying this, all the other facts recorded lose their unity, and become unreal; for it is only the purpose of God in Him that gives them order and consistence. It is full time, therefore, that the Incarnation, and the facts most closely connected with it and most distinctive of Christianity, should be set in clearest light, and be examined in all their historic relations, when this is brought into contrast with other religions. This is not the place for such an examination, but some points already touched upon may be here repeated.

Beginning with this fact, the union of the Divine and human in Christ, as that which gives direction to all God's works, creative and redemptive, and defines their order, we find in the Bible a wonderful unity and harmony. God creates man in His own likeness; but falling through disobedience under the law of sin and death, he must be redeemed. Thus two offices are to be fulfilled by the Incarnate Son: He is the Revealer of God, He is the Redeemer of men. He reveals God to men in virtue of His personality, for He is God manifest in the flesh. He is the brightness of His Father's glory, and the express image of His Person. As He cannot cease to be the Son, and abides the same yesterday, to-day, and forever, in Him God will always be revealed. And this revelation is made to all creatures: all will see the glory of God in the face of Jesus Christ. But His work as Redeemer is not eternal nor universal, for redemption is a work that necessarily comes to an end; nor does it embrace any but the fallen and sinful. To the unfallen and holy He is forever the Revealer of God, but not their Redeemer. It is of His redemptive work that the Scriptures chiefly speak; for it began with the first of our race, and continues under differing forms till all things are brought into their holy and unchangeable order. Of this work in its several successive stages, sufficient for our purpose has already been said.

The work of Christ as the Revealer of God has several distinct gradations. As the Father had spoken to men by His prophets, He also spake to them by His Son; and through Him were made known the mysteries of the Divine Being and of His counsels, as no prophet had been inspired to do; and His works confirmed His words, and were in their nature proofs and pledges of a redemption to come.

Thus He was the Revealer of God in word and work

while on the earth in mortal flesh. But having ascended to God, and been glorified, and set as Head of the Church, He has new and higher revelations to make. But how can men on earth receive them? There must be a correspondence between the revelation and the spiritual capacity to apprehend it. Light is for the eye, and the eye for light; but what man can look upon the sun shining in full splendor? The new revelations He would make, can be apprehended only by those upon whom He sends His Spirit, the Spirit of truth. (John xiv. 17.) But there is a still higher revelation to be made of the Father through the Son, when His present work as High Priest is ended, and He shall appear in the glory of the Father. Who shall be able to see the glory of God then revealed in Jesus Christ? None, except those who are lifted up into the same state of immortality and incorruption in which He now is.

Thus we see a threefold gradation of revelation by the Incarnate Son: first, through the truths He taught, and the works He did on earth; second, through the truths revealed, and works done by Him through the Spirit sent by Him from Heaven; third, through the words to be spoken and works to be done by Him at His return as the manifested King and Lord of all. And there is given to men a capacity to receive, corresponding to each of these gradations of revelation through Christ: first, in those in covenant with God to whom He spake while on earth; second, in His Church on earth, in which dwells the Spirit sent by Him from Heaven; third, in all those who are made like Him in the day when He shall sit on the throne of His glory in the Kingdom. To the other forms of revelation in word and work we may add the glory of His Person, as the Image of God, when He appears in visible majesty.

We can now see that redemption and revelation stand in close relation to each other. To the Church, indwelt by the regenerating Spirit of Christ, higher revelations of God can be made than to others on earth, because there is higher capacity to receive. To those in the Kingdom, in whom is fullness of resurrection life, the highest revelation can be made, because in them this capacity is developed in highest degree. In redeeming men, Christ does more than to restore them to the condition lost through sin, — the vision of God, and the communion with Him into which Adam was admitted. First, by making them partakers of His own life as the second Adam, He lifts them up into a higher condition than that given them at their creation; and enables them to apprehend truths that had been kept hidden till that time. Finally, when this life is perfected in resurrection, and they are made like Him in that form of humanity which is the highest form of creature being, new revelations can be made them through the Son; and they attain to a knowledge of God, and to a communion with Him, such as is possible to none beside.

It is most important to keep clearly in mind that although redemption, when consummated, brings with it that enlargement of being which enables all in Christ to be filled with the fullness of God, and capable of receiving such revelations of Him as can be made to none other; yet this new and higher stage of existence does not subvert the original constitution of man, nor necessitate any change in the essential elements of his nature. Humanity is seen in Christ to be a form of being, which, although capable of degrees of excellence, remains forever unchanged in its constituent elements. Man, however exalted, never ceases to be man. Of this we have the infallible assurance given in the Incarnation of the Son, when "manhood was taken into God." And in His resurrection is given the pledge that the body is not to be cast aside as unworthy of exaltation with man, but is itself to be transfigured and glorified. Christ's present existence as the Risen One in "the body of glory," is the assurance of our own like immortality and incorruption. "As we have borne the image of the earthy, we shall also bear the image of the heavenly." And as the body was made of the dust of the earth, its preservation is a pledge that the earth, and, we may believe, all material worlds, have their deter mined and permanent place in the still unfulfilled purpose of God.

Thus we find in Christianity, what may be rightly demanded of any religion that claims to be absolute and universal, that it gives not only such a history of the past as satisfactorily to account for the present, but also so reveals the future that we can see in them all a uniform and consistent purpose. And this purpose is one worthy of God, and looks forward to the highest manifestation of Him, and consequently to the highest good of the creature; and this without end. Of no heathen religion can this be said, much less of any philosophic cosmology. Without One Personal and Supreme God, there can be no unity of purpose, no defined line of movement, no assurance that the end can be reached, and no permanance of result. Polytheism brings only confusion, pantheism knows only of endless cycles of change; neither gives any explanation of the past, nor casts any light on the darkness of the future. Christianity alone answers to the conditions of an absolute and universal religion. It affirms a creation by the will of God, and finds the ground of this creation in His love, which has its supreme manifestation in the Incarnation of His Son, who as God and man is the eternal bond of union between the Creator and the creature, the Infinite and the finite. And having in our nature through death, won the victory over sin and death, He is, as the Risen One, the perfect Image of the invisible God, revealing Him to all creatures forever; and to be made like Him in resurrection is to reach the highest place that can be given to a creature.

Thus Christianity stands apart from all other religions in its essential features, and is infinitely above all. It presents a clear and defined purpose of God, steadily moving onward to its goal; embracing the whole universe in its scope, and yet meeting the needs of every soul, sinless or sinful.

It may truly be called the absolute religion, since it includes every region of truth, and all truth; and the universal, since it meets the needs of all created beings, fallen and unfallen, in all worlds. The redeemed will see in Jesus Christ their Saviour; the holy angels will see in Him the Image of God: to all men and angels, and other intelligent beings, if there be other, He will be the Way of approach to the Father. If any other religion knows of creation as a free act of God, it knows nothing of Incarnation, and therefore nothing of the purpose of God in creation; nor of the goal to be reached when all things are to be made new. No other religion knows any thing of fallen humanity, or of the forgiveness of sins through the sacrifice of the Incarnate Son; nothing of resurrection, and of the new and higher form of humanity thus attained; nothing of the fullness of life, and of the blessed communion with God of those who through Christ are made partakers of the Divine nature.

In Christianity every question is answered which it concerns us to know respecting man, his origin, history, and destiny. God's purpose in His Son, as declared in the Scriptures, explains man's creation, his constitution as embracing soul and body, the origin of death, the disembodied state, the resurrection, the new humanity, and eternal life. If there be confusion in the minds of any upon these points, it must arise from the failure to hold the teachings of the Scriptures in their unity and harmony. These must be interpreted in the light of their own dominant ideas; any admixture of ideas foreign and incongruous, necessarily brings discord and confusion. Of this we may find a striking illustration in the vague, uncertain, and contradictory statements in many Christian writers as to the future of the earth and of man. The biblical narrative is plain: all the material worlds were made by God; and of these the earth was especially prepared for man's habitation; and between him and his dwelling-place there was a designed and wonderful correspondence. Is this correspondence to cease, either by the destruction of the earth, or by the elimination of the material element from man's constitution? There are many that affirm this, though on very unlike grounds. Some, misapprehending the words of St. Peter, believe that the earth is literally to be burned up, to dissolve and vanish away (2 Pet. iii.); or perhaps, as in the case of Edwards, to remain ever burning, — the abode of the lost. Others, holding to the indestructibility of matter, and therefore to the earth's perpetuity, affirm a never-ending series of catastrophes and renewals; and others still, that, forsaken of all life, it will sweep on its pathway empty and desolate forever. And as to man's body, there is even greater variety of belief. There are few, indeed, who profess any faith in the Scriptures or in the creeds, that do not hold some kind of a resurrection body; but often in so intangible and shadowy a form, that it would be difficult to distinguish it from pure spirit. Some, and apparently an increasing number, consciously or unconsciously under the influence of a revived pagan or gnostic philosophy, find in the material body the cause of sin and all evil; and in deliverance from it, salvation and heaven. Thus, in one way or another, the relation of man to the earth is regarded very widely by Christians as a temporary one, believed to cease, as regards individuals, at each one's death; and, as to the race, at the day of final judgment. Having answered its purpose as a place for the temporary dwelling of men, a school for training, its future is said to be of no interest to us.

It need scarcely be said how utterly foreign are all beliefs of this kind to the whole tenor and spirit of the Scriptures. According to them, the body is an integral part of our humanity, without which man cannot possess fullness of life; and there are express declarations that, as the earth was brought under the bondage of corruption by man, so it will be redeemed, and the curse be removed. It will, indeed, be changed and made new, as will the body in resurrection; but a change of quality is not the destruction of substance. The eternal purpose of God in Christ embraces both man's body and dwelling-place; and there is no reason to believe that the earth will ever cease to be the abode of holy and happy beings.

If, through aversion to matter as defiling the spirit, or clogging and hindering it, the disembodied state is regarded as the heavenly and the highest, we import into the Scriptures a pagan notion which destroys the unity of the Divine purpose, and makes their consistent interpretation impossible. The true goal to which God points us — likeness to His Son raised from the dead and glorified — being lost, the true nature of redemption, as embracing all the elements of our humanity, body, soul, and spirit, joined in indissoluble union, is misapprehended; the resurrection becomes meaningless; and the existence of the material worlds an enigma. Mortality is not swallowed up of life, but life of mortality. The human race, like a river which pours itself forth upon the sands and disappears, sinks away in its successive generations into the depths of the grave. It need scarcely be said that a religion which exalts a transient and imperfect form of our humanity, the fruit of sin, into its perfected and permanent form; and finds in death, not in resurrection, the door into eternal life; makes open confession of its impotence to solve the problem of man's destiny. It goes backward to the vague, shadowy, ghostly future of pagan religions, that know nothing of our humanity as redeemed and ennobled in Christ, and made immortal and incorruptible; but only as abiding dismembered under the law of death. To the Christian alone it is given to see the Man Christ Jesus, radiant in resurrection life, filling with His brightness the eternal future; and with Him His redeemed, perfected in their humanity, body, soul, and spirit.

APPENDIX.

THE HIGHER CRITICISM.

SINCE this book was published, the "higher criticism" has drawn to itself more and more the attention of Biblical students. As presenting a view of the religious history of Israel in strong contrast with that ever held by the Church, it demands special notice. But nothing more can be done here than to examine very briefly the principles of the higher criticism, and note its most important results as stated by its more prominent advocates.

The higher criticism, taken in its natural connection with the lower or textual, is simply a means of getting all the knowledge respecting a book or writing which will help to explain its meaning as in the mind of the author—by whom written, the time and place of composition, its integrity, its readers, its relation to other similar writings. To know these and other particulars is of much value in forming our historical judgments in general. But the question arises at the outset, is the higher criticism equally applicable to all writings? Are we to make no distinction between the sacred, meaning those whose writers have special Divine light, and the secular? If there be such distinction, of what importance is it? How far should it modify the application of the critical methods to the Bible? This is a point which will be later considered.

Into the questions of literary criticism, the contradictions, discrepancies, interpolations, and redactions found in the sacred documents, we cannot here enter; they would require a volume. But it may be said that many of them are in dispute; and of others, that it is of no importance what judgment we form of them. The one important point is, to know whether the presentation of the history of Israel from Abraham down to Christ, as we have it in the Bible, and as the Church has always received it in its chief features, is the true one; or that which is presented by the higher criticism. We are not here concerned with the inerrancy of the Old Testament writers, or the degrees of their inspiration. The question is, are we to give up the old belief as to the Divine purpose in Israel based upon Israel's special relation to God, and accept the new based upon the theory of natural development. This theory as stated by Kuenen ("The Religion of Israel") is, that "religion began with Fetichism, then developed into Polytheism, and then, and not before, ascends into Monotheism." "This is the order of religious development among all ancient nations, and Israel is no exception."

The task which this school of critics has thus set before itself is to rewrite the history of Israel in the light of this theory, and trace its gradual progress from polytheism to monotheism. It is said by Professor Cheyne ("Jewish Religious Life after the Exile"), "The true history of the Jewish religion can only be obtained by applying the methods of modern criticism to the old Hebrew documents;" and by Professor Briggs (Introduction) that the higher criticism having eliminated the false, "rearranges truths and facts in their proper order and harmony." The first step is to subject to a sharp critical analysis the historical records of the Old Testament, and separating the truth from the error, and facts from legends, thus obtain a strong foundation on which to build the new historic superstructure. Such a foundation, it is claimed, is found in the writings of Amos and Hosea, about 760 B.C.—the earliest prophets whose writings we possess. Learning from them as credible witnesses the religious character of their time, we can go backward and see how the religion of Israel has developed itself from Abraham down.

Having made the stage of the religious development reached in the eighth century the basis of their historical investigations, the critics assure us that the theory just stated explains all the past of Israel. A good deal, indeed, of the history as we have it in the Pentateuch, when tested by this theory, has to be put aside as unhistorical; and not a little of the prophecy. The conclusion thus reached is, that beginning with polytheism, Israel after some twelve hundred years attained under the teaching of the prophets to an "ethic monotheism." This is presented to us by the higher criticism as a scientific result, and one not to be questioned.

We begin by considering the application of the evolutionary theory to the Biblical historical records.

The history of Israel begins with Abraham. He was a Semite, living about 2000 B. C. in Ur of the Chaldees. At this time, as we are told, the surrounding peoples were polytheists, and had many local gods. This was the case with the Semites of Abraham's day. Did he hold the common Semitic belief? This is said by most of the critics. We must then inquire, what did the Semites believe as to their gods and their relation to man?

We are told by Professor W. R. Smith in his elaborate work ("The Religion of the Semites," 1889), that every Semitic tribe had its local god. The progress from the fetich to this god, what his nature, and how he came to stand in this relation to a particular tribe, he does not clearly state. He says: "The fundamental of ancient religions is the solidarity of their worshippers as parts of one organic society. The social body was not made up of men only, but of men and gods." The tie that binds them together is one of kinship. "It cannot be too strongly impressed upon us that the idea of kinship was originally taken in a purely physical sense. There is nothing in the Semitic conception of the Divine nature which forbids us to take in its literal sense the kinship between men and their tribal god." [1]

We thus learn that at first the tribal god was regarded as "the physical progenitor of his people," in other words, a deified ancestor. But he was also a nature god. It is said by Tylor ("Anthropology," p. 259) that "the ghosts of the dead were looked upon as divine beings, powerful both for good and harm. They had control over the forces of nature, and so were regarded as nature spirits. The soul of every great ancestor might be worshipped as a god." Thus the tribal god might be a deified ancestor, and also a nature god. But he did not dwell in heaven, he had a special dwelling-place on earth. We are told that Jehovah was the tribal god of the Kenites, and had his dwelling at Mount Sinai. He was a nature god, the Thunderer, the god of the storm. Like other tribal gods he ruled only over the land where his kinsmen dwelt, and had no jurisdiction over other lands, or authority over other peoples.

Accepting the statements of Professor Smith as to the polytheism of the Semites, the question arises: Was Abraham, when called of God to become the father of the covenant people, a polytheist? [2]

If so, did he continue to believe that Jehovah was only a tribal god, and to be honored and worshipped as were

---

[1] In speaking of the higher criticism we know that the critics are by no means at one in their theological beliefs, or in the results to which they come. But we may take as its true representatives those who are most logical in carrying out its principles. As among the Germans, Kuenen and Wellhausen; among the English, W. R. Smith and Professor T. K. Cheyne.

[2] The more advanced critics deny that the accounts given us of Abraham are historical. Kuenen thinks he may have lived, but cannot be regarded as an historical personage. So Professor Cheyne says: "Hebrew legends may have told of an ancient hero bearing this name."

other tribal gods? Did Jehovah in calling him to a special relation to Himself give him any Divine light as to His own nature and attributes? Did Abraham from this time onward know Him to be the one only supreme God?

These and other like questions have been answered by the higher critics somewhat differently, but with general agreement that the religious beliefs of Abraham and his children down to the time of the Exodus were in substance the same as those of the polytheistic tribes about them, and also their worship.

As in worship the worshipper's conception of his god most clearly appears, let us take, in illustration, the rite of animal sacrifice. This rite was common among the Semites; what meaning had it to them? Professor Smith assures us that it finds its explanation in the kinship of gods and men. "Throughout the Semitic field the fundamental idea of sacrifice is that of communion between gods and their worshippers by the joint participation in the living or raw flesh, and the blood of a sacred victim." Later, the blood was poured out on the altar as the share of the gods, and the flesh eaten by the worshippers. Did Abraham believe that Jehovah thus participated in the food furnished by the animal sacrifices he offered? Some of the higher critics deny that his conception of the moral attributes of Jehovah was higher than that of the Semitic peoples in regard to their gods. He believed that He partook of the sacrificial food, and even that He accepted human sacrifice. Others, indeed, affirm that Abraham, though he continued to be a polytheist, had higher notions of Jehovah as a spiritual being; but fail to state with clearness in what respect his polytheism, and the worship based on it, differed from that of the peoples around him.

We come down to Moses, about five hundred years after Abraham. During all this period we learn of no religious development; but with him, as most of the critics agree, began a new stage of civil and religious history. By the union of the several tribes under him, Israel now became a nation, and Jehovah is advanced to the rank of a national god. Moses, we are told, was like Abraham, a polytheist, and did not teach Israel the truth of one righteous and supreme God. It is said by Wellhausen, that "Moses gave no new idea of God to his people." Jehovah was to him, as to Abraham, only one among many national gods, though he had a higher conception of His moral attributes. But He did not cease to be a local and limited deity. Dwelling at Sinai, he was there chosen to be Israel's god, and aided the people in the conquest of Canaan.

The higher critics do not agree as to how far we are to regard the accounts given us of Moses as historical. If we confine ourselves to the matter of worship as established by him, we are told that he doubtless prepared a tent having an altar and ark, and appointed some rites of worship, but that the ritual ascribed to him in the Pentateuch is a fiction of post-exilic priests. We are assured that he gave no authoritative law of ritual. He knew nothing of one sanctuary at which all should worship. He permitted many local sanctuaries, each having its priests, and at which sacrifice was offered. But sacrifice, which was a chief element in all ancient worship, was a part of natural religion, not appointed by God to Israel, and in which He had no pleasure.

The religious position of Israel as left by Moses was in brief this : Jehovah was a national god, having no authority or power out of Palestine. If one of His people passed out of this land, He could no longer protect him. The people had no directions as to their worship which they were bound to obey. It is said by Professor W. R. Smith, that "the whole worship of the early period was spontaneous and natural." This can only mean that they worshipped Jehovah according to their judgment of what was fitting, both as to time, place, and manner. The great point was the recognition that He was the national god. This recognition did not demand any true apprehension of His moral attributes, but was like the recognition of a king by his subjects.

It is plain that, if this was the religious position in which Moses left Israel, the people had little defence against heathen idolatry (Smith, "Old Testament," p. 347). The entry into Canaan was the time when a knowledge of Jehovah in His relations to the heathen gods, and positive and definite rules of worship, were most needed for their protection. Yet it is said no such knowledge or rules were given. Jehovah being regarded as only one among the national gods, the distinctive features of His worship, if it had any, were soon effaced. It is said by Professor Smith of the period from Moses to the prophets of the eighth century, that though "Jehovah was worshipped with assiduity as the national god of Israel, there was no clear conception of the fundamental difference between Him and the gods of the nations." "The lawful worship was corrupt to the core." "The whole service is represented by the prophets as gross, sensual, and unworthy of a spiritual deity. They worshipped other gods side by side with the national deities. Their worship of Jehovah is hardly to be distinguished from a gross polytheism." (Smith, "Old Testament," p. 350). It is said by Kuenen : "At first the religion of Israel was polytheism. During the eighth century B. C. the great majority still acknowledged the existence of many gods ; and what is more, they worshipped them. And we can add that during the seventh century, and down to the beginning of the Babylonian exile (586 B. C.), this state of things remained unaltered."

If this was the religious condition of Israel in the eighth century, had there been from Moses to this time any prophets sent by God to teach the people? Can we believe that Jehovah had in all these years given them through His prophets, or in other ways, no knowledge of

Himself as the one supreme, holy God, of His attributes of righteousness, justice, truthfulness, and mercy, and of the character and forms of His worship?[1] But if, on the other hand, He had given His people this knowledge, how can it be said that it was first made known by the prophets of the eighth century? One of these positions must be taken. The Israelites either had a knowledge of Jehovah as the one righteous and supreme God, who had given them commands compulsory, before the time of the prophets Amos and Hosea, or they had not. If they had, their sins for which the prophets so severely reproved them, were sins against knowledge; if they had not, they were sins of ignorance, and not to be severely rebuked and punished. But we find that the prophets did not look upon it as their chief mission to lay down new laws, or set up new institutions; it was to call the people to repentance for neglect and violation of the old. Repentance was in their mouth, as in that of the Baptist, the chief cry, with warnings of coming judgments.

If we accept the teaching of the higher criticism, we must believe that not till the time of Amos and Hosea—more than twelve hundred years after the call of Abraham—could God make Himself known to His covenant people as the one holy and righteous God. Neither Samuel nor David nor Solomon so knew Him. Other gods existed, and had their temples and priests and prophets. At last Israel attained to an ethical monotheism. This was reached by them, not so much by any direct revelation of Jehovah to

[1] An illustration of this is given us by Dr. Briggs, who tells us that there was no knowledge of falsehood as a sin till after the exile, and that the prophets knew nothing of the sin of speaking lies as such. "The holiest men did not hesitate to lie whenever they had a good object in view, and showed no consciousness of sin in it. And the writers who tell of their lives are as innocent as they." A people which did not put truthfulness among the attributes of their deity, could have had little confidence in his promises to them, or in the promises made to one another.

them, as by inference from His moral attributes, and especially from His righteousness.

In reading the more advanced critics it is very noticeable what small active part is ascribed to Jehovah in His relations to Israel. It is not His dealings with His people of which we are told, but of the progressive development of their ideas of Him. One would scarcely suppose that He made any more manifestation of Himself in Jewish history than in the history of any other people, or took any special interest in them. Such interest, it is said, would be "particularism," and unworthy of one who was Lord over all.

We pass from the theory of the religious development of Israel, which is the heart of the higher criticism, to some of its practical applications.

But we may first notice the dictum laid down by Professor W. R. Smith, as "the first principle of criticism;" that " as every book bears the stamp of the time in which it was produced, we understand it only as we put ourselves into the age in which it was written." That there is a large measure of truth in this has been already said ; but as stated here and applied to the historical books of the Bible, it is a virtual ignoring of a progressive Divine purpose in Jewish history, and of our knowledge of its progress.

If we accept this purpose, we cannot go back into any past stage, and say that those then living understood what God was doing in it better than any generation that should follow. Contemporaneous writers may give minute details of passing events, and the knowledge of these is instructive; but the meaning of these events, their place and importance in the Divine purpose, may be far more clearly seen by a later generation. And it is only the generation living at the end, that can see in its unity and so fully understand what God has been doing, and thus know the relations of the successive stages to one another, and the place and value of each. A man who sees for the first time the foundation of some great building laid, or its earlier stages, can have no right judgment of the structure as it will be when completed, or of the relation of its several parts. These can be known only as the building progresses, and fully known only as seen in their unity. Much less could the early patriarchs, or any generation of Israel down to the birth of the Lord, know the full significance of what God was doing in their day, and its relations to the future. All contemporary records, however full in detail, can be truly understood only by those who can see in the facts recorded, not isolated events, but the parts of the great whole.

What is true of the actings of God in Jewish history, is true also of the revelations made by word through His prophets. "He spake unto the fathers in the prophets by divers manners," or piecemeal, giving them such knowledge of the future of His purpose as He was pleased to make, and sending by them also such messages of reproof and warning as He saw His people to need. But no single utterance is to be judged of by itself. It is a part of a whole. The revelation is one. Whilst the prophetic word was addressed primarily to the generation then living, and was adapted to its needs, yet often it had a larger scope. The full meaning of their utterances as prophetic, and often pointing to a distant future, the prophets themselves did not know. "They spake as they were moved by the Holy Ghost," and their predictions had a largeness far surpassing the narrow range of their own intellectual vision.

If it is thus clear that no generation in Israel, even down to the Lord's birth, could have fully understood what Jehovah was doing in its day as preparing His way,—and also, that His purpose in the coming of His Son became clearer as the end drew nigh,—we see that nothing is gained as to the full meaning of the contemporaneous records, historic and prophetic, by putting ourselves back into the position of the writers. On the contrary, we, living when so much of the Divine purpose has been accomplished, are far better able to distinguish the permanent and the transient in the prophetic utterances, and putting aside those which were especially for the day, see in its entirety the Divine purpose. To go back to the centuries long before Christ in order to learn the meaning of God's words and acts in preparing His way, as it was understood by those then living, is to go from midday to dusky twilight.

As the Christian critic believes that God has a purpose in human history, so he believes also that this purpose has its goal in the Incarnation of His Son. The hope of the coming of the Messiah was the hope set before the covenant people from the first ; and to teach them who He was and the nature of His work, the end of all the institutions appointed them. Jewish history has, therefore, to be read in the light of this purpose in the Christ, without which it cannot rightly be understood.

If this is so, we may expect that this purpose will be made known in some way to man from the earliest times, and that the revelation of it and of the manner of its fulfillment will become more and more clear as the purpose progresses. And it is in the light of this progress that we of to-day must study all past revelations.

But there are some who say, and their words seem to find large acceptance, that we must come to the study of the Bible without any prepossessions as to its truth ; in other words, must put aside all our Christian beliefs and not allow them to affect our interpretations. In this way only can we be impartial critics. We may not assume any unity in the Biblical records based upon a unity of the Divine purpose. Each writer must be studied by himself, and we may find no more meaning in his words than the strictest literality will give.

This on the face of it is a denial that "holy men of old spake as they were moved by the Holy Ghost," and so a denial of the unity of the revelation. The Scriptures are thus reduced to the rank of literature. The Christian critic will study them as a whole. Having a purpose in the Jews, in which they are to be workers together with Him, He gives knowledge of this purpose, from time to time, through the illumination of the Holy Spirit. This does not involve perfect knowledge, much less infallibility, in their rulers or historians or prophets, but each in his own place had a measure of Divine guidance. Thus, through the Holy Ghost operating through all, the unity of the Divine purpose was preserved, though no one in his special work saw its relation to the work of others, or its bearing on what was to come. Guided by the Divine Spirit, "they builded better than they knew."

We are very often told that the first and chief requisite to get the truth is to have the love of it. But we are to remember that love of the truth is only a moral condition preparatory to the possession of it. It is absolutely essential to the learner, but he who teaches truth must first possess it. The judges who apply the law must have knowledge of the law. Critics who judge the truth of the Biblical records, must have true principles of judgment. The new can be known to be true only by its agreement with the old. A Biblical critic who, in order to be impartial, should attempt to put himself into a state of artificial ignorance, would act as foolishly as an astronomer or geologist who should ignore all that had been known before him. Every critic must say, "I already possess truth, it is the measure of my judgment." The new cannot contradict the old, but may enlarge it, enlighten it, give it new power. The truth dominating the Christian critic is the Incarnation. The fact that the Son of God was made man, and now abides man, is one we cannot ignore. Living so many centuries after the birth of the Son, we read the Hebrew Scriptures in His light. Though His redemptive work is not yet completed, yet His birth set the seal upon the past, and gives the key to its right interpretation ; and from this point, and not from the eighth century preceding, should the higher criticism have begun its critical studies.

Accepting, then, this truth, that the purpose of God in Israel has its goal in the Messiah—the Anointed One— we ask: How does the higher criticism deal with the revelations of this purpose both in their historic and prophetic features? First, of the Messiah as King. We are told that the promise made in Eden, of the Seed of the woman which should bruise the serpent's head, if historical, has no personal reference. But this promise, it is said, and those made later, to Abraham that in his Seed all nations should be blessed, and to David that the Messiah should be of his lineage and rule all nations, are unhistorical. Indeed, all that is said of a Messiah before the time of the prophets in the eighth century, B.C., is to be regarded as the expression of post-exilic beliefs projected backward. Israel knew nothing of any Messiah for many centuries after Abraham. So long as Jehovah was believed to be only a national God, the conception of a universal Messianic Kingdom was impossible.

If we now turn to the prophets themselves, how far does the Messianic element appear in their prophecies? As they now lie before us, and as the Church has always read them, they appear to speak of the Messiah very frequently and with great distinctness. But it is said by Professor Driver (Int. p. 229, note) that "among recent critics the opinion has gained ground that these writings have in many cases not been handed down to us in their original form, but that they were expanded, supplemented, and otherwise adjusted to the needs of a later age, by the scribes and editors through whose hands they passed after the exile."

We are told by one very recent critic, Rev. R. H. Charles ("Doctrine of a Future Life," London, 1899), that "most of the passages in Amos, Hosea, Isaiah, and Micah—the four great prophets of the eighth century—which promised the advent of the Messianic Kingdom, are intrusions into the text from a later time." It is said by Professor Cheyne that the notices of the Messiah in Isaiah and Jeremiah were inserted by editors. Beside these changes, supplements, and adjustments, so numerous that we do not know what was the original text, we are told that often, when mention seems to be made of an individual ruler to come, we are to understand it of a dynasty or a series of kings. Sometimes it is Jehovah who is presented in prophecy as the King, and of this kingdom the personal Messiah is not an integral part, but only a passing figure.

The question arises, were these post-exilic editors and redactors so guided by the Spirit of God that we can regard the changes in the prophecies as expressing His will? If so, we can accept them as of Divine authority, as many of the higher critics seem to do; if not, these editorial additions, post-exilic insertions, and appendices may wholly pervert the meaning of the original prophecy, and leave us no sure promise on which we can rest.

Second, we ask, What does the higher criticism teach us respecting the Messiah as a Saviour from sin? Must we not say that this is almost wholly ignored? Any fall of man, any sinfulness of human nature, are facts which the evolutionary theory of man's development wholly rejects. If there be no such sinfulness of nature, no Redeemer from sin is needed. For occasional personal transgressions the offering of an animal sacrifice is sufficient. The Messiah, therefore, could not be presented to Israel as a Redeemer from sin, nor could there be any rites of worship looking forward to His sacrifice.

But inasmuch as the sacrifice of Christ is the very foundation of His redemptive work, the place which the rites of sacrifice held among the Jews must here be considered.

According to Genesis, animal sacrifice was appointed of God immediately after the fall of Adam, and, as has been always held in the Church, prefigured the vicarious death of the Incarnate Son. All the various forms of sacrifice in the Mosaic ritual pointed to His sacrifice, but each in some partial and peculiar point of view. In general, the death of the victim is the acknowledgment that death is the penalty of sin, and that "without the shedding of blood there is no remission." Sacrifice, therefore, lies at the basis of all rites of worship offered to a holy God by sinful men, whether in the Jewish or the Christian Church. In both it is a confession that we are under the law of sin and death, and points to the sacrifice of Christ, through whose cross alone we are saved.

Assuming that sacrifice was Divinely appointed, and was based upon the fact of the sinfulness of man, and therefore the need of mediatorship, the Mosaic ritual served an immediate and present purpose, and had also a prophetic character. It affirmed that none can approach to God and be accepted of Him who do not come with confession of sin. And His people must be taught their sinfulness, and how abhorrent sin is to a holy God. To this end were appointed the rites of the brazen altar. By these the worshippers were brought to a consciousness of their sinfulness; and were also pointed to One who should be their Mediator with God, and their Redeemer from sin and death.

So far as we understand them, this reference in the Mosaic ritual to sin and deliverance from it through the sacrifice of the Messiah, is wholly ignored, if not positively denied, by the more advanced higher critics. Nor Moses nor Samuel nor David, it is said, knew anything of it. Even the position of the prophets of the eighth century toward sacrifice was, as we are told by Professor R. Smith, a purely negative one. "The prophets have no objection to sacrifice and ritual in the abstract, but they deny that these are of positive Divine institution, or have any part in the scheme in which Jehovah's grace is administered in Israel." "Sacrifice is not necessary to acceptable religion, though He may accept it." We may, then, strike out wholly from the Mosaic ritual the rite of sacrifice as not of God's appointment, and as of no real religious value. There remains, therefore, nothing in the system of religious education of Israel to teach its members of their sinfulness, and of their need of a Mediator with God. The fundamental fact on which our religion as a Divinely appointed redemptive system rests, was not taught to Israel, in word or by ritual, for more than a thousand years.

We thus see the position in which the higher criticism puts us, in regard to the Messiah. Of God's purpose in Him, either as the Saviour from sin, or Ruler of the nations, there was no revelation made for many centuries; and when in the prophets He is spoken of, we are told that most of the passages are insertions of a much later time. This is said by Cheyne of Isaiah ix. and x.

It was but a few years before the Lord came that a real belief in Him and in His kingdom became general. All the patriarchs, from Abraham down, the priests and the prophets and the kings, for many generations knew nothing of Him by whom and for whom all things were made—the First and the Last in the Divine purpose.

If we hold the Christian faith as to the Person of Christ the Incarnate Son, we can understand God's actings in the past or in the present, only as we see them in the light of the purpose of God in Him. This is true both of history and of prophecy. It is impossible that He could have held in them the very subordinate place given to Him by the critics. No one can read them aright who does not believe that "the testimony of Jesus is the spirit of prophecy," and that all done in the world is done by the Father, that He may be manifested through the Son. In His light all history and prophecy grow luminous; though the light will not be perfect, illumining all the obscurities of the past, until His work in redemption shall be finished.

Let us now examine the Levitical system, as presented in the Pentateuch and carried out in the worship of the Tabernacle, and note its special features and the evidence it gives of the twofold work of the Messiah.

In the order of events, as told in Exodus, God, after taking Israel at Sinai into special covenant relation to Himself, gives command to Moses to build Him a sanctuary, that He may dwell among them. It was His purpose that Israel should be "a kingdom of priests and a holy nation;" and that His people might fulfill their high calling, and be themselves prepared for it, He showed to Moses a pattern of the sanctuary he was to build, and which he was to follow in all its details. In this sanctuary He would manifest His presence by a visible symbol. Of the worship to be offered Him there, animal sacrifice was an essential element; and an altar for this purpose was placed in the outer court, open to all, and upon this altar the fire which came down from heaven was to be ever burning. But passing beyond this altar, we come to an enclosure, in the one part of which, known as the Holy Place, we find another altar, of different construction and for a very different use.

We now ask, what is the meaning of this second altar and of its rites, and what its relation to the first? Of the meaning of the rites on the altar of sacrifice, sufficient has been said. In the regular daily service the priest, as representative of the people, makes confession through the death of the victim, that all are under the law of sin and death; and its consumption by the holy fire on the altar is a symbol that they can offer themselves to God, through His Spirit, a living sacrifice—a whole burnt-offering—and are accepted by Him. This being done, the priest enters the Holy Place with the censer filled with coals from the altar of sacrifice, and burns the incense upon the golden altar within the veil. In this service he is alone, and no eye beholds him.

If we ask what is the meaning of the rites at the second altar, of which the offering of incense is the chief, there is general agreement that incense is a symbol of prayer. We have thus in the two altars, types prefiguring two essential and closely connected but widely differing acts of worship—the preparation of the worshippers to approach into the Divine presence, and the prayers which they then offer in His presence. And the order of these acts cannot be changed. Upon the first altar, animal sacrifice only was offered ; upon the second, incense only could be burned. No incense could be offered till the preparatory rites of sacrifice had been fulfilled. All approach to the altar of incense was by way of the altar of sacrifice, and the same holy fire was used upon both altars.

In the Mosaic ritual God thus made known to His people how they were to draw nigh to Him, and also for what purpose He had called them to be "a kingdom of priests and a holy nation." First of all, they must offer themselves to Him upon the altar of sacrifice, and be cleansed by the sprinkling of blood ; for none but the cleansed and holy can enter into the presence of the Holy One. But thus prepared by offering themselves as a whole burnt-offering, they could enter upon their priestly functions of intercession. From the very beginning of the covenant relation, the house of God was appointed to be "a house of prayer for all nations," and the fulfillment of this duty was symbolized by the burning of incense. Thus the Tabernacle and its rites were for the preparatory teaching and training of Israel, and for the present fulfilment of its priestly functions.

The Mosaic ritual had also a prophetic purpose.

It is not possible for us to consider these two altars, and the rites performed at each, and their relation to one another, without seeing a clear and most wonderful prophetic foreshadowing of the twofold work of Christ in our redemption,—His work of Sacrifice, and His work of Intercession. Coming into the world in our nature, He offers Himself to God upon the altar of sacrifice, a whole burnt-offering, the Lamb without blemish or spot. Sinless, He yields Himself to death, to deliver us from the law of sin and death. But His work of redemption was not completed at His death ; this first stage was but preparatory to another. Rising from the dead, He ascends into heaven, and enters into the Holy Place within the veil, where He burns the incense before the Father upon the golden altar. As our great High Priest, "made after the power of an endless life," He offers continual prayer for us. Thus we have set forth in the daily Tabernacle service our Lord's two great redemptive acts, His Atonement and His Intercession. One of these was finished on the cross, in sight of the whole world ; the other He is now fulfilling before the Father, unseen by mortal eye.

It is thus, in the light cast upon the Levitical ritual by the work of Christ, as already fulfilled and now fulfilling, that we can understand why Moses was commanded to make all things after the pattern showed him in the Mount. God's worship was something far too high and holy to be left to human wisdom or invention. He must Himself prescribe how sinful men should worship Him.

If we now ask the higher critics what explanation they give of the origin of this most remarkable ritual, we are told that it never was a reality. It is said by one of them : "We here assume that the Tabernacle, as described by the priestly writer, is an ideal structure, an imaginary modification of the Temple." (Encyc. Biblica.) Most agree that Moses knew of an ark and an altar and tent of meeting, and that he probably appointed some rites of worship. It is said by Professor Driver, that "the chief ceremonial institutions of Israel were of great antiquity, but the laws respecting them were gradually developed and formulated, and that in the shape in which they exist in the Priest's Code they belong to the exilic or post-exilic age." This theory of gradual enlargement does not meet the difficulty. The Tabernacle with its threefold division and its service are exactly adapted to one another. No one could have devised such a structure without knowing the nature and order of the worship to be offered in it. And it was more than a modification of some older rites.

The Mosaic ritual could not have been put together piecemeal,—a little by one generation, and a little by another. The two altars must have been co-existent in the Tabernacle service, and the meaning of each known. The higher criticism must show whence came the altar of incense, and when it was joined to the altar of sacrifice, and what was the relation of the two altars?

There are other objections to the assertion that the Tabernacle and its ritual are wholly unhistorical, and the pure invention of priests in post-exilic times. Putting aside the antecedent improbability of this on the ground of common honesty, why give such a detailed account of the Tabernacle? Why those minute numerical statements of its construction, which are all imaginary, and yet their accuracy can be verified to-day by reconstruction? Why represent a system of worship as appointed of God, and given by special revelation to Moses in the Mount, when there was no ground for it in tradition? Tradition may have known of a tent in the wilderness, but knew nothing of such a Tabernacle as the priests invented. How then could the people believe in it? They knew it to be a fiction.

We read in Numbers iv. of the taking down of the Tabernacle, and very minute directions are given how it shall be done, and by whom, and certain families are set apart for this purpose. Why was this elaborate division of labor, when the Tabernacle itself was a fiction?

There is another and sufficient reason for rejecting the assertion that the Tabernacle and its ritual were the invention of the post-exilic priests, which is found in its supernatural features as given by them, and on which they lay great stress as essential elements. Upon the brazen altar in the Outer Court burned the holy fire which came down from heaven, and was never to go out, and with which the sacrifice, and the incense in the Holy Place, were burned. Within the Most Holy Place was the Ark, and upon the Mercy-seat, between the Cherubim, was the

Visible Glory, the symbol of Jehovah's Presence. All these supernatural elements the higher critics declare to be unhistoric. Neither in the first nor in the post-exilic Temple were any of these found. The last, as all knew, had no holy fire upon its altar, no Ark in its Most Holy Place, and the Visible Glory had departed. This being the case, why should Ezra and his co-laborers invent a Tabernacle and a service, and ascribe to it a special Divine authority as the one true form of worship, and insert in it these supernatural elements, when the worship of the Temple established by themselves had none of them? If the invention of the Tabernacle and its rites was to give sanction and authority to their own worship (and it could have no other purpose), why set forth their own as so defective, by presenting the original ritual in its complete form and with all its supernatural features? To do this was gratuitous self-condemnation; the imperfect present was brought face to face with the perfect past.

We are thus forced to the conclusion that the Mosaic ritual was not made piecemeal, nor was it a fiction of the later priests. If not written down by Moses, it was prescribed by him, and preserved in the traditions of the priests and the people. In the Tabernacle at Shiloh and in the Temple of Solomon was the same threefold division, with the two altars, both having the same rites of worship. Not till the destruction of the Temple by the Assyrians did Jehovah withdraw the visible symbols of His Presence. There were changes of place. First, the Tabernacle, the movable tent fitted for the wanderings in the wilderness; the temporary Tabernacle at Shiloh; and then the permanent Temple' in the Holy City, when the nation had taken possession of the land the Lord had given it. But the order of construction was the same, and the service. After the destruction of the Temple, and the loss of the supernatural features, there could be no full and perfect worship.

We now ask, What is the value of the higher criticism, historic and religious?

As to its historic value, it will be admitted that its minute study of the history of Israel has cast much light upon some obscure portions, and yielded some valuable results. But the documents available for such study are very few and brief, and date back some two or three thousand years; and the student must remain ignorant of much that a historian would know. He is, therefore, greatly tempted to fill up the blanks by conjectures and uncertain inferences. That the higher critics have not resisted this temptation, their writings abundantly show.[1] As there are many problems in Jewish history for whose solution we have no sufficient data, the question naturally arises,

---

[1] It is said by Matthew Arnold ("God and the Bible," Preface) speaking of Protestant Biblical critics: "These are under strong temptations to produce new theories in Biblical criticism, theories marked by vigor and rigor, and for this purpose to assume that things can be known which cannot, to treat probabilities as if they were certainties, to make symmetry where one does not find it; and so to land both the teacher and the learners who trust to him in the most fanciful and unsound conclusions. There are few who do not succumb to these temptations."

He speaks, also, of the obstacles to a sound judgment on the part of those critics "who make too much a business of such inquiries, and give their whole life and thoughts too exclusively to them, and treat them as if they were of paramount importance. They are continually reading its literature, the theories of their colleagues about it, their reputation is made by emitting on the much-canvassed subject a new theory of their own. . . . Their special subject intoxicates them, they are carried away by theorizing, they affirm confidently where one cannot be sure; and in short prove by no means good and safe judges of the evidence before them. In the domain of religion, as in the domain of poetry, the whole apparatus of learning is but secondary, and we always go wrong with our learning when we forget this."

Every one who has read much of the higher criticism has met many examples of this confident affirmation without proof—the possibility of one page becoming the probability of the second, and the certainty of the third.

Why should we attempt to solve them? If it be said that it is always our duty to seek the truth simply as truth, irrespective of any good it may bring, and therefore we are to study the past, even in its minutest details, we ask: What is historic truth? How are we to attain it? We do not truly know any history until we know all that took place, even down to the minutest events; for upon events which seem very insignificant the fate of nations may turn.

If, then, perfect knowledge is impossible, and this is especially true of the long-past Jewish history, what is gained by entering into controversies that cannot be settled?

As dealing with the unchangeable past, its historical details can be of importance to us only as they cast light on the present. As regards Old-Testament history, they become important only as they work a change in our apprehension of God's purpose in His dealings with Israel, and thus affect our beliefs. But to many of the critical results of the higher criticism the legal maxim may be applied: *de minimis non curat lex*. It is plainly of no consequence to us whether a battle was fought on one battlefield or another; or whether twenty or fifty thousand men were slain. We are told that there are three differing accounts of the Exodus. Suppose it to be so; mere discrepancies of statement as to the manner of a fact do not disprove the fact itself. This is true of the Deluge, of the events at Mt. Sinai, and of many others, of which, if we have, as is said, "confused accounts," the reality is not affected. The trouble may lie solely in our ignorance. As the past is unchangeable, and as many of the points discussed with great learning and ingenuity by the higher critics can, however decided, be of no practical importance to us as regards belief or conduct, we can regard them as having only an antiquarian value.

The history of any nation presents many problems which interest historical students, but are regarded with indifference by the general public, because not affecting the life of to-day. It is so with the history of Israel. What is written is written.

If it be said that through the more accurate knowledge of the details of Old-Testament history unbelievers will be led to accept Christ and Christianity, this is very doubtful. It may rather be safely said that the higher criticism, which appeals chiefly to the intellect, will plunge more minds into doubt and perplexity than it will bring to a belief in the Incarnate Son. Already the opinion is widespread that the labors of learned scholars have shown that the Old Testament is full of errors, historic and prophetic; and that the understanding of God's purpose in Israel, as held by the Church for many centuries, is now proved to be very far from the true one. This opinion finds countenance in the general acceptance of evolution as applicable to all departments of human knowledge; for if modern science rejects much held in the past, why not also in religion? Our ever-advancing knowledge must extend to God Himself, and therefore to His revelation.

When the apostles went forth to preach the gospel to the nations, they did not take with them the Old Testament in order upon its historic records to build faith in Jesus. They preached Him, the "Living One," and the resurrection. To-day it is the same message. It is by bringing men to Him, and not by learned discussions of Old-Testament history, that men will be made His disciples.

If we believe in the Son as now having all power in heaven and earth, the several steps by which God prepared His way,—the choice of Israel as His people, and their training and spiritual education,—though always of interest, are of no religious importance as affecting our present relations and duties. A new stage of the Divine work is going on, based upon the Incarnation as an accomplished fact. The Incarnate Son is our living Lord; and our spiritual relations are with Him and the Father. We are not saved by our knowledge of Jewish history, but by our faith in Him, and obedience to His will. Our trust is not in a book, but in a Person.

Thus looking upon God's dealings with the Jews in the past as a means to attain an end, and this end having been reached in the coming of the Son, the perfect accuracy of the record of these dealings is to us of very small importance. Jesus, now the Head of the Church and Lord over all, needs no records of the past to prove His existence and power. History tells us of the dead, but He is the Living One. We are dealing with present, not mere historic facts. Christ is now His own witness, the Maker of history; and the Old-Testament records may be even wholly cast aside, or lost, but He whom they foretold lives, and can at any moment manifest Himself to the world; and all nations will then bow down before Him, and do Him homage.

From this point of view we can but regard a large part of the historic criticisms of the Old Testament as labor misdirected and useless. Its mistakes and errors, granting that they exist, do not affect the exaltation and the supreme authority now exercised by the Son. It is through communion with Him, the living Lord, that we learn to understand the actings of the Father among the covenant people in preparing His way. What now concerns us is to know the will of the Lord Christ, and to be workers with Him in the present stage of His redemptive work. "Follow me, and let the dead bury their dead," is His word to us.

The extension of the supremacy of criticism in literature has always been regarded as an ominous sign: for it tells us that a period of literary decadence is come; that productive power has ceased. Criticism is analytic; it dissects, but does not create.

This is no less true in the religious than in the literary field. The prophetic vision, the enthusiasm of hope, the power of faith, the inspiration to great deeds, are gone.

"The light that never was on land or sea" fades away; the spiritual gives place to the intellectual; faith to sight. The Bible is put upon the dissecting table; and the keen knife severs its joints and bands and leaves it a heap of disconnected fragments. A dim cloud gathers over the past history of Israel, in which we see men as trees walking. Scientific criticism will have a law of religious development which it can fully understand. Divine interpositions are an offence to the cool critical intellect; the supernatural must be relegated to the unhistorical.

It need not be said that this microscopic criticism, dealing only with the past, which does not affect the Christian life, can have no permanent place. For many centuries the Church has found in the Old Testament as we have it, a clearly defined Divine purpose, culminating in the Incarnation of the Son; a purpose which God is now carrying on to its consummation. We may confidently expect that she will not cast her belief away, and accept one directly antagonistic to it. And if she abide in her living Head, though the twilight hang over the long Past, her pathway will be in the light that shineth more and more unto the perfect day. It is her calling to follow the direction and example of the Apostles to "forget those things which are behind, and reach forth unto those things which are before."

NOTES FOR THE REVISION.

Page 34.—The objection is often made that Moses could not have given any such institutions of worship as are ascribed to him, because of the low intellectual development of the people. Monotheism, and the worship adapted to it, they were not prepared for, and centuries must elapse before such preparation could be completed. But this is to confound things that differ. To know God as a Person, having power and wisdom superhuman, whose will all must obey, and to whom the homage of all is due, did not involve the full conception of His Divine nature and attributes. They were to attain to a fuller knowledge of these by coming into communion with Him through the manifestations He made of Himself in His sanctuary. They could know Him only as He revealed Himself to them, and this would He do in increasing measure as they were prepared by the right use of the ordinances He gave them. The deep meaning of the Mosaic ritual would open more and more to them, and they come in due time to the full measure of their high calling.

As through their approach to God in the rites of worship the Hebrews were to learn to know Him, so should they also learn to know themselves as under the law of sin and death. A great end of all the Mosaic ritual, especially of the rites of sacrifice, was to teach them this, and to awaken in them the desire for cleansing and redemption, and the hope of the promised Redeemer. They were taught the holiness of Jehovah, and that they must offer themselves to Him upon the altar of sacrifice before they could bring to Him any acceptable service.

That the Hebrews did not as a people for centuries enter

into the spirit of the worship given them, is admitted ; but this does not show that they could not have done so. Moral development is only in a minor degree dependent upon intellectual. Faith goes before sight. The dwelling of Jehovah in His sanctuary, and the guidance and blessing consequent upon it, had a power far beyond the capacity of the people to understand, but not beyond the capacity of feeling ; as the child trusts its parent, so were they to trust Him. Every day's experience should thus have led them on in the knowledge of Him, and prepared them to be coworkers with Him.

Page 36.—The Theocratic ideal and the historic reality are separated by so wide a chasm that many are tempted to say that Israel could never have borne such a witness to the surrounding peoples of Jehovah's supremacy and righteousness as is here spoken of. But all who believe in the covenant relation must admit that great as His promises to His people were, they would have been fulfilled had there been faith. We may find a sad illustration in the history of the Christian Church, which, endowed with all powers and gifts of the Holy Spirit that it might go on unto perfection, has fallen so far short of its ideal, and had a history in many points like that of the Jewish Church. Israel might have fulfilled its calling to be "a kingdom of priests and a holy nation," and that it did not, was its sin ; and the captivity brought the merited judgment.

Page 86.—Date of the Prophet Joel. Until recently, Joel has been regarded as one of the earliest of the prophets whose prophecies we have, and is put by some in the ninth century B. C., but by more in the eighth. Of late some of the higher critics have brought him down to 450 or 400 B. C. For this change of date there seem to be no new grounds given; and it may be ascribed to the tendency of the critics to put as many of the prophets as possible after the exile, thinking thereby to find some support for their order of Israel's religious development. From the contents of their prophecies we may conclude that Joel was a little earlier than Amos, who is placed by many between 800 and 750 B. C.

Page 111.—The Captivity. This has always been regarded as God's act of judgment upon His people because of their sins. Very early the prophets uttered their predictions of a national overthrow unless there was national repentance. The higher criticism, however, presents the matter in a wholly different light. The Israelites, we are told, for the most part looked upon Jehovah as their national God, having their land as His special domain, and believed themselves to be in such sense His people and He their God that He would always protect them against foreign enemies. It was, therefore, necessary for Him to destroy this great illusion by giving them into captivity, and show them that His dominion was not confined to Palestine, and that He might be found in other lands. Thus He made known to them that their land was no holier than the lands of the nations around them, for He was Lord over all, and might everywhere be acceptably worshipped.

From this point of view the Captivity was a necessary step onward in the religious development of Israel. But as Jehovah dwelt alike in all lands, and could everywhere be worshipped acceptably, there was no ground why the captives should return to their own land. Why then did any return? Plainly the few who did so, returned on religious grounds. Their land continued to be to them the Holy Land, Jerusalem the Holy City, the Temple the one place where Jehovah could be most acceptably worshipped. And this was the teaching of the prophets. But, according to the critics, the captives who did not return were the larger-minded; and those who did, did so under the illusion that Jehovah had some special regard for Palestine. Yet in these all the interest of later Jewish history centres, not in the Dispersion.

ANALYSIS.

INTRODUCTION

A GENERAL STATEMENT OF PRINCIPLES.

CHAPTER I.

GOD'S REVELATION OF HIMSELF TO MEN. — The Incarnation the centre of God's actings. — To this all look forward. — Divine actings prior to it. — How men are to know God. — He must make Himself known. — His personal self-revelations in increasing degree as man is obedient to Him. — The Scriptures the record of the successive revelations of Himself to men.

CHAPTER II.

REVELATION AND REDEMPTION. — Man having fallen must be redeemed. — Redemption not possible without revelation. — Each dispensation a higher stage both of redemption and revelation. — Redemption a work limited in time, but revelation without end. — The highest revelation when redemption is completed. — Two periods of time, redemptive and post-redemptive.

PART I.

THE REVELATIONS OF GOD TO MEN BEFORE AND UNDER THE THEOCRACY.

CHAPTER I.

THE REVELATION OF GOD TO ADAM IN EDEN. — Adam's intercourse with his Creator and knowledge of Him. — The commands given Adam. — The Cherubim. — God's manifestation of Himself under sensible forms. — Adam's sin and fall. — The lessons now to be taught him. — The sense of sin. — The submission of his will and God's supremacy. — A kingdom of righteousness in the future.

CHAPTER II.

GOD'S REVELATION OF HIMSELF TO THE PATRIARCHS. — Expulsion from the garden. — The Cherubim. — Probable worship in their vicinity. — Revelations of the Divine will to the patriarchs. — The Sabbath. — Rite of sacrifice. — Moral separation of the early patriarchs, Cainites and Sethites. — Corruption of morals. — Promise of the Seed of the woman. — Belief in a future redemption. — Spread of idolatry. — Growth of nations. — Call of Abraham. — Building of Babel. — The dispersion of nations.

CHAPTER III.

THE THEOCRACY. — God's relation to a nation as its King. — Thus able to manifest Himself to the world as the One Supreme God. — Choice of the Jews. — Their separation from other peoples. — Possession of the land He had given them. — Jehovah to be their Law-giver and King. — The blessings to follow obedience. — Their mediatorial position in relation to other nations. — The judgments to come upon them if disobedient. — God's renewed grace if repentant. — Relation of Jehovah to the people. — No human representative of Him. — Under His laws and institutions the nation to be educated. — Jehovah both their God and their King. — Two spheres of His rule. — Their laws suited to their national development. — Mosaic legislation a unity. — Jehovah's relation to the land. — Its characteristics. — He its owner. — The people His tenants. — Choice of a capital city. — Possession dependent on obedience.

CHAPTER IV.

PURPOSE AND SIGNIFICANCE OF THE THEOCRACY. — God acting in redemption through elections. — A nation here elected. — Two ends to be attained. — The education of the elect people. — God's revelation of Himself by them to the nations. — Truths to be taught the people, — How to be taught. — Prophetic reference to the Messiah. — Jehovah as dwelling among them. — Its moral effects. — The law of obedience. — Power of the national witness to Jehovah upon the world. — Effect of His judgments if the people are unfaithful.

CHAPTER V.

HISTORY OF THE THEOCRATIC PEOPLE TO THE ESTABLISHMENT OF THE MONARCHY. — The wandering in the wilderness. — Its moral effect. — The conquest of their land. — Inability through want of faith to drive out the idolaters. — Want of unity of action. — Temptations to idolatry. — Worship in high places. — The tabernacle set up at Shiloh. — Defilement of His worship. — His judgments and their effect. — Spirit of prophecy in Hannah.

CHAPTER VI.

The Establishment of the Monarchy and the Davidic Covenant. — Request of the people for a king. — Grounds of this. — Action of Samuel. — Election of Saul. — Relation of the king to Jehovah. — The king to be His servant. — To carry out His will. — Kingly prerogatives. — His priestly character. — Special temptations. — Personal character an important element in national history. — Sin of Saul. — David, his character. — God's covenant with him. — It looked forward to the Messiah and His kingdom. — National apprehension of this kingdom. — National preparation for it.

CHAPTER VII.

Origin and Elements of the Messianic Belief. — Earliest promise of a Redeemer. — How far understood. — Now declared to come of David's family. — The Messianic hope. — Its three elements. — A universal kingdom of righteousness. — Place of the Jews as Jehovah's elect people in it. — Its administration by a Son of David. — All these elements in the popular conception of the future kingdom. — Questions as to the person of the Messiah, and His relation to Jehovah. — Higher spiritual blessings to be expected in the Messianic Kingdom. — Thus this kingdom an object of hope.

CHAPTER VIII.

The Preparation of the Theocratic People for the Messianic Kingdom. — Moral relations of the Theocracy to the Messianic Kingdom. — A stage of preparation for it. — The nation on trial. — So also the house of David. — How far the responsibility felt.

CHAPTER IX.

History of the Kingdom from David to its Division. — Tribal jealousies. — Character of David. — Solomon. — His tolerance of idol-worship. — Folly of Rehoboam. — Division of the kingdom.

CHAPTER X.

History of the Two Kingdoms after the Division. — Loss of national unity. — Its evil effects. — New centres of worship in the northern kingdom at Bethel and Dan. — The two kingdoms hostile. — Idolatry in the northern kingdom under Ahab. — The kingdom of Judah. — Its special advantages. — Its rulers of David's family. — Its possession of the temple. — The appointed worship carried on. — But Judah unfaithful. — First chastisement under Shishak. — General religious tendency downward. — Attempt to restore peace to the two kingdoms by marriage alliances. — Significance of Jehoram's reign. — Idolatry under Athaliah.

CHAPTER XI.

THE MESSIANIC HOPE FROM THE DIVISION OF THE KINGDOM TO THE TIME OF WRITTEN PROPHECY. — Little prophetic mention of the Messiah for near two centuries after David. — Reasons of this. — The people not prepared to hear. — The Messianic Kingdom not an object of spiritual hope. — Messianic hope in the hearts of individuals.

CHAPTER XII.

WRITTEN PROPHECY: ITS PLACE AND SIGNIFICANCE. — Why prophecy should be written down. — Place of the prophet under the Theocracy. — Written prophecy indicated the cessation of the spoken word. — Jehovah about to withdraw from them. — No speedy coming of the Messiah. — Time when prophecy began to be written. — Its peculiar character. — First announcement in Joel of the day of the Lord. — A great day of judgment. — The national overthrow seen in the distance. — All the prophets speak in like manner. — Significance of words spoken to the heathen nations, and written down.

CHAPTER XIII.

HISTORY OF THE TWO KINGDOMS TO THEIR OVERTHROW. — Increase of idolatry in both kingdoms. — Persecutions of the prophets. — Their warnings for the most part unheard. — Progress in national apostasy. — Final overthrow of the northern kingdom. — Transient reformations in Judah. — Help sought alternately from Egypt and Assyria. — Overthrow of Judah, and destruction of the city and temple.

CHAPTER XIV.

MESSIANIC BELIEF IN THE PROPHETS DOWN TO THE EXILE. — Written prophecy down to the exile. — Its chief features. — The day of God as impending. — The people to go into captivity. — The restoration of a remnant. — Its reconstitution. — The universal kingdom under Jehovah. — The several prophets in their order. — Joel. — Amos. — Hosea. — Micah. — Isaiah. — Characteristics of this prophet. — His far vision. — Deep sense of the sins of the people. — A time of penal blindness at hand. — The purification of a remnant. — Its deliverance and glory. — Jeremiah. — The covenant with Israel perpetual. — The people to be restored. — Mention of the Messiah in these prophets. — Silence of some. — Most distinctly spoken of by Isaiah. — His supernatural character. — Permanence of the Davidic covenant in Jeremiah.

CHAPTER XV.

THE NATIONAL OVERTHROW AND THE REMNANT. — National overthrow foretold by Moses as a consequence of disobedience. — First mentioned in written prophecy by Joel. — Often by the later prophets. — The captivity. — Its elements. — Cessation of the theocratic rule of Jehovah. — His withdrawal from the land and city. — Partial return from Babylon. — Not the restoration of the Theocracy. — Jehovah not dwelling again with them as at the first. — A remnant to return from Babylon. — Purpose of God in this remnant. — The Messiah to be born in His land, and here to present Himself to the people. — His rejection followed by a new dispersion. — Moral conditions of the deliverance of the future remnant. — Mention of the remnant in Isaiah. — God's chastisements to continue till it is found. — Frequent allusions to the remnant in Ezekiel and in other prophets. — Uncertainty as to the time of deliverance, and number delivered. — Relation of the deliverance of this remnant to the salvation of the nations.

CHAPTER XVI.

MESSIANIC PROPHECIES DURING THE EXILE. — Prophets of the exile. — Ezekiel and Daniel, by some, last part of Isaiah. — Ezekiel and the exiles with him. — Effect of the captivity upon the exiles. — He sees in vision Jehovah's departure from Jerusalem. — But He will return. — The two tribes and the ten tribes shall be re-united. — Jehovah will again dwell among them. — Heavy judgments before this takes place. — Gog and Magog. — A new order to be established. — A new division of the land, and new temple. — Second part of Isaiah. — Largeness of these prophecies. — Look beyond the Babylonian exile to the end of the great captivity. — The glory of the Messianic Kingdom. — Mention of the Messiah. — Daniel. — Place of the Messianic Kingdom among the world monarchies. — The Son of man and Ancient of days. — And His kingdom at the end of the days. — The Messiah a supernatural Being.

CHAPTER XVII.

THE RETURN FROM THE BABYLONIAN EXILE, AND THE PROPHETS AFTER THE RETURN. — Return from the Babylonian exile. — Decree of Cyrus. — But few returned. — Stages of rebuilding the temple and city. — Early leaders, Joshua and Zerubbabel. — Later, Ezra and Nehemiah. — Not a national restoration. — Prophets of this time, Haggai, Zechariah, and Malachi. — Distinctive character of their prophecies. — The original theocratic relation not restored. — The day of the Lord yet future. — This the day when Jehovah returns to dwell among them. — Then the Messianic Kingdom to be set up. — Haggai. — His predictions. — Allusions to the Messiah. — Zechariah. — Use of symbols. — Distinct mention of the Messiah. — The Branch. — The King riding upon the ass. — Tribulation before the Messianic Kingdom. — The nations to worship at Jerusalem. — Malachi. — Character of his prophecies. — Reproofs of the sins of the priests and the

414   ANALYSIS.

people. — Promise of the coming of the Messiah to His temple. — A preparation for Him needed. — The prophet Elijah. — Destruction of the wicked.

CHAPTER XVIII.

MESSIANIC BELIEFS IN THE PSALMS. — MESSIAH AS KING. — Psalms as distinguished from prophecies.— Messianic beliefs as found in them. — Frequent mention of the King. — Who He is. — This King in David's Psalms. — Second, twentieth, twenty-first, and one hundred and tenth. — In these he looks forward to his greater Son. — Other Messianic Psalms. — Forty-fifth and seventy-second. — Other Psalms, ninety-sixth to ninety-ninth. — Mention in them of the coming of Jehovah. — No mention of the Messiah. — General result.

CHAPTER XIX.

THE PRESENTATION IN THE LAW AND PROPHETS AND PSALMS OF A SUFFERING MESSIAH. — Knowledge of a suffering Messiah. — Its basis in consciousness of sin. — This consciousness twofold. — Of sins personal, and of corruption of nature. — Consciousness of sin before the law. — Promise of the Seed of the woman. — Rite of animal sacrifice. — Ideas of mediation and substitution. — Consciousness of sin under the law. — Knowledge of disobedience by means of the law, of holiness through the manifestation of God's holiness as dwelling among them. — The meaning of sacrifice. — Expectation of an atonement to be made by the Messiah. — How this truth to be taught the people. — The kingly work of the Messiah first to be set forth. — Time when His work as national Redeemer could be presented. — Not till near the Babylonian exile. — Grounds of this. — This redemption and its elements. — Difficulty in setting forth the true nature of His sacrifice. — Fullest revelations made by Isaiah. — Why by this prophet? — His use of the titles of "Holy One" and "God," and of "The Servant of Jehovah." — Differing significations of the last title. — The Suffering One, chap. liii. — Not understood by the Jews as of their Messiah. — The bearing of these sufferings upon all nations. — Upon the elect people and upon individuals. — Rites of the Day of Atonement and their application. — Zechariah. — Reference in this prophet to the Messiah as suffering. — References in the Psalms.

CHAPTER XX.

THE DEAD UNDER THE THEOCRACY. — God's revelations respecting the dead. — Existence of the soul after death. — The general belief of all peoples. — So of the Hebrews. — Mode of its existence. — Respecting this no Divine revelation. — Reasons for this silence. — First lesson to be taught that death a penalty for sin. — No communication to be held with the dead. — The disembodied state imperfect. — Silence respecting retribution at death. — Sheol the receptacle of all souls. — Deliverance from it. — This by resurrection. — Resurrection unknown to the heathen. — Patriarchal knowledge of a resurrection. — Later revelations. — The Psalms and the prophets. — Why these revelations not more full. — The full significance of death not known till the Redeemer died, nor significance of resurrection. — In His likeness the dead to rise. — God's purpose in redemption to be wrought out by the living. — The dead not to be invoked or worshipped. — A partial resurrection to be at setting up of Messianic Kingdom. — Individual happiness subordinate to the Divine purpose. — Distinction between biblical and heathen eschatologies.

CHAPTER XXI.

THE SCRIBES AS SUCCESSORS OF THE PROPHETS, AND THE MESSIANIC HOPE. — Things in the first temple wanting in the second. — Spirit of prophecy still continued. — Its cessation with Malachi. — Now all earlier revelations of God to be gathered up. — Work of the scribes. — Their relations to the priesthood. — Their growing influence. — Its injurious bearing on the Messianic hope. — Exaltation of the law. — This made a substitute for the Messiah. — Intellectual pride of the scribes. — Little consciousness of sin or need. — The scribes not able to prepare the Messiah's way. — A prophet must come. — Three great divisions among the people. — The Essenes, Pharisees, and Sadducees.

CHAPTER XXII.

THE MESSIAH IN THE APOCRYPHAL AND APOCALYPTIC BOOKS. — Apocryphal books. — Age and origin. — General expectation in them of Jehovah's universal kingdom. — High place of the Jews in it. — Sirach. — Baruch. — Tobit. — Judith. — First Maccabees. — Wisdom of Solomon. — Silence respecting the Messiah. — How explained. — Effect of wars of the Maccabees on the Messianic hope. — The Alexandrian school. — Philo. — Apocalyptic books. — Characteristics. — Sibylline Oracles. — Henoch. — Psalms of Solomon. — Book of Jubilees. — Apocalypses of Baruch and Ezra. — Place of the Messiah in the Apocalyptic books. — The Apocryphal and Apocalyptic books compared.

CHAPTER XXIII.

THE RESURRECTION AND THE JUDGMENT. — THE MESSIANIC KINGDOM AND THE WORLD TO COME. — Duration of the Messianic Kingdom. — Confusion respecting it. — Redemptive and post-redemptive periods. — The final judgment at end of redemption. — In which period the Messianic Kingdom to be placed. — This a time of probation. — And in the redemptive period. — As such not eternal. — Whether the Old-Testament prophets looked beyond the Messianic Kingdom. — This the great theme of prophecy. — Their divisions of time into pre-Messianic and Messianic. — A resurrection and judgment at beginning of the Messianic period. — Knowledge of the Jews as to its duration. — Prophetic declarations that it would be without end. — The Messiah to be mortal, or immortal? — Confusion of Jewish opinions. — Teaching of St. Paul. — Christ to give up the Messianic Kingdom, yet continue universal King. — Thus three periods. — Pre-Messianic, Messianic, and post-Messianic. — Final resurrection and judgment at the end of the Messianic period. — This world and the world to come. — Original significance of these terms. — Later change of use. — Condition of departed souls not the world to come.

CHAPTER XXIV.

MESSIANIC BELIEFS IN OUR LORD'S DAY AS SET FORTH IN THE GOSPELS. — Two points. — Belief as to Messiah's person. — As to His work. — Several designations of the Messiah. — Their significance. — Used with indefiniteness. — General Jewish belief respecting His person. — His work. — National deliverance the most prominent element in popular mind. — How far including deliverance from sin. — How this to be effected, indistinctly apprehended. — Words of the angels respecting the Messiah to Zacharias. — To the Virgin Mary. — To Joseph. — Utterances of the Spirit by Mary. — By Zacharias. — By Simeon. — By Anna. — Words of the Baptist.

CHAPTER XXV.

THE LORD'S OWN TEACHINGS RESPECTING HIS MESSIANIC WORK. — The Messianic Kingdom to be established. — The Messiah's Kingdom as distinguished from the Theocracy. — Still future. — To be identified with "the world to come." — Not set up till His return from heaven. — During His absence His children to be tried. — Hated of the world. — The time of great tribulation immediately before His return. — At His return as Judge, He separates the good and evil. — In His kingdom believing Gentiles will have part. — Participation in the kingdom a privilege given to such as He accounts worthy. — Correction of Jewish beliefs. — All power given to the Messiah as the Judge. — He to raise the dead. — His authority over the law. — New truths revealed by Christ. — The mystery of His person. —He Himself to be the source of life. — Thus great enlargement of the Messianic conception. — His silence respecting national restoration. — Reason for this.

PART II.

THE REVELATIONS OF GOD TO MEN IN THE CHRISTIAN CHURCH.

CHAPTER I.

THE MESSIAH IN HEAVEN. — The work of redemption to be carried on from heaven by the Messiah. — New relations into which brought by His ascension. — First, to Jehovah. — As the Anointed He becomes His perfect instrument for all future work. — Secondly, His relation to the Jews. — Not now their King. — Their new dispersion. — Teaching of St. Paul as to their national salvation. — Effect of this fall upon the place of the Gentiles. — A new election to be gathered. — In this the Gentiles to have place. — The fall of the Jews the blessing of the Gentiles. — The Jews to be grafted in again. — God's purpose in their election to be fulfilled in them. — Thirdly, to the Gentiles. — Christ's death for all. — The gospel to be preached to all. — Gives His heavenly life to all who believe. — He is both Son of David and Son of man.

CHAPTER II.

THE NEW ELECTION, AND ITS CALLING AS THE BODY OF CHRIST. — Purpose of God in the new election. — Its designation as the body of Christ. — Its Head the man Christ Jesus risen from the dead. — Vital relation of the Body and Head. — By this Body the Messiah in heaven carries on His work on earth. — As the Second Adam, a new Head of the race. — The gospel to be preached to all. — In the Church, men brought nearer to God than in the Theocracy. — God revealed in the Son, and the Son through the Church in which dwells His Spirit. — A higher stage of redemption reached in the Church.

CHAPTER III.

THE TWO ELECTIONS, JEWISH AND CHRISTIAN, COMPARED. — Essential distinction between the elections Jewish and Christian. — Points of comparison. — The Jewish election a nation. — The Christian from all nations. — In the latter a higher knowledge of God. — A deeper sense of sin — A higher spiritual standing as the dwelling-place of the Spirit. — So its ordinances and ministries. — The Jews had the pattern of heavenly things. — The Church has the substance. — Its higher worship and priesthood. — Higher forms of miraculous powers, a larger measure of spiritual endowments. — The gift of prophecy, of tongues. — The Christian election no mere continuation of the Jewish. — The body of Christ essentially new in life, constitution, and powers.

CHAPTER IV.

THE CHURCH NOT THE MESSIANIC KINGDOM. — The belief that Christ began to reign when He ascended. — Formula — The Church is the kingdom. — On what grounds believed. — Early became the general belief. — Distinction between Christ's present rule in the Church and over the nations. — The last providential, not immediate. — Christ not now seen as King of the nations. — This future, when He takes His great power, and reigns. — To affirm the Church to be the Messianic Kingdom confounds means and end. — The Church an election. — To be completed and perfected before it can reign. — Also, sets aside God's purpose in the Jews. — Also, confuses the two offices of Christ as High Priest and King. — Also, makes the Church period the last redemptive period. — If so, impossible that the apostle could have desired His speedy coming. — His words respecting the future of the Church. — Sinful and mortal men cannot reign with Christ, nor the dead reign over the living. — Practical applications of the principle that the Church now reigns. — The Church of Rome. — Her head Christ's Vicar, clothed with supreme power. — The Greek Church. — The Reformers. — Their eschatology in substance that of Rome. — Gradual change of belief. — Christ now reigning, but His rule that of a teacher of truth. — His authority moral. — Of the three elements of the Messianic conception, the first only retained. — A universal kingdom of Jehovah. — Claims to infallibility. — Position of the Anabaptists. — Two currents of opinion in our day.

CHAPTER V.

THE ETERNAL LIFE, AND THE DEAD IN CHRIST. — Jewish belief as to the life in the Messianic Kingdom. — Eternal life. — Term used in Daniel. — In common use in the Lord's Day. — The terms life and death. — Their several meanings. — Eternal life, its elements. — Only applicable to the saints after their resurrection. — Involves fullest communion with God, and highest blessedness forever. — This conception of life not possible till Christ arose. — Disembodied existence imperfect. — Influence of Greek philosophy on Jewish belief. — Expectation of a resurrection before the Messianic Kingdom. — What new elements the Lord added to the Jewish belief. — Prerogative of the Messiah to admit to eternal life. — He as the Messiah to be the source of this life. — Regeneration. — Its nature not understood till after Pentecost. — Those in Christ possess eternal life. — But not secured against death. — This not to be till He returns. — The dead in Christ. — Continue to abide in Him. — Fullness of eternal life through resurrection and translation. — Such only His helpers in the kingdom. — The dead not His helpers. — Error that the body is no essential element of the eternal life. — Undue exaltation of the disembodied condition.

CHAPTER VI.

THE APOSTASY AND THE ANTI-CHRIST. — Mention of the falling-away in the Church by St. Paul. — Revelation of the lawless one, the man of sin. — Like mention by other apostles. — The Antichrist. — The Lord's prophetic warnings. — The beast of the Revelation. — Spirit of Antichrist. — Its distinctive character. — The Antichrist appears in the Church. — His appearing not a strange phenomenon. — In Him the deification of manhood. — The highest form of human wickedness. — Antichrist as claiming the rule of the world. — His relation to Satan. — The authority given him. Conditions that make a great world monarchy possible. — Signs of its approach.

PART III.

THE REVELATIONS OF GOD TO MEN IN THE MESSIANIC KINGDOM.

CHAPTER I.

THE MESSIANIC KINGDOM: ITS NATURE AND PURPOSE. — The two elements, revelation and redemption, in the Messianic Kingdom. — A higher stage of both. — Christ then revealed from heaven in His glory. — And God in Him. — Also, a higher stage of redemption. — The dead in Christ appear with Him in glory. — The living changed into His likeness. — The Jews, then sanctified as His people, made obedient and holy. — All nations blessed under them. — The Messianic Kingdom the last stage of redemption. — The two elections completed and perfected. — God's purpose fulfilled in them. — Three distinct classes in the kingdom. — The glorified Church. — The Jews. — The nations. — Place of each. — Through these elections Christ fulfills His kingly and priestly functions. — A well-ordered system of government. — Wonderful development of humanity in all good. — True golden age.

CHAPTER II.

THE JUDICIAL ACTINGS OF CHRIST AS PREPARATORY TO THE KINGDOM AND THE DAY OF THE LORD. — The kingdom period as a day of judgment. — Its beginning and end special times of judicial action. — Two elements in Messianic judgment. — Separation. — Reward. — Process of separation at the Lord's coming. — Prevailing lawlessness at this time. — All free to show what is in their hearts. — God's testimony to His truth the means of separation. — The good and evil in three classes. — The baptized, the Jews, the nations. — Separation to be made in each. — The disobedient and the obedient gathered out. — The disobedient cut off from the earth. — This the day of the

Lord. — A time of trial. — Of God's vengeance on the wicked. — All judgment given to Christ. — His words respecting the great tribulation. — Order of this process of judgment in the Book of the Revelation. — The kingdom set up. — The first resurrection.

CHAPTER III.

THE MESSIANIC KINGDOM IN THE BOOK OF THE REVELATION. — Book of the Revelation. — Its peculiar character. — A book of symbols. — Deals with the spiritual condition of the Church. — Christ's successive actings to prepare it for the kingdom. — The Jews have no place in this book. — Terms symbolically used. — The Messianic Kingdom preceded by marriage of the Lamb. — Nature of this relation. — The binding of Satan. — Duration of the kingdom. — The loosing of Satan. — The last resurrection and judgment.

CHAPTER IV.

THE JEWS IN THE KINGDOM, AND THE NEW COVENANT. — Nature of new covenant. — When to be established. — The promises to Abraham the basis of the covenant. — These universal and special. — The last to be first fulfilled. — All to be fulfilled by the Messiah. — The covenant at Sinai. — The law added. — Failure to keep the covenant. — Its punishment. — Covenant not revoked. — Not fulfilled when Christ came. — The new covenant not a mere repetition of the Sinaitic. — Not the covenant with the Church. — This a new election. — Provision for renewal of Sinaitic covenant. — Rites of Day of Atonement. — Impossible to fulfill them after the Babylonian exile. — These to be yet fulfilled by Christ as great High Priest. — A day of national repentance to come. — The new covenant then made. — Its elements. — Forgiveness of past sins. — Perfect obedience to God's law. — All obedient. — Under the new covenant the Jews prepared to fulfill God's purpose. — Through them the nations to be taught God's will.

CHAPTER V.

THE LAST APOSTASY AND FINAL JUDGMENT. — The kingdom a time of probation. — Obedience to God of the Jews and nations. — How far perfect. — The last outbreak of wickedness. — Speedy punishment of the rebellious. — The resurrection of all the dead. — Final judgment. — The giving up of the Messianic Kingdom to the Father. — Christ as God-Man abides Universal Lord. — Distinction of relations to God and Christ among the saved during the ages to come.

CHAPTER VI.

THE NEW HEAVENS AND NEW EARTH. — Revelation of God in creation. — Higher revelation through Incarnation. — For man the earth made. — Adaptation to his spiritual education. — Correspondence in the history of man and of the earth. — The curse through Adam's disobedience. — The earth to be renewed through obedience of the Second Adam. — Prophetic words. — What meant by new earth. — Not a new creation. — A restoration and exaltation. — Adapted to the Second Adam. — This change not in conflict with geology. — Not instantaneous. — Probably several stages. — One at establishment of the kingdom. — St. Peter's words refer to the result when all change is completed. — Probable beginning of the change in the Holy Land. — Thence extends in time to all the earth. — Our solar system. — The universe. — The law of the new creation found in Christ risen and glorified. — A false spiritualism. — Edwards and the future of the earth.

CONCLUSION.

CHRISTIANITY AND OTHER RELIGIONS. — High place of the Incarnation in Christianity. — To be regarded in comparing Christianity with other religions. — Unity and harmony of the Bible. — Offices of the Incarnate Son. — Revealer of God. — Redeemer of men. — Redemption already considered in its several stages. — Degrees of revelation by Christ. — By His words and works when on earth. — By His words and works from heaven through the Church by His Spirit. — By His words and works in the Kingdom at His return. — Also, the glory of His Person then manifested. — Capacity to receive these revelations. — First, by the Jews. — Second, by the baptized. — Last, by those made like Him in the kingdom. — The Incarnation gives assurance that humanity remains ever the same in its elements. — Christ the God-Man risen from the dead. — The body to have part in the glory of man. — Christianity an absolute and universal religion. — Not so heathen religions. — Absolute as including all truth, and universal as embracing all creatures. — All questions respecting man answered by Christianity. — Foreign ideas to be excluded, e.g., the future of the earth and man. — Attempted elimination of the material element. — Unity of the Divine purpose thus destroyed. — The future filled with the glory of Christ risen and glorified. — And of His saints made like Him.